RUSSIA IN THE MIDDLE EAST

Theodore Karasik and Stephen Blank, Editors

The JAMESTOWN FOUNDATION

Washington, DC
December 2018

THE JAMESTOWN FOUNDATION

Published in the United States by
The Jamestown Foundation
1310 L Street NW
Suite 810
Washington, DC 20005
http://www.jamestown.org

For more information on this book of The Jamestown Foundation, email pubs@jamestown.org.

ISBN: 978-0-9986660-3-7

Cover art provided by Peggy Archambault of Peggy Archambault Design.

Jamestown's Mission

The Jamestown Foundation's mission is to inform and educate policy makers and the broader community about events and trends in those societies which are strategically or tactically important to the United States and which frequently restrict access to such information. Utilizing indigenous and primary sources, Jamestown's material is delivered without political bias, filter or agenda. It is often the only source of information which should be, but is not always, available through official or intelligence channels, especially in regard to Eurasia and terrorism.

Origins

Founded in 1984 by William Geimer, The Jamestown Foundation made a direct contribution to the downfall of Communism through its dissemination of information about the closed totalitarian societies of Eastern Europe and the Soviet Union.

William Geimer worked with Arkady Shevchenko, the highest-ranking Soviet official ever to defect when he left his position as undersecretary general of the United Nations. Shevchenko's memoir *Breaking With Moscow* revealed the details of Soviet superpower diplomacy, arms control strategy and tactics in the Third World, at the height of the Cold War. Through its work with Shevchenko, Jamestown rapidly became the leading source of information about the inner workings of the captive nations of the former Communist Bloc. In addition to Shevchenko, Jamestown assisted the former top Romanian intelligence officer Ion Pacepa in writing his memoirs. Jamestown ensured that both men published their insights and experience in what became bestselling books. Even today, several decades later, some credit Pacepa's revelations about Ceausescu's regime in his bestselling book *Red Horizons* with the fall of that government and the freeing of Romania.

The Jamestown Foundation has emerged as a leading provider of information about Eurasia. Our research and analysis on conflict and instability in Eurasia enabled Jamestown to become one of the most reliable sources of information on the post-Soviet space, the Caucasus and Central Asia as well as China. Furthermore, since 9/11, Jamestown has utilized its network of indigenous experts in more than 50 different countries to conduct research and analysis on terrorism and the growth of al-Qaeda and al-Qaeda offshoots throughout the globe.

By drawing on our ever-growing global network of experts, Jamestown has become a vital source of unfiltered, open-source information about major conflict zones around the world—from the Black Sea to Siberia, from the Persian Gulf to Latin America and the Pacific. Our core of intellectual talent includes former high-ranking government officials and military officers, political scientists, journalists, scholars and economists. Their insight contributes significantly to policymakers engaged in addressing today's newly emerging global threats in the post 9/11 world.

Table of Contents

About 'Russia in the Middle East' Project.......................vi

1. Introduction
Stephen Blank...1

2. The Foundations of Russian Policy in the Middle East
Stephen Blank...28

3. The Arab View of Russia's Role in the MENA: Changing Arab Perceptions of Russia, and the Implications for US Policy
Shehab Al Makahleh..61

4. Iran's Russian Conundrum
Alex Vatanka...87

5. Russia's Policies in the Middle East and the Pendulum of Turkish-Russian Relations
Mitat Çelikpala..105

6. European Assessments and Concerns About Russia's Policies in the Middle East
Pavel K. Baev...131

Cont. on next page...

...Contents cont. from previous page.

7. Imperial Strategies: Russia's Exploitation of Ethnic Issues and Policy in the Middle East
Stephen Blank..154

8. The Tactical Side of Russia's Arms Sales to the Middle East
Anna Borshchevskaya...183

9. Russia in the Middle East: Energy Forever?
Rauf Mammadov..212

10. Russia's Financial Tactics in the Middle East
Theodore Karasik...240

11. Russia in the Middle East: A New Front in the Information War?
Donald N. Jensen...265

12. 'Continuing War by Other Means': The Case of Wagner, Russia's Premier Private Military Company in the Middle East
Sergey Sukhankin...290

13. Demography's Pull on Russian Mideast Policy
Ilan Berman..319

14. Russia in the Middle East Until 2024: From Hard Power to Sustainable Influence
Yuri Barmin..338

15. Russia's Middle Eastern Position in 2025
Stephen Blank..367

16. Implications and Policy Recommendations
Theodore Karasik...414

Author Biographies...441

About 'Russia in the Middle East' Project

There is an outpouring of reporting on Russian activities in Syria, and to a lesser degree other countries in the Middle East and North Africa. But until mid-2017, there was no single effort to analyze the totality of Russian objectives, instruments of power, tactics, and strategy in the greater Middle East and their implications for US foreign policy. The Jamestown Foundation's "Russia in the Middle East" project, headed by Dr. Theodore Karasik and Dr. Stephen Blank, was launched to rectify this gap by providing the basis and material for a multi-dimensional analysis of Russian strategy and tactics in the Middle East, bringing into sharp relief the depth and scope of Moscow's strategy.

Unfortunately, Western analyses have long missed the bigger picture: Russia seeks to capture the entire Middle East market across several multi-dimensional issues. These include Russian arms sales; the formation of a working coalition or bloc with Iran, Iraq and Bashar al-Assad's Syria; the insertion of Russia as a broker in the Palestinian-Israeli conflict, efforts to regain major influence over Middle Eastern and Eastern Mediterranean gas sales, especially liquefied natural gas (LNG), to Europe; and using its newly established position in the Middle East to augment its military-economic-political influence regionally and upon Europe.

Tragically, given this absence of analysis of Russia's Middle Eastern strategy, there is a lacunae in knowledge regarding how far advanced the Kremlin's program for the Middle East really is and the metrics of such a robust Russian advance.

Approach

This book is based on the conclusions and insights arrived at over the past year in a series of expert workshops, published papers, briefings and public events within the scope of the "Russia in the Middle East" project.

Our analysis bases Russia's current trajectory on Yevgeny Primakov's activities as foreign and prime minister in 1996–1999. He may truly be described as the moving spirit and soul of the Russian policy reorientation that has come to its fullest fruition under Vladimir Putin, particularly regarding the Middle East. Putin has used Primakov's ideas and activities as a springboard for his own and continues to use them as the basis of his vision of Russia's role in the Middle East and its actions there. Backed by the military, energy firms, arms sellers, the Russian Orthodox Church, and the security services with their advances in information warfare, Russia has successfully reduced Western and US influence in the Levant and created a new strategic equation in the Middle East, Mediterranean, and Europe.

Policy Implications

Russia's intervention in Syria and the ensuing dramatic expansion of its overall Middle Eastern profile have substantive and serious implications for the US. First, both these processes betoken Moscow's determination to force Washington to acknowledge the legitimacy of its aims and status as an equal global superpower to the US. Although Putin has long sought to augment Russia's influence in the Middle East, our failure in Syria and the ensuing vacuum in Washington's policy toward the broader region—due in part to our worsening ties with Israel and the effort to pursue reconciliation with Iran—have opened up opportunities for Moscow. As a result, Russia now seeks a status comparable to the one it had in the 1970s regionally if not globally—namely, a status where, as Foreign Minister Gromyko said in 1971, no world issue can be decided without or against it.

Second, in line with centuries-old Russian strategic imperatives, it seeks to challenge the US and NATO militarily in the Levant and the Mediterranean. Russia has acquired bases in Syria, seeks them in Egypt and Cyprus, and, should its Libyan client, General Khalifa Halter, come to power in Libya, it will seek bases there. In all these cases, too, it has positioned itself advantageously to make major arms deals and arms sales with the governments in question. Similarly it has done so with both the government of Iraq and the Iraqi Kurds. And it is acquiring and demonstrating military capabilities that we had not expected it to have in these theaters. At the same time, thanks to numerous intersecting developments, Moscow is making great strides in detaching Turkey from a pro-Western orientation and from its status as an active member of NATO. Given Turkey's overall strategic position in Europe and the Middle East, that denouement would have profoundly negative international consequences.

Third, Moscow has forged a working partnership if not alliance with Iran against the US and its allies in the Middle East. And through that alliance and Moscow's support for Iranian clients, including terrorist groups like Hezbollah and Hamas, it seeks as well to rearrange the regional map to its and Tehran's benefit at our allies' expense and to the detriment of US interests. It has convincingly demonstrated enhanced military capabilities in support of its political objectives, thereby highlighting the failures of our policy and intelligence assessments that denied Russia had such capabilities.

Fourth, through the orchestration of all of its instruments of power Moscow hopes not only to leverage its Middle Eastern position to give it renewed influence on European gas and oil outcomes, it also seeks to use the Gulf states and the Middle East in general as conduits for circumventing the impact of the sanctions imposed on it due to the aggression against Ukraine.

Fifth, and finally, it also seeks to use its position in the Middle East to force the US and Europe to accept that aggression and an altered state of affairs in Europe and other locations around the world.

1. Introduction

Stephen Blank

Today, Moscow is engaged across the entire Middle East in multiple and apparently mutually reinforcing ways. Apart from its military intervention in Syria, it now holds the balance between Israel and Iran as well as between Syria and Jordan. Russia makes energy pacts with Saudi Arabia that eclipse the Organization of the Petroleum Exporting Countries (OPEC). In Iraq, Moscow has leverage with both the Iraqi government and the Iraqi Kurds. Russia has established a robust partnership with the United Arab Emirates (UAE) that transcends the Middle East to include Sub-Saharan Africa. And Russia has done all this while simultaneously making economic deals and negotiating arms sales with the Qataris, the UAE and Saudi Arabia's Gulf rival. Russia also now polices the Golan Heights.[1] At the same time, it apparently now aspires to play a mediating role in the Israeli-Palestinian conflict that has defied generations of international efforts at conflict resolution and is being called upon on by the Arab League to undertake just such a role.[2] In North Africa, Russia is simultaneously mediating Libya's civil war and being invited to make a decisive move on behalf of the east-based Libyan National Army, led by General Khalifa Hafter, one of the warring parties there.[3] In Morocco, it is now trying to play a part in the diplomatic skirmishing going on around the war in the Western Sahara.[4] Yet, at the same time, the Kremlin has sold Algeria weapons with which it could confront Morocco.[5] Furthermore, Russia is apparently trying to play a

1

mediating role in Yemen's Civil War as well.

Meanwhile, it is seeking naval and air bases in Cyprus, Egypt, Libya, Syria, Sudan and Yemen.[6] Russia is also selling arms to Egypt, Iran and Turkey, as well as negotiating future sales with Qatar and Saudi Arabia.[7] And thanks to the impending breakdown of Turkey's relations with the United States, Turkish political figures are not only proclaiming defiance toward Washington but also threatening to evict the US from the Incirlik Air Base and even leave the North Atlantic Treaty Organization (NATO). Such outcomes would inestimably boost Russia's already high influence in and upon Turkey. Moscow is presumably advocating for both, if not in public then behind closed doors.[8] Indeed, Russia is apparently developing plans to counter US economic warfare against it, Iran, and Turkey by creating regional currency blocs or payment unions.[9]

All these manifestations of Russia's presence, therefore, highlight the comprehensive, even multi-dimensional engagement of Russian power in all of its forms—military, diplomatic, informational and economic—with the entire Middle East. Moreover, this large-scale engagement has developed over several years, so it is process of long duration and will not end anytime soon. If anything, Moscow's engagement with the Middle East is likely to grow in scope and depth through 2025. Indeed, the scope of Russia's regional engagement has finally galvanized at least some of the upper echelons of the US military and political leadership to express open concern about Russia's role across the entire Middle East, from the Maghreb to Iran and from Sudan and Yemen to Turkey.[10] At the same time, these examples (which do not include all of the forms in which Russian power is engaged there) show Moscow's flexibility where it can provide arms to one or another side in a civil conflict yet also pose as a mediator or valuable interlocutor to both sides in that same conflict. We see this phenomenon in Morocco, as stated above; but since 2012, we have also seen it in Iraq, where Moscow is playing both sides against the middle in its engagement with the government in Baghdad and the Kurdistan Regional government (KRG) in Erbil.[11]

Yet, even now there is still an insufficient appreciation of the extent of Russian activities across this huge expanse, an inadequate awareness of the flexibility Moscow now commands in its approaches to the Middle East. In addition, there is an unwillingness to accept that Moscow is not just being opportunistic but that it may actually have a strategy with relatively crystallized political objectives in mind behind all this activity. Indeed, one recent study by the Rand Corporation manages to contradict itself by saying simultaneously that Moscow has a strategy but that it is astrategic and has no strategy.[12] Similarly, other US analysts find it hard to grasp that Moscow uses force because it has a discernible political objective in mind.[13]

Precisely because too many analysts have been too reluctant or unready to acknowledge the depth and extent of Moscow's regional engagement, The Jamestown Foundation's "Russia in the Middle East" project is both timely and necessary. We aim to provide both a synoptic assessment of the multiple dimensions of Moscow's regional presence with functional analyses of key areas—energy, finance, arms sales, information warfare, etc. (i.e., the instruments that Moscow employs)—to communicate to readers just how deep and deep-rooted Russia's involvement actually is with Israel, Turkey, Iran, and the Arab world. Indeed, Moscow never really left the Middle East; although in the 1990s, when its power was at its nadir, it could hardly sustain the role it had previously and now presently imagined for itself.

Nevertheless, and especially from the moment Yevgeny Primakov became Russian foreign minister in 1996, Moscow's undeviating goal has been the restoration of its Cold War status and presence in the area. Indeed, it is arguable, as Stephen Blank suggests, that the visible continuity in Russian policies that we see from the Cold War to the present is Primakov's legacy; his ideas have, in large measure, outlived him and still form the intellectual basis of Russia's regional policy here.[14] Primakov long argued that it is essential for both Russia and the Middle East that the United States not be the exclusive the regional hegemon there.[15] Russia must constitute an equal and opposing presence. In 1991, on a mission to the area to save the Soviet Union's regional position, he said that Middle Eastern leaders "consider it necessary that a united economic and military-strategic area of the USSR [Union of Soviet Socialist Republics] be preserved." He continued,

> They wanted a USSR presence in the Middle East because this would preserve the balance of power. Nobody wants some power to maintain a monopoly position there. These states understand that our country creates an area of stability in this region with its new policy of non-confrontation with anyone, a policy oriented toward searching for ways of making interests coincide with those of other countries.[16]

That precept naturally comports with the equally long-standing Russian belief, already articulated quite cogently in the 1990s, that Russia cannot be content with anything other than a role equivalent to that of the United States. Sergei Rogov, director of the USA Institute and an advisor to the government and foreign ministry, wrote in 1997 that,

> First of all, Moscow should seek to preserve the special character of Russian-American relations. Washington should recognize the exceptional status of the Russian Federation in the formation of a new system of international relations, a role different from that which Germany, Japan, or China or any other center of power plays in the global arena.[17]

Similarly, Dmitri Trenin of the Carnegie Endowment observed then that Russian analysts argue that current difficulties are transient but

Russia is *entitled* to this "presidium seat" in Europe, the Middle East, Asia, and on global issues.[18] And to this day, as many analysts now acknowledge, this drive for equivalency of global status through regional confrontation with Washington drives Moscow's foreign policy. Essentially Moscow's ultimate, though not proximate, objectives in intervening so strongly in the Middle East and in other key regions is to create regional bipolarities with the US and its allies that will force Washington (and them) to take Moscow at its own self-valuation and acknowledge a truly multipolar world with Russia as the US's equal. Thus, today, analysts as disparate as the Israeli scholar and former ambassador to Moscow, Zvi Magen, and Dmitri Trenin both argue that the overriding objective of Russian foreign policy in the Middle East is the achievement of recognition of a restored superpower or great power status.[19]

In pursuing this global objective Moscow also concurrently pursues serious regional objectives by using all the instruments of power that it possesses. While the intellectual foundation of policy arguably lies in the Primakovian legacy, Vladimir Putin, by pursuing this policy in his own way, has added to and deepened it and placed his personal stamp upon it. The deployment of these instruments of power and policy, therefore, represent a kind of mélange of Tsarist, Soviet and contemporary Russian attributes united into one. Consequently, the chapters following the depiction of the Primakovian legacy display how and to what ends Moscow has used these attributes of its state and also examine what has been the reaction to them.

As the Russian economy rebounded in 2000–2008, from its nadir in the 1990s, it allowed the state to gain both new capabilities and new standing to play the foreign role its leaders and elites believed they should play. And this trend was observable in the Middle East as well as elsewhere. Already we see substantial advances in Moscow's ability and willingness to sell arms abroad to Arab states and use those relationships to foster new ties between Russia and regional actors. As

Anna Borshchevskaya shows in her paper for this book, Russian leaders have always understood the importance of arms sales as a factor enhancing ties to clients and Russia's standing in states who buy those weapons and associated services. Nor is this merely a question of heightened Russian capabilities. The internal dynamics of a highly conflict-prone Middle East lead its leaders to come to Russia to buy more and ever newer weapons:

> As Sergei Chemezov, chief of the powerful state industrial holding Rostec, said in February 2015, "As for the conflict situation in the Middle East, I do not conceal it, and everyone understands this, the more conflicts there are, the more they [clients] buy weapons from us. Volumes are continuing to grow despite sanctions. Mainly, it is in Latin America and the Middle East."[20]

But Russia's capacity to attract Arab interest or simultaneously to engage Middle Eastern states in a positive way are not exclusively restricted to arms sales. As Stephen Blank shows in his paper, Moscow has gone back to employing tactics and strategies for dealing with Muslim peoples at home and abroad that have stood it in good stead throughout the entire checkered history of Russian empire building, imperial collapses, and now an attempted rejuvenation of the empire or at least its great power status.[21]

Consequently, since 2000, a complex process has arisen whereby both Moscow and leading Arab states seek to influence each other's domestic and Islamic elites for the purpose of enhancing each side's political-economic-ideological interests. While Moscow has allowed for substantial financial investments by Arab sovereign funds (about which more is stated below), it has also secured opportunities for using the Chechen government under its client, Ramzan Kadyrov, to carry out sensitive missions and spread positive information about Russian policy in the Middle East. Thus, Moscow has updated its long-standing imperial tactic that dates back to its inception as a state: finding elites from among Islamic societies who are willing or even eager to be coopted into Russian state service and using them as the *avant-garde* of its efforts to integrate them into the Russian state. And at least from Soviet times, Moscow has used Muslim scholars to attract Middle Eastern elites to Soviet and now Russian achievements.[22]

Thus, Russia's Middle Eastern policy has, for some time, expressed the general process in Russian policy of a greater identification with the East in order to resolve or at least tackle pressing political challenges. International relations scholar Andrej Kreutz observed in this context that, for Putin,

> The sheer size and ferocity of the Islamic challenge had an impact on the new Russian leader and persuaded him that a new political approach was necessary in order to solve the conflicts with the Muslim population of the country and have a closer link with the Islamic nations.[23]

Similarly, political analyst and Russia editor of *Al Monitor*, Maxim Suchkov, commented,

> As an external power, Russia needs regional partners to master its own Islamist challenges in the Caucasus, the Volga region, and the Urals, to name a few. Thus Moscow is in constant pursuit of a balance between a pragmatic foreign policy in the Middle East and its own domestic problems in this regard.[24]

Among those Islamist challenges is Russia's own restive Muslim population, whose numbers are growing while those of the "Slavic cohort" are falling quite rapidly. As Ilan Berman points out in his contribution to this book, the danger of radicalism is an ever-present concern to the Russian government and one of the prime motivations that it has given and that external observers attribute to it for intervening in Syria. But this fear of Islamic terrorism migrating through the Middle East back to Russia also prompted Russia to intervene in Libya against Islamist forces. But at the same time, as Berman argues, the Kremlin will come under increasing domestic pressure to work with Muslim governments in the Middle East and alleviate the domestic conditions of its Muslim population, whose demands for more enfranchisement are inevitable.[25] Whether Moscow can square that latter circle is a moot point; but the existence of a swelling Muslim population is already a fact of life that affects Moscow's policies. Indeed, in 2003, Putin told the Mufti of Tajikistan that Russia "could be regarded as part of the Islamic world in some sense"; and a year later, it filed a formal application to join the Organization of the Islamic Conference, clearly as a nod to domestic realities. The determination to shelter Russia from Islamic terrorist influence relates to Moscow's sense of the vulnerability of Russia's Muslim population to the siren song of Islamism.[26]

It is not a surprise then that, in 2003, Putin defined Russia as an Islamic country and joined the Organization of Islamic Countries (OIC) to establish Russia as a bridge between Europe and the Islamic world and to "do everything to promote the idea of the similarity of the Russian and 'Islamic' approaches to many international issues."[27] Everything since then has only reinforced elite opinion that Russia must persevere along this course for its own security against terrorism and due to its particular demographic profile.[28] And as that demographic profile becomes more skewed or weighted toward a large Muslim influence in Russian politics as well as the danger of internal terrorism, Russia will have little choice but to pursue a proactive course in the Middle East—not unlike what it has been doing for several years.

Adding to the continuing utility of arms sales and the tactics of using Muslim elites in Russia and in the Middle East to resolve urgent challengers is Moscow's enhanced economic and informational capabilities, which have grown in magnitude since 2000, notwithstanding long-term structural defects in Russia's economy. Donald Jensen, writing in this book, elucidates the channels by which

Russia conducts the same kind of information warfare (IW) in Syria that it has done in Europe and the United States. And it is clear from Jensen's analysis (as well as from other papers) that Moscow has successfully garnered a large audience for its media presentations of its policies and of international relations in the Middle East and elsewhere. The extent to which Middle Eastern audiences trust what Moscow presents is quite unclear, but there can be no denying the extent of Moscow's informational reach and the fact that there are receptive audiences for its message.[29]

Similarly, in his paper for this collective work, Shehab Al-Makahleh confirms that Arab youth and other audiences evidently view Moscow's intervention in Syria in a favorable light, especially when juxtaposed against the US interventions in Libya and Iraq. He also points out that that China is apparently abetting Russia's penetration of the Middle East. Given the growing strategic comprehensive partnership, if not alliance, between Beijing and Moscow, that trend could have portentous implications for the region and world politics.[30] China's power potential in the Middle East, to be sure, is primarily economic. But there are signs that it is ready to intervene in some still-unspecified but decisive way to sustain Bashar al-Assad's rule in Syria.[31] And the China connection forces us to look as well at the economic instruments that Russia has crafted for sustaining its intervention in Syria and broader regional presence in spite of its visible economic weakness.

Thus, Theodore Karasik, in his contribution, finds that, since 2007 (if not before), Russia has astutely created mechanisms to tie Arab wealth to its politics and create durable financial and energy linkages that create lasting economic-political communities of interest across the Middle East with Russian elites. These instruments of economic power are:

- Creating a "north–south" corridor of economic connections based on a confluence of Russia's historical and cultural drive to achieve a rightful place in the Middle East;
- Pushing connectivity through soft power instruments such as "Roadshows" but also through the activity of Russian business councils;
- Signing Russia-Arab finance agreements, especially between Sovereign Wealth Funds (SWF) and other Gulf Arab government–owned investment vehicles;
- Printing currency for distribution in Middle East war zones.[32]

The mechanisms thus created not only facilitate lasting commercial and investment ties but also, as Karasik observes, create a basis for Russia's increasing economic-political penetration into Africa.[33] For example, Russia's successes in the Middle East have led the UAE's Crown Prince, Mohammad Bin Zayed, to say that both governments share open communication channels on all issues of international affairs and will form a strategic partnership to promote their relationship.[34] And thanks to their economic and political partnership, the UAE is helping Russia penetrate Africa as well.[35] Presumably, as the UAE visibly increases its capabilities for projecting its influence abroad, it will likely bring Russia into at least some of those arenas, like Africa.[36] This certainly makes for a long-time relation that imparts significant economic and political resources to Russia for the benefit of its quest for great power standing in the Middle East. In this context, the north-south corridor is a strategic reality that allows Russia's relationship with Arab states to serve as a jumping-off point for Russian economic initiatives in Africa and the global South.

And, of course, these financial and investment relationships are not the only or even primary source of Russian economic presence in the Middle East. That place obviously belongs to the energy relationships that Russia has forged and is forging across the entire area. As we have long known, energy is a primary weapon of Russian foreign policy and seen as such by Moscow. As Russia's Energy Strategy Through 2035 states explicitly, "Russia as a responsible state considers external energy policy not form the exporter's narrow point of view, intended to maximize short-term revenues, but as a tool to solve both national and global problems."[37]

As Rauf Mammadov observes in his paper found in this book, Russia's goals regarding energy in the Middle East are to:

- Find new markets for its oil and gas.
- Attract investment for an economy whose capital from the West has dried up from sanctions.
- Work with other energy exporters to stabilize international oil prices.
- Undermine Europe's efforts to diversify its natural gas supplies.
- Help Russia deliver more oil and gas to Asia.[38]

In other words, Russia's Middle Eastern policies go beyond the Middle East to include Europe and Asia. It is not just a question of energy but also of geopolitical ambition, as reflected in Russia's energy policies and the ongoing acquisition of air and naval bases from which to project power and deny NATO access to the Eastern Mediterranean and Black Sea.[39] But on a daily basis, the most consequential economic relationship between Moscow and Middle Eastern states is the energy tie. Moscow is now building the TurkStream pipeline to Turkey and, from there, throughout the Balkans. The pipeline is meant to ship gas that heretofore has been traversing Ukraine. Morover, Russia has signed energy deals with both the Iraqi government and the Kurdish Regional Government in Erbil that have given it enormous leverage between those rival parties as well as Turkey, which has a vital interest in the status of the Iraqi Kurds.[40]

Beyond that, as Mammadov points out, Russia is engaged with Algeria, Libya and Egypt's energy sectors, including nuclear energy. It has also made large-scale energy deals with Saudi Arabia and is cooperating with it in trying to regulate global oil production, essentially supplanting OPEC.[41] At the same time it has made major energy deals with Qatar and has obtained major concessions regarding Syrian energy assets and pipelines.[42] But Russia's energy deals do not end there. It has made major efforts to insert itself into the large-scale deposits found in the Mediterranean by Cyprus, Egypt and Israel. And it has signed several major deals with Iran since 2016.[43] In addition, there are unconfirmed reports of a still larger $50 billion recent deal with Rosneft.[44]

And yet, flexible diplomacy, the exploitation of elite cleavages that attract Muslim elites to Moscow, information warfare, financial deals and arms sales are not the full extent of Russian initiatives toward the Middle East. Moscow has also displayed an intelligent military strategy to complement or facilitate its larger multi-dimensional strategy to assure itself of regional prominence and demand global equivalence with the US. This strategy, according to the Israeli scholar Dmitry Adamsky, is a "multi-dimensional strategy of coercion to compel audiences to accept the Kremlin's self-valuation and objectives."[45] But within the purely military sphere, Moscow has both innovated creatively and succeeded in Syria beyond most analysts' and maybe even its own expectations.

As Yuri Barmin notes in his paper for this book, it is hard (i.e., military) power that has enabled Russia to achieve what amounts to a battlefield victory and, prospectively, a political resolution of Syria's civil war. Thus military victory is now being translated and expanded into a lasting political presence. Indeed, as he crucially notes, not only has Moscow enhanced its reputation and standing throughout the Middle East, it has created and is now fulfilling Middle Eastern expectations that it will remain a major actor there for a long time to come.[46] Thus as he and Stephen Blank argue, Moscow is now not only consolidating but also expanding its position in the Middle East into one of sustainable influence through 2025 if not beyond.[47] Moreover, they both see clearly that by virtue of its victory in the Middle East, Moscow is now able to generate the multi-dimensional elements of influence and even coercion mentioned above. In particular, they both emphasize the importance of the network of air and naval bases that Russia is now building in the Mediterranean and Red Sea and around the Middle East. This network of military facilities both allow Moscow to project its own power as well as push NATO back from the Levant and the wider Black Sea region, thus obstructing the North Atlantic Alliance's own ability to project power into those regions, if not beyond.[48] Furthermore, they both point to the fact that Moscow's enhanced capabilities to project power and impose escalation control upon wars like Syria's—capabilities that had long been complacently dismissed by numerous observers—now allow the Russian Federation to expand its purview into Africa, as it is now doing.[49]

For the future, we should note that Vladimir Putin has already directed the forces at his disposal to increase Russia's presence in Africa by saying that, "Africa cannot be on the periphery of international relations" given its security problems, which affect all of the international community.[50] For that reason we should not be surprised at the expansion of Russian influence into Africa that is now occurring in the wake of its Middle Eastern ascendancy.[51] But the connection between Moscow's military intervention into Syria's civil war and Africa does not end here.

Although it might in some manner be emulating the US use of private contractors during its wars in Iraq and Afghanistan, Russia has also creatively fashioned its own version of so-called "private military companies" (PMC). These companies are deeply rooted in Russian military history under both Tsarism and Soviet power, as Sergei Sukhankin demonstrates in his chapter to this book; and they also solve domestic as well as foreign policy issues.[52] The use of such forces, most notably the Wagner Group (so named because its founder, Dmitry Utkin, is a fan of German composer Richard Wagner's operas), has occasionally ended in calamity, such as Wagner's deadly defeat when facing US-led forces in Syria in early 2018. Nonetheless, Moscow is clearly committed to the continued employment of these PMCs not only in Syria but also Africa.[53] The murder of three Russian journalists in the Central African Republic (CAR) as they were investigating the Wagner PMC's operations there, casts a potentially lurid light upon such "private" security activities. More importantly, it shows how these PMCs are executing Russian policy in Africa, for example in the CAR and Sudan.[54] Thus, as Sukhankin has written elsewhere,

> In this regard, it is worthwhile to take a look at an assessment presented by the French expert Didier François, who expressed confidence that Russian "instructors" will be deployed to the Central African Republic, on the border with Sudan, specifically to the "area containing gold, uranium and diamonds." This will allow the Russians to kill two birds with one stone—"securing Russia's economic interests and expanding its military-political presence in East-Central Africa." Incidentally, a statement presented by the Russian Ministry of Foreign Affairs identified the "exploration of locally based deposits of natural resources" and the "realization of concessions in the mining sector" as key elements that originally enticed Russia to begin cooperating with Sudan.[55]

In other words, Moscow will build on its successes in the Middle East and diffuse them across that region into North and Sub-Saharan Africa. The African continent is notably becoming more important to Russia following Putin's injunction above. As such, Moscow is utilizing its capabilities not only to enhance its influence and leverage there but also to regionally challenge Europe by exploiting energy supply links with African countries as well as exacerbating the flows of northward-bound refugees. By thus creating a tense domestic situation in European countries overwhelmed by migration from the south, Moscow enables its local clients (subsidized political parties) to then exploit those political-social tensions against competing local pro-American forces.[56] Therefore, here again we see the linkages between Middle Eastern and European security (and arguably African security as well). This assessment suggests a critical dimension to Russia's overall security strategy in the Middle East as well as elsewhere. Moscow intends to make its presence felt, forcefully, if necessary, in regional security affairs by means of systematic multi-dimensional coercion and influence campaigns against the Western liberal order in order to force acceptance of it as a great global power.[57] As former Israeli ambassador to Russia Zvi Magen puts it, "Putin's long-term goal is not just an empire but global superpower status, at least equal to the US—in promoting this goal, he has to achieve influence in every regional crisis on the international arena."[58] Or if we say it epigrammatically, Russia intends to force regional bipolarity upon the West in order to compel the acceptance of global multi-polarity. As Vergil wrote in *The Aeneid*, "If I cannot move heaven, I will raise hell."[59]

Western policymakers and analysts now seem to grasp this aspect of Moscow's objectives. Assistant Secretary of State A. Wess Mitchell testified that,

> Moscow's primary aims in Syria are not really about the Syrian people or the stability of the region. Moscow wants to retain its presence in Syria as an entry point through which to influence future events in the Levant and Eastern Mediterranean. It also wants to inflict globally visible defeat on the United States: to create a negative "demonstration effect" of thwarting our aims here to dishearten our friends abroad and to drive wedges between us and our allies.[60]

Similarly, Mark Katz and Phillipp Casula also have written that Russia cannot relate to the Middle East without relating to the West. "In no other part of the world is Russia's foreign policy as "influenced by the development and behavior of Western nations." Thus, the competition with Washington or the broader West is not only in the Middle East but also for the Middle East.[61] They also note that Moscow's participation here is not directed toward creating or recreating some new order in the Middle East but in merely taking advantage of its travails to ensure Russian presence there and thwart the West. The rivalry in the region, therefore, necessitates a search for a US strategy that can enlist the efforts of local governments, just as Moscow has done.[62]

Indeed, precisely because of the inherent limitations upon Russian power and capability, plus the external sanctions that have been levied upon it since 2014, Moscow requires partners and even enablers in order to achieve its objectives in the Middle East and beyond. We have already cited the case of the UAE. But two other key partners or even enablers of Russian policy are Turkey and Iran. This does not mean these states work with Russia as a cohesive bloc. Rather, Moscow has invested heavily in its relations with them in order to find the basis for a long-term continuous working relationship allowing for the resolution of commonly perceived tasks, challenges and goals.

To be sure, Turkey and Iran are much more difficult partners to work with than the UAE, for example, which, as noted above, facilitating Russian policies in the Middle East and Africa.[63] In Iran's case, the relationship with Russia is notably marked by mutual distrust, historic suspicions if not enmity, and numerous tensions. And yet, Russian analysts and elites have long believed that Moscow must, nevertheless, find a way to work with Tehran when necessary and possible and to some degree stand in the way of US threats toward the Iranian Republic.[64] Indeed, in his paper, Iranian expert Alex Vatanka finds that Russia needs regional partners or allies (at least on a case by case basis, not a formal alliance); and Iran's utility, by virtue of its hostility to the US, makes it eminently suited to play that role, despite the divergence in policies between both sides.[65]

Yet, at the same time, it seems clear that if the opportunity to build a strong relationship with Washington is on the table, Moscow will show little hesitation in sacrificing Tehran to that cause. Thus, at the US and Russia's July 2018 Helsinki summit, President Putin evidently agreed with President Donald Trump that Iran should not play a role in postwar Syria but that it was very hard to enforce that outcome.[66] In this fashion, Putin can make a deal with Washington but also play an equivocal role in simultaneously restraining Iran and delaying or softening the blow.

As in so many other cases, Russia tries to be simultaneously Iran's prosecutor and defense counsel. Nevertheless, Iran and Russia signed a military agreement in early 2015 and that remains operative: Moscow even obtained an Iranian base at Hamdan in 2015—until it publicly admitted that fact in 2016, putting Tehran under domestic political pressure to stop that practice.[67] Therefore, for US allies, Moscow's ties to Tehran remain a consistent preoccupation even as they strive to partner with Russia on other issues or find a modus vivendi in Syria. Indeed, it is a tribute to Russia's achievements and flexible diplomacy that, in case after case in the Middle East, Moscow has been able to intervene on one side of a dispute and then employ the leverage it has accrued to play a mediating or partner role with both sides.

This characteristic is amply discernible with regard to Turkey, despite centuries of strife and suspicion between it and Russia. For instance, Russia has utilized the Kurdish and Armenian cards against Turkey since 1890, if not before.[68] Yet, by virtue of its ability to be simultaneously a sponsor of Kurdish terrorism and a major provider of energy to Turkey—actions that give Moscow enormous leverage over Kurdish movements in Iraq and Turkey, as well as its intervention in Syria—Moscow has essentially compelled Ankara to cooperate. And since Syria is, in Turkish eyes, a test of Western support for Turkey's domestic political structure as well as its security and foreign standing, and the West has consistently failed Turkey (as it sees it) here, Ankara has had no choice but to gravitate to Moscow. Or at least that is the Turkish narrative, as Mitat Çelikpala demonstrates in his paper.[69] This narrative preceded the recent steep and apparently accelerating decline of US-Turkish relations that is attributable to many factors on both sides beyond Syria. But arguably, even if all the other issues at stake in the Washington-Ankara rift are resolved, until the US fashions a Middle Eastern and Syrian strategy that in some measure answers Turkey's needs, Moscow will have all too easy an opportunity to intensify its efforts to drive Turkey out of the West.

Conclusion

As virtually every observer has now grasped, Russia is in the Middle East to stay.[70] As we have argued, Moscow's intervention in Syria and subsequent enlargement of its Middle Eastern standing are not things that happened out of the blue or a mere brilliant tactical improvisation. Indeed, John Parker's study of Russian policy for the National Defense University (NDU) makes clear that Russia was already escalating its presence in Syria from 2013 on. While other sources point out that planning for the actual intervention began in January 2015, at Iran's request, given al-Assad's visible loss of territory and power.[71] And beyond that linkage, it appears from Parker's analysis that the steady ratcheting upwards of arms transfers to Syria in 2011–2013 through a naval screen prepared the ground for (and was linked in Putin's mind to) the need to prevent another "color revolution" in Ukraine. In other words, the successful and stealthy employment of the navy and other organs to increase arms supplies to Syria helped convince Putin to invade Ukraine as did the linkages between preventing the triumph of revolutions in areas of importance to Moscow.[72] And before that, as this book's following chapters and other sources make clear, the ideas and programs that have paved the way for the enlargement of Russian capacity were under way and missed by the West. Just as the West "slept through" the Russian buildup—feeling unjustly complacent that Russia could not challenge the West in the Middle East or project power there—it still is reluctant to grasp the scope of Moscow's achievement in this region or the opportunities accruing to it in neighboring Africa. As a result, and as noted above, it is only now that some officials have awoken from their lethargy to grasp that Moscow's activities in the Middle East constitute a challenge to US policies there as well as in Africa and Europe. If the essays here serve to awaken readers to the current challenge and stimulate the search for a viable and strategic response to Russia's challenge, then the collective "Russia in the Middle East" project will have served its purpose.

ENDNOTES

[1] "Russian Military Police To Create Eight Outposts Near Syrian-Israeli Border," *TASS*, August 10, 2018.

[2] Zach Battat, "Peace In the Middle East: Russia's Role In the Israeli-Palestinian Conflict," Russian International Affairs Council, ww.russiancouncil.ru/en, August 13, 2018; "Arab League Expects Russia to Propose Initiatives to Resist US Steps – Envoy," *Sputnik News*, August 16, 2018, https://sputniknews.com/middleeast/201808161067252260-arab-league-russia-us-unilateral-steps/.

[3] "Libya's East-Based Army Calls For Stronger Russia Ties," *BBC Monitoring*, August 9, 2018.

[4] Jacques Rousselier, "A Role For Russia In the Western Sahara?" Carnegie Endowment, August 9, 2018, http://www.carnegieendowment.org/sada/76532.

[5] Casablanca, *Akhbar Al-Youm Al-Maghrebiya Online*, in Arabic, October 30, 2013, *Open Source Center, Foreign Broadcast Information Service, Central Eurasia ,* (Henceforth, *FBIS SOV*), October 30, 2013.

[6] Stephen Blank, "Russia's Middle Eastern Position in 2025," The Jamestown Foundation, November 20, 2018.

[7] Anna Borshchevskaya, "The Tactical Side of Russia's Arms Sales to the Middle East," The Jamestown Foundation, December 20, 2017.

[8] Ben Aris, "Moscow Blog: Turkey's Crisis a Golden Opportunity For the Kremlin," BNE Intellinews, August 13, 2018, http://www.intellinews.com/moscow-blog-turkey-s-crisis-a-golden-opportunity-for-the-kremlin-146777/; "Kremlin Speaks About Possibility Of Providing Assistance To Turkey," News.am, August 14, 2018, https://news.am/eng/news/466144.html.

[9] Maziar Motamedi, "Russia-Led Payment Network could Blunt US Sanctions On Iran," *Al-Monitor*, August 22, 2018, https://www.al-monitor.com/pulse/originals/2018/08/iran-russia-regional-payment-network-sanctions-pressure.html; "Russia Says Dollar's Days Numbered As Global Trade Currency," *Reuters*, August 14, 2018; Ben Aris, "Russia and Turkey Step Up Fight Against Dollar's Dominance In Trade," *BNE Intellinews*, August 13, 2018, http://www.intellinews.com/russia-and-turkey-step-up-fight-against-dollar-s-dominance-in-trade-146995/; "Russia Proposes Deal With Turkey To Ditch US Dollar For Lira-Ruble Trade Amid Currency Crisis," *RT*, August 15, 2018, https://www.rt.com/business/435978-russia-turkey-ditching-dollar/.

[10] Anwar Iqbal, "Russia's Growing Influence Cause Of concern: U.S. General," *Dawn*, August 13, 2018, https://www.dawn.com/news/1426686.

[11] *FBIS SOV*, October 30, 2013; Stephen Blank, "Energy and Russia's High-Stakes Game in Iraq," EGS Working Paper 2015-2-1, Center for Energy Governance and Security, Hanyang University, 2015.

[12] James Sladden, Becca Wasser, Ben Connable, and Sarah-Grand Clement, *Russian Strategy In the Middle East*, Rand Corporation, 2017.

[13] Samuel Charap, "Is Russia An Outside Power In the Gulf?" *Survival*, LVII, No. 1, February 2015, p. 154.

[14] Stephen Blank, "The Foundations of Russian Policy in the Middle East," The Jamestown Foundation, October 5, 2017.

[15] Blank, "The Foundations of Russian Policy in the Middle East."

[16] Quoted in, Alvin Z. Rubinstein, "Moscow and Teheran: The Wary Accommodation," Alvin Z. Rubinstein and Oles M. Smolansky, Eds., *Regional Power Rivalries in the New Eurasia: Russia, Turkey, and Iran*, Armonk, New York: M.E. Sharpe, Inc. and Co., 1994, pp. 31–32.

[17] Sergey M. Rogov, "Russia and NATO's Enlargement: The Search for a Compromise at the Helsinki Summit," Center for Naval Analyses, Alexandria, VA. CIM 513/ May, 1997, p. 10.

[18] For Trenin's views and other such expressions see: E-mail Letter from Darrell Hammer, Johnson's Russia List, February 5, 1997, Dmitry Trenin, "Transformation of Russian Foreign Policy: NATO Expansion Can Have Negative Consequences for the West," *Nezavisimaya Gazeta*, February 5, 1997, E-Mail Transmission; J. Michael Waller, "Primakov's Imperial Line," *Perspective*, VII, No. 3, January-February 1997, pp. 2–6; "Primakov, Setting a New, Tougher Foreign Policy," *Current Digest of the Post-Soviet Press* (Henceforth *CDPP*), XLIX, No. 2, February 12, 1997, pp. 4–7.

[19] Zvi Magen, *Russia and the Middle East: Poliycy Challenges*, Institute of National Security Studies (INSS), Memorandum, NO. 127, 2013, pp. 9–10.

[20] "Glava Rostekha Soobshchil of Roste Prodazh Chem Bol'she Korose Prodazh," Newsru.com, February 23, 2015, http://www.newsru.com/russia/23feb2015/chemezov.html; as quoted in Borshchevskaya, "The Tactical Side of Russia's Arms Sales to the Middle East."

[21] Stephen Blank, "Imperial Strategies: Russia's Exploitation of Ethnic Issues and Policy in the Middle East," The Jamestown Foundation, December 20, 2017.

[22] Alec Nove and J.A. Newth, *The Soviet Middle East: A Model for Development?* London: Routledge (Routledge Revivals), 2013; Alexandre Bennigsen, Paul B. Henze, George K. Tanham, and S. Enders Wimbush, *Soviet Strategy and Islam*, Macmillan, London, 1989.

[23] Andrej Kreutz, "Bilateral Relations Between Rusia and the Gulf Monarchies: Past and Present," Marat Terterov, Ed., *Russian and CIS Relations With the Gulf Region: Current Trends In Political and Economic Dynamics*, Dubai, Gulf Research Center, 2009 p. 44.

[24] Maxim A. Suchkov, "Russia Rising," *Al-Monitor*, October 15, 2015, https://www.al-monitor.com/pulse/originals/2015/10/russia-campaign-syria-options-leadership.html.

[25] Ilan Berman, "Demography's Pull on Russian Mideast Policy," The Jamestown Foundation, March 8, 2018.

[26] Witold Rodkiewicz, *Russia's Middle Eastern Policy: Regional Ambitions, Global Objectives,* Warsaw, Centre For Eastern Studies, OSD Study No. 71, 2017, p. 18.

[27] Leonid Gankin and Vladimir Serebryakov, "Islam Receives Vladimir Putin," Moscow, Kommersant, in Russian, October 16, 2003; *FBIS SOV*, February 7, 2005.

[28] "Islam In Politics: Ideology Or Pragmatism?" pp. 100–105.

[29] Donald Jensen, "Russia in the Middle East: A New Front in the Information War?" The Jamestown Foundation, December 20, 2017.

[30] Shehab al-Makahleh, "The Arab View of Russia's Role in the MENA: Changing Arab Perceptions Of Russia, and the Implications For US Policy," The Jamestown Foundation, October 5, 2017.

[31] Logan Pauley and Jesse Marks, "Is China Increasing Its Military Presence in Syria?" *The Diplomat*, August 20, 2018, https://thediplomat.com/2018/08/is-china-increasing-its-military-presence-in-syria/.

[32] Theodore Karasik, "Russia's Financial Tactics in the Middle East," The Jamestown Foundation, December 20, 2017.

[33] Stephen Blank, "Russia Returns To Africa," *GIS Reports Online*, August 17, 2018, https://www.gisreportsonline.com/opinion-russia-returns-to-africa,politics,2631.html.

[34] Theodore Karasik and Giorgio Cafiero, "Russia and the UAE: Friends With Benefits," *Intropolicydigest.org*, April 26, 2017, https://intpolicydigest.org/2017/04/26/russia-uae-friends-benefits/.

[35] Blank, "Russia Returns To Africa."

[36] Camille Lons, "Battle Of the Ports: Emirates Sea Power Spreads From Persian Gulf To Africa," *Newsweek*, August 6, 2018; "UAE Ready To Take On Greater Security Burden In Middle East, Minister," *Reuters*, July 28, 2018.

[37] Quoted in Vira Ratisborynska, "Russia's Hybrid Warfare in the Form of Its Energy Manoeuvers Against Europe: How the EU and NATO Can Respond Together?," NATO Defense College Research Papers, No. 147, June, 2018, p. 3.

[38] Rauf Mammadov, "Russia in the Middle East: Energy Forever?" The Jamestown Foundation, March 8, 2018.

[39] Blank, "Russia's Middle Eastern Position in 2025."

[40] Blank, "Energy and Russia's High-Stakes Game in Iraq."

[41] Mammadov, "Russia in the Middle East: Energy Forever?"

[42] Ibid.

[43] Ekaterina Pokrovskaya, "Russia and Iran Sign Flurry of Energy Deals: What's Next," *Oilprice.com*, November 10, 2016, https://oilprice.com/Energy/Energy-General/Russia-And-Iran-Sign-Flurry-Of-Energy-Deals-Whats-Next.html; Callum Wood, "Russia and Iran Sign $30 Billion Energy Deals," November 10, 2017.

[44] "Russia ready to invest $50 billion in Iran's oil & gas projects," *Neftegaz.ru*, July 16, 2018, https://neftegaz.ru/en/news/view/173310-Russia-ready-to-invest-50-billion-in-Iran-s-oil-gas-projects.

[45] Dmitry Adamsky *Cross-Domain Strategy: The Current Russian Art of Strategy*, Institut Francais Des Relations Internationales (IFRI), Proliferation Papers, No. 54, 2015.

[46] Yuri Barmin, "Russia in the Middle East Until 2024: From Hard Power to Sustainable Influence," The Jamestown Foundation, March 8, 2018.

[47] Barmin, "Russia in the Middle East Until 2024: From Hard Power to Sustainable Influence"; Blank, "Russia's Middle Eastern Position In 2025."

[48] Ibidem.

[49] Ibidem.

[50] "Putin Zayavil Chto Afrika Ne Mozhet Byt' Na Peripferii Mezhdunarodnykh Otnoshenii," *RIA Novosti*, October 27, 2016, https://ria.ru/world/20161027/1480166410.html.

[51] Blank, "Russia Returns To Africa."

[52] Sergei Sukhankin, "'Continuing War by Other Means': The Case of Wagner, Russia's Premier Private Military Company in the Middle East," The Jamestown Foundation, July 13, 2018.

[53] Sukhankin, "'Continuing War by Other Means': The Case of Wagner, Russia's Premier Private Military Company in the Middle East"; "How

'Wagner' Came To Syria," *The Economist*, November 2, 2017, https://www.economist.com/europe/2017/11/02/how-wagner-came-to-syria; Adam Taylor, "What We Know About the Shadowy Russian Mercenary Firm Behind an Attack on U.S. Troops in Syria," *The Washington Post*, February 23, 2018, https://www.washingtonpost.com/news/worldviews/wp/2018/02/23/what-we-know-about-the-shadowy-russian-mercenary-firm-behind-the-attack-on-u-s-troops-in-syria/?utm_term=.9e783dd63e68.

[54] Daniel Brown, "3 Countries Where Russia's Shadowy Wagner Group Mercenaries Are Known To Operate," *Business Insider*, April 27, 2018, https://www.businessinsider.com/russia-wagner-group-mercenaries-where-operate-2018-4.

[55] Sergey Sukhankin, "Beyond Syria and Ukraine: Wagner PMC Expands Its Operations To Syria," *Indian Strategic Studies*, May 5, 2018, http://strategicstudyindia.blogspot.com/2018/05/beyond-syria-and-ukraine-wagner-pmc.html.

[56] Pavel Baev, "European Assessments and Concerns About Russia's Policies in the Middle East," The Jamestown Foundation, October 5, 2017.

[57] Rodkiewicz, p. 20; Dmitri Trenin, *What Is Russia Up To In the Middle East?* Cambridge: Polity Press, 2018.

[58] Quoted in Joshua Spurlock, "'Emperor' Putin's Middle East, Russia's Ongoing Role in the Region," *The Mideast Update*, https://www.bridgesforpeace.com/article/emperor-putins-middle-east-russias-ongoing-role-in-the-region/, May 8, 2018.

[59] "Flectere si nequeo superos, Acheronta Movebo!" as quoted in *Virgil's Aeneid*, book VII.312.

[60] Testimony by Assistant Secretary Wess Mitchell, House Foreign Affairs Committee, "Hearing on U.S. Policy Toward a Turbulent Middle East," House.gov, April 18, 2018.

[61] Philipp Casula and Mark N. Katz, "The Middle East," Andrei N. Tsygankov, Ed., *Routledge Handbook of Russian Foreign policy*, London: Routledge, 2018, p. 295.

[62] Casula and Katz, "The Middle East," p. 301.

[63] Karasik and Cafiero, "Russia and the UAE: Friends With Benefits."

[64] John W. Parker, *Russia and the Iranian Nuclear Program: Replay or Breakthrough?* INSS Strategic Perspectives No. 9, 2012, http://ndupress.ndu.edu/Portals/68/Documents/stratperspective/inss/Strategic-Perspectives-9.pdf.

[65] Alex Vatanka, "Iran's Russian Conundrum," The Jamestown Foundation, October 5, 2017.

[66] Amir Tibon, "Trump and Putin Agree That Iran Needs To Pull Out of Syria, Says U.S. Official," *Haaretz*, August 17, 2018, https://www.haaretz.com/world-news/.premium-trump-and-putin-agree-that-iran-needs-to-pull-out-of-syria-1.6387415.

[67] Anne Barnard and Andrew E. Kramer, "Iran Revokes Russia's Use of Air Base, Saying Moscow 'Betrayed Trust,'" *The New York Times*, August 23, 2016, https://www.nytimes.com/2016/08/23/world/middleeast/iran-russia-syria.html; Vatanka, "Iran's Russian Conundrum."

[68] Michael A. Reynolds, *Shattering Empires: The Clash and Collapse of the Ottoman and Russian Empires 1908-1918*, Cambridge: Cambridge University Press, 2011.

[69] Mitat Çelikpala,"Russia's Policies In the Middle East and the Pendulum of Turkish-Russian Relations," The Jamestown Foundation, October 5, 2017.

[70] Chuck Freilich, "In the Middle East the Russians Aren't Coming: They Are Back," *The National Interest*, August 13, 2018, https://nationalinterest.org/feature/middle-east-russians-aren%E2%80%99t-coming-they-are-back-28672.

[71] John W. Parker, *Understanding Putin Through a Middle Eastern Looking Glass*, Institute for National Strategic Studies, National Defense University, Fort Leslie McNair, Washington, D.C, 2015.

[72] Parker, *Understanding Putin Through a Middle Eastern Looking Glass*, pp. 25–39.

2. The Foundations of Russian Policy in the Middle East

Stephen Blank

Summary

There is little doubt that Russia is winning in the Middle East at the expense of the United States. This strategic development has a lengthy history:

- As foreign minister and later prime minister, Yevgeny Primakov laid the intellectual and political foundations for Vladimir Putin's current policies in the Middle East.

- Putin has adroitly refined and modified that framework where and when necessary, e.g. to confront the threat of terrorism and develop Russia's capabilities.

- The framework is intrinsically anti-American and motivated by an obsession to recover Russia's great power status of bygone times.

- Russia regards the Middle East as a prime area for achieving both critical domestic and foreign policy goals that are also increasingly linked together by Moscow.

Introduction

Few American officials and analysts believe that Vladimir Putin has a strategy, and even fewer discern a Russian strategy for the Middle East beyond Syria.[1] The myth of Putin as a mere tactician or poor strategist dies hard.[2] This chapter attempts to remedy that shortcoming by demonstrating Russia's long-standing, dynamic, and evolving strategy for the entire Middle East since the times of former spymaster, foreign minister and then prime minister of Russia, Yevgeny Primakov. Although Primakov functioned as leader during the nadir of Russian influence and bequeathed to Vladimir Putin a strategy born of weakness; since Moscow intervened in Syria's civil war in 2015, Russia has proceeded with growing confidence, retaining the core precepts of Primakov's approach while adding and refining them in the light of Putin's perceptions and experience. In essence, we must remember that Russia's intervention in Syria's civil war did not occur in a void but rather takes place within a definite and discernible context.

From Primakov to Putin

Although Primakov's vision emanated from Russian weakness, its core precept is that Russia must regain its standing as a great power. Consequently one enduring driver of Russian policy here is the constant effort to remind everyone that Russia is a great power globally and has critical equities in the Middle East that must be respected. But Russia must also act and be seen as a great power globally and regionally to counter the United States—its principal rival if not enemy. Russia's return as a pole of the emerging multipolar world is "a natural desire in the multipolar world."[3] Therefore, Russia must act as and become a counterforce to the US in the Middle East.[4] Upon becoming foreign minister in 1996, Primakov told *Rossiyskaya Gazeta,*

> Russia's foreign policy cannot be the foreign policy of a second-rate state. We must pursue the foreign policy of a great state—the world is moving toward a multipolar system. In these conditions, we must pursue a diversified course oriented toward the development of relations with everyone and, at the same time, in my view, we should not align ourselves with any individual pole. Precisely because Russia itself will be one of the poles, the "leader-led" configuration is not acceptable to us.[5]

Thus, rivalry with the US has been the core of foreign policy for over 20 years, not least in the Middle East. In fact, Russia acts as if it itself is at war with the North Atlantic Treaty Organization (NATO), and not just the United States. On January 18, 2005, Russian Defense Minister Sergei Ivanov told the Academy of Military Sciences, the official institutional locus of systematic thinking about contemporary war, that, "There is a war against Russia under way, and it has been going on for quite a few years. No one declared war on us. There is not one country that would be in a state of war with Russia. But there are people and organizations in various countries who take part in hostilities against the Russian Federation."[6] In that light, Russia's failure to achieve great power status and a lack of recognition abroad means, first of all, a defeat in this war. Moreover, Moscow creates domestic pressures that threaten the foundations of Russia's own statehood. Consequently if Russia is not a great power, then Moscow is nothing. The effort to deploy and sustain Russia's military and political presence in the Middle East and Eastern Mediterranean has been, since Catherine the Great, a structural feature and obsession for many Russian statesmen.[7]

In order to reassert Russia's greatness, Primakov and Putin aimed ultimately at strategic denial, denying Washington sole possession of a dominant role in the Middle East from where US influence could expand to the Commonwealth of Independent States (CIS). For both men the Middle East was and remains, as Soviet leaders insisted, an area close to Russia's borders, despite the retraction of those borders from the Middle East after 1991. Such statements highlight the fact that for both men and their disciples, Russian security in key ways equates to Soviet security and policies.[8] Russia's Middle Eastern policy is therefore a critical component of a global or multi-vector strategy to reassert Russia's parity with the US globally and regionally. Regional "bipolarity" supposedly will facilitate American recognition of multi-polarity, i.e. Russia's equal standing to Moscow both in the Middle East and at large. Russia's assertive Middle Eastern policies arguably furnish its domestic and elite audiences with proof of Russia's continuing great power vitality and supposed anti-terrorist resolution; and for this reason alone, those policies command respect. This point is particularly important in the context of Putin targeting Sunni terrorism in Syria against President Bashar al-Assad as linked to the Arab Spring.

Achieving great power status in the Middle East was essential for Primakov and subsequently to Putin because Russia's transition to democracy remains incomplete. Put another way, Russia's unsettled internal constitution requires attainment of great power status in the Middle East to deflect demands for greater democratization at home. Therefore, when Chechnya exploded, Putin found it necessary to gain Middle Eastern support for Russia so that those governments could add their influence in favor of preserving Russia's integrity. Achieving and preserving great power status in the Middle East not only ensures internal stability in Russia, the Caucasus and Central Asia, it also mandates that Russia be able to offer Middle Eastern governments something in return for their support for its domestic "tranquility." Indeed, Primakov and Putin have both argued that despite the US victory in the Cold War and ensuing hegemony, there remains an opportunity for Russia to balance America in the Middle East.[9] As Anna Borshchevskaya argues, Putin's anti-American disposition has been a constant in his Middle Eastern policy.[10] And for some time now, Putin and his spokesmen have explicitly seen the US as a power in decline, adding momentum to the Kremlin's design for the Middle East.

Iraq, Afghanistan, Libya and Syria convinced Moscow the US is a type of "rogue elephant" that acts unilaterally and is overly prone to violence; yet, for all its power and tactical proficiency, which Russia respects and admires, in Moscow's view the US does not know how to bring these wars to positive strategic conclusions. From Russia's perspective, America has failed to curb its ways and represents a growing threat to Russia because the US refuses to accept its own decline and disregards what Moscow deems to be legitimate Russian interests. Ongoing American efforts to force its views upon recalcitrant powers despite its decline generate possibilities for Russian advances. But to exploit its opportunities, Russia must be able to offer something tangible beyond mere diplomatic support to countries in the Middle East.

This last point highlights both the evolution and one significant difference from Primakov to Putin. Primakov asserted as best he could Russia's traditional standing in the region but failed. Russia's weakness deprived him of anything to offer except "good offices." So he could not present a credible regional alternative to Washington or compel the US to take Russia seriously. Putin, coming to power amidst a war that threatened Russia's integrity, had to offer local governments something tangible to obtain genuine support from them against the Chechens and other terrorists. So he had to build up the state and launch economic reforms that were borne aloft by surging energy prices during 1999–2008. Those actions enhanced Russia's economic power and attractiveness, allowing Putin to launch a regional diplomacy offering trade advantages, energy deals, arms sales, and other opportunities in return for support against the Chechens and terrorism. Those tradeoffs characterized Russia's regional policy from 2000 to 2008.[11]

First, throughout this period, Putin offered trade deals to virtually every Arab country. And by 2007, when he toured the region, these trade packages included nuclear reactors, exploiting their fear of the Iranian nuclear program.[12] Second, by 2005, Russia repudiated its post-Soviet policy of not selling arms on credit, forgave Syria's debts, and began selling Damascus weapons on credit.[13] Similarly this period witnessed revived arms sales to North African and other Arab states. These arms sales are linked not only to Russia's unremitting efforts to regain its former regional standing but also to its strategy to become the world's dominant natural gas exporter and gain decisive leverage upon Europe through access to and control over Middle Eastern and African energy sources.[14] Access to Arab states through arms sales and gas deals are correlated, and often this combination has led to Russian bases. Consequently, Russia tried for a long time to consummate a major arms deal with Libya and Algeria, whom Moscow regarded as potential gateways to the broader African and Arab markets.[15] We can expect a repetition of this phenomenon should Russia be able to sell arms to Egypt and if its proxy, Field Marshal Khalifa Hafter, prevails in Libya.[16]

Before the Arab Spring Libya had expressed interest in many weapons.[17] Finally, in October 2009, Libya signed a total of five contracts with Russia to include equipment and spare parts for the Army and Navy as well as the modernization of its T-72 tanks.[18] Russia concurrently also sought access with the Italian energy company ENI to Libyan gas fields and assets and announced a $1 billion sale of aircraft to Rome.[19] This approach is part of a global strategy that Russia also applies wherever Moscow discerns possibilities for exploiting regional disturbances in order to leverage itself as both a global and regional power in that region, e.g. the CIS, the Balkans and the Middle East.[20] We see a similar pattern of the nexus among arms sales, energy deals, and Russia's quest for naval or air bases in Vietnam, Syria and Cyprus.[21] Similarly, since 2013, Russian arms sales to Iraq have been labeled as a vital priority for Russia in conjunction with its energy deals there.[22] Russian arms sales to Egypt are now apparently coordinated with a deal that will revive tourism, after terrorists detonated a bomb on a Russian flight over Egypt in 2015.[23]

Thus, strategic continuity from Primakov to Putin remains the dominant though not exclusive trend. Most importantly, both leaders argued that for Russia to play its "assigned" regional role, Moscow had to offer a contrast if not a counter to US interests and rally Arab voices that they confidently believed were opposed to America's exclusive hegemony in the Middle East. Accordingly, when the US slipped, Russia could then exploit its opportunities. They both relied on this trend, arguing that such "multi-vector" diplomacy epitomized the transition to multi-polarity that they allegedly saw.[24] It is well known that Putin and Foreign Minister Sergei Lavrov have subsequently consistently developed, refined, and implemented this global diplomacy in service of a supposed multi-polar world order. Consequently when Russia could display hard power in 2015 and directly challenge Washington, Moscow could do so with impunity while conducting an effective dialogue with every regional government, even though that capability did not and still does not guarantee the attainment of all of Russia's objectives. Meanwhile, Moscow also possessed the economic leverage to compel Turkey to embrace Russia, even without threatening energy supplies to Turkey, after Ankara shot down a Russian plane in 2015. This simultaneous ability to speak to every regional government while also possessing visible coercive power is a critical asset of Putin's policy and now a cornerstone of the strategy. And this is his personal achievement even if the broader framework for policy remains Primakov's creation.

Iran

Primakov and Putin sought partnership with Iran to counter US pretensions in the Middle East. But Russia has compelling domestic motives for doing so as well. Russia fully grasps Iran's capacity for fomenting unrest in the Caucasus and Central Asia, and that is one reason why Russia refrains form provoking Iran even when both sides' policies have not been jointly aligned. At the same time, Moscow knows Iran aspires to be a regional great power, will always be there, and has an immense potential to make trouble for Russia if it so chooses.[25] Critically, both leaderships fully grasp that Iran's implacable opposition to US interests in the Middle East makes Tehran available to Moscow as a partner against Washington since the Islamic Republic clearly needed great power support.[26] Even if Iran, unlike China is not a "strategic partner" of Russia as many Russian and even Iranian academics argue, the evidence of policy coordination in Syria and elsewhere is very strong.[27] And Moscow's growing influence includes collaborating against Washington in Afghanistan.[28]

Primakov and Putin recognized that Moscow must always have close relations with Tehran even though Iran could ultimately threaten Russia because of its missile and nuclear programs.[29] Russian experts also argue that Moscow must always be able to engage Tehran, even in difficult times.[30] Indeed one reason why Russia sells Iran weapons is its awareness of the latter's potential to disrupt the Caucasus, Central Asia, and Afghanistan. Moscow realized it had to blend arms sales with close monitoring of Iranian activities.[31] Moscow's economic calculations to keep its defense industry markets selling to Iran is also part of a strategy to push away US and European influence in the Islamic Republic because Moscow believes that if Russia did not sell arms to Iran its competitors would wrest that market away from Russian companies. Therefore, arms sales to Iran have always been a Russian tool to prevent an Iranian challenge to Russian power; and from Moscow's point of view, this strategy has succeeded handsomely.[32]

In the 1990s, Russian analysts clearly argued that while Russia opposed the Iranian nuclear program, cooperation with Iran could serve as a model for dealing with other proliferation issues, e.g. North

Korea.[33] Subsequently, under Putin, Russian thinking evolved to the point where Chief of Staff General Yuri N. Baluyevsky stated that Washington's claim that Russia now admitted to an Iranian threat was a misinterpretation. While Russia never denied a global threat of proliferation of missiles, "we insist that this trend is not something catastrophic, which would require a global missile defense system deployed near Russian borders."[34] Defense Minister Anatoly Serdyukov stated that, "We don't share all the West's views on the capacities of the Iranian nuclear program."[35] Foreign Minister Lavrov and his deputy, Sergei Ryabkov, stated that though sanctions might become inevitable if Iran does not comply with the International Atomic Energy Agency (IAEA) regading enrichment of uranium, Iran represents no threat to Europe or the United States. Moreover, Moscow has no evidence of its planning a military nuclear program that would justify missile defenses.[36] And since the adoption of the Joint Comprehensive Plan of Action (JCPOA) in 2015, Russia has consistently been Iran's defense attorney, strategic partner, arms seller and energy trader.[37]

Furthermore, in some respects Russia's attitude toward Iranian proliferation resembles Andrei Gromyko's concerning reports of Iraqi proliferation in the 1980s. For Gromyko, these reports suggested major instabilities in the Middle East, but those would be US and Israeli headaches that would lead them to come to Moscow on their knees to help stop these new conflicts.[38] Alexei Arbatov further observes that,

> There is a broad consensus in Russia's political elite and strategic community that there is no reason for their nation to take US concerns closer to heart that its own worries—in particular if Washington is showing neither understanding of those problems of Russia, nor any serious attempts to remove or alleviate them in response for closer cooperation with Russian on non-proliferation subjects. [39]

Russia does not view Iran as a potential enemy. Iran is a major consumer of Russian arms, an extremely important Russian geopolitical partner, as well as a growing "regional superpower" that balances out the US military and political presence in the Black Sea/Caspian region and Middle East, while simultaneously containing Sunni extremism in the North Caucasus and Central Asia.[40] Russia also views Iran as the dominant regional power in the neighborhood that can project power into the Caucasus, Central Asia and the Persian Gulf. Therefore, Moscow repays Iran for refraining from doing so by upholding Russia's pro-Iranian policies.[41] Neither does Russia take the proliferation threat nearly as seriously as do the US and its allies in Europe and the Middle East.[42]

Obviously Russia's robust economic interests in Iran as well as the nuclear, energy and defense industry lobbies that benefit from those interests greatly influence Moscow's policies today as they have in the past. But beyond those lobbies, Russia's fundamental strategic interests lie in promoting Iranian-US hostility, not cooperation. Official Russian statements advocate strengthening Iran's role as a legitimate actor in a Middle East security system even as Iranian leaders threaten to destroy Israel and promote state-sponsored terrorism. Lavrov even went beyond this region and said that Iran should be invited to participate in any security system for the Black Sea region.[43]

For over two decades, Russian pundits and officials have openly stated that they want Iran to be a partner of Russia and not the US lest the US consolidate its position as the *Ordnungsmacht* (law enforcement agency) in the Middle East, where Moscow still desperately desires to be seen as a great power capable of influencing regional trends. Iranian-American hostility precludes such consolidation by Washington and permits Russia to exercise influence by supporting the maintenance of a system of controlled tension that benefits the Kremlin. Iranian rapprochement with the West undermines Russia's use of the energy weapon to subvert European security institutions and governments because large quantities of Iranian gas and oil would then be shipped to Europe. An Iranian reorientation to the West would also likely stimulate foreign investment to and access from Central Asia through Iran to the Persian Gulf and the Indian Ocean, allowing the free flow of Central Asian energy to the entire world, bypassing Russia and undermining its ability to control Eurasian energy and trade flows. Therefore, the presumption that we can expect any genuinely serious cooperation from Moscow regarding Iran is unfounded, and even mischievous. Not surprisingly Iran now stands with Russia against the US in Afghanistan as well.[44]

By adopting this stance, Russia has obstructed Western efforts to win over Iran against Russian interests that are threatened by any Western hegemony in the Middle East. From very early on, the Russian-Iranian partnership—as expressed, for example, by Iran's help in winding down Tajikistan's civil war in 1992–1997—was characterized by the notion that Tehran reckoned with and refrained from jeopardizing Moscow's vital interests, which, in turn, helped achieve the domestic consolidation sought there by Moscow.[45] Moreover, given Iran's extensive connections to Syria and, after 2003, a Shiite-led Iraq, Tehran could become the core for a pro-Moscow bloc in the Middle East to enhance Iranian and thus indirectly Russian influence at the expense of the United States. Not accidentally, this emerging Shiite bloc, now clearly visible, recalls the Rejectionist Front of 1978-1979 against the Camp David Treaty. Accordingly, Primakov advocated removing all US troops from the Persian Gulf as part of a broader Gulf security plan.[46] Russia still supports this plan, opposing "NATO-like alliances" in the Gulf.[47] So even if Iran is as a tactical partner and strategic rival in Syria, Moscow will keep Iran as a partner as long as it can because the rewards of doing so are great and the risks of failure are even greater.[48]

We see this adherence to an Iranian orientation in Moscow's skepticism toward President Donald Trump's and some Sunni Arab states' concept of an "Arab NATO," which Russia sees as an anti-Iranian alliance and worse yet as an effort to create a Sunni bloc that will inevitably generate new fissures within the region given its overtly anti-Shiite character.[49]

Turkey

Primakov's consistent approach to Iran, which was improved under Putin, also applies to Russian policy toward Turkey. Putin advanced Primakov's outlook to encompass Turkey and move Ankara away from a pro-Western to a pro-Russian orientation.[50] Putin's Turkey policy has aimed all along to neutralize any possibility for Turkey to project power either in the Caucasus, Central Asia or in the Middle East, while binding Turkey closer to Russia through economic and political ties—particularly trade and energy. The internal collapse of Kemalism and the rise of Turkish President Recep Tayyip Erdoğan and his Islamic anti-Western view have been inestimable boons that Putin has adroitly exploited since coming to power.[51]

These policies, along with Russia's century-old cultivation of the Kurds in Turkey, Iraq and now Syria to generate pressure on Ankara or Baghdad whenever necessary, is now the norm. The impressive economic leverage upon Turkey that Moscow then displayed after 2015, plus its tactical flexibility in then dealing with Turkey in Syria once Turkey restored ties on Russia's terms, demonstrates the range of instruments that Putin has built up to manage Turkey and exploit its domestic currents to his benefit.[52] Those anti-Western and anti-democratic currents also have gone far to neutralize Turkey as a potential threat to Russia in the Caucasus or as a NATO member.

Concurrently Putin, utilizing Russia's rising economic capability, arms sales and energy deals, including nuclear energy, has assiduously courted every Middle Eastern government to create good or at least solid working relationships with all of them and establish Moscow's regional bona fides. By 2008, Russia had achieved viable linkages to all of the Middle East but clearly was still playing well back in the orchestra. A decade later, with US policy adrift and unmoored, Russia is acting confidently and forcefully throughout the region using a strategic plan based on Primakov's thinking.

Terrorism

The global threat of both Sunni and Shiite terrorism emerged in the 1970s. Whereas in the Soviet period Moscow assiduously cultivated and spawned many of the terrorist groups that have evolved into today's organizations, the wars in Chechnya brought home the danger posed by Salafi terrorism to Russia.[53] Russian officials saw the possibility of relaunching the "Soviet-style" sponsorship of terrorism against the West. This threat and awareness of the potential threat against the West has led to the evolution of a wholly "instrumentalized" view of terrorism.

On the one hand, Putin strove consistently to estrange the Chechen terrorists from potential or even actual sponsors in the Middle East by means of combining threats and blandishments that Russia's rising economy offered him. As Moscow has itself often claimed, its perspective on the overall Middle East is closely tied to its threat perception, particularly Islamic terrorist threats, to its domestic stability.[54] Moreover, this commingling of internal with external threats is part of the officially sanctioned approach to national security and foreign policy in Putin's Russia. As the Russian 2008 Foreign Policy Concept states, "Differences between domestic and external means of ensuring national interests and security are gradually disappearing. In this context, our foreign policy becomes one of major instruments of the steady national development."[55]

Putin also simultaneously pursued alignment with the US against terrorism, in 2001–2003, in the wake of the 9/11 attacks. Putin also sought to enhance Moscow's position as an interlocutor with every

Middle Eastern state, including Israel. He used all of Russia's instruments of power to impress upon Middle Eastern audiences that Russia, too, was an Islamic state. Russia even became an associate member of the Organization of Islamic Countries (OIC), advocating cooperation while building ties with every Middle Eastern government. This association has reached the point where the OIC has now named Putin a friend of Muslims, and he reassures Muslims that they can count on Russia.[56] In other words, Putin is courting the Muslim World in innovative ways.

At the same time, Putin has long sought and continues to portray Russia as the West's partner in the campaign against Islamist terrorism. One key motive of his activities in Syria has been to show the West why it should collaborate with Russia against what Putin believes is terrorism. Nadezhda Arbatova and Alexander Dynkin write that,

> The main goal of Russia's involvement is to show that Moscow's assistance may play a crucial role in the settlement of major issues, such as the Syrian conflict and international terrorism, and to underline the point that the Islamic State (also known as ISIS or ISIL) is the greatest threat the world faces. Any improvement in Russia-West relations through cooperation on such issues would increase the chances of a lasting peace in Ukraine.[57]

Certainly, Putin and the Russian leadership have embraced this idea to the point of calling the Islamic State the main threat to Russia when it suits them (for actually the US is that threat).[58] But the Russian intervention in Syria may arguably have been also intended as a riposte to what Putin sees as an American global conspiracy against Russia.[59] This understanding becomes particularly important because Putin's regime explicitly regards its domestic security as unstable and the state as having failed to achieve the "necessary level of public security."[60] And this instability is traceable, in no small measure, to

Islamic terrorism and criminality associated with terrorism.[61] Therefore, preventing the spread of terrorism beyond the North Caucasus and ultimately eliminating terrorism are major state priorities, especially with the 2018 presidential elections around the corner. Moscow reiterates endlessly that it intervened in Syria to prevent terrorists from returning home and turning Russia into a new Iraq. This claim clearly has a basis in reality and implicitly underscores the connection from internal to external security—even if, in 2013–2014, Moscow facilitated the terrorists' movement to Syria to reduce the incidence of terrorism in the North Caucasus.[62]

> Of course, we did. We opened borders, helped them all out and closed the border behind them by criminalizing this type of fighting. If they want to return now, we are waiting for them at the borders. Everyone's happy: they are dying on the path of Allah, and we have no terrorist acts here and are now bombing them in Latakia and Idlib. State policy has to be pragmatic; this was very effective.[63]

This view gained prominence because Putin, at the end of the day, argued that the Arab Spring constituted an American-made threat against Russia. The long-standing desire to restore Russia to its previous Cold War prominence in the Middle East at Washington's expense dovetailed nicely with the implosion of the post–World War II Middle East order. As Russian prime minister, Putin quickly voiced fear that the revolutions in Tunisia, Egypt and Libya would "inevitably" trigger greater violence in the North Caucasus.[64] Similarly, then-President Medvedev expressed the belief that the Arab Spring was the direct result of a foreign conspiracy against Russia. As *Al Jazeera* reported,

> 'The situation is tough. We could be talking about the disintegration of large, densely populated states, talking about them breaking up into little pieces,' [Medvedev] said in comments broadcast on state television. 'These are not simple states and it is

highly probable that there will be difficult events, including fanatics coming to power. This will mean fires for years and the spread of extremism in the future. We need to look this straight in the eyes.' […] 'They have prepared such a scenario for us before, and now more than ever they will try and realize it. In any case, this scenario won't succeed,' he said[65]

Since 2011, Moscow called the Arab Spring a real threat to its domestic order and has repeatedly justified intervention.. Clearly, Moscow considers all opposition to Russian allies and/or interests as inherently terrorist and that assessment justifies virtually any kind of response in order to protect Russian state interests even outside normal international jurisdiction lines.

On the other hand, combining this threat perception with its "instrumentalizing" of terrorism leads Moscow to sponsor terrorism for its own purposes and not only in the Middle East but also in Ukraine and even Latin America..[66] This tactic also coincides with centuries of experience in inciting ethnic tensions in targeted societies. The ability of the Russian state to manufacture, incite, and exploit ethnic or other conflicts among the peoples on Russia's periphery dates back to the very inception of the Russian state.[67] Nor was this tactic confined to Russian subjects. This policy was a hallmark of Russian policy toward the Kurds and Armenians in the late Ottoman Empire and remains so today. Moscow's policy makes clear Russia's attitude toward the Kurds varies with the prospects for Russian ties to Turkey and Iraq.[68]

> Russia is more than willing to tolerate instability and economic weakness in the neighboring countries, assuming they are accompanied by an increase in Russian influence. In fact, Russia consciously contributes to the rising instability and deterioration of the economic situation in some, if not all, of these countries.[69]

Indeed, Russia's overall national security strategy and tactics do not respect accepted ideas of sovereignty or territorial integrity, seeing them as instrumentalized weapons—just like Moscow sees terrorism.[70] Indeed, Moscow "instrumentalizes" "Gray area diplomacy" as an acute form of non-linear destabilization—and not only in Ukraine or Georgia, but in Syria, Iraq and elsewhere.

> The notion encompasses the systematic use of a given territory to destabilize the central state form within, create a new status quo, use legal precedents and diversion to give a smokescreen of legitimacy, ensure political control form within, and finally force the central state to accept the new situation with no possibility to come back to the status quo ante. Through controlled tension, Moscow can "reheat" the proverbial buffer zones at will and keep them unstable militarily and politically.[71]

Simultaneously, Moscow is the principal armorer through Syria and Iran of Hezbollah, the Houthi in Yemen, and the Syrian Kurdish Democratic Union Party (PYD), which Ankara considers to be a terrorist group affiliated with the Kurdisant Workers' Party (PKK) in Turkey.[72] Russia also refuses to recognize either the PKK or Hamas as terrorists, although Turkey and Israel recognize them as such. Finally, Russia is evidently supplying the PKK with weapons, even though this Kurdish group's military operations in Syria clearly involve terrorist acts, including the bombing of civilian targets.[73] Despite valuable trade relations with Russia, Israel's government openly views Russia's support for Hamas and Hezbollah, to whom Russian arms are going, as a classic example of a double standard, whereby Moscow denounces terrorism but supports its proxies as not being terrorists.[74]

Terrorism and Israel-Palestinian Issues

In 2007, Russia's ambassador to Israel, Andrei Demidov, stated that Israel must talk with Hamas. But when queried about Russia's refusal to talk with Chechen terrorists, he said that the Chechen problem is an internal Russian one: "We decide how to settle the problem." Moreover, he mendaciously claimed that Moscow settled Chechnya by peaceful means and created a government, parliament and judicial system there. He even recommended that Israel learn from Russia's example.[75]

Demidov's hypocritical statement shows Russia's true *Realpolitik* calculations along with the implicit belief that Israel is not truly a sovereign state while Russia is. So while Russia's sovereignty is inviolable, Moscow can tell Israel to negotiate with terrorists who seek its destruction. Not surprisingly, Israel replied that Hamas is no different than Chechen terrorists.[76] But Moscow rejected this argument. This statement also shows Moscow's wholly utilitarian attitude toward terrorists: Moscow's attitude is "I decide who is a terrorist." Thus, if terrorist groups like Hezbollah or Hamas suit Russian interests, so much the worse for supposed cooperation with the West.[77]

Russia has also consistently maintained that the Palestinians should unite. As such, in Moscow's view, Hamas should take part in the discussions leading to any peace conference and ultimately be a member of the unified Palestinian delegation. Deputy Foreign Minister Andrei Denisov said, in 2007, "National unity in Palestine is the main determining condition for an independent Palestinian state."[78] Consequently, Moscow regularly expresses its desire for this unity and dismay whenever the perennial strife between the Palestinian Authority (PA) and Hamas undermines the two groups. Accordingly, Russia constantly urges Hamas to support the PA but deals openly with Hamas while advocating Israeli negotiations with the PA and Hamas' participation in those talks.[79]

However, in pursuing this goal, Russia has also had to maintain, in open defiance of the facts, that Hamas is not a terrorist organization. Since 2006, when President Putin invited Hamas' leadership to

Moscow after their election victory, Russian authorities have allegedly tried to convince Hamas to renounce terrorism, recognize Israel, and abide by all previous Israeli-Palestinian agreements. Yet, Moscow imposed no conditions on the visit or subsequently on Hamas and seemed unfazed by the fact that Hamas' leadership continues to express its determination to destroy Israel.[80] Putin even stated earlier that Russia did not recognize Hamas as a terrorist organization on its list of such groups. This emphasis on pushing Hamas and the PA to unite continues to be a key point in Russian diplomacy.[81] Yet, nothing has changed Hamas' outlook or modus operandi.

Other less obvious reasons also exist for Russia's steadfast engagement with Hamas and Hezbollah. According to the influential senator and chairman of the Federation Council's Foreign Affairs Committee, Mikhail Margelov, the idea that Russia has good relations with Hamas is merely an illusion. The real reason for opening those ties is that Moscow cannot afford to forego contacts with any potentially important player lest Russia be deprived of leverage over them and have to adjust to other players' initiatives. This posture highlights Russia's regional weakness not its strength. Margelov stated,

> We are in communication, which is mostly of an informational nature for us. When there is a player on the political arena, it would be just too fantastic for those backing this player if we allowed them a monopoly in using it. Therefore, it is better to speak with HAMAS directly than to depend on the Iranians or Syrians, who will dictate to us their conditions for talking with HAMAS. But we are under no illusion about the fact that HAMAS is heterogeneous: in Gaza, in a more subdued state in the West Bank, and in Syria.[82]

It is also clear that there are factions in Russia who would go further in supporting Hamas. In 2006–2007, then–Chief of the General Staff Yury Baluevsky even intimated that Russia might sell Hamas weapons, only to be corrected by Defense Minister Sergei Ivanov, who stated that Russia would only do so if Israel approved.[83] Yet, Israel's intelligence community reported by 2010 that despite the 2008–2009 war with Israel, Hamas had amassed 5,000 rockets and modified some of these rockets that Hamas acquired from Iran. Israel concluded that Hamas has not only rearmed but is looking to extend the range of its missiles and fire multiple tubes from vehicles. Hamas has also acquired Russian SA-7 and SA-14 anti-air missiles as well as AT-3 and AT-5 anti-tank weapons, either from Iran or Syria. As a result, Israel's military then assessed that war with Hamas was likely in 2010; but the war came instead in 2012.[84] It is inconceivable that Moscow did not know about these transfers to Hamas or Hezbollah.

Meanwhile, Hamas continues its terrorist operations and rocket attacks against Israel despite Russian urging to desist from this course.[85] But none of Hamas' terrorism has changed Russia's outlook on Palestinian unity or the need for Hamas to play a role in the peace process. Sponsoring Hamas helps ensure Russia's presence and leverage in the peace process. Russia regards its contacts with Hamas as its "contribution" to peace talks and will continue pursuing them despite Hamas' inflexibility on Israel.[86] When then-President Medvedev met in Damascus with Hamas leader Khaled Meshaal in 2010, he urged not just reconciliation with the PA but also that Israel engage with Hamas who should be part of the peace process.[87] And that stance remains in force today.

Israeli Ambassador Zvi Magen observed that what disturbs Russia about Hamas is not its attacks on Israel but its refusal to unite with the PA. Moscow clearly distinguishes between internal terrorists, whom Russia regards as its exclusively internal affair, and groups like Hamas that it wishes to cultivate. Therefore, and to safeguard its ability to maintain contacts with everyone, Moscow seeks to prevent further Hamas rocket attacks on Israel. But those rocket attacks are irrelevant to the issue of terrorism in its eyes.[88] Russia has advanced numerous reasons for inviting Hamas to Moscow and conducting an annual round of meetings with Foreign Minister Lavrov and its representatives. In 2006, after Hamas' election victory, Putin said that Hamas was the winner in a democratic election that Moscow must respect; the Russian president added that Moscow never recognized Hamas as a terrorist movement and that Russia tries to work with all sides.[89] More accurately, Putin saw in Hamas' election win in 2005 an American defeat as well as an opportunity for Russia to make gains at the US's expense.[90] So despite Lavrov's consistent urging of Hamas to reconcile with the PA, adopt a more flexible tone with Israel, and desist from radical terrorist acts, those admonitions have gone nowhere.[91]

This instrumentalized outlook represents a consistent Russian policy.[92] Former Ministry of Foreign Affairs official Andrei Kovalov wrote that, "When working on the staff of the Russian Security Council, in 1997, I encountered schemes by the special services to direct Islamic extremism and Islamic terrorism against Europe and the United States on the pretext that these phenomena were supposedly created by them and aimed against Russia."[93] He also observed that under pressure of the Chechen threat in the 1990s, the security services and many officials were unable to confront the realities of terrorism and concluded that the West exported Islamic terrorism into Russia to tear the country apart.[94] Therefore, suggesting that Russia export terrorism back to the West was not a stretch.

Conclusion

Russian foreign policy since Primakov contains both continuity and innovation. Primakov formulated the basic intellectual framework and threat assessment regarding terrorism. He and his successors also restored the anti-American and neo-Soviet outlook in Russia's overall national security policy. Elsewhere, this author has argued that Russian policy retains its Leninist imprint, particularly in its threat assessments and modus operandi.[95] That policy's evolution in the Middle East clearly shows the enduring Soviet-like if not Tsarist worldview that drives Russian foreign policy. And for the most part, except perhaps in Moscow's current quest to stabilize Syria, Russia's policy welcomes ongoing regional conflict.

As Niall Ferguson has written, "Russia, thanks to its own extensive energy reserves, is the only power that has no vested interest in stability in the Middle East."[96] Indeed, even in regard to Israel, with whom Russia conducts a thriving economic relationship, Moscow clearly believes that Israel's security and sovereignty are disposable, contingent realities and that it reserves to itself alone the right to determine who are the terrorists. In 1998, this author characterized Primakov's policy as one motivated by what Johann Wolfgang von Goethe called the spirit of eternal negation. Not only does Moscow count on unending strife, it can only succeed if that strife continues, whatever form it might take. Negation, not construction, is its real policy. Moreover, since Russian policy in the region is deemed to be essential to the domestic stability of the regime, whatever else Russia might be in the Middle East it is not, cannot, and will not be a partner for peace.

ENDNOTES

[1] Jon Alterman, "Russia, the United States, and the Middle East, https://www.csis.org/analysis/russia-united-states-and-middle-east, July 21, 2017; Jon Parker, *Putin's Syrian Gambit: Sharper Elbows, Bigger Footprint, Stickier* Wicket, Strategic Perspectives, No. 25, Institute for National Security Studies, National Defense University Press, Washington, D.C., 2017; James Sladden, Becca Wasser, Ben Connable, Sarah Grand-Clement, *Russian Strategy In the Middle East,* Rand Corporation, Washington, D.C., 2017, https://www.rand.org/pubs/perspectives/PE236.html.

[2] *Ibid.*, Fiona Hill and Clifford G. Gaddy, Mr. *Putin: Operative in the Kremlin,* Washington, D.C.: Revised and Expanded Edition, 2015.

[3] Moscow, *Diplomaticheskii Vestnik*, in Russian, No. 7, July, 1996, *Foreign Broadcast Information Service, Central Eurasia* (Henceforth *FBIS-SOV*)-96-211, October 31, 1996, Coit D. Blacker, "Russia and the West," Michael Mandlebaum, Ed., *The New Russian Foreign Policy*, New York: Council on Foreign Relations Press, 1998, p. 183, *Johnson's Russia List*, no. 2097, March 8, 1998, *davidjohnson@erols.com*.

[4] Alvin Z. Rubinstein, "Moscow and Teheran: The Wary Accommodation," Alvin Z. Rubinstein and Oles M. Smolansky, Eds., *Regional Power Rivalries in the New Eurasia: Russia, Turkey, and Iran*, Armonk, New York: M.E. Sharpe, Inc. and Co., 1994, p. 31.

[5] "Interview With Foreign Minister Yevgeny Primakov," Moscow, *Rossiyskaya Gazeta,* in Russian, December 17, 1996, *FBIS SOV*, December 17, 1996.

[6] M.A. Gareyev, *Srazheniya na Voenno-Istoricheskom Fronte*, Moscow: ISAN Press, 2010, p. 729 cited in MG I.N. Vorob'ev (RET) and Col. V.A. Kisel'ev (Ret), "Strategies of Destruction and Attrition," Moscow, *Military Thought*, in English, NO. 1, 2014, *Open Source Center, Foreign Broadcast Information Service, (FBIS SOV)*, January 1-2014-March 31, 2014, accessed, June 2, 2014.

[7] Christopher Clark, The *Sleepwalkers: How Europe Went To War In 1914*, New York: Harper Perennial, 2014, p. 251.

[8] We still find Putin's people saying the Middle East is close to Russia's borders, just as Primakov did as if the Soviet Union did not end and the same justifications for policy exist today as in 1970.

[9] Rubinstein, pp. 31–32.

[10] Borshchevskaya

[11] See the essays in Marat Terterov Ed., *Russian and CIS Relations With the Gulf Region,* Dubai, Gulf Research Centre, 2009.

[12] Ariel Cohen, "Putin's Middle East Visit: Russia is Back," http://www.heritage.org/europe/report/putins-middle-east-visit-russia-back, March 5, 2007.

[13] "Russia To Sell Arms Only to 'Solvent Countries'," *ITAR- TASS*, May 13, 2006; Stephen Blank, "Bashear Assad Comes to Moscow, Seeking Gifts," *Eurasia Daily Monitor*, January 26, 2005.

[14] Stephen Blank, "Russia's Mideast Role," *Perspectives*, XVIII, No. 3, May, 2008.

[15] Dmitry Litovkin, "Russian Arms Are Going to Africa Once Again," Moscow, *Izvestiya*, in Russian, October 8, 2009, *FBIS SOV*, October 8, 2009.

[16] LTC Michael Segall (Ret) "Russia Seeks Another Mediterranean Naval Base In Libya," Jerusalem Center for Public Affairs, XVII, No. 2, January 22, 2017, http://jcpa.org/article/russia-cultivates-strongman-libya-seeks-another-mediterranean-naval-base/.

[17] Litovkin as cited above in note 15

[18] "Russia Has 5 Arms Deals With Libya, "-Rosoboroneksport," *RIA Novosti*, October 7, 2009, http://www.en.rian.ru/military_news/2009/1007/156383869.html.

[19] "Russia has five arms deals with Libya – Rosoboroneksport," *RIA Novosti*, October 7, 2009, http://en.rian.ru/mlitary_news/20091007/156383869.html; "DJ Libya To Buy Russian Fighter Jets In $1 Bln Arms Deal – Report," AFP, October 19, 2009, http://english.capital.gr/News.asp?id=834835; "Libyan Leader Seeks Energy Deals With Russia," *Reuters*, November 1, 2008.

[20] Russian foreign policy in the Balkans is the subject of forthcoming articles by Stephen Blank see also Stephen Blank, "Russian Strategy and Policy in the Middle East," *Israel Journal of Foreign Relations*, VIII, No. 2, May 2014, pp. 9–25.

[21] Stephen Blank, "Russia Seeks Naval and Air Bases in Cyprus," *Eurasia Daily Monitor*, July 17, 2013; Stephen Blank, "Russia's Growing Ties With Vietnam," *The Diplomat*, www.thediplomat.com, September 19, 2013.

[22] "For Russia, $4.3 Billion Arms Deal With Iraq Is Vital," www.upi.com, July 16, 2013.

[23] "Egypt to Buy Russian Jets in Deal That May Revive Tourism," *Radio Free Europe Radio Liberty*, February 3, 2016.

[24] Interview With Foreign Minister Yevgeny Primakov. "Interview With Foreign Minister Yevgeny Primakov," Moscow, *Rossiyskaya Gazeta*, in Russian, December 17, 1996, *FBIS SOV*, December 17, 1996 same as note no. 5

[25] Jon W. Parker, *Persian Dreams: Moscow and Tehran Since the Fall of the Shah*, Washington, D.C.: Potomac Books, 2009.

[26] *Ibid*, p. xi.

[27] For a thorough discussion of Russo-Iranian relations see the discussion among Russian and Iranian experts in, Russian International Affairs Council and The Institute for Iran-Eurasia Studies, *Russia-Iran Partnership: An Overview and Prospects For the Future,* Report NO. 29, 2016.

[28] Shoshanna Kranish, "Iran and Russia To Enhance Military Ties After New US Sanctions," *Jerusalem Post*, August 6, 2017, www.jpost.com; "Iran and Russia Upgrade Cooperation," *Operational Environment Watch,* May, 2017, p. 9, https://fmso.leavenworth.army.mil/OEWatch/Current/current.pdf.

[29] Parker, *Persian Dreams,* pp. 135, 146, 307–308, for example.

[30] *Ibid*.

[31] *Ibid*. Passim; Stephen Blank, "Russia and Iran in a New Middle East," *Mediterranean Quarterly*, III, no. 4 Fall, 1992, pp. 124–127

[32] Parker, *Persian Dreams* passim.

[33] Stephen Blank, "The Spirit of Eternal Negation: Russia's Hour in the Middle East," Stephen J. Blank, Ed., Mediterranean Security Into the Coming Millennium, Carlisle Barracks, Pa.: Strategic Studies Institute, U.S. Army War College, 1999, pp. 484–485;
"The Foundations of Russian (Foreign) Policy in the Gulf," Marat Terterov Ed., Russian and CIS Relations With the Gulf Region, Dubai, Gulf Research Centre, 2009, pp. 229–258.

[34] *RIA Novosti*, June 21, 2007.

[35] "Russia Says It Wants "Equal" Involvement in Missile Shield," *Global Security Newswire*, www.nti.org, October 25, 2010.

[36] Moscow, *RIA Novosti*, in Russian, March 10, 2010; Open Source Center, *Foreign Broadcast Information Service Central Eurasia,* (Henceforth *FBIS SOV)*, March 10, 2010;
"UN to Address Sanctions Against Iran 'soon'—Russia's Lavrov," *RIA Novosti,* April 29, 2010; Moscow, *Interfax*, in English, April 21, 2010, *FBIS SOV*, April 21, 2010.

[37] Stephen Blank, The Spirit of Eternal Negation: Russia's Hour in the Middle East," Stephen J. Blank, Ed., Mediterranean Security Into the Coming Millennium, Carlisle Barracks, Pa.: Strategic Studies Institute, U.S. Army War College, 1999, pp. 484–485.

[38] Quoted in Yuri E. Fedorov, "Russia's Relations With the West,' Bertil Nygren, Bo Huldt, Patrick Ahlgren, Pekka Sivonen, Susanna Huldt, Eds., Russia *On Our Minds: Russian Security Policy and Northern Europe*: Stockholm: Swedish National Defense University, 2010, p. 13.

[39] *Ibid.*

[40] *Ibid.*

[41] Thomas E. Graham, "The Friend of My Enemy," *The National Interest*, No. 95, May–June, 2008, pp. 36–37.

[42] Alexei Arbatov, "Terms of Engagement: WMD Proliferation and US-Russian Relations," paper prepared for the U.S. Army War College Conference "US and Russia: Post- Elections Security Challenges," Carlisle, PA, March 6-7, 2008, in Stephen J. Blank, ed., *Prospects for U.S.- Russian Security Cooperation*, Carlisle, PA: Strategic Studies Institute, U.S. Army War College, 2009, pp. 147-149; Matthew Kroenig, *Beyond Optimism and Pessimism: The Differential Effects of Nuclear Proliferation*, Managing the Atom Working Paper Series Working Paper No. 2009-14, Belfer Center, November 2009, pp. 34–35.

[43] Moscow, *Vremya Novostey*, in Russian, September 11, 2006, *FBIS SOV*, September 11, 2006; Transcript of Russian Minister of Foreign Affairs Sergey Lavrov Interview to Turkish Media, Moscow, May 29, 2006, www.mid.ru.

[44] Carlotta Gall, "Iran Gains Ground in Afghanistan as U.S. Presence Wanes," *New York Times,* August 6, 2017, https://www.nytimes.com/2017/08/05/world/asia/iranafghanistan-taliban.html?rref=collection%2Fsectioncollection%2Fworld&action=click&contentCollection=world&region=rank&module=package&version=highlights&contentPlacement=2&pgtype=sectionfront.

[45] *Russia-Iran Partnership: An Overview and Prospects For the Future,* Passim.

[46] Blank, "The Foundations of Russian (Foreign) Policy in the Gulf," Marat Terterov Ed., Russian and CIS Relations With the Gulf Region, Dubai, Gulf Research Centre, 2009, pp. 229–258.

[47] "Russia Opposed To NATO-Like Alliances In Gulf- Lavrov," *Interfax News Agency*, May 18, 2017, Retrieved from *BBC Monitoring*.

[48] Parker, *Putin's Syrian Gambit* 2017.

[49] Yoel Guzansky, "An 'Arab NATO' including Israel can exist if it stays quiet," *The Hill Blog*, May 24, 2017, http://thehill.com/blogs/pundits-blog/foreign-policy/334922-an-arab-nato-including-israel-can-exist-if-it-stays-quiet.

[50] Fiona Hill and Omer Taspinar, "Turkey and Russia: An Axis of the Excluded," *Survival*, XLVIII, No. 1, Spring, 2006, pp. 81-92; Fiona Hill and Omer Taspinar, "Russia and Turkey in the Caucasus: Moving Together to Preserve the Status Quo," *Russie. Nei. Visions No. 8*, IFRI, Paris, 2006.

[51] *Ibidem.*

[52] The Jamestown Foundation, "Erdogan and Putin Expand Military, Economic, and energy Relations," www.oiprice.com, August 5, 2017.

[53] Christopher Andrew and Vasili Mitrokhin, *The World Was Going Our Way: The KGB and the Battle for the Third World*, New York: Basic Books, 2005; Uri Ra'anan, Robert Pfaltzgraaf, Igor Lukes, Ernst Halperin, Eds., *Hydra of Carnage: International Linkages of Terrorism: The Witnesses Speak*, Lanham, Md: Lexington Books, 1985.

[54] Edict of the Russian Federation President, "On the Russian Federation's National Security Strategy," December 31, 2015, http://www.ieee.es/Galerias/fichero/OtrasPublicaciones/Internacional/2016/Russian-National-Security-Strategy-31Dec2015.pdf.

[55] "The Foreign Policy Concept of the Russian Federation, 2008, www.fas.org/nuke/guide/russia/doctrine/concept.htm.

[56] "OIS nazvala Vladimira Putina liderom, pokazavshim «druzheskiye» zhesty islamu i musul'manam," (The OIC Calls Putin a leader showing Friendship to Islam and Muslims)," http://rusisworld.com/religiya/ois-nazvala-vladimira-putina-liderom-pokazavshim-druzheskie-zhesty-islamu-i-musulmanam, July 28, 2017; "Putin, "Islamskii Mir Mozhet Rasschitivat' Na Podderzhu I Sodeistviee Rossii," www.islamrf.ru, May 17, 2017.

[57] Nadezhda K. Arbatova and Alexander A. Dynkin, "World Order After Ukraine," *Survival,* LVIII, NO. 1, 2016, p. 72; Marc Galeotti, "Why Russia and the West Should Fight Terrorism Together," *Moscow Times,* May 24, 2017, Reprinted in *Johnson's Russia List,* May 24, 2017.

[58] "Patrushev Names Biggest Threat To Russia," *Vestnik Kavkaza,* July 28, 2017, http://vestnikkavkaza.net/news/Patrushev-names-biggest-threat-to-Russia.html; Moscow, *RIA Novostei,* in Russian, November 1, 2011, *FBIS SOV,* November 1, 2011.

[59] Maxim Trudolyubov," The View From the Kremlin: Survival is Darwinian," www.nytimes.com, August 5, 2017.

[60] "Concept of Public Security in the Russian Federation," Moscow, www.kremlin.ru, November 20, 2013, *FBIS SOV,* January 25, 2014.

[61] *Ibid.*

[62] Michael Weiss, "Russia Is Sending Jihadis to Join ISIS," http://www.thedailybeast.com/articles/2015/08/23/russia-s-playing-a-double-game-with-islamic-terror0.html, August 23, 2015; International Crisis Group, *The North Caucasus Insurgency and Syria: An Exported Jihad?* http://www.crisisgroup.org/en/regions/europe/north-caucasus/238-the-north-caucasus-insurgency-and-syria-an-exported-jihad.aspx, March 16, 2016, pp. 16–17.

[63] *Ibid,* p. 16.

[64] Moscow, *Interfax,* in English, February 24, 2011, *FBIS SOV,* February 24, 2011.

[65] "Medvedev Warns Arabs of 'Extremism' http://www.aljazeera.com/news/europe/2011/02/2011222142449923896.html, February 22, 2011.

[66] In Ukraine this can be seen in the post-2014 attacks on Odessa and Khar'kiv while in Latin America, Stephen Blank Younkyoo Kim, "Russia and Latin America: The New Frontier for Geopolitics, Arms Sales, and

Energy," Problems of Post-Communism, LXII, NO. 3, May-June, 2015, pp. 159–173.

[67] John P LeDonne, *The Grand Strategy of the Russian Empire, 1650-1831*, pp. 61-81, 198-212, 219-233, New York and Oxford; Oxford University Press, 2004; Boris Nolde; La Formation De 'Empire Russe, Paris, Institut d'Etudes Slaves, 1953.

[68] Stephen Blank, "Energy and Russia's High-Stakes Game in Iraq," EGS Working Paper 2015-2-1, Center for Energy governance and Security, Hanyang University, 2015; Igor Delanoe, Les Kurdes : un Relais d'Influence Russe au Moyen-Orient ? "Russie.Nei.Visions", n° 85, June 2015, Institut Francais des Relations Internationales (IFRI), 2015; Michael A. Reynolds, *Shattering Empires: The Clash and Collapse of the Ottoman and Russian Empires, 1908–1918*, Cambridge: Cambridge University Press, 2011.

[69] Susan Stewart, "The EU, Russia and Less Common Neighborhood, "SWP Comments, Stiftung Wissenschaft Und Politik, January, 2014, pp. 2–3.

[70] *Ibid;* James Sherr, *Hard Diplomacy and Soft Coercion: Russia's Influence Abroad:* London: Chatham House, 2013, pp. 61-62; Matthieu Boulegue, "The Russia-NATO Relationship Between a Rock and a Hard Place: How the 'Defensive Inferiority Syndrome' Is Increasing the Potential For Error," *Journal of Slavic Military Studies*, XXX, No. 3, 2017, p. 371.

[71] *Ibid.*, p. 376.

[72] Serkan Emitras, "Turkey Warns US, Russia Over Arms Supply to Syrian Kurds." Hurriyet Daily News, http://www.hurriyetdailynews.com/turkey-warns-us-russia-over-arms-supply-to-syrian-kurds.aspx?pageID=238&nID=89820&NewsCatID=510, accessed on May 2, 2016.

[73] "Russia Supplies Weapons to PKK Terrorists in Turkey," *Middle East Observer*, May 2, 2016.

[74] Stephen Blank, "Putin Embraces Double Standard, in Middle East Crisis, *Eurasia Daily Monitor*, July 20, 2006.

[75] Herb Keinon, "Interview With Andrei Demidov," Jerusalem, *Jerusalem Post*, in English, February 16, 2007, FBIS *SOV*, February 16, 2007.

[76] Barak Ravid and News Agencies, "Israel to Russia: Hamas is Like the Chechen Terrorists," www.Haaretz.com, May 13, 2010.

[77] Evgeny Biyatov, "IS Poses Threat to Russia, Moscow Ready to Cooperate With the West: Official," *Sputnik*, January 14, 2015.

[78] Marianna Belenkaya, "Russia Hopes Palestinian Unity Will be Restored," Moscow, I RIA Novosti, in English, August 1, 2007, *FBIS SOV*, August 1, 2007.

[79] Vladimir Radyuhin, "Russia Backs Abbas, Talks to Hamas," *The Hindu*, August 1, 2007; Avi Isacharoff, "Hamas official: Russia Invited us to Moscow in Coming Days," *Ha'Aretz.com*, August 3, 2007; Moscow, *Interfax*, in English, January 21, 2008, *FBIS SOV*, January 21, 2008; Moscow, *Ministry of Foreign Affairs Internet Version*, in English, January 23, 2008, *FBIS SOV*, January 23, 2008.

[80] "Moscow Hopes Hamas Will Sign Up To Previous Agreements," *Interfax*, March 3, 2006; "No Pressure Exerted While Discussing 'Road Map-Hamas Delegation Member," *Interfax*, March 3, 2006.

[81] "Turkey, Russia Call for Talks With Hamas," *China Daily*, May 13, 2010, www.englihs.cri.cn/6966/2010/05/13/189s/569393.

[82] Shimon Briman, "Interview with Senator Mikhail Margelov," www.Izrus.com in Russian, January 27, 2010, *FBIS SOV*, January 27, 2010.

[83] "Hard Talk Awaits Lavrov in DC," www.kommersant.com/page.asp?id=654562, March 3, 2006.

[84] "Israel Intel: Hamas Has Amasses 5,000 Rockets Since 2009 War," www.worldtribune.com, January 28, 2010.

[85] "Hamas Chief; "No 'Prospect' of Israeli-Arab Peace Deals," www.einnews.com, February 9, 2010.

[86] Moscow, *Interfax-AVN Online*, in English, December 9, 2009, *FBIS SOV*, December 9, 2009.

[87] "Russia Spurns Israeli Rebuke Over Hamas Meet," http://www.ynetnews.com/articles/0,7340,L-3889325,00.html, May 13, 2010.

[88] Zvi Magen, "Russia Between Terrorism and Foreign Policy," Tel Aviv, *Institute for National Security Studies,* in English, April 18, 2010, *FBIS SOV*, April 21, 2010.

[89] Moscow, *Rossiya TV*, in Russian, February 9, 2006, *FBIS SOV*, February 9, 2006; Pavel K. Baev, "Moscow's Initiative: Your Terrorist is Our Dear Guest," *Eurasia Daily Monitor*, February 13, 2006.

[90] *Ibid.*

[91] "Russia to Urge Hamas to Abandon Radicalism-Russian ME Envoy, www.kuna.net.kw, February 10, 2006; "Lavrov Asks Mish'al To Sign Reconciliation Agreement Quickly. PA Rejects Arab Pressure Before HAMA Sings Egyptian Document," Gaza, *Quds net* in Arabic, February 9, 2010, *FBIS SOV*, February 9, 2010; Moscow, *ITAR-TASS*, in English February 8, 2010, *FBIS SOV*, February 8, 2010.

[92] "Israel Slams Medvedev's Hamas Call," *www.aljazeera.net*, www.einnew2s.com, May 13, 2010.

[93] Andrei A. Kovalev, *Russia's Dead End: An Insider's Testimony From Gorbachev to Putin*, Lincoln, Nebraska: Potomac Books Under the Imprint Of the University of Nebraska Press, 2017, p. 308.

[94] *Ibid.*, p. 131.

[95] Stephen Blank, "Lt. Kizhe Rides Again: Magical Realism and Russian National Security Perspectives," *Journal of Slavic Military Studies*, XXVII, No. 2, Spring, 2014, pp. 310-357, reprinted in Roger N. McDermott, Ed., *The Transformation of Russia's Armed Forces: Twenty Lost Years*, London and New York, Routledge, 2014, pp. 4–50.

[96] Quoted in Gordon G. Chang, "How China and Russia Threaten the World," *Commentary*, June 2007, p. 29.

3. The Arab View of Russia's Role in the MENA: Changing Arab Perceptions of Russia, and the Implications for US Policy

Shehab Al Makahleh

Summary

- In late September 2015, Russia made a great comeback to the Middle East scene when Russian Armed Forces, on President Vladimir Putin's order, intervened in the Syrian conflict, at the request of the sitting Syrian government.

- Putin's address at the 70th United Nations General Assembly (UNGA) in 2015 was a clear and unequivocal expression of Russian indignation at the dismal state of global affairs, in particular regarding the US-led military interventions in the Middle East.

- Russian military intervention in Syria—only two days after President Putin's UNGA speech in 2015—signaled to the West, the international community and the Arabs in particular, that the current regional trajectory of instability is no longer tolerable and that Russia will not stand by idly watching the Middle East collapse under the scourge of Islamist terrorism.

- The Russian resolve has taken the Western world, the US in particular, by surprise. Then-US President Barack Obama underplayed and underestimated the importance of the event that eventually turned the tide of the Syrian conflict by stating that Russia would face certain defeat in Syria.

- Whether Russia's return to the Middle East was aggressive or not, it has been a stunning, sudden success—and a setback to Western power and prestige.

- Obama's prediction of the outcome of the Russian intervention proved dismally wrong. Two years on, Russia is all but victorious, and the Syrian Army at the time of writing is rapidly recapturing the territory seized by the Islamic State (ISIS) and other terrorist factions fighting on the ground. Contrary to Obama's misplaced comments, Russia's intense diplomatic and military efforts have produced nearly unimaginable results, including collaboration with the United States on the Syrian battlefield, where now Moscow, not Washington, is calling the shots.

- The key diplomatic successes of Russian peacemaking efforts include the agreement with Iran and Turkey on the establishment of several ceasefire zones in Syria. The culmination of Russian efforts in Syria, aided by Jordanian mediation and support, has been the Trump-Putin agreement on the establishment of de-escalation zones in southwestern Syria, signed on the sidelines of the G20 Summit in Hamburg, on July 7, 2017.

- Most Arab states do not like to see the rapprochement between Ankara and Tehran. Others such as Doha prefer this, considering it a victory for Qatar and behind them their master, Russia, which planned for this new alliance that is against the interests of other MENA states. These developments pave the way for Moscow's greater presence in the Middle East.

Introduction

The Russian presence in the Middle East, in particular in the Levant and parts of North Africa, spans over two centuries, back to the time of the Russian Empire. And despite frequent interruptions and upheavals, it has lasted to this day. By the time the United States was first entering the region, following the end of World War II in 1945, during President Harry Truman's administration, Russian influence and presence in the Middle East had already been long established, although it had ebbed and flowed over time.

According to international law, the Russian intervention in Syria is legitimate, since it was launched at the request of the Syrian government. Yet, the Western powers have accused Russia of aggression and expansionism.[1] This rebuke likely stems from the fact that the United States and other Western powers feel that they are losing influence in the Middle East, while Russia is gaining strategic advantage in this crucial region, which Moscow considers its "near abroad." For Russia, the Middle East is instrumental to its national security, especially along Russia's mostly Muslim-populated southern border areas, whose citizens have in their scores joined various terrorist factions in both Syria and Iraq.

Meanwhile, the annual survey of Arab youth[2] ages 18–24 shows that young Middle Easterners' attitudes toward Russia and the West are in flux, whereby the two rivals seem to be reversing roles. In the same survey conducted last year, respondents from just four Arab countries—Iraq, Yemen, the Palestinian territories and

Lebanon—considered the United States an enemy. This year, the number of countries to echo this negative opinion about the US has doubled to include Qatar, Libya, Algeria and Egypt. Coincidentally, all these are either countries in conflict with the US, due to its military interventions, and/or at the same time, more or less, traditional Russian allies from the Soviet era.

These trends simultaneously indicate an increasingly positive image of Russia in young Arab minds—a fact that can be attributed to Moscow's role as a protector of Syrian people against the menace of terrorism.[3] The opinion of many Syrians, though some are against Bashar al-Assad and his policies. The US, on the other hand, is being regarded as unfriendly or even as the most dangerous nation in the world, in a growing number of countries globally. In Turkey, a traditional American ally for the past half century, over 70 percent consider the US a top threat, superseding the Islamic State.[4]

Decades of US interventions in the Middle East, in particular the invasion and subsequent destruction of Iraq, and later Libya, have put the United States in a position of being blamed by both the terrorist factions and the ordinary Muslim public for the crisis embroiling the region. The changing attitudes of the new generations of Arabs, as well as non-Arab Middle Eastern nations, should be taken in consideration in shaping future US policy in the region. The new American Middle East policy should be built on a platform based on regional grassroots sentiments, national priorities and socio-economic and cultural aspirations—which are not necessarily in line with the existing American perceptions about the region and its needs.

Russia's cultural and religious ties to both the Muslim and the Christian populations in the Mediterranean part of the Middle East (present-day Lebanon, Syria, Jordan and Palestine) were particularly strong during the Russian imperial era. The collapse of the Ottoman Empire changed these dynamics. These broad shifts negatively affected Russia's presence and regional influence, while establishing the British and the French as the new regional overlords, from an Arab perspective.

While the Anglo-Russian and Franco-Russian rivalry in the region dates back to Tsarist Russia, especially the reign of the Romanov dynasty (1613–1917), the clash and rivalry with the United States in the region, is a much more recent phenomenon and is linked to the Cold War period. Soon after the dissolution of the Soviet Union, and particularly the 1990s, the period was marked by Russian passivity and near-absence from the region. Changes in Moscow's policy orientation chiefly focused on solving internal socio-economic issues, thus pushing Russia to withdraw from the outer regions, including the Middle East, Africa and Central Asia, previously considered by the Soviets to be of strategic importance to the country's interests abroad.[5]

With the subsequent ascent of Vladimir Putin to the Russian presidency in 2000, Russia again started to play a more assertive role in these crucial regions, however. Notably, the Middle East again took on a key focus within Russian foreign policy. This shift in orientation toward the Middle East and Russia's "near abroad" (as Moscow refers to the other countries of the post-Soviet space) in the early 2000s, as Russia began to reemerge from the rubble of former Soviet collapse, was made manifest in the high-level visits organized in 2005 by Yevgeny Primakov to a number of Middle Eastern countries, including Iran, Syria, Lebanon and even Jordan. These visits were part of the new "Putin Doctrine," which emphasized repositioning Russia as a "great power" and developing a new geopolitical discourse placing Russia vis-à-vis the US.[6]

But after 2010 and the advent of the so-called "Arab Spring," the chain of events that ensued signified a systemic crisis across the region. At this point, Russia decisively stepped in, ostensibly to counter American hegemony, regime change and Washington's approach of "spreading democracy."[7] For Russia, the so-called "Arab Spring" revolutions were reminiscent of the "Color Revolutions"—the various related movements that developed across a number of countries in the former Soviet Union and the Balkans in the early 2000s. Russia has strongly opposed such demonstrations, which the Kremlin considered a major threat to Russian national security and the stability it fought to regain in the decade following the collapse of the USSR.

Parallel with the "Arab Spring" events, changing European Union and US policies toward the region left room for Russia, the only country seeking a larger presence in the Middle East since it had lost many of its strategic bases in the MENA after the fall of some regimes in the region. These events have given the Russians an opportunity to "fill the vacuum left for an honest external broker in resolving regional problems"[8] at the expense of the US and in a manner distinctively different from the Western one. In contrast, the US was distancing itself from MENA issues and trying not to become involved in the local conflicts, believing that the best policy was to remain neutral. Russia, on the other hand, thanks to efforts by Deputy Foreign Minister Mikhail Bogdanov, managed to set a course to return to the Middle East through rebuilding relations with various countries. Specifically, Bogdanov played a key role in winning friends and influencing people, from Egypt's President Abdel Fattah el-Sisi, to Turkish President Recep Tayyip Erdoğan, to Libya's Field Marshall Khalifa Haftar. Russia's updated approach to the Middle East offers an alternative diplomatic vision: an image of a steadfast ally respectful of national identities[9] and the existing state order in the extremely volatile and unstable region. One should remember the last words Obama said on December 16, 2016, in his final press conference as president: the Russians cannot change the Americans or weaken them, because Russia is a weaker country and their economy does not produce anything that anybody wants to buy, except oil and gas and arms.

Moscow's alternative vision appeals to many in the Arab world, much more than the Western approach that seeks to upend the status quo and impose, by the application of both soft and hard power, neoconservative, liberal democracy to the region. Due to the failures that US interventions of the past two decades have brought upon a range of Middle Eastern countries, from Afghanistan and Iraq, to Libya and Syria, to name but a few, the region seems to be more susceptible to fresh approaches; and Russia, with silent backing from China, seems to be offering that alternative.

Unlike Soviet foreign policy, which was strongly ideological[10] in nature and sought to spread Communist ideas across countries of interest, post-Soviet Russian policy is markedly non-ideological and pragmatic in nature, apparently based on Vladimir Putin's political philosophy of "pragmatic nationalism,"[11] with national security and sovereignty at its core. This approach focuses on economic and security integration and strengthening relations without imposing Russian values, either politico-ideological or cultural, on the partner-countries.[12] What is remarkable is that Arab governments are increasingly seeing Russia's actions in a positive light.

Russo-Arab Ties: From the Soviet Union to Putin's Russia and the 'Arab Spring'

Russian policy toward the region has remained nearly constant since the era of the Russian Empire. And this fact is despite the fact that the state system in present-day Russia has changed drastically several times in the course of the last century and, consequently, so did Russian foreign policy priorities, including those regarding the Middle East and adjacent regions.

The Russian Empire regarded the Middle East to be important due to the Romanov dynasty's approach to the Holy Land. Russian Tsar Peter the Great considered himself a protector of the Middle Eastern Christians and the benefactor of the region's holy sites. Meanwhile, the Ottomans ruled the area and oppressed not only Christians but

Muslims alike. The same Russian foreign policy orientation and regional significance remained a constant throughout Romanov rule, up until the Bolshevik Revolution and the formation of the Soviet Union in 1917.

Due to its large Muslim population, Russia has over the centuries, up until current times, sought to build bridges with the Islamic World, despite the two bitter wars with Chechnya in the early 2000s. Today, as seen on the Syrian battleground, the experience of fighting and overcoming terrorists in Chechnya has proven extremely valuable. In less than two years, Russian military advice as well as material and humanitarian support to the Syrian government have achieved more to suppress and eliminate terrorist groups and restore stability in many parts of the embattled Arab country, than have 16 years of American operations in Afghanistan and Iraq.

The Cold War period in the Middle East, in contrast, was marked by a sharp rivalry between the United States and the Soviet Union. At the time, the region was essentially divided into two blocs, one supportive of and supported by the US, and the other by the Soviet Union which was a strong backer of the pan-Arab movement that rode the waves of nascent Arab socialism, which itself had appealed to the ideologically driven Soviet foreign policy. This period saw the Soviet Union support its allies in many ways, including though financial and military aid as well as training in Soviet institutions. Soviet allies during this time included: Egypt, Libya, Syria, Lebanon, Palestine and Yemen.

Following the 1991 collapse of the Soviet Union, former Russian President Boris Yeltsin's Russia turned inward, nearly crumbling due to its political, economic and military weaknesses. Yeltsin's Russia focused on domestic issues and, in foreign policy matters, on relations with Europe and the United States. The Yeltsin era, 1991–1999, marks a Russian withdrawal to near-absence from the Middle East, with the exception of Turkey and Iran.[13]

On the eve of the new millennium, another change was on the horizon in Russia, and it came with Yeltsin's resignation and the nomination of Vladimir Putin as his successor. Putin's rise to power in 2000 marks a new era in Russian Middle East policy. Markedly different from the Soviet approach, Putin's Middle East policy is based on *Realpolitik* and is focused on strengthening ties with a range of Middle Eastern states. Those relationships are based on the arms and energy trades along with political and diplomatic support to regional allies in key matters where Russian and partner interests converge.

During a high-profile tour of the Middle East in 2005, Putin himself visited the region, accompanied by top executives from Russian military corporations (MiG and Rosoboronexport),[14] in a quest to bolster economic ties and reestablish Russia's status as a major arms supplier—the role it lost during the Yeltsin's "low key" Middle East policy period. Besides renewing ties with traditional allies from Soviet times—Egypt, Iran, Iraq, Syria—Putin added to his Middle Eastern agenda relations with Jordan, the Gulf Cooperation Council (GCC), Israel and Turkey.

Since his early days as Russian head of state, Putin has consistently followed specific principles related to his multi-vector Middle East policy orientation: the protection of sovereignty, economic gain (oil, gas and the arms trade), and the expansion of the Russian influence in the Western-dominated region.

Drastic transformational changes in the political life of several Arab republics, labeled as the "Arab Spring," displeased Russia for their resemblance to the "Color Revolutions" that swept across several former Soviet republics, most notably Ukraine and Georgia, in the early 2000s. Bruised by its own bitter experiences with revolutions and anti-terrorist wars in Russia's southern Muslim republics of Chechnya and Dagestan, Moscow strongly opposed these transformations—especially since it viewed them as outside-imposed rather than homegrown solution. In 2011, Russia abstained from United Nations Resolution 1973, yet it did not veto it,[15] fearing that a repetition of NATO's operations in Yugoslavia would be enacted in Libya after the imposition of a no-fly zone. The Russian approach to the Libyan crisis at the UN Security Council (UNSC) was manifest in the public exchange between then-President Dmitry Medvedev and Prime Minister Putin, the latter calling the Resolution a "medieval call for crusades." Russian fears turned into reality, and Libya has become an ongoing disaster and a de-facto failed state after the NATO intervention toppled long-standing Libyan leader Muammar Qaddafi, which pushed the country into a civil war.

In the Libyan case, Russia tried to stay neutral and exert its influence via the UNSC, rather than by acting more forcefully to assert a different position in the Libyan case. This hesitation on Russia's part may be attributed to the fluctuating relationship the Kremlin had with the Libyan leader, as well as the attempt not to again sour relations with Washington, which had suffered in the aftermath of the Russo-Georgian war in 2008. Following the NATO intervention in Libya, it was evident that Russia had chosen a wrong path, and this mistake was even publicly admitted: Russian officials stated their disappointment with the Western behavior in Libya. After realizing Russia's mistake in Libya, the Kremlin then tried to contain its economic losses in the embattled country. But this became increasingly difficult as several competing parties took over and effectively split Libya into three different spheres of interest, none to Russia's advantage.

In Syria, however, having learned from its mistakes in Libya, Russia took an unwavering stance from the outset of the upheaval by positioning itself as a protector intent on preventing the Libyan disaster from playing out in Syria. By choosing this strategy, Russia openly positioned itself in confrontation with the US and Europe. Russian interests and stakes in Syria were much higher than in Libya, which is part of the reason for a markedly different Russian approach.

According to *The Moscow Times*, Russian investment in Syria in 2009 amounted to $19.4 billion, while the 2005 canceling of 73 percent of Syria's Soviet debt equaled $13.4 billion.[16] In addition to these two key economic factors, Damascus was a major buyer of Russian weapons, and Moscow could ill afford to lose such a long-time, trusted partner. Moreover, the dubious nature of the roots of the Syrian "rebellion" saw a revival of Russian fears of Islamist terrorism spilling over to its trouble-prone southern regions. Taken together, these were the major security factors driving Russian policy toward Syria.

The Key Countries in Russian Middle Eastern Focus

In light of the rapidly changing global geopolitical and economic order as well as the declining role of the West, especially the US, in the Middle East and Asia, Russia is seeking to reposition itself as a global power. In particular, Moscow is trying to raise its profile in the post-Soviet Central Asian space and in a number of Middle Eastern countries. The Russian focus for the coming decade is centered on reestablishing and strengthening cooperation with its traditional Middle Eastern strategic partners, such as Algeria, Libya, Egypt, Syria, Iraq and Yemen, in addition to new countries, including Jordan, the United Arab Emirates, Oman and Qatar. Moreover, Russia's partnerships with two non-Arab Middle Eastern countries, Turkey and Iran, despite some hiccups and occasional disagreements on several regional issues, seem to be rapidly strengthening in recent years.

As a member of the BRICS—a political-economic bloc of major developing economies Brazil, Russia, India, China and South Africa—Russia is not alone in its pursuit of influence in the region. China is silently backing most Russian moves. And despite assessments to the contrary by some Western policy analysts and think tanks, there is little room for speculation about a Sino-Russian rivalry in this region or elsewhere. What China lacks, Russia has and vice versa. Thus, each member of this duo perfectly complements the other, together building a strong foundation for long-term partnership across the board.

Chinese financial might and the size of its economy, in addition to its energy dependence on both Russia and Iran, among others, make the duo perfect partners for creating a new world order in this crucial region. This point has been made clear by Chinese announcements of investments in Syrian post-war reconstruction.[17]

Washington's moves to impose fresh sanctions on Russia, as well US efforts to put pressure on Iran and Turkey, are achieving results that may run contrary to established American policy. Specifically, those actions may draw Russia, China, Iran and Turkey closer together into an unbreakable Eurasian alliance that has the potential to change the political discourse for decades to come. The case in point is the admission of India and Pakistan as full members of the Russian- and Chinese-led Shanghai Security Cooperation Organization (SCO)[18]; while Iran is poised to join soon, likely followed by Iraq, and Turkey in the near future.

Devoid of ideological undertones, including "exporting democracy" and military interventionism, which underpin Western attitudes toward the region, the Russia-China duo's regional approach is markedly pragmatic and focuses on four key pillars of cooperation:

- Military,
- Security,
- Economic, and
- Political/diplomatic cooperation on regional and global issues.

While Russia is rising politically and militarily as a key global player, China is expanding economically, ascending at the expense of other economic giants such as Japan and Germany. Both countries are

seeking strategic partnerships in crucial regions and developing markets, including the Middle East—for its energy resources—as well as developmental and infrastructural investments, the latter being particularly attractive to China in pursuit of its larger global agenda.

Security is of vital interest to the Middle East, which has been embroiled in conflict for over half a century now. And in particular, following the disastrous consequences of the American invasion of Iraq, NATO's interventions in Libya, and the West's covert and overt support for Syrian "rebels," the solutions for regional security presented by organizations like the SCO, seem increasingly attractive to a number of Middle Eastern powers.

Russian modernized weaponry and military capabilities have been tried and tested effectively in the Syrian conflict—putting Russia back at the forefront as the guarantor of stability as well as the protector of state sovereignty and the principles of the existing international order. One of the tangible results from the Syrian intervention has been the numerous orders Russia received for its state-of-the-art S-300 and S-400 air and missile defense systems. Besides Syria and Iran, Turkey has signed purchase agreements with Russia,[19] while Qatar has expressed strong interest[20] in becoming a buyer, too.

In addition to the military, economic and social security as well as investment that the BRICS offer as a group, Middle Eastern states also value certain contributions that China and Russia may proffer individually. In particular, the Chinese multi-billion, mega-development project "One Belt One Road" (OBOR)—which encompasses a number of regional countries, including Syria, Jordan and Turkey—is extremely attractive to key regional states.

China and Russia have principally devised their economic and political ties based on a sprouting cluster of strategic partnerships that involve economic and military cooperation at all levels.[21] The strong ties between China and Russia are temporary, but they share their expansionist tactics together on various continents including Asia, Africa and South America, where China is cultivating a strong presence that can serve as a springboard for its future economic leap at the expense of the US. China, of course, cannot proceed or vie for the international market without fully being supported by Russian, which itself seeks to control many continents regardless of American interests.

In the political and diplomatic arena, the Arab World has now, for half a century or so, suffered dire consequences, not least due to the seemingly intractable Israeli-Palestinian issue. This conflict, which the Arab World has for several decades tried to resolve with American and European assistance, has to date resulted in little to no positive outcomes. The issue of "historic injustice"—as the Palestine problem is deemed by many Arabs and other Muslims—has been at the forefront of Russia's Middle Eastern agenda, including during the Cold War. While the US has traditionally sided with the Israelis, Russia has for a while stood as the advocate for the Palestinian cause, and has earned the respect of the Arab street for its support.

As terrorism started spreading across the Middle East and beyond, various militant factions based their rhetoric and ideology around the Palestinian issue, often citing the Western occupation of the Arab and the Muslim world as the key grievance that leads many of the militants to "jihad" in the belief that they are fighting for the liberation of their Muslim brethren. Russia has been advocating renewed efforts for finding a lasting solution to the Israeli-Palestinian standoff. Russian President Putin's approach is based on the belief that the solution lies in returning to political negotiations based on the existing international agreements and laws,[22] while Palestine should be granted its own long-overdue statehood. Moreover, Palestine has been included among the users of the common preference system of the Eurasian Economic Union (EEU), signaling future trajectories in regards to Russian Palestine policy.

Russia and the Wider Middle East: Forging New Alliances

The great transformation in the Middle East, including the collapse of state structures as well as the breakout of revolutions and wars, is ongoing. These transformations also include a growing rift between Iran and the US, a rift between Egypt and Iran because of the spat between Qatar and other GCC states, and a rift between a number of key world powers over Syrian crisis. All these have been forcing diverse actors into new alliances in the military, energy and food security spheres, among others.

Among regional actors, Egypt, for example, has approached Iraq to purchase oil, following a stalemate in its relationship with Saudi Arabia. The Egyptian request was soon followed by daily pumping of Iraqi oil to Egypt, to compensate for a one million barrel shortage on the Egyptian market. The Cairo-Riyadh conflict stems from an ongoing dispute over two Red Sea Islands and Egyptian President Abdul Fattah Sisi's stance on several regional issues, including his rejection of the overthrow of Syrian President Bashar al-Assad, whom Sisi considers the legitimate leader of the country.

Furthermore, both Egypt and Iran are major markets for Russian weapons. The fact that Russia has entered agreements with both states on sales of its sophisticated weaponry indicates that they are deemed solid allies.

In addition to Egypt and Iran, Russian ties with Turkey have significantly improved in the past year and are poised for further growth. Particular success was reached by the Russian, Turkish and Iranian negotiators in Astana, Kazakhstan, on the settlement of the Syrian crisis, through the implementation of several ceasefire zones across the Arab country. Moreover, Turkey has ceased its support for the militants in northern Syria, paving the way for a cessation of hostilities. In turn, the Russian Federation has removed restrictions on trade and tourism, which were imposed on Turkey in December 2015, following the Turkish downing of a Russian Su-24 tactical bomber.

As the trilateral Russia-Turkey-Iran alliance gains traction, Russia, due to its advantage as a major world power, is securing access to the whole of Africa, the Levant, the Arabian Peninsula, and major parts of Europe. By locking Iran within the alliance, together with China, Russia is gaining access to strategic sea-lanes and maritime choke points, therefore developing an upper hand in countering possible Western-led disruptions in energy supplies. Adding to the Russian Arab alliance is Qatar, which of late has been courting both Russia and Iran in light of the GCC diplomatic crisis. By coming together, Russia, Iran and Qatar—the three top world producers of liquefied natural gas (LNG)—can effectively control global gas supplies, and by extension gain a significant say over much of the global geopolitical discourse.

In addition to the Gulf Arab states and key countries in the southeastern Mediterranean and the Levant, Russia has been building bridges and relationship with a whole host of North African countries (Arab Maghreb), that include traditional Soviet allies Algeria and Libya, but also Morocco, Tunisia and Mauritania.[23]

During the Soviet era, relations with the Maghreb states were based on ideological affiliations, hence the strongest were with Algeria and Libya by virtue of the nature of their regimes. However, Vladimir Putin's presidency changed Russian foreign policy toward North African Arab states, and the relations are no longer limited to Algeria and Libya, but are increasingly moving towards closer cooperation with other countries, especially Morocco, despite competition there with the United States and France.[24]

As in the rest of the Middle East, Russia's policy is focused on investment opportunities, trade exchanges, coordination in the areas of gas production and trade, and nuclear technology for peaceful, industrial purposes, as well as the strengthening of security cooperation in the fight against terrorism, against the backdrop of the Libyan crisis.[25]

Middle East Between East and West: In Search of Identity, Security and Independence

Following the demise of the Ottoman Empire that ruled most of the Middle East and the Arabian Peninsula for over four centuries, Arab peoples in the region have failed to gain real independence, despite the creation of the modern nation-states under Anglo-French control. Not all, but many of the problems that beset the region in the past century can be attributed to a large extent to the imperial designs and arbitrary drawing of the Middle Eastern map. Other factors contributing to the lack of stability in the region can be attributed to the forceful expulsion of Palestinians and the creation of the state of Israel. Sectarian issues, which the West mistakenly puts at the core of the Middle Eastern strife, are perhaps the last of the destabilizing factors in the region.

Over the past century in the Middle East, the unchanging constant remains a lack of stability and frequent armed conflicts. Thus, the powers that want to have a lasting positive impact on the region are the countries that put national, energy and food security at the forefront of their Middle East policy approach. It is more than evident at this juncture that the Western countries, led by the US, have failed in this task. Rather than bringing stability to the already inflamed region, the United States is creating more chaos that nobody seems to be able to control.

For a long time, the Middle East was not a self-sufficient region in terms of guaranteeing its own security. Security (and the majority of security threats) tended to be a kind of regional import provided by external forces. The Middle East was and has until recently remained one of the "major components of the bipolar world, an arena of competition and limited cooperation between the two global powers. Starting from the end of Desert Storm in 1991 up to the beginning of the Arab Spring in 2010–2011, the region was characterized by US hegemony and its attempts to preserve and even strengthen this hegemony."[26]

The Arab Spring changed this trajectory, principally due to Russian active involvement in the Syrian conflict. Russian involvement in Syria has in the beginning split the Arab world in two camps: pro- and anti-Russian or pro- and anti-United States. Today, a majority of the Arab states, voluntarily or involuntarily have to admit that US foreign policy in Iraq, Libya, Syria and elsewhere, has failed to bring stability. On the contrary, it has unleashed waves of instability and facilitated growth of a plethora of terrorist and extremist groupings across the Muslim world—a problem that will likely take another decade or two to eradicate.

The Appeal of Russian Policy Approaches to Middle Eastern Issues

What Russia seems to have understood about Arab needs, and Western powers have missed, is this vital need for security and partnership reliability. According to some Arab sources,[27] Arab views on Russia and its role in the region are not all in agreement. However, there are significant points worth mentioning, where views of a number of Arab actors converge.

It is noteworthy to compare these key points with the official Russian foreign policy concept,[28] as they are centered on same crucial points:

1. Support for the nation state and state sovereignty.
2. Fill the strategic security vacuum caused by the decline of American power.
3. Partner in Syrian settlement.

4. Partner in war on terrorism.
5. Be a reliable alternative provider of weaponry and armaments.
6. Partner in economic development.

1. Russia's support for state sovereignty:

Russia's Foreign Policy Concept still places importance on the idea of the state and traditional sovereignty in international relations, and pursues policy of not intervening in the affairs of other countries, except at the request of the legitimate authorities, as was the case with Syria. This aspect of the Russian foreign policy is appreciated by a number of Arab states, together with the Russian stance against exposing societies to internal disintegration in pursuit of democratic demands. For some Arab governments and societies, Russia represents a safe superpower in contrast to the United States. [29]

2. Filling the strategic vacuum:

Amid the decline of US power in the Middle East, Arab thinking about Russia, as an alternative power capable of filling the strategic vacuum left by American disengagement from the region, is starting to emerge. There are signs of an emergence of a comprehensive Russo-Arab relationship, and one not solely confined to military and security cooperation. Along with military agreements, many Arab countries have concluded economic, educational, technological and cultural agreements with Russia. However, there is fear in the Gulf, in particular, that Russian traditional partners, Iran and Syria, are reaping the most benefits at their expense.

To improve its standing in the eyes of the skeptical Gulf countries, Russia needs to address this fear by reassuring them about the Russian orientation that favors strengthening international peace and global security and stability, establishing a fair and democratic international system that addresses international issues on the basis of collective decision-making and the rule of international law, as well as creating equal partnership relations among states on bilateral and multilateral bases.

3. *Partner in crises settlement:*

As a key player in the Syrian settlement process, following the success of its anti-terrorism strategy, Russia is now expected to facilitate political settlements in Syria, Yemen, Iraq and Libya, execute the settlement agreements and post-settlement processes of state reconstruction, as well as consolidate internal peace and national security. At the moment, there is a lack of confidence in Washington's ability to settle these matters in the Gulf; yet, there is no general Arab consensus on the Russian role. However, as the ceasefire agreements in Syria—initially reached through Russian efforts with Turkey and Iran, and later with the US and Jordan—seem to be bearing fruit, the key countries that initially supported the overthrow of the Syrian government have changed their rhetoric and have ceased supporting the "rebel" groups.

4. *Partner in the war on terrorism:*

Russia is the one of the foremost opponents of the jihadist groups. One of the major motives for Russian military intervention in Syria was fear of the impact that the armed terrorist groups in Syria and Iraq would have on Russian Muslim republics, and the destabilizing effect that the returning jihadist elements could cause in Russia. Therefore, Moscow's strategic interest in the war on terrorism lies at the center of policy. Hence, extending north-south intelligence and security cooperation between Russia and the Arab World is a lasting prospect for years to come. However, diversity in Arab states' assessments of terrorist organizations and groups is a hindrance to this cooperation. The current situation in Syria indicates a difficulty in reaching a common Arab point of view on what constitutes terrorism, so work on helping Arabs find common language is a task that Russia and other Arab states intend to work upon.

5. *The armaments provider:*

The volume of Arab military spending and arms purchase deals over the past two years indicate that a significant share of arms bought by some Gulf States and Egypt originate from Russia. There is a clear tendency in the Arab countries to entice Russian interest toward more comprehensive partnerships with the Arab world in this sphere. Saudi Arabia and the United Arab Emirates have funded an initial agreement between Russia and Egypt to purchase military equipment, including 24 MiG-29s, Buk-M2s and Tor-M2s. According to some reports, the deal ranges between $2 billion and $4 billion. Saudi Arabia also donated $1 billion to support the Lebanese army in August 2014, some of which went to buy helicopters and Russian air defenses. Russia supplied Bahrain with Kornet-EM anti-tank missiles. The UAE and Saudi Arabia have also concluded independent arms deals for their own military purposes.

6. *The economic partner:*

Beyond military areas, Arabs consider Russia an important economic partner and a promising market for investment, as shown by the quality of the agreements concluded between Russia and the Gulf Arab states in 2014 and 2015. Russian-GCC governmental committees for commercial, economic, technical and scientific cooperation, as well as joint business councils and investment forums have been formed for some time. For example, an agreement to establish an investment fund worth up to $4 billion, to finance joint projects and contribute to the development of trade and economic relations between Saudi Arabia and Russia, was signed during the meetings of the Russian-Saudi Joint Committee for Economic and

Commercial Cooperation between the two countries in November 2015. Another investment fund, worth $10 billion, had been agreed upon in July 2015. At the fifth meeting of the joint UAE-Russia committee in November 2015, an agreement on enhancing cooperation in the field of tourism, transport and investment was signed. Two additional memorandums of understanding were also signed, in the fields of sports cooperation and intellectual property. The Abu Dhabi Crown Prince's visit to Russia in September 2013 saw the UAE and Russia signing a memorandum of intent to establish a joint investment partnership between the Department of Finance in Abu Dhabi and the Russian Direct Investment Fund, to invest up to $5 billion in Russian infrastructure projects.

All of the above are positive indicators of the areas for future collaboration between Russia and the Gulf Arab states in particular. Similar areas of common interest can be found in other Arab and non-Arab states in the Middle East. Beyond pursuit of economic and military cooperation, and in accordance with the official Russian foreign policy concept, development of bilateral and multilateral cultural relationships with the Arab world should be an area of focus in the post-conflict Middle East era.

Conclusion: Russia's Role in Middle East in the Coming Decade

Following the breakout of armed conflicts in Syria and other Middle East countries, Russia is increasing its involvement in the region in order to protect its own national security interests. Increased Russian engagement is noticeable through its calibrated military intervention in Syria and the formation of alliances with a number of Middle Eastern states, even at the expense of the United States due to Washington's withdrawal from the region under Obama's presidency.

When the Arab Spring turned into civil wars in Syria and Libya, Russia returned to the Middle East on a self-defense policy platform, seeking to counter Western ambitions in the region. This grand strategy required an application of diverse tactics in order to achieve its goals, all while benefitting from the weakness of the European Union and the distancing of the US from the Middle East in favor of the Pacific region.

Russia's return to the region on the counterterrorism platform was justified by the Middle East's close proximity to Russia's southern borders. This geographic closeness and the gravity of the terrorist threat gave Russia the right to intervene to safeguard its own national security, while simultaneously cooperating with key regional powers such as Iran, Turkey, Egypt and Algeria, in an attempt to reestablish the equilibrium of power in the conflict-ridden region.

Despite official narratives echoed by the media in parts of the Middle East and the West in particular, many Middle Easterners do not view Russian intervention in the region as something negative, nor do they see Russian presence in the region as colonialist or intruding. On the contrary, they view the Russian role in the region as *a fait accompli*, a situation that cannot be easily challenged or transformed. At the same time, Arabs understand that each of the major world powers pursues its own objectives in this strategically located region, which controls most of the global energy resources.

Overall, based on this understanding of the regional problems and needs, the coming decade will not see a decrease in Russian regional influence. Rather, Moscow can be expected to place more efforts on enhancing Russia's media presence and strengthen its influence through culture, art and education, in order to familiarize Middle Easterners with Russian civilization and values. Traditionally more conservative than the liberal and secular West, Russia has many more things in common with the Middle Eastern ways of life. And both Russia and the Middle East could reap great benefits from enhancing their cultural ties in the coming years, even while challenging American interests.

It is expected that Russia will be interfering in many countries' politics, especially those which were part of the former Soviet Union in a bid to annex them. It will also start exploration in the North Pole for oil and gas in order to use energy as a weapon against other countries. After the Syrian civil war ends, Russia, along with Iran, Qatar and Syria, will be exporting more than 70 percent of the world's gas. This factor is a serious threat to many countries, including the US, because gas will be used to twist the arms of many countries. The next decade will prove to be confrontational, with Moscow and Arabs agreeing on many issues that will challenge America.

ENDNOTES

[1] Reza Parchizadeh, "The Historic Roots of Russian Expansionism in the Middle East," *American Thinker*, October 18, 2015.

[2] ASDA'A Burson-Marsteller, Arab Youth Survey 2017, http://www.arabyouthsurvey.com/.

[3] ASDA'A Burson-Marsteller, Arab Youth Survey 2017, http://arabyouthsurvey.com/ar/about-survey.html.

[4] Pew Research Center, Spring 2017, Global Attitudes Survey. www.pewresearch.org.

[5] Dağı, Z., "Russia: Back to the Middle East," *Perceptions*, Spring 2007: 123–141.

[6] Dağı, Z., p.128.

[7] Ekaterina Stepanova, "La Russie a-t-elle une grande stratégie au Moyen-Orient?" *Politique étrangère*, 2016/2 (Summer 2016), p. 2.

[8] Dağı, Z., ibid.

[9] Clement Therme, "Russia's influence in the Middle East: On the rise or inevitable decline?"*Ètude de l'IRSEM*, No. 33. www.defense.gouv.fr.

[10] Ilya Bourtman, "Putin and Russia's Middle Eastern Policy," *Middle East Review of International Affairs*, Vol. 10, No. 2, (June 2006).

[11] Olena Bagno-Moldavsky, "Russian Foreign Policy in the Middle East: No Change in the Offing". *Strategic Assessment*, Vol. 15, No. 4, January 2013, p. 121.

[12] Stepanova, p. 2.

[13] Anna Borshchevskaya, "Russia in the Middle East: Motives, consequences, prospects," *Policy Focus 142*, February 2016, Washington Institute for Near East Policy, www.washingtoninstitute.org.

[14] Ilya Bourtman, "Putin and Russia's Middle Eastern Policy," *Middle East Review of International Affairs*, Vol. 10, No. 2, (June 2006).

[15] Margarete Klein, "Russia and the Arab Spring: Foreign and Domestic Policy Challenges". *SWP Comments 3, February 2012*. German Institute for International and Security Affairs.

[16] Klein, p. 4.

[17] Pepe Escobar, "The New Silk Road will go through Syria," *Asia Times*, July 13, 2017, www.atimes.com/article/new-silk-road-will-go-syria/.

[18] "India and Pakistan join SCO," *TASS*, June 9, 2017. http://tass.com/world/950697.

[19] Sputnik International, "Russia, Turkey sign documents on S-400 supplies – Erdogan," July 25, 2017,

https://sputniknews.com/military/201707251055862009-turkey-russia-s400-supplies/.

[20] Anadolu Agency, "Embattled Qatar eyes Russian air-defense systems". August 23, 2017, http://aa.com.tr/en/middle-east/embattled-qatar-eyes-russian-air-defense-systems/892332.

[21] Shehab Al Makahleh, "Sino-Russian Ties, Not Easy to Break," *Group of Strategic Vision "Russia-Islamic World,"* April 10, 2017.

[22] Press statements following Russian-Palestinian talks. May 11, 2017. President of Russian Federation. http://en.kremlin.ru/events/president/news/page/22.

[23] Zuhair Hamdani, "Russia develops relations with the Maghreb states through economy and arms deals," *Al-Jazeera* [Original in Arabic: روسيا تطور علاقاتها المغاربية من بوابة الاقتصاد والسلاح], April 27, 2017.

[24] Ibid.

[25] Ibid.

[26] I. Ivanov. *Is a Collective Security System Possible in the Middle East? Russian International Affairs Council (RIAC),* February 9, 2016, http://russiancouncil.ru/en/analytics-and-comments/analytics/tri-korziny-dlya-blizhnego-vostoka/.

[27] Mutaz Salameh, "The future of Russo-Arab relations," [Arabic original: مستقبل العلاقات العربية - الروسية], February 8, 2016, http://www.siyassa.org.eg/.

[28] Foreign Policy Concept of the Russian Federation (approved by the President of the Russian Federation Vladimir Putin on November 30, 2016), The Ministry of Foreign Affairs of the Russian Federation http://www.mid.ru/en/foreign_policy/official_documents/-/asset_publisher/CptICkB6BZ29/content/id/2542248.

[29] M. Salameh, "The future of Russo-Arab relations," 2016.

4. Iran's Russian Conundrum

Alex Vatanka

Summary

Following Russia's decision in September 2015 to intervene militarily in the Syrian war, speculation has been rife in Washington that President Vladimir Putin's ultimate end-goal is to eclipse America's long-held dominance in the Middle East. To that end:

- Moscow needs regional allies that can abet its ambitions.

- At least in American eyes, no other state can be more useful to Russian machinations than the ardently anti-American Islamic Republic of Iran.

- Given the fluid state of geopolitics in the Middle East—defined by ongoing conflicts in a number of theaters and uncertainty among US partners and allies about Washington's commitment to the region—the question of Iran as a conduit for Russian ascendency is both timely and proper.

That said, Iran's checkered history with the Russian Federation since 1991 informs that while Tehran and Moscow have common interests at times, the path toward a possible strategic partnership is bound to be long and arduous at best.

Historical Context

One might believe that Iran and Russia today enjoy a semblance of "strategic cooperation." Defenders of such grand assertions most often point to the ongoing joint Iranian-Russian military campaign to keep Syria's Bashar al-Assad in power. In reality, Russian and Iranian officials have labeled their bilateral relations "strategic" as early as the dawn of the 1990s. It was then, during the presidencies of Boris Yeltsin and Akbar Hashemi Rafsanjani, when major defense and economic agreements were first announced.

In other words, those championing closer Iranian-Russian ties will argue that this so-called fraternity did not begin in Syria in 2015 but that it came to a climax in that Arab state's civil war: at that point, Tehran and Moscow's interests dovetailed to a great extent. Even assuming that the Iranian-Russian partnership has been gradually in the making since the early 1990s, it still does not amount to an untroubled relationship. And signs of trouble were evident from the earliest of days after the collapse of the Soviet Union, while Moscow desperately was seeking to rekindle its relations with the outside world.

The principal example of that was arguably the secret June 1995 agreement between Vice President Al Gore and Prime Minister Viktor Chernomyrdin, which stipulated Moscow to end all military sales to Iran by 1999.[1] When the Iranians found out about the secret pact between Washington and Moscow years later, a sense of perplexity hit Tehran given the years of overtures they had made to the Russians. Then–Iranian President Akbar Hashemi Rafsanjani had personally prioritized Russia as a new anchor for Tehran's foreign policy. Within about two weeks of becoming president in late June 1989, he visited Moscow as his first international trip. Besides the significant symbolisms of the gesture, Rafsanjani had traveled there with high hopes and with concrete goals in mind.[2]

Following the death of the Islamic Republic's founder, Ayatollah Ruhollah Khomeini, in June 1989, Rafsanjani was eager to quickly put an end to the previous decade's isolation, which had been overwhelmingly brought about due to Tehran's own revolutionary intransigence and its commitment to export its Islamist model. And with Khomeini's death coinciding roughly with the Soviet military withdrawal from Afghanistan in early 1989—an occupation that had mobilized much of the Islamic world against Moscow—Rafsanjani should have been forgiven for believing the timing for a new chapter in relations with Iran's northern neighbor was ripe. Tehran's later deep disappointment in finding out about the Gore-Chernomyrdin agreement has to be seen in this context.

The Russians have always measured this Iranian anger mostly through the financial losses it subsequently incurred on Russian exporters. Still, from Russia's perspective, Moscow should be forgiven for wanting to prioritize its ties with the United States—which has long maintained a policy of seeking Iran's isolation—against Tehran's high hopes for what Russia could do for Iranian fortunes. As *The Moscow Times* put it, Russia's relations with Tehran "took a backseat to the post-Cold War reconciliation between Russia and the US."[3] In the process, Russia not only lost about $4 billion in unfulfilled military contracts to Iran, but the Gore-Chernomyrdin agreement left behind a deep sense of mistrust among Iranian officials. Over the following decade and half, three other issues further deepened this distrust in Tehran.

First, the Russians were seen by the Iranians to deliberately be holding up the completion of the Bushehr nuclear power reactor, which had been awarded to Moscow in a 1995 contract. The project was not a golden goose for Moscow as such. The Iranians believed this Russian delay was partially due to Western pressures on Moscow but also stemmed partly from an assessment in Moscow that delaying the completion of Bushehr kept Iran's nuclear program alive as a controversy. This would in turn prolong Russia's role as a mediator and give it the global eminence it craved. More specifically, the Iranians correctly believed that Moscow was playing its Iran cards as it balanced its interests with Western states and particularly as a way to extract concessions from Washington elsewhere in their bilateral relations. After repeated delays, the Bushehr nuclear plant was finally operational in September 2011, about ten years after the original deadline and with a number of contract cost increases in between.

Second, the Russians had first agreed in 2007 to sell Tehran a number of S-300 anti-air missile systems. In 2010, however, President Dmitry Medvedev banned the sale, which compelled the Iranians to bring a $4 billion lawsuit against Russia at the International Court of Arbitration in Geneva.[4] The psychological fallout from this episode is perhaps the most significant. Tehran's $800 million purchase of the sophisticated air-defense systems—one of the biggest single arms deals the Islamic Republic has ever signed—had come at a time of intense American signals that Washington might unilaterally strike Iran's nuclear facilities. The S-300 systems were meant to be an answer to Iran's prayers for an impenetrable defense shield. Medvedev's sudden ban again signified to the fidgety Iranians that Moscow was a fair-weather friend at best. Russia was certainly proving reluctant to be perceived as the guardian of an Islamic Republic that, at the time, insisted on pushing ahead with its questionable nuclear ambitions.

Third, the Russian stance during the international negotiations to find a solution to Iran's controversial nuclear program also created an impression in Tehran of Russian equivocation. Over a four-year period, from June 2006 to June 2010, Russia voted to sanction Iran at the United Nations Security Council on six occasions for its nuclear activities.[5] Not once did Russia abstain or veto sanctions against Tehran at the UN. The Russians let the irritated Iranians know that, each time, they had been frantically watering down the punitive impact of the sanctions on Iran behind the scenes. This was Russia's rationale for its actions at the UN, but Tehran has never openly accepted this Russian explanation. The heyday of Russian support for international sanctions on Iran came after the arrival of President Mahmoud Ahmadinejad in 2005. Iran not only had restarted nuclear enrichment in April 2006[6], which it had suspended in 2004, but Ahmadinejad's bombastic approach to international affairs—including labeling the Russians "good cops" when the US ostensibly played the "bad cop" in subduing Iran—did little to please Moscow.

Put simply, the above-mentioned examples sit at the heart of today's Iranian mistrust in Russia as a partner. As one member of the Iranian parliament put it in 2010, "No other country has wronged Iran as much as Russia."[7] These kinds of sentiments are regularly expressed by Iranian officials and commentators. If nothing else, the Iranians have been guilty of mismanaging their own expectations about Russia as a potential partner. As a shortcoming, harboring unrealistic goals is a phenomenon that has impacted the highest levels of power in Tehran.

False Strategic Premises vs. Tactical Advantages of Cooperation

Nearly 20 years after President Rafsanjani paid homage to Moscow in a bid to turn Russia into Iran's guardian—and despite the fact that Tehran has had a very mixed record to show for it—the country's most powerful figure took another gamble on Moscow. In January 2007, Supreme Leader Ayatollah Ali Khamenei, who is the ultimate authority in Tehran, told a visiting Igor Ivanov, the head of the Russian Security Council, that Tehran wanted to form a "strategic alliance against common adversaries" and proposed that the two countries share between them responsibility for the future of the Middle East and Central Asia. A month later, Khamenei dispatched his top foreign policy advisor, Ali Akbar Velayati, to Moscow with a detailed plan to brief Putin himself. Meanwhile, there was no Russian response as such.[8]

Putin was in Tehran in October that year to attend a security conference by the states of the Caspian Basin. It was the first time since 1943 that a Russian leader had been in Tehran.[9] And yet there was still no sign of a Russian receptivity to Iranian overture that were continuing to come from the highest power in the byzantine system of the Islamic Republic. Instead of contemplating an implicit pact with Tehran, the Russians were at the time more concerned about what they believed to be lack of Iranian cooperation to find a resolution on Iran's nuclear program.

And more importantly, at the heart of this conundrum lies an implicit Iranian call that Moscow should effectively side with Tehran in rolling back American power in the Middle East and Central Asia, whenever possible. Moscow was not prepared to entertain such Iranian ambitions since Russian interests—and hence the need to have a working relationship with the United States—go well beyond Asia's western regions. Not even major dips in Russian-Western relations—such as heightened tensions following Russia's intervention in Georgia in 2008—altered this basic coolness Moscow displayed toward Tehran's call for a united anti-American front.

The uneasy twists and turns in relations, however, should not be the only barometer. On a tactical level, where Iranian and Russian interests have overlapped in regard to narrow policy objectives, the track record of cooperation has been much brighter. Immediately after the Soviet pullout from Afghanistan, Tehran and Moscow became de facto partners in supporting the Northern Alliance against the Pakistani and Saudi-backed Taliban movement in the Afghan civil war. In the 1990s, Tehran and Moscow were also largely on the same side in the civil war in Tajikistan. This fact was also true in the case of Russia and Iran both wanting to counter Turkish inroads in the South Caucasus, where Ankara was backing Azerbaijan in its conflict against Armenia, which was backed by Tehran and Moscow.

Overall, the Iranians have been careful not to upset Russian interests in the former Soviet South, a zone Moscow jealously labels and guards as its "Near Abroad." Perhaps most notably, Iran—as a large Muslim state—played a highly accommodating role in the context of Russia's two bloody military interventions in suppressing a national movement in Chechnya, Russia's most rebellious Muslim-populated republic. Whereas there was much condemnation in the Islamic world of Russian actions in Chechnya, Tehran used its chairmanship of the Organization of Islamic States (OIC) to basically provide a cover for Moscow.

As the then Foreign Minister Kamal Kharazi put it, Iran was merely ready to "collaborate with Russia to establish stability in the North Caucasus, including Chechnya."[10] This position hardly amounted to a censure of Russia, a step that pleased Moscow but tarnished Iran's image as a self-declared defender of Muslim rights on the international stage, a role Tehran has been loudly touting since 1979.

Nonetheless, in Tehran's calculations, the cost-benefit analysis was straightforward and Iran was not about to irk Moscow over the Chechen question. Also around this time, in the early 2000s, Russian commentators started to frequently refer to Iran as Moscow's most important ally in the Middle East.

One can argue that Tehran has viewed the Russian question and role in much bigger terms than just as a provider of arms and technology or as the occasional geopolitical ally or, conversely, even as a Christian-majority state with a complicated set of relations with its own Muslim minorities or its Muslim neighbors to its south and east. At its core, Iran has been judging Russia also as an important building block in the anti-Western global front that the Islamic Republic so desperately has wanted to see emerge to challenge the Western-dominated international system. Even though Iran's experiences with Russia on this matter have not always met Tehran's expectations, it would be wrong to ignore "anti-Westernism" as a partial driver in their bilateral relations.

The idea of constructing a new set of international norms that reflect the practices, worldview, and aspirations of the ruling authorities in Tehran is as old as the Islamic Republic. In its earliest days, the revolutionary theocratic government targeted both the US and the Soviet Union. The one slogan that epitomized this sentiment was "No to the East [Soviet Union]; No to the West [United States]; [But only the] Islamic Republic." It was a coarse attempt to catapult Khomeini onto the world stage, though the concept was itself hardly worked out in detail even by its bickering supporters in Tehran. By Khomeini's death, the Islamic Republic was no longer aspiring to change to the world. The Iran-Iraq War (1980–1988) had exhausted the revolutionary fervor. Tehran was further disillusioned by its failure to capture the imagination of the masses in the Islamic world.

Instead of seeking to export its model, Tehran's pursuit of the alternative norm continued only as an effort to enhance the Islamic Republic's legitimacy. It was in this framework that other political systems outside the Western orbit—the "Russias" and the "Chinas" of the world—were identified by Tehran as fellow travelers in a crusade to push back against the global mainstream norms the West had systematically advocated since the end of the Second World War. From recasting the conventional principles of human rights and political participation, to launching alternative international media, and working to reshape and restrict access to the Internet, Tehran's effort to manipulate counter-norms began to move ahead and continues to go on unabated. In the course of these efforts, it has been seeking global partners that share its agenda. Tehran found Moscow to be useful role model, facilitator, and collaborator.

Today, President Putin and Ayatollah Khamenei probably agree that the very notion of "democracy" is an undesirable Western concept. In the case of Iran, Khomeini and later Khamenei have insisted that

"Islam itself is democratic" and proceeded to define democracy the way they have deemed fit to serve their narrow political interests but cast as a defense of the country's national interests. Despite one being a Shiite Muslim theocracy and the other an Orthodox Christian revisionist power, the Iranian Islamists share the same antipathy toward the Western liberal model as do the top officials in the Kremlin; and both are equally alarmed by Western intentions.

Moreover, while on the global stage Tehran's assertion that Iran is an "Islamic democracy" is unpersuasive at best inside the country; yet, this has never prevented the Islamic Republic from seeking to assert its values on the global scene. As is evident from the frequent public speeches of Khamenei himself, Iran does so on the pretext of defending local non-Western cultural values. In the course of promoting substitutes for democratic norms, the authorities in Tehran frequently attack the accepted standards of human rights—a particular weak spot of the Islamic Republic. And instead of withdrawing from international human rights bodies, where it comes under criticism, Tehran has rather wanted to reshape those very same institutions. In order to do so, Tehran has looked to form tactical partnerships with like-minded countries in order to confront Western norms. Again, from Tehran's perspective Russia fits the bill as a like-minded companion on this journey.

Iran has already seen the fruits of such investments. For example, when the UN Human Rights Council voted, in March 2014, to renew the special rapporteur's mandate to investigate Iran's record, 21 states supported the motion, but nine opposed it. Among the nine that came to Iran's aid were Russia, China, Cuba and Venezuela. In another revealing example, from October 2014, Russia—along with countries such as China, Syria and Cuba—refrained from censuring Iran's record at the UN Universal Periodic Review of Tehran's compliance with basic human rights standards. By now, it has become routine for Tehran to rely on sympathetic states in such forums.

In most cases, Iran's ties with other non-democratic states first developed as a way to satisfy material needs and gain geopolitical support aimed at countering the country's isolation as instigated by the United States. Although these remain key priorities, Iran is now also seeking to form alternative blocs within international forums, and it views like-minded non-democratic countries as collaborators in this quest. Tehran's courting of other revisionist powers, such as China and Russia, therefore rests on two pillars—material needs and diplomatic cover. First, this approach seeks to meet Iran's basic economic, military and trade needs given that its behavior at home and abroad has made Western states wary of dealing with it. One example of such a policy is Iran's trade relationship with China. Trade between Iran and China increased from $4 billion in 2003 to $36 billion in 2013, making China Tehran's biggest trading partner by far. More recently, in the aftermath of Russia's falling out with the West over the crisis in Ukraine in early 2014, Tehran and Moscow have penned numerous economic agreements although bilateral trade remains small. Still, the driver is unmistakable and is aimed to circumvent troublesome Western states that are at loggerheads with Iran and Russia, albeit for different reasons.

Second, forging ties with other revisionist powers provides Tehran with a diplomatic comfort zone and a claim to international inclusion, even if it fails to convince the West. For example, Tehran has earnestly sought to join the Shanghai Cooperation Organization (SCO), a six-member bloc led by Russia and China that touts itself as a counter to the West. Iran currently has observer status in the organization. The Iranians see the SCO as another mechanism to negate Western-led pressures. More recently, Iran's expressions to join the Russia-led Eurasian Economic Union (EEU) are rooted in the same basic calculations in Tehran.

Furthermore, as is evident elsewhere in the fields of defense and nuclear cooperation, not all of Iran's dealings with revisionist powers such as Russia rest on symbolisms only. Plenty of evidence can be found of other tangible cooperation. For example, Iran—which in 2003 became the first country to prosecute a blogger—works closely with Russia and China in the field of surveillance technologies and cyberspace monitoring. In 2010, Iran's largest telecommunications firm purchased a "powerful surveillance system capable of monitoring landline, mobile and internet communications"[11] as part of a $130 million contract with a Chinese company. The deal was signed only a few weeks after the European Union (EU) decided to impose restrictions on the sale of communications equipment to Iran following Tehran's crackdown on the Green opposition movement in the summer of 2009.

If Iran shares with Russia a common interest in regulating cyberspace as a purportedly defensive strategy against Western machinations, it also shares with Moscow an equally strong desire to go on the offensive in the realm of international broadcasting. Tehran has long considered this arena worthy of investment in order to counter the influence of Western broadcasters such as the *BBC* and *Voice of America*. The launch of Iran's 24-hour English-language *Press TV* in 2007 followed two years after Russia's *RT* (formerly *Russia Today*) was launched in 2005. The *modus operandi* is simple: They defend Iran's policies and those of its allies, while criticizing Western policies. The programming on both stations includes a pervasive questioning of the basic international norms of political and human rights.

Overall, despite the many ups and downs in bilateral relations since 1991, Tehran finds Russia to at a minimum share its intrinsic opposition to what they both perceive to be Western diktat. It is why the Iranian government—an Islamist regime that claims to be carrying out Allah's wishes on Earth and preparing the ground for the coming of the Mahdi (the Messiah)—counts among its most treasured foreign partners an atheist China and a Russia led by Putin, a self-declared champion of Christianity. It is not a common set of values that brings them together, but rather the desire to preserve their own power and to limit their sense of isolation in the international arena. If there is a succinct way in which to describe the goal of such alliances, it is what has been aptly called the doctrine of "democracy containment."

As mentioned above, this approach has already brought Russia and China to Iran's aid in UN human rights forums, and Tehran is eagerly pursuing membership in the SCO, an organization whose outlook on political and human rights mirrors that of the Islamic Republic. Joining forces with the SCO and with states such as Russia and China at least offers Ayatollah Khamenei's system (*nezam*) a means of avoiding global ostracism. For sure, given the dissimilarities that exist between Iran and its international partners, few in Tehran presumably expect a real strategic partnership to emerge from their country's cooperation with its revisionist allies. Yet, a common bond of sorts is arguably in the making.

Crimea and Arab Spring

On the question of Russian and Iranian collaboration in the Middle East, a number of developments in the last five years are significant. There was the 2012 return of Putin—seen by many as a Eurasianist who comes with a big dose of skepticism about Western intentions— to the presidency. In Tehran, the Russians perhaps welcomed the departure of the irksome Ahmadinejad, who was succeeded by the moderate hand of Hassan Rouhani in 2013. But there can be no doubt that two particular events—the onset of the Arab Spring in 2011 and Russia's annexation of Crimea in 2014—are the key factors that have boosted the Iranian-Russian fellowship in the Middle Eastern theater.

Russia, fearful that the West, via its pro-US Arab allies, was going to emerge as the winner from the Arab upheavals, quickly recognized that they shared a deep common interest with Iran in wanting to keep al-Assad in power in Damascus. It was, however, after the West imposed sanctions on Russia in response to its 2014 annexation of

Crimea, that Moscow deployed military assets to Syria in defense of al-Assad.

But as has been evident elsewhere in the relations, even this Iranian-Russian compact about Syria has not been without hiccups. While the Iranians welcomed the Russian military presence on the ground in Syria, a suspicion that Moscow could at an opportune moment undercut Iran's interests in Syria—by for example reaching a separate understanding with the US or Turkey—has been pervasive in Tehran. Such nagging doubts have only been further fueled by unilateral Russian actions. For example, Moscow announced, in January 2016, that it was pulling out of Syria in a step that most likely was not coordinated with the Iranians. Later, and as the Russian withdrawal did not materialize, Moscow unilaterally revealed that it was using an Iranian airbase for its operations in Syria. This was hugely embarrassing to Iran given that the Islamic Republic's constitution bars the use of its soil by foreign militaries.

The Russian indiscretion led to much anger in Tehran. Iranian Defense Minister Hossein Dehghan summarized it best when he called the Russian action a case of "betrayal." Meanwhile, the Iranians continue to monitor Russia's Syria agenda nervously. On the one hand, they are tactical partners—as manifested via joint military actions on the ground in Syria as well as through such joint sponsorship as the Astana round of peace talks about the future of Syria. And yet, it can only trouble the Iranians that Moscow has a freer hand than Iran in seeking to cut deals with an array of other actors—such as the Americans, the Turks, the Israelis and even Tehran's arch regional rivals, the Gulf Arabs. As *Kayhan*, the Islamic Republic's equivalent to the Soviet *Pravda*, put it, "Iran did not make so many sacrifices and offer so many martyrs in Syria for five years to allow it to become a chip in a deal between Moscow and Washington."

It goes without saying that the Russians too have misgivings about Tehran's game plan. President Rouhani's persistent overtures to the West since 2013 have created doubt in Moscow if the Iranian regime as a whole is still serious about the kind of strategic alliance that Ayatollah Khamenei had touted back in 2007. A mirror fear exists in Moscow that Iran is using its Russia cards in its own geopolitical haggle with the Western powers. It goes beyond geopolitical calculations. The Rouhani government's conspicuous preference for Western goods and services is a sore point in Moscow. In one telling case, a Russian minister canceled a trip to Tehran in anger over Iran's bias for Boeing and Airbus over Russian-made aircraft.

Conclusion

The Islamic Republic's ideological commitment to compete with the United States in the Middle East and beyond has certainly been a major geopolitical boon for Moscow since 1979. It is a reality that in effect weakens Iran's hand—as Tehran's stance on the US is a non-starter for a majority of the states in the region that enjoy close ties with Washington—and compels the Iranians to turn to Russia for a host of military, economic and diplomatic requirements. And yet, some quarter of a century after the fall of the Soviet Union, Iranian opinions on Russia vary greatly.

When it comes to the generals from the Islamic Revolution Guards Corps (IRGC)—the political-military guardians of the Islamic Republic and Moscow's principal Iranian collaborators in the Syrian war—one will mostly hear praise vis-à-vis Russia. These are the stakeholders in the Iranian state that speak of a "strategic overlap" of interests with Moscow in everything from combatting Sunni terrorism to rolling back American power in the Middle East. Still, even among such pro-Russia voices in Tehran, the relationship is not always easy to justify, as was conveyed by Defense Minister Dehghan's statement about Russian "betrayal."[12]

Even the limited tactical partnership with Moscow is not cost-free. The IRGC, which portrays itself as a revolutionary Islamic force, was tellingly silent throughout Moscow's military campaigns in Chechnya. For the IRGC, it is the flow of Russian arms, intelligence cooperation and other practical benefits that Moscow offers that make it a special partner. If Iran's Islamist credentials take a dent in the process, so be it. Meanwhile, the IRGC's key rival inside the Islamic Republic, the moderate government of President Rouhani, has a far less rosy view of Russia, and it is not beholden to Moscow as a transactional partner as is the IRGC top brass.

The Rouhani team has since 2013 largely looked at the new US-Russian cold war following the fallout from the annexation of Crimea as an opportunity to push its own agenda—not as an opportunity to move closer to Moscow per se, but to play the Russia card as a way to prod Washington to reassess its overall posture toward Iran. Indeed, on the question of Russia, one can detect a genuine difference of opinion between the elected president and the unelected Supreme Leader Khamenei. After his tepid visit to Tehran in 2007, Putin returned once more to Tehran in November of 2015. Here he gave Khamenei an ancient manuscript of the Koran as a gift.[13] By then, Russian troops were fighting alongside Iranians in Syria and a case for a strategic alliance—as Khamenei had first brought up in 2007—was considerably stronger. At best, however, Putin's November 2015 trip to Tehran reflected continuity in relations, and there has been no public sign of an emergence of deeper strategic convergence since.

Rouhani's key goal is the transformation of the Iranian economy, and his elected government recognizes the United States as a pivotal obstacle that one way or another has to be placated. For them, Russia does not have the financial or technological edge to be a game-changer in the beleaguered Iranian economy. And while it is good to have Russian support for when the next time Iran's human rights record is up for a vote at an international forum, the Rouhani team's preoccupation is not diplomatic symbolism but real renewal of the Iranian economy. The IRGC generals do not share this view, and claim legitimacy based not on how many jobs they can create, but on their military prowess in the many conflicts around the Middle East.

Nonetheless, both camps in Tehran quietly agree that Russia has historically taken far more from Iran than it has ever contributed to its national interests. In recent years, the Russians upset the Iranians to no end by voting repeatedly against Tehran's nuclear file at the United Nations; by deliberately delaying the completion of the Bushehr nuclear plant in order to use Iran as a pawn in Moscow's broader talks with Washington; and by systematically absorbing Iran's global oil market share when the country was under sanctions. And yet, for the hardliners in the ranks of the IRGC and elsewhere in the Iranian regime, the Rouhani government's proclivity to favor the West over the East is more ominous.

They see Rouhani as a man who might look to cut more deals with Washington at the expense of the influence and agenda of the hardline camp. Moscow's ability to find a way to fly its bombers out of an Iranian airbase has to be seen in the context of this power struggle in Tehran. From Washington's perspective, the question is whether this Iranian-Russian cooperation poses a fundamental and long-term threat to US interests in the Middle East. America has had plenty of time to ponder this question. Iran and Russia signed a military cooperation agreement in January 2015, which has so far been met by little response of any kind from Washington. The United States might see this mounting Tehran-Moscow axis as a cursory build-up. That is not necessarily how US allies in the Middle East will see it, and that alone should matter to Washington.

ENDNOTES

[1] John M. Broder, "Despite a Secret Pact by Gore in '95, Russian Arms Sales to Iran Go On," *The New York Times*, October 13, 2000, http://www.nytimes.com/2000/10/13/world/despite-a-secret-pact-by-gore-in-95-russian-arms-sales-to-iran-go-on.html?mcubz=1.

[2] "The Shadow of Mistrust in Iranian-Russian Military Relations," *Radio Farda*, https://www.radiofarda.com/a/f8-iran-russia-military-cooperation/26864535.html.

3 Matthew Bodner, "Mistrust Dogs Russia-Iran Arms Talks as Shoigu Heads for Tehran," *The Moscow Times*, January 19, 2015, https://themoscowtimes.com/articles/mistrust-dogs-russia-iran-arms-talks-as-shoigu-heads-for-tehran-43011.

4 "Russia & Iran reach agreement on S-300 air defense systems delivery – deputy foreign minister," *RT*, August 19, 2015, https://www.rt.com/news/312804-russia-iran-s300-delivery/.

[5] See time-table: "Resolutions on Iran," *Global Policy Forum*, accessed November 21, 2018, https://www.globalpolicy.org/security-council/index-of-countries-on-the-security-council-agenda/iran/49102.html.

[6] See time-table: "Iran's Nuclear Development," *The Washington Post*, January 17, 2006, http://www.washingtonpost.com/wp-dyn/content/custom/2006/01/17/CU2006011701017.html.

[7] See TABNAK, May 30, 2010, http://www.tabnak.ir/fa/news/101428/%D9%87%D9%8A%DA%86-%D9%83%D8%B4%D9%88%D8%B1%D9%8A-%D9%85%D8%AB%D9%84-%D8%B1%D9%88%D8%B3%D9%8A%D9%87-%D8%A8%D9%87-%D8%A7%D9%8A%D8%B1%D8%A7%D9%86-%D8%B8%D9%84%D9%85-%D9%86%D9%83%D8%B1%D8%AF%D9%87.

---

[8] Mark Katz, "Russian-Iranian Relations in the Ahmadinejad Era," *Middle East Journal*, Vol. 62, No. 2, Spring, 2008, pp. 202–216.

[9] Nazila Fathi and C. J. Chivers, "In Iran, Putin Warns Against Military Action," *The New York Times*, October 17, 2007, http://www.nytimes.com/2007/10/17/world/middleeast/17iran.html?mcubz=1.

[10] Shireen Hunter, *Islam in Russia: The Politics of Security and Identity*, ME Sharpe, 2004.

[11] Steve Stecklow, "Special Report: Chinese firm helps Iran spy on citizens," *Reuters*, March 22, 2012, http://www.reuters.com/article/us-iran-telecoms/special-report-chinese-firm-helps-iran-spy-on-citizens-idUSBRE82L0B820120322.

[12] Dehghan comes from the ranks of the IRGC.

[13] "From Putin To Khamenei: A Koran Copy With Its Own History" *RFE/RL*, November 23, 2015, https://www.rferl.org/a/putin-khameni-koran-russia-iran-history-islam/27382730.html.

5. Russia's Policies in the Middle East and the Pendulum of Turkish-Russian Relations

Mitat Çelikpala

Summary

The Turkish authorities have always considered Russia to be a counterweight to the West. Turkish-Russian bilateral relations, mainly based on economics, developed from the mid-1990s up to November 24, 2015. Importantly:

- Turkish decision makers see Russia as either supportive of Ankara's regional security or as an obstacle.

- Similarly, Russian authorities consider Turkey as either a locomotive of cooperation or an adversary preventing the advancement of Russian interests in its neighborhood.

- The escalation of disagreements in the Middle East between both countries, especially the so-called "plane incident," the downing of a Russian bomber by a Turkish fighter jet on November 24, 2015, had direct negative consequences on the almost two-decade-old Turkish-Russian modus vivendi.

- Syria is the top security issue for Turkish foreign policy–making, not only because of its direct consequences for Ankara's diplomatic and security relations with the West and Russia, but also due to its effects on Turkey's regional position as well as domestic developments.

- A long list of priorities exists, including the re-emergence of the PYD/YPG/PKK as an international actor, the existence of al-Qaeda derivatives on Turkey's borders, the future of Sunni regions after the Islamic State, the increasing legitimacy of the al-Assad regime in Syria, the situation of the refugees, and the future of the pro-Turkish opposition in Syria.

Within this context, as long as the Syrian conflict remains unresolved, despite its deceptive role as a political partner, Russia will hold a decisive balancer role in the realization of Turkey's interests in Syria. Turkish decision-makers feel they need Russian support to force the United States to change its attitude toward the YPG in Syria. Thus, as long as the Kurdish issue remains an obsession for the Turkish establishment and the US attitude toward the Democratic Union Party and People's Protection Units (PYD, YPG) remains unchanged, Russia will play a stronger and decisive role in shaping Turkish foreign policy in the Middle East.

This complex web of relations results in an unbalanced, obscure and, at times, self-contradictory Turkish foreign policy. The Kurdistan Regional Government's (KRG) independence referendum on September 25, which Ankara describes as an "irresponsible act," as well as the Kurdish entities' potential role both in Syria and Iraq will determine Turkey's relations with both the US and Russia for the foreseeable future.

Introduction

Turkish-Russian bilateral relations developed with a constant acceleration from the mid-1990s up to November 24, 2015. Turkey and Russia, while considering each other rivals in all neighboring regions in the early 1990s, have changed their perceptions with the aim of establishing a "new strategic partnership in the new century" and started to come closer with a focus to concentrate on the flip-side of relations. What does this aspect mean?

To be sure, this view means that Turkish decision-makers see Moscow as either supportive of Ankara's regional security or as an obstacle. Similarly, Russian authorities consider Turkey as either a locomotive of cooperation or an adversary preventing the advancement of Russian interests in its neighborhood. In order not to harm pre-defined Turkish interests vis-à-vis Russia, Ankara displayed a sensitivity since the collapse of the Soviet Union. For the sake of not offending Russia, Turkey maintained this cautious attitude toward the Russian War on Georgia in 2008 as well as during the ongoing Russian-Ukrainian conflict, even after the invasion of Crimea. Nevertheless, the escalation of disagreements in the Middle East between both countries, especially the so called "plane incident," the downing of a Russian Su-24M tactical bomber by a Turkish F-16 fighter jet on November 24, 2015, had direct negative consequences on the almost two-decade old Turkish-Russian *modus vivendi*. The increasing disagreements, competition, and insecurity in the region put any improvements in the political, economic and security-related arenas into a tight spot. At the same time, rising tensions between the West and Russia compromised the already fragile regional balance. Ankara appeared to be stuck in the middle.

Nevertheless, on July 16, 2016, the Turkish people woke up to a different country—one traumatized by the failed coup attempt the day before. It had only been weeks since commentators had begun to speak of a *normalization* or *reset* of Turkish foreign policy, following the resumption of bilateral ties with Israel (for the first time since the *Mavi Marmara* incident in May 2010) and Russia (President Recep Tayyip Erdoğan had just sent a letter to President Vladimir Putin, expressing his regrets for the downing of the Russian jet in November 2015). Erdoğan spoke of these changes in terms of a win-win approach for Turkey's relations with the world. Turkish Prime Minister Binali Yıldırım hinted at cautious policy shifts vis-à-vis Iraq, Syria and Egypt as reflection of a new foreign policy after April 16, 2016, with the motto of "earning more friends than enemies."

One month later, President Erdoğan paid his first visit abroad in the aftermath of the failed coup to St. Petersburg on August 9, 2016. This visit marked a milestone in the bilateral relations between the two nations after an almost nine-month break, which was labeled as the *annus horribilis* in Turkish-Russian relations. After their meeting in St. Petersburg, the two leaders highlighted their substantial and constructive dialogue on all issues of mutual interest and outlined a roadmap for restoring ties to a pre–"plane incident" level. Both leaders agreed that regional problems needed to be resolved through joint initiatives, implying that this should happen under the tutelage of Turkey and Russia.

Following the St. Petersburg meeting, the Russian chief of the General Staff, General Valery Gerasimov, visited the Turkish capital Ankara on September 15, 2016. The Russian general's visit was the first top-level military-to-military contact after the two countries had worked out their differences over the downing of the Russian tactical bomber. Gerasimov was also the first Russian chief of the General Staff to visit Ankara after an 11-year lull. According to official statements, Gerasimov and his Turkish counterpart, General Hulusi Akar, discussed military developments in Eurasia. While Turkish military sources described the meeting as "fruitful," most observers focused on the prospects of developing a common stand for the resolution of problems in the Middle East, namely the Syrian conundrum. In addition to the ongoing normalization of bilateral relations, it seems that Turkey finally managed to secure an understanding with Russia on Syria, from which Moscow began to reap benefits beyond its southern borders. The turn of events in Syria and the operational developments related to Operation Euphrates Shield, which the Turkish military launched to clear Syria's northern border area of extremists, could be seen as a reasonable clue for assuming that Ankara received a positive response from Moscow. Since then, the war in Syria was a major focus of the leaders' discussion in each and every top-level meetings. Moreover, Syria continues to affect Turkey's relations with its neighbors and traditional allies not only in the Middle East but also to the north, especially the Black Sea and the Caucasus.

This paper aims to analyze the last two years' turbulent Turkish-Russian relations, being shaped, more than anything else, under the multi-layered pressures of the Syrian crisis, and providing a prognosis about the future. What are the key drivers first of contention and then rapprochement? What are the limits of Russian-Turkish reconciliation/cooperation while the factors of contention still prevail in Syria? For that aim, the chapter will approach Turkey's perception of Russian policies in the Middle East from a historical Turkish-Russian relations perspective of competition vs. cooperation.

Turkish-Russian Relations: A Brief Historical Perspective

The Turkish authorities have always considered Russia to be a counterweight to the West and have played the Russia card in their negotiations with Washington and Brussels on different issues. Turkish-Russian bilateral relations developed with a constant acceleration from the mid-1990s. Despite budding relations between the two countries, it is not easy to say that the legacy of historic distrust between them has been successfully removed from their political relations. Ankara and Moscow could not manage to establish fully harmonious relations on some basic political issues such as the Kurdish issue, the Cyprus conundrum, or Armenia-related disagreements. Turkey's NATO membership and the tricky European Union accession process are also concerns for the Russian side.

Turkey's alienation from the US and the EU is a positive development from Moscow's point of view. Similar to the current political and security environment in the Middle East, Turkey is quarrelling with its Western allies especially over Iraq and the Kurdish issue since the early 2000s; this approach and attitude is shaping Ankara's policy toward Moscow. Turkey disappointed the US because of Ankara's reluctance to help topple Saddam Hussein, while the US alienated Turkey because of American forces' active engagement with the Kurds without having Turkish consent. The Turkish parliament's rejection of the deal that would allow US troops to move through Turkish territories to open a northern front in the war in March 2003 created a major crisis in Turkish-American relations. The decision was a severe blow to US war plans, which the US military was compelled to change while troop ships waited offshore and out of sight of the Turkish port of Iskenderun. This was a turning point in US-Turkish military relations, which hit rock bottom when the Turkish Special Forces compound in Süleymaniye was stormed by their American counterparts. US Special Forces humiliated the Turkish military by hooding the Turkish soldiers they apprehended. This event left a notable scar in the memory of the Turkish military as well. The current discomfort between CENTCOM and the Turkish Army in Syria and Iraq stems from almost 20 years ago with the Kremlin watching carefully.

The lack of progress in Turkey-EU relations and problems between Russia and the EU regarding the urgency to fight against extremism, namely by Kurds and Chechens, contributed to changing perceptions. It is now apparent that both parties have started to see each other as potential partners with a capacity to open up bright futures in Eurasia.

In November 2015, the downing of the Russian plane erased fifteen years of progress in bilateral relations in almost 20 seconds. A patriotic fury erupted in Russia that caught Ankara off guard. Putin warned of "serious consequences" for what he described as "a stab in the back" by "terrorist accomplices."[1] He commented, "It appears that Allah decided to punish Turkey's ruling clique by depriving them of wisdom and judgment." The escalation in rhetoric was followed by a series of quick and harsh economic measures against Turkish companies and exports. Over the next days, the two countries effectively froze diplomatic ties, hostility prevailed in the public domain, and the absence of some four million Russian tourists dealt a significant blow to Turkey's tourism industry. Combined with the declining number of European tourists due to Islamic State attacks, Turkish tourism suffered its worst period since the Iraq war. This crisis resulted in bilateral trade dipping to $23.3 billion in 2015 from 31.5 billion in 2014.[2]

What turned best friends into the worst of foes overnight was mainly the two countries' uncompromising perspectives towards Syria. Syria had been the top political issue for Turkey and Russia since 2012. Both Ankara and Moscow failed to find a mutually acceptable solution to the war in Syria at the high-level discussions between the two countries during 2012–2015. While Ankara remained dedicated to the idea of regime change in Damascus and continued to support opposition groups along its borders, Russia was determined from the beginning not to allow Syria to become another Libya, where multilateral action led to regime change that was a step into the unknown, with Moscow remaining unwavering in its support for the al-Assad regime.[3] As a result, Russia conducted its first military intervention beyond the borders of the former Soviet Union since the end of the Cold War. For Russia, the al-Assad regime's survival is its main interest in Syria while Moscow saw Iran as a natural and most trustworthy partner in the flow of events in Syria. Moreover, Erdoğan's vibrant support for the Arab Spring and the uncompromising Turkish attitude concerning the al-Assad regime in Syria have been the main obstacles to advancing Russian interests in Syria.

Russia in Syria and Turkish-Russian Relations

From a Turkish point of view, Russia is one of the principal actors in defining regional stability and security in the Middle East since the Cold War years. Russia's main concern in the region is to consolidate and maintain its power while restricting the presence of the other powers. Naturally, this attitude is a reflection of Russian assertiveness in its neighborhood and has always been a concern for Turkish authorities. Among the other Middle Eastern countries, Syria has always been a priority for Russia. Russian influence in Syria was reduced after the collapse of the Soviet Union, but Russia managed to hold on to its naval supply base of Tartus, which was established during the 1970s and continued to ship in arms and ammunitions to the regime's military forces. Russian support to the Syrian regime increased dramatically when the Arab Spring began in 2011. Russian-Syrian ties strengthened rapidly because of the legacy of the Cold War relationship and Syria, next to Iran, was perceived as a natural ally in the Middle East. In order to prevent unilateral Western involvement in the resolution of uprisings across the Middle East, Russia decided to take part in all those events actively. Moscow's interpretation of Libyan President Muammar Qaddafi's removal in 2011 is seen by the Kremlin as directly undermining Russia's global role and influence in the Arab World. Russia failed to take control of the flow of events in Libya; so in order to show its decisive role in the Middle East developments, the Kremlin decided to enter Syria. Putin's action was one of the direct ways of showing that Russia is a strong power.

The first serious sign of Turkish-Russian political disagreements emerged just after the Russian invasion of Crimea. Turkey acknowledged Russia's annexation as illegal and the referendum illegitimate, and thus Ankara does not recognize the de-facto situation in Crimea.[4] Turkish commentators question the limits of Turkish-Russian relations when Moscow is acting aggressively in Turkey's close neighborhood.

Turkey also sees Russia throwing its weight around in Syria, which has emerged as a new but more vibrant arena of conflicting interests and expectations. In reality, Erdoğan and Putin consistently failed to find a mutually acceptable solution to the war in Syria between 2012 and 2015. That Russia sought to intervene in Syria occurred at the same time as Turkey's press began to discuss a prospective military intervention is deemed to be a coincidence. When the first news of Russian military's operational build-up in Syria hit the headlines in Turkey in September 2015, Turkey started to feel the hindering impact of Russia's opposition to its policies in Syria.[5] Following a meeting with Turkish Foreign Minister Feridun Sinirlioğlu, in Sochi, on September 17, 2015, Russian Foreign Minister Sergei Lavrov openly expressed Russian doubts regarding Turkey's policies in Syria, especially when it came to the decision to join the US-led anti–Islamic State (formerly Islamic State of Iraq and Syria, ISIS)—and at the time, at least by implication, anti-al-Assad—coalition. This reaction was unmistakably triggered by Turkey's decision to open the İncirlik Base, in Turkey's southern province of Adana, to the US military for operations against ISIS. In Russia's view, this act completely failed to take Moscow's concerns into account.

However, in reality, there is little to suggest that the Turkish decision to make İncirlik available to the anti-ISIS coalition had much to do with Turkey's strategic calculus when it comes to creating a direct impact on Russian-US relations. Rather, the Turkish decision seems to have been motivated by a concern related to Turkey's desire to harness international support for its own aspiration of establishing No Fly Zones in support of the opposition groups fighting against the al-Assad regime, largely modeled on the No Fly Zones established in Iraq following the Gulf War of 1992. In that regard, the Turkish decisions of the period may be understood in terms of trying to secure US support for its own agenda and priorities in Syria. Given the course of events, this does seem like an exercise largely in vain (if not totally) due to a misreading of US prerogatives in Syria. In this context, and in line with the current state of Turkish-US relations, it is important to note that large parts of Turkish society, and an important number of opinion pundits close to the government in Turkey, have interpreted the situation as one that involved the deliberate misleading of Turkish foreign policy by the US. It also has to be noted that this rhetoric played a critical role in shaping the internal discourse in Turkey.

President Erdoğan's Moscow visit to open the renovated 111-year-old Grand Mosque, on September 23, 2015, served to remind Russia of Turkey's priorities in Syria. The Turkish leader began his speech with a quote from Tolstoy: "The most significant endeavor in life is Goodness." He then continued, alluding to his disagreement with the Russian Air Force's indiscriminate bombings in support of the regime in Syria:

> Tolstoy, in another one of his stories, said that fire in a single house risks burning an entire village. We should analyze all developments in our region from that perspective. The flames in the Middle East must be extinguished with kindness, justice and conscience. That is why we have welcomed two million refugees and have been helping people on our territory for the past four years. The solution to the refugee issue is not closing borders but guaranteeing a peaceful life in their homes.[6]

This speech marked Erdoğan's signaling his displeasure with Russia's stance directly and in front of a Russian public, for the first time.

Nevertheless, Russian fighter jets soon began violating Turkish airspace around the province of Hatay and carried out coordinated air strikes against anti-al-Assad forces in Syria, especially against

Turkish-supported forces, including the Turkmens in the north of Syria, as early as October 2015. These Russian violations were clearly undermining Turkey's self-declared rules of engagement after Syrian missiles shot down a Turkish Phantom jet off the Mediterranean coast in 2012; they signaled the possibility of a deadly encounter between the parties. President Erdoğan's statement just after his return from Russia and before flying to Strasbourg to attend an anti-terrorism meeting organized by the Union of European Turkish Democrats in early October 2015 hinted at a further escalation of tensions:

> Turkey could not endure Russian violations of Turkey's airspace in its campaign in Syria. This campaign would isolate Russia in the course of events. Russia is taking those steps despite Turkey, and that makes us sad and disturbed. Russia has no border with Syria. What is Russia trying to do here? It is doing so since the regime in Syria demanded [to intervene in the country], but there is no obligation to conduct such an operation with each regime's demand.[7]

It was during this period that Erdoğan started to talk with a raised tone of voice after NATO condemned the increasing violations of Turkish airspace:

> There some people who display sensitivity as far as to end the war in Syria or Syrian crisis. State terror caused the death of almost 350,000 people in Syria. But some actors are still trying to secure the regime. Iran is among them. Russia is another one. NATO has issued a stern ultimatum. We cannot endure it. Some steps that we do not desire are being taken. It is not suitable for Turkey to accept them. This is also beyond the principles of NATO. Our [good] relations with Russia are obvious. But they would lose us. If Russia loses Turkey, it would lose a lot.[8]

In addition, Prime Minister Ahmet Davutoğlu said that "Turkey's rules of engagement were clear about whoever violates its airspace. Turkey maintains the right to take military action against any object that enters its territory. I should express it clearly, even if it is Syria, Russia or any other country's planes, Turkey's military engagement rules are valid for all." Davutoğlu also asserted that Russia assured Turkey that its airspace would not be violated again. Such declarations heralded Turkey's realization, once again, that in the face of increasing disagreement and harassment of Turkey's airspace by Russia, the only balancing act could come from its traditional alliances.

The clearest message from those statements was Turkey's readiness to take the risk of even suspending bilateral relations with Russia for the sake of realizing Ankara's priorities in Syria. Nevertheless, despite the nominal support of its NATO allies against certain security concerns, Turkey failed to convince its Western partners to advance its interests in Syria, including establishing mechanisms to respond to the growing ISIS threat and creating security zones by enforcing No Fly Zones in northern Syria.

In November 2015, Russia increased its aggressive air strikes against Turkish-backed opposition groups in Idlib and Latakia, in particular against the Türkmen Dağı in the Jabal Turkman region. Suddenly, the position of Turkmen opposition forces became a major topic in the Turkish media and the issue morphed in the popular imagination with "Russians attacking Turkmens," especially in the pro-government media. Both Prime Minister Davutoğlu and President Erdoğan made passionate pleas about the plight of the Turkmens and the bombardment of civilians, publicly calling on Russia to halt its campaign. The Russian ambassador to Turkey, Andrei Karlov, was summoned to the Turkish Ministry of Foreign Affairs on November 19, 2015, and warned of the consequences, while Ankara tried to enlist NATO support over repeated Russian violations of its airspace.[9] While the Russian media was enjoying the spectacle of a resurgent military fighting "terrorists" and "jihadists" in Syria, the Turkish public became polarized: pro-government newspapers focused on the plight of the Turkmens and complained of Russian-Kurdish connections, while anti-government commentators relished the collapse of Turkey's Syria policy. Ankara decided to take its case regarding the bombardment of Turkmen civilians to the United Nations. But events on the ground were moving faster than policies.[10] The Russian/Syrian advances were successful in repelling opposition forces. In a front-page headline on November 21, 2015, Islamist newspaper *Yeni Şafak*, which has close ties to the Turkish government, reported: "Turkmen Mountain Falls!"[11]

The aforementioned flow of events in the final months of 2015 at last brought the two parties to the "plane incident" on November 24. This new stage in Turkish-Russian relations was a historic event for Russia and, as previously mentioned, President Putin described the incident as "a stab in the back" by "terrorist accomplices."[12] He warned of "serious consequences" as "It appears that Allah decided to punish Turkey's ruling clique by depriving them of wisdom and judgment."[13]

Despite strong statements by top Turkish officials, neither the Russian authorities nor Turkey's Western allies were anticipating such a strong response from Turkey. The basic question that has to be answered at this point is: Why did Erdoğan resort to an aggressive response instead of opening diplomatic channels? As a matter of fact, it is still a tough endeavor to answer the question why two countries, despite the existence of official mechanisms to swiftly bring top decision makers together, failed to apply the tradition of "concentrating on the flip-side of relations" on this matter.

The answer to this question lies mainly in the structural design of Turkish-Russian relations. For a long time, the two parties sustained their relations on the principle of compartmentalization—that is, geopolitical issues and economic cooperation were segregated as not only separate but distinctive agendas. Such a "seconderization" of geopolitics looks strange when one considers the strategic cultures of both parties, which are heavily laden by grand geopolitical narratives. Expectedly, in an environment where geopolitics had returned to the agenda, it did so in an overwhelming manner, threatening the real previous gains regarding bilateral trade and energy relations. We may classify the quick game changers of Turkish-Russian relations as domestic and external factors, as far as the Syrian crisis was concerned.

Domestic Factors

When the plane incident happened in late 2015, Turkey had already been facing controversial domestic developments that negatively affected political stability within the country. As mentioned above, Erdoğan and his ruling party enthusiastically supported the Arab Spring. But this support turned bitter in 2013, after the start of the Gezi Protests across Turkey. The leadership and pro-government media took a particularly critical stance against the revolutions and began to allege "Western involvement" in all those events. The second Tahrir Square rebellion, which led to the collapse of the Morsi government in Egypt, was a signal to the Erdoğan government to take an unsympathetic tone toward mass protests on Turkish streets. And with the Ukrainian Maidan revolution and mass protests all over the country in February 2014, the reservations by Turkish authorities toward popular street demonstrations were enhanced.

Erdoğan presented the establishment of direct presidential system as a solution to the unstable political environment in Turkey. He was elected President of the Turkish Republic with 51.8 percent of the votes on August 10, 2014, in the first ever direct presidential elections since the establishment of the Republic.

As far as the Kurds were concerned, Erdogan pursued a policy of social reconciliation and launched a policy of "Kurdish Opening" during his term as prime minister. The detente ended in July 2015, with members of the Kurdistan Workers' Party (PKK) killing Turkish policemen and soldiers, following two years of relative calm. The reasons behind the PKK's reversal of its strategy might be summarized as follows: Firstly, with the increasing "success" of its Syrian branch, the PYD, in the northern parts of Syria, the terrorist organization believed it saw an opportunity to position itself as an international political actor. The active cooperation with the US in the latter's campaign against ISIS in Syria emboldened the PKK regarding its operations in Turkey. Another important factor may have been linked to US materiel support and military training, which the PKK felt enhanced its capabilities and fighting skills. The PKK also apparently felt that there was room for it to build on the public credibility it had garnered fighting against ISIS in Syria and leverage its reputation. This element was thought to work for increasing its support in the West. Another potentially influential element was the PKK's fall-out with KRG President Masoud Barzani, in northern Syria. The PKK, for the first time, felt that, after expelling ISIS, it could secure territorial domination that could not only provide an alternative logistics base to Kandil, but also serve as a test case for its vision of a political system, after years of terrorism activities in Turkey.

Most importantly, after the HDP's strong performance in the June 2015 election, the military cadre of the PKK in Kandil seems to have felt that it was losing the initiative when it came to dominating the "Kurdish cause" in Turkey. In the immediate aftermath of June elections, as the HDP increased its vote share and enlarged its base, a renewed discourse around the HDP becoming a "Party of Turkey"—rather than a single agenda, ethnic political entity—was taking shape. The leadership of the PKK seems to have taken little, if any, pleasure from that development, which simply fueled its appetite for a renewed militarization of its conflict with Turkey. Under the impact of these factors, the PKK started a new urban campaign called the "war of ditches and barricades." The Turkish government's quick response was to return to traditional military methods: specifically, the Turkish army stormed urban centers such as Sur, Silopi and Cizre in southeastern Turkey to prevent the PKK from becoming entrenched there.

Ankara's "new" understanding of security, combined with its growing fight against terrorism within Turkey's borders, had a natural spillover effect on Turkey's policymaking in Syria. When Russian forces arrived in that war-torn country, the Syrian issue, interwoven with the fight against the PKK, had already become a domestic matter of concern for Turkey. Moreover, the Turkish government heavily used this argument of pairing ISIS with the PYD/PKK as a strategy to delegitimize the PKK's image in the West; Ankara's goal was to have the PYD in Syria also included on the list of legitimate and internationally recognized terrorist targets. Nevertheless, the political disagreements between Turkey and the US and, of course, with Russia for a time prevented Turkish forces from deploying beyond the country's borders in any land or air operations—Turkey's military was limited to cross-border artillery fire.

External Factors

Turkish nationalist and conservative security circles traditionally believe in the existence of external forces that continually seek to disperse and destroy Turkey. Therefore, they allege, it is necessary to defend the state and Turkish territorial integrity against this danger. For these circles, the Western powers are continually looking to "weaken and carve up Turkey." Russia's indifferent attitude, even after the aforementioned open calls by Erdoğan for joint operations in Syria as well as the US's prioritization of the PYD/YPG/PKK role in its anti-ISIS campaign were seen as "evidence" of these intentions.

The most striking example of this robust narrative was the famous phrase "precious loneliness," penned by President Erdogan's chief policy adviser, Ibrahim Kalın. These words were meant to express Turkey's "honorable stance" against coups and slaughters, as opposed to the world's ignorance of the conflicts in Egypt and Syria.[14] During the early years of Justice and Development (AK) Party government, Turkey embraced the foreign policy perspective of Ahmet Davutoglu, characterized by the motto "zero problems with neighbors." But in time, Turkey had few neighbors left with which it did not have problems. Notably, it fell out with Israel, Egypt, Syria, and Iraq and saw its friendly relations with its Western partners compromised by a lack of trust and common ground. Russia might be singled out as the only significant foreign actor that did not enforce pre-conditions on Turkey when it came to deepening strategic and economic relations.

The Turkish authorities already understood as early as 2015 that Bashar al-Assad was not going to give up power any time soon, and Ankara's priorities shifted toward the single issue of how to stop the PYD/YPG from conquering more territory adjacent to Turkey's border in northern Syria. This factor is an internal part of the Turkish plan to prevent not only the aspirations of PKK separatism, but also any separatist Kurdish movement beyond Turkey's borders. Consequently, when Russian operations began targeting Turkish-trained forces in Syria that were fighting both against ISIS and the PYD/YPG/PKK, from Turkey's point of view, this indiscriminate Russian approach diminished Turkey's operational influence in Syria—and this was not to be tolerated anymore.

What Happened Afterwards?

The first immediate result of the November 2015 downing of the Russian jet was that the Turkish population rallied around its government and the president himself. Yet, Turkish leaders approached the situation with a conciliatory tone, putting forward a narrative of defending Turkey's basic right to secure its borders. Meanwhile, the tone in pro-government media was less restrained and presented a view that "foreign powers" want to destroy Turkey's territorial integrity and international reputation. For some, "Turks taught Putin a lesson and Erdoğan destroyed Putin's charisma as a world leader," or, "Turkish eagles warned Russia like this." Some columnists even welcomed the plane incident as a clear sign that Turkey was becoming increasingly free in foreign policy terms for the first time since the Cold War. Yıldıray Oğur said, "Turkey is making its own way [...] it is constructing and defending its own position by staying within the alliances. ...Erdoğan's and Davutoğlu's self-confident and down-to earth new foreign policy perspectives are behind this success."[15]

However, were these observations accurate? When we look at what happened afterwards, the flow of events shows a totally different picture. First of all, the incident sparked animosity in Russia. The Russian media ran negative reports and accused Ankara of supporting ISIS, even claiming that Erdoğan and his family were involved in reselling ISIS oil. Furthermore, Russian targeted Turkey with economic sanctions. The tourism, agriculture, construction, and to a lesser degree, energy sector were the first that felt the direct results of these actions. Both countries' unique approaches to "greatness" were fully on display.

More importantly, Russia's reemergence as a decisive factor in shaping the key outcomes of the Syrian conflict made Turkey's situation more fragile as far as the Kurdish factor was concerned. Russia, along with the US, intensified its contacts with both Turkish and Syrian Kurds and, accordingly, undermined Turkey's room for maneuver in Syria. Within a month of the incident, the Russian media began reporting on the Kurdish question and the plight of the group inside Turkey and in Syria, discarding the tacit agreement between Ankara and Moscow to stay clear of Kurdish and Chechen issues. In January 2016, the Russian foreign ministry spokesperson, Maria Zakharova, publicly supported a petition signed by Turkish academics condemning human rights abuses in Ankara's fight against the PKK. In a surprise move, Russia also extended a warm welcome to the Turkish pro-Kurdish party HDP, and invited its leader, Selahattin

Demirtas, to meet with Russian Foreign Minister Lavrov in Moscow that December. The meeting marked the beginning of a series of contacts between Moscow and Kurdish groups; Syrian Kurds were even invited to open offices in Moscow and Yerevan. These developments clearly signaled to Turkey that the linkage and balance established between the Kurdish and Chechen issues was broken under the weight of the two countries' differences in Syria that had reached a climax with the downing of the Russian Su-24M. At this stage, Turkey found its hands tied and, therefore, turned and found refuge in its traditional alliances.

The immediate impact of the deterioration in Turkish-Russian relations was Turkey's quick U-turn to its historical allies—the US and NATO. As was the case just after the Second World War, when Soviet territorial claims pushed Turkey toward the West and opened a path to NATO membership, Turkish authorities immediately asked their Alliance partners for solidarity and protection against a probable Russian assault. Although Ankara was unable to persuade NATO to evoke Article 5 on collective defense, the North Atlantic Alliance expressed its support for Turkey's territorial integrity. Ankara felt the need to return to the Western security architecture rather than "going it alone," as per the idea penned by Ibrahim Kalın at the height of the Arab Spring.

Domestic developments were also not promising in those days. Erdoğan's expectations he would be able to establish a direct presidential political system that clarified the powers of the head of state, as well as his need and to achieve the "Turkey 2023" program, necessitated a decisive shift in power. In order to facilitate a brand-new domestic and foreign policy, Erdoğan enhanced his cooperation with nationalist factions, intensified his fight against the so-called "parallel state" and, replaced Davutoğlu with a new AK Party chairman and prime minister, Binali Yıldırım, in May 2016. Prime Minister Yıldırım hinted quickly at policy shifts *vis-à-vis* Iraq, Syria, and Egypt as a reflection of a new Turkish foreign policy after April 16, 2016. The government's new foreign policy motto would be "earning more friends than enemies."

As a reflection of this new foreign policy perspective, Ankara first initiated talks with Israel to normalize bilateral relations. Then, in order to mend bilateral ties between Ankara and Moscow, President Erdoğan sent a letter to President Vladimir Putin expressing regret for the downing of the Russian Su-24. Erdoğan, in his letter, expressed Turkey's readiness to restore relations with Moscow by calling Russia "a friend and a strategic partner." Prime Minister Yıldırım saying noted that Ankara was ready to compensate Russia for the downing of the plane.

This foreign policy behavior is a sea change in Turkish foreign policy–making since the plane incident. Moreover, an increased number of ISIS attacks on Turkish soil and the failed July 2016 coup further distracted Ankara from Syria and quickened the pace of events in the direction of rapprochement with Moscow.

Erdoğan took these steps because of Ankara's perceived lack of Western support in tackling the attempted coup. Turkey remained upset and strongly critical of the US and EU response to the coup attempt, while Russia saw it as an opportunity to provide a supportive shoulder for Turkey.

More importantly, while the internal fight against PKK terrorism was ascending on a daily basis, preventing the PYD/YPG/PKK from expanding their operations west of the Euphrates became a new red line for Turkey. Meanwhile, the US's insistence on cooperating with the PYD on the battlefield, together with Washington's continued arming of the Syrian Kurdish forces even with heavy equipment, and the appearance of pictures in the Turkish media of US special operations forces wearing the insignia of the YPG in Syria were accepted as tangible signs of US support for separatist Kurdish groups.

Turkish public opinion started to acknowledge the PYD/YPG as the US "combat boot" in Syria, which aims to establish a Kurdish state along the southern borders of Turkey.

Increasing anti-US sentiment in public opinion contributed to the Turkish government's search for a new partner on the Syrian issue. Under these undesirable circumstances, a well-known historical "lesser evil," Russia, emerged as a balancer to realize Turkey's interests in Syria. Russia, despite its declared support for al-Assad's regime, which before had contributed to the souring of Turkish-Russian relations, nevertheless now appeared as a much better alternative to the "pro-separatist PYD supporter"—the United States. The Russian choice also prevented Turkey's isolation in the region by bringing Iran into the equation on Turkey's side. Iran had always been a potential natural ally for Turkey when it came to the Kurdish issue. As a result, Turkey's old rivals, Iran and Russia, though key backers of Syrian regime, quickly became Ankara's new allies against the US-led coalition.

The launch of Operation Euphrates Shield by the Turkish Armed Forces, on August 24, 2016, is the most tangible result of the Turkish-Russian rapprochement to date.[16] The operation's main objectives were to maintain border security and confront ISIS terrorism within the framework of the UN Charter. The Turkish authorities were also targeting the PKK terrorist organization and its affiliates, the PYD/YPG, by saying that the terrorists "will not be allowed to establish a corridor of terror on Turkey's doorstep." Operation Euphrates Shield is being conducted in coordination with the US and Russia, but the main factor that has allowed Turkey to carry it out is the normalization of relations with Russia. Specifically, Turkey was able to reach a tacit agreement with Russia that enabled Turkish forces to operate in and near Syrian airspace. Russian cooperation has been persistent, since for the Turkish military campaign in Syria to proceed, Russia first had to ease its anti-access/area denial (A2/AD) measures against Turkey. Turkish-Russian coordination has enabled Turkey to act with a relatively free hand in Syria after a hiatus of months. Ultimately, Euphrates Shield allowed the Turkish army to embed itself in Syria and create a buffer zone preventing the PYD/YPG from gaining strategic depth and expanding its area of influence to Turkey's borders west of the Euphrates River. The operation also contributed positively to the Turkish army's shattered morale after the coup attempt and distracted the military's attention from domestic political issues to external, security-related priorities.

Thanks to Operation Euphrates Shield, Turkey reemerged as an actor able to secure its borders via land and air operations. Turkish forces took control of the Azez-Cerablus-El Bab triangle and became a military force on the ground, giving it greater claim to negotiate with the big powers against the smaller and non-recognized belligerent entities in Syria.

The diplomatic consequence of this Turkish military show of force has been Turkey's role in the Astana peace process, held in the Kazakhstani capital. After almost a year, Turkish officials managed to find an effective position for Turkey in the diplomatic arena and, together with their Russian and Iranian counterparts, issued a joint statement in Moscow on December 20, 2016, in which the parties declared that they agreed on the steps to revitalize the political process to end the Syrian conflict.[17] The three governments declared their support for the territorial integrity of the multi-ethnic, multi-religious and non-sectarian Syrian Arab Republic and called for a non-military solution to the Syrian conflict under UNSC Resolution 2254. More importantly, Turkey, together with Russia and Iran, declared its readiness to facilitate and become the guarantor of the prospective agreement/peace accord being negotiated between the Syrian government and the opposition. This approach is a clear elevation of Turkey's diplomatic status in the resolution of the Syrian issue since the start of the civil war. Turkey's position shifted significantly as a result of the Astana process, although Ankara is beholden to Moscow for making such a triumvirate possible.

Despite some brief interruptions caused by disagreements regarding whether the negotiating parties represented the real military opposition in Syria or not, talks in Astana and between Russia and Jordan have resulted in an agreement on the creation of several de-escalation zones in Syria. The agreement proposes the establishment of such zones in Idlib, the Turkmen mountains, parts of the Homs governorate, and areas on the outskirts of Damascus, including Ghouta and in Deraa in the south. This result, undoubtedly, was in line with the Turkish policy of establishing security/buffer zones in Syria to prevent the flow of refugees and to protect the Turkmen population without giving any advantageous position to the Kurds in Syria.

Conclusion

In sum, Syria is currently the top security issue for Turkish foreign policy, not only because of its direct consequences for Ankara's diplomatic and security relations with the West and Russia, but also due to its effects on Turkey's regional position as well as domestic developments. As was mentioned above, the Turkish government faces a long list of Syria-related priorities, including the re-emergence of the PYD/YPG/PKK as an international actor, the existence of al-Qaeda derivatives on Turkey's borders, the future of Sunni regions after the defeat of the Islamic State, the increasing legitimacy of Bashar al-Assad's regime in Syria, the situation of the refugees, and the future of the pro-Turkish opposition in Syria.

Among these priorities, the immediate concern for Turkey is the military, diplomatic, and political support that the United States and Russia had been providing to the PYD/YPG/PKK since the beginning of the Syrian crisis. After the Turkish-Russian rapprochement, the

Turkish authorities have been more vocal in their complaints about the US providing weapons and ammunitions to the PKK and its affiliates in Syria. The authorities now assert that Russia better understands Ankara's sensitivities concerning this issue and has stopped giving military support to the YPG. Within this context, as long as the Syrian conflict remains unresolved, Russia will play a decisive balancer role in the realization of Turkey's interests in Syria—despite Moscow's deceptive role as a political partner. Turkish decision-makers feel that they need Russian support to force the US to change its attitude toward the YPG in Syria. While the Kurdish issue remains an obsession for the Turkish establishment and as long as the US attitude toward the PYD/YPG remains unchanged, Russia can be expected to play a strong and decisive role in shaping Turkey's foreign policy in the Middle East. The flow of events and Ankara's diplomatic initiatives indicate that Turkish officials are trying to keep Iran and Russia on the Turkish side in Syria. This paradoxical attitude is the result of the three parties' longtime geopolitical competition in the region, which drives their periodic conflicts as well as their cooperation. These current developments apparently have made Turkey an actor again on the Syrian battlefield; but in return, Russia is playing the Kurdish card with a much louder voice, thereby making Moscow a factor in Ankara's relations with the West. This complex web of relations results in an unbalanced, obscure and, at times, self-contradictory Turkish foreign policy. The KRG's upcoming independence referendum on September 25—which Turkey describes as an "irresponsible act"—combined with the Kurds' potential role both in Syria and Iraq will determine Turkey's relations with both the US and Russia for the foreseeable future.

ENDNOTES

[1] "Putin sırtımızdan bıçaklandık," *NTV*, November 24, 2015.

2 "Türkiye-Rusya Ticaret Hacminde Büyük Düşüş," Milliyet, February 12, 2016.

3 Asli Aydintasbas, *With Friends Like These: Turkey, Russia, and the End of an Unlikely Alliance*, ECFR Policy Brief, June 2016.

4 See Turkish Foreign Ministry's statements e.g. "Kırım'da Düzenlenen Referandum Hakkında," No:86, March 17, 2014 and "Kırım'daki Son gelişmeler Hk.," No:77, March 6, 2014.

5 Rob Crilly, "Russia is Building Military Base in Syria," *Daily Telegraph*, September 5, 2015.

6 "Cumhurbaşkanı Erdoğan, Putin ile birlikte Moskova Merkez Camii'nin açılışını yaptı," *Hürriyet*, September 23, 2015.

7 "Cumhurbaşkanı Erdoğan'dan Rusya Açıklaması," *Ntv.com.tr*, October 4, 2015.

8 "Rusya Türkiye'yi kaybederse çok şey kaybeder," *TRT Haber*, October 6, 2016, http://www.trthaber.com/haber/gundem/rusya-turkiyeyi-kaybederse-cok-sey-kaybeder-207330.html..

9 Deniz Zeyrek, "Turkey warns Russia over border security," *Hürriyet Daily News*, http://www.hurriyetdailynews.com/turkey-warns-russia-over-border-security.aspx?PageID=238&NID=91568&NewsCatID=510. Ambassador Karlov was shot dead by a Turkish police officer in protest at Russia's involvement in Aleppo on December 19, 2016. The incident happened a day after protests in Turkey over Russian support for Syrian President Bashar al-Assad. Both leaders, Erdoğan and Putin agreed that the incident was an act of provocation aimed at disrupting the normalization of bilateral ties and peace process in Syria.

10 Asli Aydintasbas, *With Friends Like These: Turkey, Russia, and the End of an Unlikely Alliance*, ECFR Policy Brief, June 2016.

[11] "Türkmen Dağı Düştü!" Yeni Şafak, November 21, 2015. For an online version see http://www.yenisafak.com/dunya/turkmen-dagi-dustu-2344150.

[12] "Putin çok ağır konuştu: Terör işbirlikçileri tarafından sırtımızdan bıçaklandık," Diken, November 24, 2015, http://www.diken.com.tr/putin-cok-agir-konustu-teror-isbirlikcileri-tarafindan-sirtimizdan-bicaklandik/.

[13] "Uçak krizi patladığından beri Erdoğan ve Putin neler söylediler?" CNN Turk, November 30, 2015, http://www.cnnturk.com/dunya/ucak-krizi-patladigindan-beri-erdogan-ve-putin-neler-soylediler?page=5.

[14] "Turkey not 'lonely' but dares to do so for its values and principles, says PM adviser," Hurriyet, August 26, 2013, http://www.hurriyetdailynews.com/turkey-not-lonely-but-dares-to-do-so-for-its-values-and-principles-says-pm-adviser-.aspx?pageID=238&nID=53244&NewsCatID=338.

[15] Yıldıray Oğur, "Hayır diyebilen hatta jet düşürebilen Türkiye," Türkiye, November 25, 2015, http://www.turkiyegazetesi.com.tr/yazarlar/yildiray-ogur/588965.aspx.

[16] For a detailed account of the operation in Turkish see Ahmet Kasım Han and Behlül Özkan, "Fırat Kalkanı Sünni Hilaline Döner mi?" Birgün, September 9, 2016, https://www.birgun.net/haber-detay/firat-kalkani-sunni-hilaline-doner-mi-127729.html.

[17] Statement by the Foreign Ministers of the Islamic Republic of Iran, the Russian Federation and the Republic of Turkey on agreed steps to revitalize the political process to end the Syrian conflict, December 20, 2016, http://www.mfa.gov.tr/joint-statement-by-the-foreign-ministers-of-the-islamic-republic-of-iran_-the-russian-federation-and-the-republic-of-turkey-on-agreed-steps-to-revitalize-the-political-process-to-end-the-syrian-conflict_-20-december-2016_-moscow.en.mfa.

6. European Assessments and Concerns About Russia's Policies in the Middle East

Pavel K. Baev

Summary

European perspectives on Russia's proactive policies in the Middle East are diverse across countries, political forces and public opinions, and tend to become less compatible with one another. Moscow is perfectly aware of these disagreements, so intrigues in the Middle East, and the Syrian intervention in particular, have become a major instrument for Russia's policy of simultaneously building bridges with and putting pressure on the European Union (EU). In the great variety of views, it is possible to distinguish four key European perspectives:

- Russia's power projection in Syria is a part of the evolving confrontation between the West and Russia and aims at exposing weaknesses in the US strategy in the Middle East. At the same time, Russia's entanglement in the Syrian war puts heavy pressure on its military and diverts capabilities from the task of establishing dominance on the Black Sea theater;

- Russia could be a useful partner in the struggle against terrorism, and the intervention in Syria opens opportunities for cooperation. At the same time, Moscow's initiatives in joining efforts against the threat of terrorism are mostly self-serving, and Russia's track record in counter-terrorism is dismal;

- Russia is a big part of the humanitarian problem in the Middle East and has no interest in being a part of any solutions. Moscow can claim a role to play in the region only as long as there are violent conflicts; and as the work proceeds to post-conflict reconstruction, this role evaporates;

- Russia expands its involvement in oil and gas projects in Iraq and the Eastern Mediterranean, and delivers on its part of the cartel agreement with OPEC on production cuts. At the same time, its main interest is in preventing new volumes of gas from coming to the European market and in ensuring an increase in the oil price.

What hampers significantly the development of EU responses to Russia's steps and intrigues is the disappearance of US leadership aggravated by increasingly typical opposition in Europe to Trump's gestures and initiatives.

Introduction

Russia's ambitions to turn its military intervention in Syria into a powerful lever for strengthening its positions and influence in the wider Middle East have generated strong and various responses in Europe, which remains unable to generate a coherent policy in this conflict-rich region. The countries more directly exposed to Russian military pressure, like Poland, tend to perceive Russia's activities as an element of global confrontation and interpret them as hostile advances against Western interests. Countries less threatened by Russian military power, particularly in Southern Europe, are inclined to see Russia as a stake-holder in conflict management and put emphasis on possible cooperation in counter-terrorism. There is a wide and strong disapproval, particularly in the left-leaning part of European public opinion, of Russia's disregard of the humanitarian problems in the region, exemplified by the airstrikes that decided the outcome of the battle for Aleppo. There is also a significant business interest to the deal-making of Russian oil and gas corporations in the Eastern Mediterranean and in Iraq, as well as to the cartel arrangements between Moscow and the Organization of Petroleum Exporting Countries (OPEC). These different perspectives are often in conflict with one another, and the Russian leadership has space for maneuvering between European political positions and actors, while at the same time struggling to ensure sustainability of its own policies. Aggravating discord in Europe and disagreements between the United States and the European Union (EU) is in fact one of the key goals of Russia's policies in the Middle East.

This paper aims to evaluate the scope of differences in European views on Russia's policy in the Middle East by juxtaposing four key perspectives: a) traditional security perspective focused on the military aspects of Russian intervention in Syria; b) modern security perspective concerned with the threat of terrorism and avenues for cooperation with Russia in counter-terrorism; c) humanitarian perspective narrowing particularly on the problem of refugees; and d) the business perspective exploring the opportunities for joint projects in the oil and gas industry. The main proposition is that as these differences deepen, Moscow redoubles its efforts to exploit them, looking for additional opportunities created by the erosion of US leadership.

Intervention as a Part of Confrontation

The assessment of Russia's maneuvering in the Iraq-Syria war zone as an element of its strategy of confrontation with the West is prevalent in those European circles that put the focus on the task of containing the Russian threat. There are, indeed, good reasons to see the exercise in power projection targeting Syria as a manifestation of Moscow's preference for using military force as a key and indispensable instrument of policy. Every doctrinal document issued by President Vladimir Putin in the last two years, from the Military Doctrine (2014) to the "Basic Principles of State Naval Policy until 2030," defines US and NATO policies as the main source of threat to Russia and directs efforts and resources to countering them.[1] The proposition on confronting and defeating the US and NATO policies in the Middle East is spelled out in many mainstream commentaries in Russian media.[2] For that matter, Moscow's tentative involvement in the chaotic civil war in Libya is interpreted by many European experts as attempts at sabotaging the EU efforts at bringing this violent mess to an end.[3]

The main clash of Russian and Western interests is certainly happening in Syria, where Moscow's massive support for President Bashar al-Assad's regime forces European states, including France, to moderate their stance on removing it from power. The Russian intervention was launched partly with the aim of distracting attention from the deadlock in the Donbas war zone, but has, during two years of non-stop airstrikes, turned into a self-propelling enterprise, which shapes rather than serves Moscow's aims in the region. The first direct contention happened in November 2015, when Turkey requested and received support from NATO in the course of the crisis triggered by the lethal intercept of a Russian Su-24M bomber.[4] Tensions eased as President Recep Tayyip Erdoğan opted for reconciliation after the failed coup in July 2016, but several new spikes were registered in April 2017, for instance, after the US missile strike on the Shayrat airbase.[5]

These spasm of tensions involved Russia and US, and European states generally preferred to express only cautious support to US actions.[6] The introduction of new sanctions against Russia by the legislation initiated by the US Congress and signed into law by President Donald Trump on August 2, has raised the level of confrontation and upset many Europeans.[7] At the same time, there is a peculiar twist to the intrigue as Syria now turns out to be the only place where military cooperation between US and Russia continues to function.[8] The new US sanctions regime covers Russia as well as Iran, and European politicians seek to preserve the parameters of the July 2015 nuclear deal with Tehran while at the same time discouraging a deepening strategic partnership between Russia and Iran.[9]

Changeable current European responses to the mutating Syrian disaster add color to the basic strategic picture of NATO building up capabilities for containing Russia's aggressive behavior in the Baltic Sea and Black Sea theaters. In this perspective, the grouping of Russian forces deployed in Syria is a major challenge to NATO's goal of enhancing stability in the Eastern Mediterranean.[10] More importantly, however, the open-ended operation in Syria makes it necessary for Moscow to divert resources and attention from the two main theaters on the Western "front," so that the Black Sea Fleet cannot concentrate on the task of establishing dominance in its area of immediate responsibility and has to deal with the hard task of servicing the sea line of communication from Novorossiysk to Tartus via the Turkish Straits.[11] Russia's "victory" in Syria turns into a costly and high-risk entrapment, which lessens the pressure on such European states as Romania, which is committed to the plan of building the European missile defense system.

Elusive Cooperation in Counter-Terrorism

The start of the Russian intervention in Syria coincided with a wave of terrorist attacks in Europe, including the coordinated multiple-casualties attack in Paris on November 13, 2015. That deterioration of domestic security prompted many European politicians to reconsider Putin's invitation to build a "broad anti-terrorist coalition," spelled out in his September 2015 UN General Assembly speech. French President François Hollande made a visit to Moscow and sought to establish practical military cooperation in the air attacks on Islamic State targets in Syria.[12] Yet, NATO support for Turkey during the sharp escalation of tensions with Russia caused by the downing of the Russian bomber that November effectively undercut that fledgling cooperation. And the management of that emotionally charged crisis gradually made it clear that Moscow can hardly be a reliable partner in the struggle against terrorism.[13] The Brussels bombing on March 22, 2016, for that matter, failed to produce any new initiatives on developing cooperation with Russia.

Reconfiguring and coordinating their policies in countering terrorism, major European states encountering this threat, including Germany, directed their expanded efforts on two inter-connected goals. The first one was suppression of terrorist networks created by their citizens returning home after partaking in fighting in the Iraq-Syria war zone and facilitated by radical Islamic propaganda. The second goal was defeating ISIS in its core territory in Iraq and Syria; and European states directly and mostly indirectly contributed to the war efforts of the US-led coalition. Russia has been of no relevance in the struggle on European domestic fronts, and of some but dubious help in Syria.

The work on exterminating the terrorist networks in Europe was seriously complicated by the evolving problem of migration, which reached crisis proportions in late-2015–early 2016, but has been only partly mitigated by the EU deal with Turkey reached in spring 2016.[14] Russia attempted rather awkwardly to play on that problem, which backfired badly in the European public opinion, even if the accusations of Moscow "weaponizing" the migration problem were rather inflated.[15] More important was the difference in dealing with the traffic of potential volunteers for the Jihadist cause in Iraq and Syria. European states, in particular France and Belgium, focused their efforts on preventing their citizens from traveling to the war zone and on investigating the recruiters for ISIS.[16] Moscow, to the contrary, saw no reason to check the flow of rebels from the North Caucasus to the Middle East and even facilitated it via FSB channels, expecting that this emigration would improve domestic security.[17] This encouragement of departure has started to backfire, but Moscow remains reluctant to admit it. For that matter, French President Emmanuel Macron had expressed his condolences regarding the knifing in Surgut in August 2017, several days before the Russian authorities admitted that it was indeed an ISIS-inspired terrorist attack.[18]

One new development in this problem is the growth of extremist networks among migrants from Central Asia, which manifested itself in terrorist attacks in Istanbul (January 1, 2017), Stockholm (April 7, 2017), and St. Petersburg (April 3, 2017). Europeans have good reasons to be worried about it, suspecting that Moscow is the main recruiting hub for these networks; but the Russian authorities remain uncooperative, not least because a major source of radicalization is the severe exploitation of labor migrants from Central Asia in Russia.[19]

Russia simultaneously presented itself as a major force in the fight against ISIS in Syria, but refused to join the US-led coalition, asserting that focusing narrowly on ISIS allows other terrorist groups to grow. This reasoning is not without merit, but when Foreign Minister Sergei Lavrov converted it into an accusation that the US always "spared" Jabhat An-Nusra (affiliated with al-Qaeda) in order to use it to overthrow the al-Assad regime, a reasonable assessment became an exercise in dirty propaganda.[20] Moscow was careful to target this attack on US policy, making it possible for Lavrov to suggest to EU High Representative for Foreign Affairs and Security Policy Federica Mogherini to put aside the "artificial obstacles" in Russia-EU relations, first of all sanctions, and to concentrate on the real agenda of counter-terrorism.[21] Mogherini was not exactly enthusiastic about this idea, knowing that, in reality, the situation was exactly the opposite: Sanctions are a manifestation of deep disagreements between the EU and Russia on the norms and values underpinning the European security system, and the prospects for cooperation in counter-terrorism are actually slim. What stands in the way of such cooperation is the plain fact that Russia is firm set on treating all anti-Assad forces in Syria (with a possible exception of the Kurdish YPG) as terrorist organizations.[22] This strategy of winning the war for al-Assad by camouflaging the extermination of rebels of all persuasions as counter-terrorism remains unacceptable for Europeans.

Humanitarian Disconnect

What constitutes a major negative influence over European views on Russia's policies in the Middle East and, in particular, on the Russian intervention in Syria is Moscow's complete and sincere disregard of the humanitarian consequences of its actions. The EU places a strong emphasis on the humanitarian agenda of its foreign and security policy, which is prioritized by Germany. Even small European states, such as Norway and Sweden, take pride in their reputations as "humanitarian superpowers."[23] Moscow seeks to counter accusations of indiscriminate violence by alleging that the US is covering up the "collateral damage" from its airstrikes, particularly in the battles for Mosul and Raqqa.[24] This propaganda cannot whitewash Russia's reputation as an accomplice in multiple and continuing crimes against humanity.

The issue of the deliberate targeting of civilian populations in Russian airstrikes emerged in the European media already in the first weeks of the intervention, but the most charged outcry was caused by the protracted battle for Aleppo. Moscow's flat denials of strikes on humanitarian convoys compelled even left-leaning commentators to condemn its "barbaric" methods of waging war and to expose the lies of Russian propaganda.[25] French President Hollande made an emotional speech at the UN General Assembly in September 2016 on the plight of the "martyred city" of Aleppo and asserted that "enough is enough."[26] Putin had to cancel a visit to Paris but was not particularly impressed with Hollande's hollow stance, so the offensive on Aleppo continued until full "liberation." Another outcry of anxiety followed the chemical attack on Khan Shaykhun, on April 4, 2017; British officials instantly called for holding Russia responsible for that crime.[27] The EU Foreign Service was particularly upset because the shock from the use of chemical weapons overshadowed the long-prepared donor conference in Brussels, where pledges for aid to Syria amounted to $6 billion, much below $12 billion pledged in 2015.[28]

This indignation against Russian intervention makes most Europeans suspicious of Moscow's ongoing efforts at managing the Syrian conflicts by establishing the so-called "de-escalation zones." They are seen as both an attempt to consolidate the gains on the ground and legitimize the victory of the al-Assad regime. Furthermore, those "de-escalation zones are seen as a draft for splitting up the Syrian state, which is freely discussed by Russian commentators.[29] European attitudes toward the negotiations in the so-called "Astana format" involving Russia, Turkey and Iran are certainly far from coherent. On the one hand, many European politicians, particularly in France, as well as in the EU Headquarters, resent being excluded from the peace-making process, the parties to which tend to take for granted the prospect that Europe will provide the bulk of funding for the post-war reconstruction.[30] On the other hand, the discourse on a stronger EU role in Syria typically camouflages the reluctance of many European actors to shoulder any direct responsibility for bringing the devastating war to an end.[31] The new French President Macron performs a tricky diplomatic dance, first confronting Putin on his backing for the Syrian regime, then noting that there is no "legitimate successor" to al-Assad, and then complimenting Trump on his back-channel deal with Putin on a ceasefire in the southeastern corner of

Syria. But Macron's own stance on the continuing humanitarian disaster is ambivalent at best.[32]

European views on the mutating Syrian war and Russia's role in it are significantly influenced by the evolving refugee crisis, which for such states as Italy and Germany constitutes the main humanitarian dimension of this protracted catastrophe. The escalation of the refugee problem in 2015–2016 produced a strong drive for a greater EU role in Syria, but presently the stabilization of the outflow of refugees results in a slackening of that drive.[33] The main part of this problem is now the maritime trafficking of migrants from Libya to Italy. Russia can, in principle, be a part of the solution, but prefers to play a low-cost spoiler role. Moscow has granted tangible support to "Field-Marshal" Khalifa Haftar in Tobruk, who contests power with the "Government of National Accord" (GNA) in Tripoli led by Fayez al-Sarraj. When Italy reached an agreement with the GNA on deploying its Navy to interdict the traffickers, Haftar promptly rejected it. And while he has no capacity to "repel" Italian patrol crafts, he is firm set to deny them access to ports in Eastern Libya.[34]

In general, while Moscow perceives its ability to squeeze European sensitivities to humanitarian problems as an important political advantage, in many European states, from Norway and Finland to Germany and Italy, there is a growing indignation about Russia's attempts to aggravate the need for aid and to exploit the refugee crisis as means of manipulation of conflicts.

Energy Matters the Most

A very particular perspective on Russia's policies in the Middle East comes from those European business circles that are engaged in, or evaluating the prospects of joint ventures in energy projects in the Eastern Mediterranean or in the Persian Gulf. Understanding is growing that the newly-achieved US energy self-sufficiency diminishes Washington's interest in engaging with the Middle East, while Europe continues to be dependent on oil and gas imports from the region and Russia is keen to cut into this dependency.[35]

While Russian propaganda typically presents the US "occupation" of Iraq as an execution of the desire to take control over its oil reserves, in fact, Gazprom-Neft, Rosneft and Lukoil are successfully developing production and exploration projects in both southern Iraq and Iraqi Kurdistan. In a similar way, the newly-discovered gas resources of the Eastern Mediterranean are usually described in Moscow as a subject of fierce competition, which precludes their development for the European market, while in fact, Russian companies are aggressively expanding in this area.[36] New sanctions legislated by the US Congress are targeting particularly joint energy projects with Russia and so cause much anxiety in the European oil and gas milieu.[37]

The Russian energy sector is generally known to be badly affected by the price dynamics on the oil market, so the readiness of Rosneft and Gazprom-Neft to invest in new projects in northern Iraq in 2017 has taken many European stakeholders by surprise.[38] The main destination of the new crude is the European market (an expansion of the Kirkuk-Ceyhan pipeline is in progress), so a partnership with such "usual suspects" as Total and ENI could be mutually beneficial. The problem with this enterprise is that the deal was signed by Rosneft directly with the Kurdish Regional Government, and this constitutes a direct encouragement from Moscow to the cause of independence of Iraqi Kurdistan.[39] The EU is cautiously opposed to the prospect of a break-up of Iraq, but is seeks primarily to ensure that Iran proceeds with opening up for business on the condition of the full implementation of the July 2015 nuclear deal. And in that, European interests are fully compatible with Russia's stance.[40]

In the Eastern Mediterranean, Russia spins a convoluted energy intrigue, showing the seriousness of its intentions by partaking in the gas development in Egypt, where Rosneft paid ENI as much as $1.13

billion for a 30 percent stake in the "Zohr" project at the end of 2016.[41] This deal is endangered by the new sanctions, so European lobbyists managed to persuade the US Congress to exempt from punishment joint projects in which Russian companies own less than 33 percent of shares.[42] The peculiar business-political paradox here is that while Russia shows eagerness to partner with ENI, Total and Noble Energy in the development of various gas fields, including "Aphrodite" in Cyprus and "Leviathan" in Israel, it is fundamentally not interested in the arrival of this gas to the European market, because it will inevitably reduce its own export niche.[43]

Another new development that has not been as yet quite comprehended by Russia's European business partners is the first-ever workable agreement between Moscow and OPEC on oil production cuts. The deal has not yielded the expected results in terms of pushing the oil price up, but Russian officials tried to convince Putin that a great success had been achieved.[44] European experts venture mixed opinions about the prospects of this cartel arrangement, which certainly violates the principles of free trade but cannot significantly weaken the trend of abundant supply on the global oil market.[45] The real issue with this deal is that it adds to the problems in the Russian energy sector, where sustained under-investment is aggravated by mismanagement and corruption. Rosneft is most severely affected by these problems; yet, its CEO, Igor Sechin, made the decision to grant the insolvent Venezuela a pre-payment of $6 billion, which Russian experts can only explain as a cover-up for embezzlement.[46] European companies, including BP, which owns some 20 percent of Rosneft shares, have to evaluate carefully the risks of partnering with this crony-captured company, particularly as the sanctions regime is tightened.

Current affairs in the oil and gas business in the Middle East are always tumultuous, and Russian companies are eagerly fishing for opportunities in these murky waters. Still, the basic imperative for Moscow, about which European stakeholders are fully aware, is ensuring a significant increase in the oil price. Cartel deals on production cuts cannot deliver this result, so Russia's only hope is a major armed conflict in the Persian Gulf, which is by no means an impossible proposition.

Conclusions and Implications

Disarray and discord are nothing new in European foreign policy–making and in debates on most key issues, so the spectrum of different views on Russia's policy in the Middle East is presently perhaps only marginally wider than at the start of this decade, when the arrival of a new cold war appeared to be an improbable scare. What makes a big difference now is the erosion or even complete disappearance of US leadership, which used to be (with some significant exceptions, like the beginning of the Second Gulf War) a major formatting influence on European views and policies in the greater Middle East. European political and business elites, as well as fractured public opinions, are at a loss about the trajectory of interactions between US and Russia in the Middle East, and so they miss a key reference point for assessing the consequences and risks of Moscow's policies in the region. There is now in Europe (with the notable exception of Greece) a widespread and well-deserved mistrust of Putin's intentions, but the unique feature of the political landscape is that Trump is trusted even less.[47]

The introduction of new US sanctions has extinguished the initially exuberant expectations in Moscow regarding a cultivation of special relations between Putin and Trump, and has made it essential for the Kremlin to focus greater political effort and propaganda attention on Europe, in order to exploit the sharply increased trans-Atlantic disunity. Intrigues in the Middle East, and the Syrian intervention in particular, have been a major instrument for Russia's policy of building bridges with and putting pressure on the EU.[48] The application of this instrument is set to intensify, and Moscow will try its best to advance the proposition on the need for, and usefulness of cooperation in counter-terrorism. One example of such re-energized efforts is the initiative of the semi-official think tank Russian International Affairs Council to develop a channel with the European Commission for dialogue on the theme "Russia and the EU in the Greater Middle East."[49] In the Europeans' view, talk and dialogue are always good, but the rationale for cooperating with Russia in the hard struggle against terrorism has proven to be weak, and Moscow's pronounced disregard of humanitarian problems remains deeply disagreeable.

One particular issue pertaining to European perspectives is the highly unstable pattern of Russia-Turkey relations. The EU has arrived at an awkward and dubious position as it has to sustain the process of Turkey's accession but at the same time make it clear to the member states that there is no prospect of actually admitting it in. Poignant European criticism of the curtailing of democratic rights in Turkey since the failed coup in July 2016 has brought estrangement and tensions, particularly in German-Turkish relations.[50] Putin, to the contrary, has expressed full support to Erdoğan and proceeds with rehabilitating the partnership interrupted by the November 2015 air skirmish crisis. Concerns abound in many European quarters that further censure of Erdoğan's semi-authoritarian regime, justified as this reproach may be from the point of view of human rights violations, may push Turkey further into an alliance of sorts with Russia.[51] In the oscillating but progressing confrontation between NATO and Russia in the Black Sea theater, Turkey's position is pivotal, so there is a strategic need to strengthen its commitment to and engagement with NATO, despite all the disarray in its severely purged military. The nearly done deal on purchasing the Russian S-400 surface-to-air missiles for the Turkish air defense system is certainly not making this task any easier, because the interoperability with NATO forces is set to suffer.[52]

The pragmatic proposal to ensure an efficient management of the new confrontation with Russia often transforms in many European political circles into a denial of the reality of this confrontation, and this ambivalence, in turn, muddles the assessments of Russia's policies in the Middle East. Many Europeans, for that matter, find Putin's ability and readiness to maintain dialogue with all important parties to regional conflicts, from Israel and Saudi Arabia to Hamas and Iran, highly commendable and fitting with their preferences for carefully negotiated political solutions.[53] Middle Eastern actors are glad to talk with Putin, but there is little trust in his good will, so Moscow is unable to act as a mediator either in the old Israel-Palestinian conflict, or in the new Qatar crisis. An understanding also exists that Russia can claim a role to play only as long as there are violent conflicts; but as the political work proceeds to post-conflict reconstruction, this role evaporates.[54] This propensity for conflict manipulation, combined with the appraisal of military force as the most useful instrument of policy, and compounded with the need to ensure an increase in oil prices, makes Russia a very particular kind of stakeholder in the overlapping Middle Eastern areas of turbulence.

Overall, European views on Russian activities in the Middle East tend to become more diverse between countries and political forces of different orientations and less compatible with one another. Moscow tries to pursue proactive opportunistic policies using the Syrian intervention as a lever for entering other developing situations, and this makes the European policies reactive, slow and often incoherent. What significantly hampers the development of EU responses to Russia's steps and intrigues is the disappearance of US leadership, aggravated by increasingly typical opposition to Trump's gestures and initiatives. The EU capacity for developing a coherent foreign and security policy is hardly going to increase. And regarding the Middle East, the weakness of German leadership is particularly apparent. Russia is at a great and deepening disadvantage in its confrontation with the West, so it cannot afford to miss opportunities for aggravating the trans-Atlantic discord, as well as the divisions inside the EU, emerging in the chaotic Middle East.

ENDNOTES

[1] The latter document, approved on July 20, 2017, is available at http://publication.pravo.gov.ru/Document/View/0001201707200015?index =0&rangeSize=1; one useful evaluation is Dmitry Gorenbrg, "Russia's new and unrealistic naval doctrine," *War On the Rocks*, July 26, 2017, https://warontherocks.com/2017/07/russias-new-and-unrealistic-naval-doctrine/.

[2] See for instance, Vladimir Mukhin, "Russia outplays USA in Syria," *Nezavisimaya Gazeta* (in Russian), July 21, 2017, http://www.ng.ru/world/2017-07-21/1_7034_siria.html.

[3] Mattia Toaldo, "Russia In Libya: War Or Peace?" European Council on Foreign Relations, August 2, 2017, http://www.ecfr.eu/article/commentary_russia_in_libya_war_or_peace_722 3.

[4] A typical Polish assessment is Mateusz Chudziak, "Turkey Goes For Broke: Tensions After a Russian Bomber Is Shot Down," OSW Analyses, November 25, 2015, https://www.osw.waw.pl/en/publikacje/analyses/2015-11-25/turkey-goes-broke-tension-after-a-russian-bomber-shot-down.

[5] European reflections on these incidents were rather mixed; see Tom Batchelor, "Russia 'Targeting' US Jets In Syria After America Shoots Down First Assad Regime Warplane," *Independent*, June 19, 2017, http://www.independent.co.uk/news/world/middle-east/russia-shoot-down-all-flying-objects-in-syria-us-regime-warplane-isis-terror-a7797101.html.

[6] Jefferson Chase, "Merkel, German Government Say US Missile Strikes In Syria 'Understandable,' " *Deutsche Welle*, April 7, 2017, http://www.dw.com/en/merkel-german-government-say-us-missile-strikes-in-syria-understandable/a-38341124.

[7] Edward Lucas, "A House Divided: Some Europeans Are Cool To New US Sanctions On Russia. They Shouldn't Be" CEPA *Europe's Edge*, July 31, 2017, http://cepa.org/EuropesEdge/A-house-divided.

[8] Igor Subbotin, "Pentagon May Save the Russia-US Relations," *Nezavisimaya Gazeta* (in Russian), July 28, 2017, http://www.ng.ru/world/2017-07-28/1_7039_pentagon.html.

[9] One critical opinion on this diplomacy is Alejo Vidal-Quadras, "Mogherini's Attendance At Rouhani's Inauguration Encourages Iranian Impunity," *EurActiv*, August 4, 2017, http://www.euractiv.com/section/global-europe/opinion/mogherinis-attendance-at-rouhanis-inauguration-encourages-iranian-impunity/.

[10] Margherita Bianchi et al., "Projecting stability in NATO's Southern neighbourhood," Istituto Affari Internazionali, July 2017, http://www.iai.it/en/pubblicazioni/projecting-stability-natos-southern-neighbourhood.

[11] Boris Toucas, "NATO and Russia In the Black Sea: A New Confrontation?" *CSIS Commentary*, March 6, 2017, https://www.csis.org/analysis/nato-and-russia-black-sea-new-confrontation.

[12] Hugh Schofield, "Hollande In Moscow: A New Era In Russian-French Relations?" *BBC News*, November 26, 2015, http://www.bbc.com/news/world-europe-34931378.

[13] Janusz Bugajski, "Russia Is a Fake Partner Against Terrorism," *CEPA Europe's Edge*, June 6, 2017, http://cepa.org/EuropesEdge/Russia_is_a_fake_partner_against_terrorism.

[14] Kondylia Gogou, "The EU-Turkey Deal: Europe's Year Of Shame," *Amnesty International*, March 20, 2017, https://www.amnesty.org/en/latest/news/2017/03/the-eu-turkey-deal-europes-year-of-shame/.

---

[15] The term was coined by Andrew Rettman, "Russia 'Weaponising' Refugees Against EU," *EU Observer*, March 2, 2016, https://euobserver.com/foreign/132526.

[16] Daniel L. Byman, "The Vicious Circle Of French Terrorism," *Order from Chaos*, July 15, 2016, https://www.brookings.edu/blog/order-from-chaos/2016/07/15/the-vicious-cycle-of-french-terrorism/.

[17] The data on this outflow, estimated at a few thousand, is scant; see "The North Caucasus Insurgency and Syria: An Exported Jihad?" *Report No. 238*, International Crisis Group, March 16, 2016, https://www.crisisgroup.org/europe-central-asia/caucasus/north-caucasus/north-caucasus-insurgency-and-syria-exported-jihad.

[18] Andrei Kamakin, "Knifing In Surgut and Political Correctness: Covering Up the Truth," *Moskovsky Komsomolets* (in Russian), August 21, 2017, http://www.mk.ru/social/2017/08/21/reznya-v-surgute-i-politkorrektnost-nado-li-utaivat-pravdu.html.

[19] Mark Youngman, Cerwyn Moore, "After S. Petersburg: Russia and the Threat From Central Asian Terror Networks," *RUSI Commentary*, April 20, 2017, https://rusi.org/commentary/after-st-petersburg-russia-and-threat-central-asian-terror-networks.

[20] Lavrov made this accusation after the meeting with US State Secretary Rex Tillerson in Moscow; see "Lavrov: Russia Suspects That USA Protect An-Nusra In Order To Overthrow Assad," *RIA Novosti*, (in Russian) April 12, 2017, https://ria.ru/syria/20170412/1492127468.html.

[21] Mogherini visited Moscow two weeks after the US missile strike; see "Lavrov Notes Anti-Russian Sanctions Brought Up During Talks With Mogherini," *TASS*, April 24, 2017, http://tass.com/politics/942883.

[22] On Russian ambivalent support for the Kurdish cause see Robert Fisk, "Secret Russian-Kurdish-Syrian Military Cooperation Is Happening In Syria's Eastern Desert," *Independent*, July 24, 2017, http://www.independent.co.uk/voices/syria-isis-russia-kurdish-ypg-happening-in-secret-a7857471.html.

[23] There is always a dose of humility in this branding; see Tor Kjolberg, "Sweden – the Humanitarian Superpower," *Daily Scandinavian*, March 3, 2017, https://www.dailyscandinavian.com/sweden-humanitarian-superpower/.

[24] See for instance, Aleksandr Sharkovsky, "The Value of Human Life In the Middle East Is Miniscule," *Nezavisimaya Gazeta* (in Russian), July 28, 2017, http://www.ng.ru/kartblansh/2017-07-28/3_7039_kartblansh.html.

[25] A typical exasperation with this propaganda is Alec Luhn, "Russian Media Could Almost Be Covering a Different War In Syria," *Guardian*, October 3, 2016, https://www.theguardian.com/world/2016/oct/03/russia-media-coverage-syria-war-selective-defensive-kremlin.

[26] See "United Nations General Assembly: France's 3 Appeals," *Gouvernement.fr*, September 21, 2016, http://www.gouvernement.fr/en/united-nations-general-assembly-france-s-3-appeals.

[27] Joe Watts, "Russia Responsible For Syria Chemical Attack, UK Defence Minister Michael Fallon Says," *Independent*, April 9, 2017, http://www.independent.co.uk/news/uk/politics/michael-fallon-russia-syria-chemical-weapons-attack-air-strikes-donald-trump-vladimir-putin-a7674831.html.

[28] Georgi Gotev, "Donors Pledge Billions At Syria Aid Conference, NGOs Say Too Little," *EurActiv*, April 6, 2017, https://www.euractiv.com/section/development-policy/news/donors-pledge-billions-at-syria-aid-conference-ngos-say-too-little/.

[29] Aleksandr Sharkovsky, "The End of 'Caliphate' Is the Beginning Of the War For Dividing Syria," *Nezavisimaya Gazeta* (in Russian), August 8, 2017, http://www.ng.ru/armies/2017-08-08/7_7046_siria.html.

[30] Experts insist on a better political use of aid; see Julien Barnes-Dacey, "Time to Play the Money Card In Syria," European Council on Foreign Relations, March 30, 2017,

http://www.ecfr.eu/article/commentary_time_to_play_the_money_card_in_syria_7261.

[31] One example of this discourse is the Press Release of the European Commission "Towards an Even Stronger EU Role For Syria, Reinforcing EU Efforts To Build Peace," March 14, 2017, available at http://europa.eu/rapid/press-release_IP-17-561_en.htm.

[32] Curt Mills, "Why Emmanuel Macron Is Now the Man To Watch In Syria," *National Interest*, July 18, 2017, http://nationalinterest.org/feature/why-emmanuel-macron-now-the-man-watch-syria-21586.

[33] Marc Pierini, "In Search Of an EU Role In the Syrian War," *Carnegie Europe*, August 18, 2016, http://carnegieeurope.eu/2016/08/18/in-search-of-eu-role-in-syrian-war-pub-64352.

[34] On Russian encouragement, see Ravil Mustafin, "Haftar Has Shown To Rome Who Is the Boss In Libya," *Nezavisimaya Gazeta* (in Russian), August 4, 2017, http://www.ng.ru/world/2017-08-04/6_7044_livia.html.

[35] James Henderson, Ahmed Mehdi, "Russia's Middle East Energy diplomacy," *Foreign Affairs*, June 20, 2017, https://www.foreignaffairs.com/articles/middle-east/2017-06-20/russias-middle-east-energy-diplomacy.

[36] One typical risk-exaggeration is "War For Gas In the Mediterranean: Turkey vs Greece," *Vesti-Finance* (in Russian), July 17, 2017, http://www.vestifinance.ru/articles/88237.

[37] One sound view is Natalie Nougayrede, "As the US and EU Square Off Over Russia Sanctions, Only Putin Can Win," *Guardian*, July 31, 2017, https://www.theguardian.com/commentisfree/2017/jul/31/europe-us-russia-sanctions-putin-washington-eu-donald-trump.

[38] Viktor Katona, "Putin's Newest Oil Play: Russia Gains Foothold In Iraqi Oil Patch," *OilPrice.com*, June 13, 2017,

http://oilprice.com/Geopolitics/International/Putins-Newest-Oil-Play-Russia-Gains-Foothold-In-Iraqi-Oil-Patch.html.

[39] Mahmut Bozarslan, "Iraqi Kurdistan-Russia Oil Deal Could Have Major Implications For the Region," *Al-Monitor*, June 12, 2017, http://www.al-monitor.com/pulse/originals/2017/06/turkey-iraqi-kurdistan-russia-moscow-eyes-kurdish-oil.html.

[40] On the ambivalent EU position on the Kurdistan problem, see Georgi Gotev, "EU Tight-Lipped On Kurdish Referendum," *EurActiv*, June 16, 2017, https://www.euractiv.com/section/global-europe/news/eu-tight-lipped-on-kurdish-referendum/.

[41] Elena Mazneva, Stephen Bierman, "Rosneft Snaps Up Stake In ENI's Giant Egyptian Gas Discovery," *Bloomberg*, December 12, 2016, https://www.bloomberg.com/news/articles/2016-12-12/rosneft-to-pay-up-to-2-8-billion-to-join-eni-egyptian-gas-block.

[42] Jorge Valero, "Eight European Projects To Be Hit By US Sanctions On Energy Sector," *EurActiv*, July 25, 2017, https://www.euractiv.com/section/energy/news/eight-european-projects-to-be-hit-by-us-sanctions-on-energy-sector/.

[43] See on that "EU To Cut Gas Dependency On Russia With Israel Pipeline," *Deutsche Welle*, April 3, 2017, http://www.dw.com/en/eu-to-cut-gas-dependency-on-russia-with-israel-pipeline/a-38269274.

[44] See the transcript of Putin's meeting with the members of government on July 28, 2017 (in Russian), available at the Kremlin website, http://kremlin.ru/events/president/news/55179.

[45] James Henderson, "Room For Cynicism and Hope In Russia's Deal With OPEC," *Oxford Institute for Energy Studies*, December 2016, https://www.oxfordenergy.org/publications/room-cynicism-hope-russias-deal-opec/.

[46] Mikhail Krutikhin, "The Deal Is Intended As a Nice Purloin," *Newsru.com* (in Russian), August 9, 2017, https://blog.newsru.com/article/09aug2017/rosneft.

[47] Richard Wike, Bruce Stokes, et all, "Less Confidence In Trump Compared With Merkel and Other World Leaders," Pew Research Center, June 26, 2017, http://www.pewglobal.org/2017/06/26/less-confidence-in-trump-compared-with-merkel-and-other-world-leaders/.

[48] My more elaborate examination of this can be found in Pavel Baev, "Pressure Points: The Syria Intervention As an Instrument Of Russia's EU Policy," *PONARS Eurasia Policy Memo* 470, April 2017, http://www.ponarseurasia.org/memo/pressure-points-syria-intervention-instrument-russias-eu-policy.

[49] Natalya Evtikhevich, "The Middle East For Russia and the EU: Bone Of Contention Or Cause Of Peace?" Russian International Affairs Council, August 2, 2017, http://russiancouncil.ru/en/analytics-and-comments/analytics/the-middle-east-for-russia-and-the-eu-bone-of-contention-or-cause-for-peace-/.

[50] German angst is spelled out in Katrin Elger, Maximilian Popp, Christian Reiermann, "Can the German-Turkish Relations Be Saved?" *Spiegel Online*, August 10, 2017, http://www.spiegel.de/international/europe/a-1162037.html.

[51] One good representation of these concerns is "Views From the Capitals: What To Do About Turkey?" *European Council on Foreign Relations*, May 22, 2017, http://www.ecfr.eu/publications/summary/vfc_views_from_the_capitals_what_to_do_about_turkey.

[52] Kerry Herschelman, "Finalising S-400 agreement with Russia, Turkey rejects NATO interoperability argument," *Janes' Defence Weekly*, vol. 54, no. 32, August 9, 2017, p. 13.

[53] On this Russian cultivation of dialogue channels, see Nikolay Pakhomov, "Russian-style Diplomacy Can Break the Middle Eastern Impasse,"

National Interest, June 14, 2017, http://nationalinterest.org/feature/russian-style-diplomacy-can-break-the-middle-eastern-impasse-21156.

[54] Hayder al-Khoei, Ellie Geranmayeh, Mattia Toaldo, "After ISIS: How To Win the Peace In Iraq and Libya," *European Council on Foreign Relations*, January 4, 2017, http://www.ecfr.eu/publications/summary/after_isis_how_to_win_the_peace_in_iraq_and_libya_7212.

7. Imperial Strategies: Russia's Exploitation of Ethnic Issues and Policy in the Middle East

Stephen Blank

Summary

Russia has been an empire throughout its history. Accordingly, the mechanisms and practices of imperial management, particularly Russia's ability to coopt potential elites from minorities with whom it is interacting, have remained central to its political behavior at home and abroad. And it has expanded to create linkages—or what Celeste Wallander has called "trans-imperialism"—between members of Russia's Islamic population and Middle Eastern elites, e.g. the use of Ramzan Kadyrov as an agent of Moscow in the Middle East. At the same time Russia has also sought expanded investment by Middle Eastern governments in projects aimed at benefitting Russia's Muslims.

But beyond attempting to create these kinds of trans-imperial linkages and coopt Muslims at home and abroad, Russia has actively exploited both domestic and foreign ethno-religious cleavages throughout its history to expand its power, territory, wealth and influence. Vladimir Putin's regime is no exception, especially in Syria and the wider

Middle East. The Kurds furnish a particularly revealing example of how Moscow has exploited these cleavages in Syria, Turkey and Iraq to gain energy rents, strategic access, wealth, and political influence over those governments to enhance its strategic position in Syria. Finally, as long as such opportunities present themselves to Moscow, it is unlikely that it will desist from exploiting this time-honored tactic of imperial aggrandizement and management, even if empire and imperial strategies invariably entail war and risk the security of Putin's state.

Introduction

Since its inception as a state, Russia has been and remains an empire. In 2000, Alexei Malashenko observed that Russia's war in Chechnya is logical only if Russia continues to regard itself as an empire.[1] Similarly Alexander Etkind remarked in 2011 that Russian history remains one of internal colonialism.[2] Meanwhile in the course of building and then losing at least two empires and striving again to recover its lost legacy, Russia has acquired an immense amount of experience in so-called wars of imperial management, counterinsurgency, and power projection beyond Russia's borders. One hallmark of this historical experience is a repeated pattern of cooptation of domestic and foreign and ethnic minority elites. A second element is an accompanying unending tactical flexibility that exploits ethno-religious (or other) divisions among Russia's neighbors, or attempts to break up hostile or targeted states—or at least neutralize their ability to resist Russia's strategies for advancing its national interest.[3] This is certainly the historical and present case as regards both Russian and foreign Muslims. Putin's policies have shown his awareness that, "for the contemporary Russian government, managing Islam and Muslim religious authorities is central to the functioning of Putin's state."[4] In this context, Afghanistan in 1978–89 stands as an exception that proves the rule: in that instance, Moscow coopted an elite (the Afghan Communist Party and its various factions) that could not remain cohesive or deliver the population. And militarily, Moscow could not isolate the theater as it has successfully done in all its successful wars of counterinsurgency. Therefore, the Soviet Union lost the war and had to retire from that scene.

Examination of Tsarist, Soviet, and current Russian foreign policy reveals a pattern: that despite its own autocratic proclivities, Russia has generally advocated for a democratic solution in disrupted states in order to preserve a pro-Russian party either in power or at least in a position of influence in those areas. It then could use that faction to advance its own interests or even assimilate the entire country into Russia's empire. This is now happening in Syria if not Iraq, too, as seen in Moscow's stance on those countries' Kurdish issues. This exploitation and cooptation of ethnic minorities to promote a larger strategy of imperial assertion continues today in Russia's efforts to regain at least some of the perquisites of empire and great power standing across the Middle East that it lost in 1991. But today's strategic environment requires that Moscow adapt to the possibility of its own Muslim population playing a larger role in its Middle Eastern policy, and to the realities of influence travelling back and forth between Russia's own Muslims and Middle Eastern Muslim populations. Even before the Syrian insurgency began Moscow had seized every opportunity to ingratiate itself with Arab and other Muslim countries as a fellow Muslim country based on its sizable minority of co-religionists. For example, it became a member of the Organization of Islamic Countries (OIC) in 2005. Subsequently, in 2014, Russia signed a framework agreement for cooperation with it.[5] Already in 2003, Putin told the OIC that Muslims were "an inseparable part" of the "multiethnic Russian nation."[6]

The Cooptation Tactic

As Alfred Rieber has written, "For Russia there was no hard and fast distinction between colonial questions and the process of state building. This was not true of any other European state."[7] Today, given the permeable boundaries of Islamic societies, cooptation of tractable domestic and foreign elites who are ethnically or religiously connected can be used abroad both to resolve domestic issues and at home to resolve foreign issues. Today Moscow utilizes domestic Islamic elites, for example Chechens, for resolving Middle Eastern issues to Russia's benefit. In Soviet times Moscow showcased Central Asia as a potential model for modernization of Arabic societies.[8] But Moscow also uses its relations with Middle East countries to prevent them from supporting domestic Islamic terrorism.[9] Meanwhile Middle Eastern governments now also seek to influence Central Asian states; for example, Saudi Arabia's investments and mosque building in Tajikistan have allegedly led Dushanbe to veto Iran's membership in the Shanghai Cooperation Organization.[10] Meanwhile Tajikistan openly solicits such Arab investments.[11]

Celeste Wallander called this process of coopting foreign elites "trans-imperialism" although the label is less important than the imperialistic reality.

> Trans-imperialism is the extension of Russian patrimonial authoritarianism into a globalized world. Russia can trade and invest without being open and permeable by selectively integrating transnational elite networks in the globalized international economic system and replicating the patron-client relations of power, dependency, and rent seeking and distribution at the transnational level. Russian foreign policy is increasingly founded on creating transnational elite networks for access to rent-creating opportunities in the globalized international economy. Moscow functions as the arbiter and control point for Russia's interaction with the outside economy to ensure that Russia is not exposed to the liberalizing effects of marketization, competition, and diversification of interests and local power. If that were to happen, the political system that keeps the present

leadership in power would be at risk of failing. In this sense, globalization is a threat not to Russian national interests but to the interests of Russia's political leadership.[12]

Accordingly exploitation of ethno-religious and other fissures in targeted societies has become a staple of Russian foreign policy and simultaneously a means for insulating its own society from such influences by eliciting Arab support for Russia's domestic and foreign policies. A recent Chatham House study by Keir Giles emphasized Russia's ability to purchase or co-opt business and political elites to create compliant networks," that is, generate "agents of influence" or "Trojan horses" in foreign governments and institutions that offer Russia leverage over them.[13] This is particularly notable where ethnic and/or religious cleavages furnish Russia with the means for exploiting those fissures, as is now happening with Muslim migration to Europe.[14] For Russia, nationalism begs to be instrumentalized for the state's benefit in the Balkans as in the Middle East. In the Balkans and Europe's East, Moscow supports the Hungarian minority against Ukraine, and Serbs against Kosovo, Albania, Montenegro and Bosnia—even to the degree of launching a coup in 2016–17, in Montenegro, using Serbs.[15]

At the same time Putin has sought outside elites' support to quell domestic insurgency and Islamic uprisings in the North Caucasus. This was a major objective of Putin's early diplomacy in the Middle East.[16] And it still figures in Russian policy. For instance, in 2016, Moscow openly solicited Iranian investment in the North Caucasus republic of Dagestan.[17] Today, although the original policy clearly continues, Putin has also redirected it to use Russia's Muslims in Syria and Libya to legitimize Russia's military intervention there.[18] Moscow also has justified its Syrian intervention by often invoking the alleged public opinion of its own Muslim population to support Bashar al-Assad's regime, though this allegation cannot be tested or verified. But Moscow has clearly obtained such domestic support, at least from Russia's official Islamic establishment.[19] For example, Putin also has entertained the idea of using Chechen forces in Central Asia and also tried to arrange for Kazakh and Kyrgyz peacekeepers in Syria,[20] in addition to sending Chechens to serve Russian policy goals in Libya and Syria as described below. Indeed, it appears that the request for peacekeepers from the Collective Security Treaty Organization (CSTO) may actually resonate within that organization.[21] Moreover, now that foreigners are allowed to serve in the Russian military, Putin might send Sunni Central Asian *Gastarbeiter* (guest workers) to Syria as part of the Russian Army.[22] Andrej Kreutz observed in this context that, for Putin,

> The sheer size and ferocity of the Islamic challenge had an impact on the new Russian leader and persuaded him that a new political approach was necessary in order to solve the conflicts with the Muslim population of the country and have a closer link with the Islamic nations.[23]

Similarly Maxim Suchkov has noted,

> As an external power, Russia needs regional partners to master its own Islamist challenges in the Caucasus, the Volga region, and the Urals, to name a few. Thus Moscow is in constant pursuit of a balance between a pragmatic foreign policy in the Middle East and its own domestic problems in this regard.[24]

Historically, Russian leaders, including Putin, have been hypersensitive to the prospect of foreign ethnic or ideological influence upon the regime's security, given the shaky loyalties to Russia of its ethno-religious minorities. But now Russia cannot close off its own Islamic population or those of former Soviet republics to foreign influences, especially when they all, including Russia, enlist Arab investment and political support. Yet, simultaneously, Russian elites also remain attuned to the opportunities that cross-border ethnic fragmentation provides for expanding the empire or at least enhancing Russia's global standing. Thus Kreutz wrote in 2009,

> Iran abuts directly to the South Caucasus and Moscow has always considered this region a strategic interest priority zone. Russian analysts perceive that, "whoever controls the Transcaucasus [South Caucasus] also controls the Caspian Sea and access to Central Asia and the Middle East. In addition, ensuring influence and stability in the Transcaucasus countries is seen as a necessary precondition for Russia's internal peace and for its territorial integrity. Russia itself is also a Caucasus state. Seven regions of the Russian Federation (Adygea, Ingushetia, Dagestan, Kabardino-Balkaria, Karachaevo-Cherkessia, North Ossetia, Chechnya) are located in the North Caucasus and four more are on the steppes adjacent to the Caucasus (Krasnodar and Stavropol territories, the Rostov region, and Kalmykia). With Muslims constituting more than 15 percent of the Russian population any potential American and allied invasion of Iran and the ensuing clash of civilizations would put pressure on Russia's domestic issues and might threaten its territorial integrity.[25]

Moscow's stratagem of using its ethnic minorities as instruments of Russian influence abroad while coincidentally protecting itself from having those same minorities used against Russia is rooted deeply in Russian imperial history, and it forms at least part of the context of Russia's current involvement in the Middle East. For example, even before the Syrian insurgency began, Moscow had seized every opportunity to ingratiate itself with Arab and other Muslim countries as a fellow Muslim state based on its sizable minority of co-religionists. Moscow's pursuit of membership in the Organization of Islamic Cooperation (OIC) paid off.[26] In 2003 Putin told the OIC that Muslims were "an inseparable part" of the multiethnic Russian nation."[27] And in 2014, Russia hosted The 6th International Economic Summit of Russia and OIC countries in Kazan, the capital of Tatarstan.[28] Having established connections with the OIC, Moscow then initiated "a tango with Islamists," "defining some as bad and others as good." It may be seeking to elicit Western or Muslim state concessions but it also is clearly attempting to coopt external Muslims in support of its domestic policies and foreign policies.[29]

The Foreign Policy Dimension and Its Link to Domestic Policy

In the Middle East this cooptation tactic is part of a larger overall approach to the "national question" that prizes tactical flexibility in manipulating reality to serve Russian state objectives. Thus James Sherr of Chatham House writes that,

> While Russia formally respects the sovereignty of its erstwhile republics; it also reserves the right to define the content of that sovereignty and their territorial integrity. Essentially Putin's Russia has revived the Tsarist and Soviet view that sovereignty is a contingent factor depending on power, culture, and historical norms, not an absolute and unconditional principle of world politics.[30]

This is what is now happening *de facto* in Syria as Moscow tries to take a leading role in defining exactly what the contours of Syrian statehood will be. Sherr subsequently adds, "For 20 years the Russian Federation has officially—not privately, informally or covertly, but officially—equated its own security with the limited sovereignty of its neighbors."[31] This certainly includes its Muslim neighbors, including Turkey.

Similarly the manufacture, incitement, and exploitation of ethnic or other conflicts is not confined to peoples inside the empire. It was and is a hallmark of Russian policy toward the Kurds and Armenians in the late Ottoman Empire as well as today. Recent studies of Russian policy toward the Kurds and toward Iraq make clear Russia's attitude vis-à-vis the Kurds varies with the prospects for its ties to Turkey and

Iraq.[32] Moscow's ties to the Syrian Kurds (YPQ) who support al-Assad and also check Turkey's regional ambitions are not a new phenomenon as Russia's previous support for them going back to the 1890s shows.[33] Russia essentially exploits pre-existing tensions in targeted areas. Those groups that cooperated with Russia themselves represented the fragmentation processes occurring within them and sought to use their connection with Russian power to advance their own objectives.

The Middle East: Syria's Kurds

In Syria, Moscow began with several strategic advantages that it then converted into positive strategic outcomes. First, Russia benefits from supporting a government possessing the rudiments of an army and state, which has also attracted support from Iranian and Hezbollah elements. This constellation of forces has proven strong enough to regain the initiative from the insurgents and ensure Bashar al-Assad's victory.

Second, al-Assad's enemies are mostly Sunnis, while his regime is mostly Alawite, an untypical form of Sunni Islam that is close to Shi'ism. Consequently his regime has apparently gained the support of Syria's religious minorities, who have good reason to fear an assertive Sunni regime, especially one influenced if not led by the Islamic State (IS). Evidently religious minorities—e.g., Shiite Muslims, Christians, Alawites, Druze, Ismailis and Kurds—fear IS and Sunni extremists more than they dislike al-Assad.[34]

These groups have formed their own militias to protect themselves from the Hobbesian state of nature that Syria has progressively become, but those militias fight mainly for ethnic or ethno-religious self-protection while cooperating with al-Assad, Russia and Hezbollah or Iranian forces.[35] Syria's Kurds have much to lose from any overthrow of al-Assad, as a Sunni Arab state would suppress their efforts to create or associate with some kind of independent

Kurdistan. Seeing Assad's weakness and dependence upon their support and Turkey's opposition to him as both an opportunity and a threat, they are predisposed to cooperate with Moscow and anyone else that can promote their interests. Thus, they are perforce dependent on Moscow, and both sides are cognizant of this fact.[36] Therefore, there are ample areas of opportunity in Syria among its ethno-religious minorities with which Moscow can work.

Moscow has stated that it pays special attention to the Kurdish issue.[37] In early 2017, Russia called for "cultural autonomy" for ethnic Kurds in any postwar Syrian state, in the constitution it is sponsoring for that country.[38] Russian scholars are thinking about applying a Bosnian model based on the Dayton peace accords for the former Yugoslavia to Syria. This would permit integration of the various militias into a postwar Syrian army, but would also ensure a weak central state that tolerates diverse cultures and peoples, including the Syrian Kurds and their political arm, the Kurdish People's Protection Units (YPK). This formula would allow Moscow to interfere in Syria for years to come, as it does in Bosnia.[39] Yet, at the same time, Russia has been building a military facility in YPG-controlled territory at Afrin, evidently to train Kurdish military units—against the Islamic State for now, but probably also to support Russia in the future.[40] Certainly such a force obstructs Turkish military designs in Syria, particularly Ankara's determination to prevent any kind of cohesive Kurdish political community. Likewise, any future Syrian government must also pay heed to Moscow's clients in any future state.[41]

Building on such actions, Moscow has allowed the YPG's political arm (the PYD) to open an office in Moscow and is allowing the YPG to expand its territorial remit inside Syria. Since many observers believe the PYD and YPG to be subsidiaries of the PKK—the Kurdish movement inside Turkey, President Recep Tayyip Erdoğan's bête noire—this effectively raises the specter of Moscow supporting both Syrian and Turkish Kurds either against Ankara or, in the future, against Damascus. The point of all these moves is not that Moscow supports such open state-building efforts, but rather that it is consolidating leverage over any future Kurdish developments in Syria and Turkey. As a result, it can use the Kurds, as it has for over a century, to weaken Turkey as well as keep Syria in a state of dependence upon Moscow, and thereby gain leverage over both states—and over the Kurds, as their main foreign protector. Thus, Russia retains maximum flexibility and maneuverability in attempting to meet any and all future contingencies. In other words, Russia can preserve its leverage to protect all of its military-economic-political investments in Syria and Turkey by being able to threaten or support those states, as it deems necessary.[42]

Moscow also plays the Kurdish card in Iraq and Turkey. It seems clear that from the outset Moscow sought to bring as many possible opposition groups, including the Kurds, into, the political process of peacemaking in Syria.[43] This conforms to the traditional practice of supporting weak, multi-ethnic or multi-confessional states in targeted areas to secure lasting Russian influence. Similarly Putin has said that since the Kurdish factor is a real one in Syria and Kurdish forces are among the most efficient opponents of the Islamic State, Russia must work with them if only to deconflict its forces (Russian and Kurdish forces), a clear sign that Moscow intends to constrain Turkey, whose opposition to any form of contiguous Syrian Kurdish territory or political assertion is obsessive (at least from the Western point of view).[44]

Moscow has also supported YPG military actions in Syria to constrain Turkish military actions in Syria.[45] Earlier in 2017, it seemed that there was a real possibility the YPG and Turkish forces could come into a direct clash around Afrin canton. Since Putin's and al-Assad's forces needed to move into territory occupied by Turkish forces around Idlib, it appeared that Moscow was then inclining to meet Ankara's needs at the expense of its Kurdish allies.[46] This episode demonstrated what Moscow gains by playing the Kurdish card. It keeps Turkey and the Syrian Kurds in a state of dependence upon Moscow and on Moscow's terms. Russia can deploy either the Kurdish or Turkish card as needed to advance its aims—in this case the pacification of Syria and avoidance of a full-scale clash with Turkey. But those entities that depend on Russian support invariably pay a high price for the attainment of even part of their objectives. Thus, in this particular case, Syrian Kurdish leader Ilham Ahmed hoped that Moscow, when devising disengagement zones with Turkey and Iran, would obtain guarantees for Kurds in a postwar state. Clearly Moscow is in a highly advantageous position vis-à-vis both Syria and Turkey thanks to its patronage of both the Syrian and Turkish Kurds.[47]

Moreover, in Turkey proper, President Erdoğan has accused Russia in the past of arming PKK militants.[48] So Moscow possesses a weapon that it can use whenever it wants to turn up the heat on the government in Ankara. Indeed, Turkey, as it now proceeds in Syria, faces numerous potential challenges involving the Syrian Kurds, and one of them is the "potential implications of a military confrontation with Kurdish militias for relations with Russia, who is supposed to play a role in disengagement on the Turkey-Syria border in accordance with the trilateral talks held with both Turkey and Iran in Astana."[49] Meanwhile, Russia—similar to the way it deals with Hamas and Hezbollah, groups it denies are terrorists—claims that neither the PKK nor the YPG are terrorist organizations.[50] Therefore, it has no reason to shun them. Moscow alone decides who the terrorists are.

Russia and the Iraqi Kurds

Russian involvement with Iraqi Kurds is, if anything even deeper than with Syria's Kurds, longer lasting, and more far-reaching. In Iraq, Russia appeals to the Kurds' hope for independence and statehood. It manipulates both Baghdad and the Kurds using leverage over energy and arms deals, ultimately in ways that support Russian strategic and economic interests. Russian interest in Kurdish energy started once the European Union expressed a similar interest in 2010.[51] In 2012, Exxon-Mobil gave up its project in West Qurna because it could obtain better terms from the Kurdistan Regional Government (KRG) in northern Iraq. This decision triggered great anger in Baghdad, which was and is determined to prevent Kurdistan from entering into foreign energy deals independently of its authority. Baghdad it depends on those energy revenues to finance its governmental operations. So to replace Exxon-Mobil, the central Iraqi government looked to Russian and/or Chinese firms.[52] However, Moscow, true to its stated policies of having a card to play with everyone, and complete flexibility regarding issues of states' territorial integrity and self-determination, has been active ever since in energy deals in Kurdistan. Illustratively, today, Lukoil plays a major role as an energy exporter in Kurdistan.[53]

Additionally, in 2012, Russia's Gazpromneft (a subsidiary of Gazprom) inked two deals with Kurdish authorities, becoming the fourth major oil company to enter Iraqi Kurdistan. Gazpromneft acquired a 60 percent share in the 1780KM2 Garmian Block and 80 percent of the 474KM2 Shakal Block.[54] This deal came about even as Russia was negotiating with Iraq over arms sales and access to the West Qurna field. Iraq then sought to force Gazprom to cancel its deals with Kurdistan in November 2012 or else lose access to the Badra oilfield near Iran that it had acquired in 2009 and that was supposed to begin production in August 2013. Iraq's government termed any contract with Kurdistan illegal, as the Iraqi government did not approve it.[55]

Nevertheless, Moscow decided to retain and even expand its dealings with Kurdistan, even though that antagonized Iraq. Russia hosted the president of the Kurdish region, Massoud Barzani, in February 2013. At these meetings, both sides discussed key political questions and energy issues as well as possibilities for further Russian energy contracts with Kurdish authorities.[56] Also at those talks, and despite Baghdad's remonstrations with Moscow, Gazpromneft signed a deal to enter into a Kurdish oil project, the Halabja Block.[57] This deal duly marked the third Russian energy project in Kurdistan.

Despite the February 2013 and subsequent deals with Kurdistan, President Putin apparently kept the Iraqi government informed of what it is doing. He may have done so to distance Iraqi Kurdistan from a flirtation with Turkey—both Russia and Iraq oppose Turkey's claims to being an energy hub and have a shared interest in keeping Turkey from obtaining unmediated access to Kurdish energy holdings.[58] But this entire sequence illustrates that Moscow can exploit the tensions between the KRG and the Iraqi government. Such maneuvering allows the Russia to gain leverage over Baghdad's and the KRG's energy and foreign policies—and potentially over Turkey as well. Thus, Russia's ties to Iraqi Kurdistan enhance its capabilities to effectively influence Turkey. The ability to manipulate ethnic rivalries here adds to Russian wealth and influence. Indeed, were Turkey to become a major energy hub, it would be able to export that gas or oil to other European countries, thus undercutting Russian exports that enhance Moscow's influence throughout the Balkans and Eastern Europe. But there are larger dimensions to this Russia-Turkey-Iraq triangle beyond that fact.

Turkish freedom from more dependence on Russian energy not only limits Russia's influence, it also enhances Azerbaijan's smaller but competitive project of selling the Balkans and Central Europe gas from the Trans-Anatolian Pipeline (TANAP), which will connect at the Turkish-Bulgarian border to the Trans-Adriatic Pipeline (TAP). Russia needs to keep Turkey as dependent as possible on its gas in order to retain a means of pressure and influence on Turkey, but also to preserve its position in the Balkans and even to some degree in the Caucasus and the Middle East. And if it cannot prevent the Kurds from selling their gas to Turkey, its goal then becomes to have a foot in both the Iraqi and KRG camps, thus ensuring that Russia receives its cut or rents for the sale of Kurdish and Iraqi gas to Turkey. And of course, to the extent that it can use Kurds against Turkey, Russia also keeps Turkey from reducing its dependence upon Russian energy. In other words, Russian policy is completely opportunistic, obstructive of genuine stability in the Middle East, as well as intended to maximize Russian flexibility and freedom of maneuver without committing itself irrevocably to any one side—except insofar as they oppose the United States.

Simultaneously, Moscow's leverage upon the Iraqi Kurds also gives it enhanced leverage upon Baghdad, which has repeatedly been forced to hold its tongue and not protest about Russian coercive pressures or its engagement with the KRG and the deprivation of the Iraqi budget of revenues from those energy platforms in Kurdistan. Precisely because it fears what Moscow could do to embolden the Iraqi Kurds and promote their centrifugal tendencies regarding independence from Iraq, Baghdad has repeatedly had to give in to Russian terms or not protest Russian encroachments upon it.[59] Moreover, that Russian engagement with Iraq's Kurds is growing: Rosneft has signed a new agreement with the KRG. Apart from plans to explore for more oil and gas holdings in Kurdish territory, "Rosneft will get access to the major regional transportation system with the throughput capacity of 700 thousand bbl. [barrels of oil] per day, which is planned to be expanded up to 1 [million] bbl. per day by the end of 2017."[60] Beyond granting Rosneft access to the KRG pipeline and ability to expand its capacity, Rosneft will then refine this oil in Germany. Also, according to Jabbar Kadir, an advisor to former KRG prime minister Barham Salih, the Russian oil giant promised to invest $3 billion in the KRG in exchange for access to 700,000–1,000,000 bbl. per day that it would ship abroad.[61] Consequently, Turkey has now been displaced from managing the KRG's energy affairs.[62]

Even as the fallout of the September 25, 2017, Kurdish referendum on independence was occurring, Rosneft signed deals with the KRG for 80 percent equity in five oil blocks, conservatively estimated at a total recoverable 670 million barrels of oil.[63] That $400 million deal came on top of earlier loans of $1.2 billion to Kurdistan earlier this year. And it was soon followed by Rosneft's agreement with the KRG to acquire majority interest and thus control of Kurdistan's main oil pipeline for another $3.5 billion.[64] This deal evidently aims to prevent Iraq and or Turkey from taking control of that pipeline and suffocating the KRG's independence drive. Instead they will now have to deal with Russia and the fact that it has clear title to that pipeline. Even if Iraq recovers that pipeline, it will clearly have to pay off Russia as well. Thus, Moscow maintains its leverage over both Iraq and the KRG.

The Kurdish question in Iraq (and by implication in Syria and Turkey) assumed even greater importance in the wake of the independence referendum. Russia here too has danced with both sides. On the one hand, it supports the integrity of the Iraqi state; and when the Iraqi government with Iranian (and Turkish) backing subsequently seized Kirkuk and its oil field, Foreign Minister Sergei Lavrov announced that Moscow is committed to a unified Iraq.[65] Clearly, Moscow cannot afford simultaneously to alienate Turkey and Iran as well as sanction a new civil war in Iraq's territory by supporting Kurdish independence in a Kurdish state carved out of their territories. Yet, on the other hand, Russia simultaneously was and remains (especially after these deals) Kurdistan's largest foreign source of financial support; and this will not change. For what is critical is not whether or not the Kurds obtain a state but whether or not they remain usable for Russia to give it leverage over each of the four regional states where this minority is present—Turkey, Syria, Iraq and Iran.[66] Indeed, it appears that Moscow's grand design is to retain its hold on the Kurds and their energy in order to keep Iraq in line and off balance as well as to gain further energy leverage over Turkey. According to Russian Minister of Energy Aleksandr Novak, Moscow intends to connect Kurdistan's oil and gas pipelines, which it now controls, to the Black Sea and thus to its projected Turkstream pipeline, thus dominating Turkey's imports.[67] This last point of

Novak's remains an aspiration but one with potentially far-reaching political consequences if it materializes.

Clearly, Russia utilizes the Kurdish card in Syria and Turkey not just to promote restive minorities to weaken targeted states but also to put diplomatic pressure on Ankara and Damascus on behalf of its own interests, obtain energy rents, and gain lasting leverage over the Iraqi, Kurdish, Syrian, and Turkish economies and political systems. As a recent paper observes, "You do not need ISIS to prevail for as long as Turkey has an ongoing conflict with the Kurdish nation in the broader region."[68] In Syria, Moscow's Kurdish game also balances Syrian and Turkish considerations viewed from Moscow.

The Chechen Card in the Middle East

Moscow's utilization in Libya and Syria of Chechen forces loyal to the pro-Kremlin local government in Grozny underscores the reciprocal interaction among the Russian government and its agents. In this case, those key agents for Moscow are Chechen leader Ramzan Kadyrov, Russia's Muslim population, and Middle Eastern and Central Asian governments. Putin's use of Kadyrov and Chechens in this way evokes previous efforts cited above to use Muslims as bearers of Moscow's message.[69] For instance, Moscow has raised the idea of sending Chechen policemen to patrol captured areas of Syria, and is now talking to Kazakhstan and Kyrgyzstan about them sending troops as well.[70] But it also inverts the policies cited above by which Putin sought outside Muslim support against *jihadi* and Sunni terrorism in Chechnya during the war of 1999–2007.[71]

However one views the relationship between Putin and Kadyrov, it remains the case that the Chechen strongman, though he clearly possesses some discretion, acts primarily as Putin's agent in the Middle East. As *The New York Times* observed, the "Grozny-Kremlin relationship is calculated, controlled, and mutually beneficial."[72] By showing himself as a prominent leader and conductor of Russian foreign policy abroad, Kadyrov enhances his own standing at home and abroad, reinforces his value in Putin's eyes by signaling Muslim support for his policies, and undoubtedly profits personally as well. He also establishes linkages to foreign governments who might be potential benefactors for him and Chechnya in the future and will, he hopes, testify in Moscow to his utility and "indispensability." Meanwhile, Moscow obtains tangible support of thousands of battle-hardened Muslim forces that it can send to Syria or elsewhere in order to soften the impact of its military presence while demonstrating Russian support for Muslim self-assertion. Troops like the Chechen forces loyal to Kadyrov that were sent to Syria also testify to the success of Putin's policies in suppressing the earlier insurgency and then reconstructing Chechnya. Thus the approximately 1,000 Chechen troops in Syria carry a high propaganda value in and of themselves and establish a vital and potentially lasting connection to Chechen émigrés in Syria who have supported al-Assad.[73]

Through this channel, Ramzan Kadyrov establishes his credentials as a Kremlin policymaker and representative who can negotiate on behalf of Moscow with Arab governments; can help them clarify their positions vis-à-vis Russia; and elicit from them investments in Chechnya and/or other Muslim regions. Kadyrov has also become involved in Kremlin diplomacy toward Afghanistan,[74] and he is now organizing an international center for the training of special forces, no doubt with Russian backing. Since Kadyrov currently participates in most if not all high-level meetings with Middle Eastern leaders, he can credibly present himself as a real Russian power broker.[75]

Kadyrov's standing as an important power broker in Russian Middle Eastern policy also emerges in Libya. By 2015, he was negotiating with Libyan authorities to free Russian sailors who had been seized by Tripoli. Since then, he has taken part in high-level negotiations among the factions in Libya and Russian officials who monitor the Libyan situation daily. Kadyrov is pushing efforts to cement ties with Libya's business community, even as he conducts negotiations with representatives of Libya's opposing factions. Meanwhile Moscow provides decisive military support to the faction led by General Khalifa Haftar. Kadyrov's role here is obviously important, and we can expect that Moscow will turn more attention and political resources to this war-torn North African state. Russia may use Kadyrov to show outside audiences that it can work with all relevant factions in Libya, as in Syria. But Moscow's ultimate objective, as in Syria, is expanding Moscow's long-term role and presence in Libya's politics, economics and energy as well as, presumably, obtaining a base in Libya: one of Joseph Stalin's aims in 1945.[76]

Conclusion

These examples show just how tactically flexible Moscow can be in its use of Muslims, at home and abroad. The continuation of these strategies and tactics in service of a broader strategy to advance Russian interests, even in a maelstrom like Syria, shows the continuity of the cooptation tactic when applied to Islamic peoples through Tsarist, Soviet and now Putinist Russia. Russia's actions reflect not just an essential tactical continuity and flexibility but also the enduring imperial mindset of divide and rule. Russia clearly still behaves as if the Middle East is, as it was in Soviet times, a region close to Soviet (Russian) borders—even though those borders are now 1,000 kilometers further away. And it employs tactics and conducts policies toward the Middle East that reflect the ongoing continuity between Tsarism, Soviet power and the current Russian Federation. Indeed many Russian analysts underscore that a major reason for Moscow's intervention in Syria has been to leverage Russia's seeming ability to fight Islamic terrorism in order to compel Washington to acquiesce to Russia's earlier invasion of Ukraine.[77]

Moscow continues to seek to govern and be seen by others as not just a great power but as an empire. And empire, as revealed, inter alia, in the persistence of imperial tactics of elite cooptation, ultimately also means protracted wars. Already in 2004, Rieber wrote a fitting epitaph underscoring the essential link between empire and war:

> If imperial boundaries have no intrinsic limitations and are solely established by force, then they are bound to be heavily and persistently contested. The universal claims of empires, whatever the practical constraints may be in carrying them out, cannot by their very nature be accepted as legitimate either by the people they conquer or their rivals for the contested space. There can be no community of empires as there is a community of nation states. All empires share a common problem of legitimizing boundaries. As perceived through the prism of the community of nations, imperial frontiers appear problematic because they are sustained by force, even though solemn treaties might have recognized them from time to time.[78]

The Middle East, of course, was historically part of various, competing empires and the legacies of those empires are still not yet resolved. Thus, Rieber's admonitions apply to it. But they also apply to Russia, which remains an empire in outlook and state structure. Indeed, as we have seen, its external power projection is closely tied to the dilemmas of assuring Russia's own internal security. Moscow's ingrained resort to this cooptation tactic in all of its guises and its overall imperial strategy in Eurasia and the Middle East are therefore not harbingers of a newly stabilized and legitimate Russian empire based on elite integration as was true previously. Rather it is a call to arms at home and abroad. Indeed, it is a summons to permanent war, even if it may take a non-kinetic informational aspect rather than a purely military character. But in either case, this summons to perpetual war ultimately is also not just a landmine under the current international order. It also a landmine under the continuity of the very Russian state Putin seeks to preserve and extend.

ENDNOTES

[1] Maura Reynolds, "Moscow Has Chechnya Back--Now What,?" *Los Angeles Times*, June 19, 2000.

[2] Alexander Etkind, *Internal Colonization: Russia's Imperial Experience* (London: Polity Press, 2011).

[3] For one long-running example in non-Muslim areas see Serhii Plokhy, *The Gates of Europe: A History of Ukraine*, New York, Basic Books, 2017.

[4] Robert D. Crews, "A Patriotic Islam? Russia's Muslims Under Putin," *World Politics Review*, https://www.worldpoliticsreview.com/articles/18150/a-patriotic-islam-russia-s-muslims-under-putin, March 8, 2016; Robert D. Crews, *For Prophet and Tsar: Islam and Empire In Russia and Central Asia*, Cambridge, MA: Harvard University Press, 2009.

[5] "OIC and Russia Sign Cooperation Agreement," https://www.middleeastmonitor.com/20140130-oic-and-russia-sign-cooperation-agreement/, January 30, 2014.

[6] Sophie Lambroschini, "Russia: Putin Tells OIC That Muslims Are 'Inseparable' Part Of A Multiethnic Nation," *Radio Free Europe Radio Liberty*, www.rferl.org,October 16, 2003.

[7] Alfred J. Rieber, ""Persistent Factors in Russian Foreign Policy: An Interpretation," Hugh Ragsdale, Ed., *Imperial Russian Foreign Policy*, Washington D.C. and Cambridge: Woodrow Wilson Center Press and Cambridge University Press, 1993, p. 346.

[8] Alec Nove and J.A. Newth, *The Soviet Middle East: A Model for Development?*, London: Routledge (Routledge Revivals), 2013; Alexandre Bennigsen, Paul B. Henze, George K. Tanham, and S. Enders Wimbush, *Soviet Strategy and Islam*, Macmillan, London, 1989.

⁹ See the essays in Marat Terterov Ed., *Russian and CIS Relations With the Gulf Region,* Dubai, Gulf Research Centre, 2009.

¹⁰ "Tajikistan: Saudis Give Loans To Build Schools, But Why?" *Eurasia Insight,* www.eurasianet.org, October 3, 2017.

¹¹ "President Urges Arab Countries To Invest In Tajikistan," www.asia-plus.com, October 16, 2017
¹² Celeste A. Wallander, "Russian Trans-Imperialism and Its Implications," *The Washington Quarterly,* XXX, No. 2, 2007, pp. 117–118.

¹³ Keir Giles, *Russia's New Tools For Confronting the West*: Russia's 'New' Tools for Confronting the West: Continuity and Innovation in Moscow's Exercise of Power, https://www.chathamhouse.org/publication/russias-new-tools-confronting-west, 2016, p. 40.

¹⁴ John R. Schindler, "How the Kremlin Manipulates Europe's Refugee Crisis," http://observer.com/2016/04/how-the-kremlin-manipulates-europes-refugee-crisis/, April 6, 2016.

¹⁵ Joel Harding and Kseniya Kirilova, "Plans for a "Great Serbia" and the Kremlin's hybrid war in the Balkans," https://toinformistoinfluence.com/2017/01/23/plans-for-a-great-serbia-and-the-kremlins-hybrid-war-in-the-balkans/, January 24, 2017.

¹⁶ Terterov, Ed.

¹⁷ Valery Dzusati, "In Courting Iran, Russia Seeks Politically Safe Investment for the North Caucasus," *Eurasia Daily Monitor,* May 4, 2016, www.jamestown.org.

¹⁸ Andrej Kreutz, "Bilateral Relations Between Rusia and the Gulf Monarchies: Past and Present," Marat Terterov, Ed., *Russian and CIS Relations With the Gulf Region: Current Trends In Political and Economic Dynamics,* Dubai, Gulf Research Center, 2009, pp. 32–62.

¹⁹ Crews, "A Patriotic Islam."

---

[20] "Russia Has Leading Role To Play In Helping Resolve Libya Crisis Says Maetig," https://www.libyaherald.com/2017/09/15/russia-has-leading-role-to-play-in-helping-resolve-libya-crisis-says-maetig/, September 15, 2017; Maxim Suchkov, "What's Chechnya doing in Syria,?" http://www.al-monitor.com/pulse/originals/2017/03/russia-syria-chechnya-ramzan-kadyrov-fighters.html#ixzz4uGlNyKJt; Valery Dzutsev, ""Russia May use North Caucasus For Hybrid Warfare in Central Asian and European Conflicts," *Jamestown North Caucasus Weekly*, XV, No. 19, October 17, 2004, pp. 3-5; "CSTO Rift Grows Between Moscow and Astana," www.rferl.org, August 6, 2017.

[21] Joshua Kucera, "CSTO Ready, But Not Yet Willing, To Send Troops to Syria," *Eurasia Insight*, December 1, 2017, http://www.eurasianet.org/node/86291.

[22] Paul Goble, "Moscow to Send Central Asian Gastarbeiters to Fight in Syria, Chablin Says," Window on Eurasia – New Series, October 15, 2017, http://windowoneurasia2.blogspot.com/2017/10/moscow-to-send-central-asian.html.

[23] Kreutz, p. 44.

[24] Maxim A. Suchkov, "Russia Rising," www.al-monitor.com, October 15, 2005.

[25] Andrej Kreutz, "Russian Relations With Iran and Iraq," Marat Terterov, Ed., *Russian and CIS Relations With the Gulf Region: Current Trends In Political and Economic Dynamics*, Dubai, Gulf Research Center, 2009, p. 89.

[26] "OIC and Russia Sign Cooperation Agreement," https://www.middleeastmonitor.com/20140130-oic-and-russia-sign-cooperation-agreement/, January 30, 2014.

[27] Sophie Lambroschini, "Russia: Putin Tells OIC That Muslims Are 'Inseparable''Part Of A Multiethnic Nation," *Radio Free Europe Radio Liberty*, www.rferl.org,October 16, 2003.

[28] "Sixth International Economic Summit of Russia and OIC Countries (Kazan Summit 2014)," http://www.sesric.org/event-detail.php?id=1036, June 5–6, 2014.

[29] Stephen Blank, "The Foundations of Russian Foreign Policy In the Gulf," Marat Terterov, Ed., *Russian and CIS Relations With the Gulf Region: Current Trends In Political and Economic Dynamics*, Dubai, Gulf Research Center, 2009, p. 247.

[30] James Sherr, Hard Diplomacy and Soft Coercion: Russia's Influence Abroad: London: Chatham House, 2013, pp. 61–62; see also Stephen Blank, "The Values Gap Between Moscow and the West: the Sovereignty Issue," Acque et Terre, No. 6, 2007, pp. 9–14 (Italian), 90–95 (English).

[31] Quoted in Brian Whitmore, "Fighting the Long War," Radio Free Europe Radio Liberty, June 16, 2015, www.rferl.org.

[32] Stephen Blank, "Energy and Russia's High-Stakes Game in Iraq," EGS Working Paper 2015-2-1, Center for Energy governance and Security, Hanyang University, 2015; Igor Delanoe, Les Kurdes: un Relais d'Influence Russe au Moyen-Orient? "Russie.Nei.Visions", n° 85, June 2015, Institut Francais des Relations Internationales (IFRI), 2015; Michael A. Reynolds, *Shattering Empires: The Clash and Collapse of the Ottoman and Russian Empires, 1908-1918*, Cambridge: Cambridge University Press, 2011.
[33] *Ibid.*

[34] "Assad Banking On Support From Minority Groups,' *Deutsche Welle*, June 13, 2012, www.dw.com; Oren Kessler, "Religion –The Overlooked Motive Behind Syria's Uprising," *Jerusalem Post*, May 20, 2011, www.jpost.com; Alison Meuse, "Syria's Minorities: Caught Between Sword of ISIS and Wrath Of Assad," www.npr.org, April 18, 2015; Bastian Berbner, "Syria's Christians Side With Assad Out Of Fear," www.spiegel.de, November 30, 2011.

[35] *Ibidem.*

[36] Patrick Martin, "Syria's Bashar Al-Assad Losing Faith Of Religious and Ethnic Minorities," *The Globe and Mail*, June 14, 2011.

[37] "Russia Paying Special Attention To Kurdish Issue," https://sputniknews.com/politics/201706021054240590-russia-kurds-lavrov/, June 2, 2017.

[38] Carlo Munoz, "Russia Calls For 'Cultural Autonomy' For Ethnic Kurds In Postwar Syria," http://www.washingtontimes.com/news/2017/feb/2/russia-calls-cultural-autonomy-ethnic-kurds-postwa/, February 2, 2017.

[39] Anton Mardasov, "Applying the 'Bosnian Model' To Syria's Crisis," www.al-monitor.com, June 6, 2017.

[40] "Syrian Kurds Say Russia To Build Base In Afrin," www.al-jazeera.com, March 21, 2017.

[41] James Pothecary, "Russia a Fair-Weather Friend For Syria's Kurds," *Jamestown Terrorism Monitor*, www.jamestown.org, XV, NO. 11, June 2, 2017; A Kurdish-Russian Deal Against Turkey!" www.aranews.net, March 5, 2017.

[42] Reynolds; Michael A. Reynolds, "Vladimir Putin, Godfather of Kurdistan,?" www.nationalinterest.com, August 4, 2017.

[43] "Russia's Lavrov Urges Dialogue With Government By Syrian Opposition," *RIA Novosti*, August 31, 2015, Retrieved From BBC Monitoring.

[44] Ahu Ozyurt, "White House vs. Kremlin House," *Hurriyet*, May 17, 2017, Retrieved From BBC Monitoring.

[45] James Pothecary, "Russia a Fair-Weather Friend For Syria's Kurds," *Jamestown Terrorism Monitor*, www.jamestown.org, XV, NO. 11, June 2, 2017; A Kurdish-Russian Deal Against Turkey!" www.aranews.net March 5, 2017.

[46] Metin Gurcan, "Ankara's offer To Moscow: Give Us Afrin For Idlib," www.al-monitor.com, July 3, 2017; Sami Mousayed, "New Front In Syria As Turks Rout Kurds With Putin's Blessing," *Asia Times Online*, www.atimes.com, July 7, 2017.

[47] "Syrian Kurdish Leader Hopes Russia Didn't Betray the Kurds Through Turkey Deal," www.aranews.net, May 7, 2017.

[48] "Turkey's Erdogan Accuses Russia Of Arming PKK Militants," www.reuters.com, August 3, 2017.

[49] "Changing Priorities: What are the Goals of Turkey's Military Intervention in Syria?" https://futureuae.com/en-US/Tag/Index/176/uae, October 15, 2017.

[50] "Russia Says Kurdish PKK, YPG Not Terrorist Organizations: Official," http://ekurd.net/russia-pkk-ypg-not-terrorist-2017-02-09, February 9, 2017.

[51] Aziz Barzani, "Russia and the Kurdistan Region: a Rapprochement," www.impr.org.tr, accessed on January 7, 2014; Eldar Kasayev, "Iraqi Kurdistan and the Future of the Russian Gas Business," www.en.internationalffairs.ru, October 9, 2010.

[52] "Iraq Wants Russians to Replace Exxon at West Qurna: Report," *Reuters*, Moscow, October 11, 2012.

[53] James Sherr, Hard *Diplomacy and Soft Coercion: Russia's Influence Abroad:* London: Chatham House, 2013, pp. 61–62.

[54] Sinan Salaheddin, "Russia's Gazprom Neft Inks Deals With Iraq Kurds," *Seattle Times and Associated Press*, August 2, 2012, www.seattletimes.com.

[55] "Iraq Pressures Russia's Gazprom to Quit Kurdistan," *BBC News*, November 9, 2012.

[56] M.K. Bhadrakumar, "Russia Renews Kurdish Bonds," *Asia Times Online*, February 25, 2013, www.atimes.com.

[57] "Russian Gazprom Neft Takes 60% Stake in Iraqi Kurdistan Oil Project," www.ekurd.net, February 27, 2013; "Russia Gazprom Neft Signs Kurdistan Oil Project Deal-Reports," *Reuters,* February 26, 2013.

[58] M.K. Bhadrakumar, "Russia Renews Kurdish Bonds," www.valdaiclub.com, February 27, 2013.

[59] Blank, "Energy and Russia's High-Stakes Game in Iraq."

[60] "Rosneft and Iraqi Kurdistan Government Agree to Expand Strategic Cooperation,' https://www.rosneft.com/press/releases/item/186811/, June 2, 2017.

[61] "Russia Joins US as a Key Player in Iraqi Kurdish Oil, http://russia-insider.com/en/politics/russia-joins-us-key-player-iraqi-kurdish-oil/ri20138, June 18, 2017.

[62] Mahmut Bozarslan, "Iraqi-Kurdistan-Russia Oil Deal Could Have Major Implications For Region," www.al-monitor.com, June 20, 2017.

[63] "Russian Oil Giant Signs Production Deal With Iraqi Kurdistan," *Radio Free Europe Radio Liberty*, October 18, 2017, www.rferl.com.

[64] Dmitry Zhdannikov and Dmitri Soldatkin, "Russia's Rosneft To Take Control of Iraqi Kurdish Pipeline Amid Crisis," *Reuters*, October 20, 2017.

[65] "Moscow Calls On Iraqi Kurds To Act In Cooperation With Baghdad," *Radio Free Europe Radio Liberty*, October 23, 2017, ww.rferl.org.

[66] Dmitry Zhdannikov, "Russia Becomes Iraq Kurds' Top Funder, Quiet About Independence Vote," *Reuters*, October 20, 2017, https://www.reuters.com/article/us-mideast-crisis-kurds-referendum-russi/russia-becomes-iraq-kurds-top-funder-quiet-about-independence-vote-idUSKCN1BV1IH.

[67] Mewan Dolamari, "Russian Minister: Moscow to Connect Kurdistan's Oil, Gas Pipelines To Black Sea," www.kurdistan24.net, October 8, 2017.

[68] Hakan Gunneriusson and Sacha Dov Bachmann, "Western Denial and Russian Control: How Russia's National Security Strategy Threatens a Western-Based Approach To Global Security, the Rule of Law, and Globalization," *Polish Political /Science Yearbook*, XLVI, No. 1, 2017, p. 21.

[69] Nove and Newth.

[70] Joshua Kucera, "Russia In Talks With Kazakhstan and Kyrgyzstan Over Military Deployment to Syria," *Eurasia Insight*, June 22, 2017, www.eurasianet.org; Neil Hauer, "Putin Has a New Secret Weapon in Syria: Chechens," http://foreignpolicy.com/2017/05/04/putin-has-a-new-secret-weapon-in-syria-chechens/, May 4, 2017; Maxim Suchkov, "What Chechnya Doing In Syria?" http://www.al-monitor.com/pulse/originals/2017/03/russia-syria-chechnya-ramzan-kadyrov-fighters.html, March 26, 2017.

[71] Kreutz, p. 44.

[72] Ekaterina Sokirianskaia, "Is Chechnya Taking Over Russia,?" www.nytimes.com, July 8, 2017.

[73] Neil Hauer, "Putin Has a New Secret Weapon in Syria: Chechens," www.foreignpolicy.com, May 4, 2017; Theodore Karasik, "Chechnya In the Shadow Of Russia's Mideast Strategies," www.englishalarabiya.net. October 19, 2015.

[74] *Ibidem;* Maxim A. Suchkov, "What Is Chechnya's Kadyrov Up To In the Middle East,?" www.al-monitor.com,November 30, 2016.

[75] *Ibidem.*

[76] Karasik; Suchkov, Vasily Kuznetsov, "Moscow Welcomes Libya's Fighting Factions," www.al-monitor.com September 24, 2017.

[77] Interview With Russian Political Analyst Sergey Karaganov: The Four Reasons Why Russia Intervened in Syria," www.memri.org, Special Dispatch no. 6335, March 2, 2016;

Nadezhda K. Arbatova and Alexander A. Dynkin, "World Order After Ukraine," *Survival,* LVIII, NO. 1, 2016, p. 72.

[78] Alfred J. Rieber "The Comparative Ecology Of Complex Frontiers," Alexei Miller and Alfred J. Rieber, Eds., *Imperial Rule,* New York: Central European University Press, 2004, pp. 199–200.

8. The Tactical Side of Russia's Arms Sales to the Middle East

Anna Borshchevskaya

Summary

Russia is the world's top arms exporter, second only to the United States. The Middle East and North Africa (MENA) region has emerged in recent years as Moscow's second most important arms market after Asia. Moscow has made great strides in this region since Vladimir Putin came to power, and especially in recent years, after it embarked on major military reform following August 2008. Arms sales matter to the Kremlin because they are a major source of financial gain, but these arms sales are also a tactical foreign policy instrument for wielding influence.

Russia's arms—generally speaking—are well made, sometimes on par with the US, and well suited for the region's needs. These platforms and armaments are also more affordable than Western weaponry. The US simply will not sell weapons to certain countries, which, therefore, turn to Moscow. Politically, Russian arms come with few strings attached and thus are a great choice when a country wants to diversify away from the West, or at least signal such an intent. Moscow has made inroads with traditional clients such as Iran, Syria and Egypt, but also diversified toward countries closer to the West, such as the Arab Gulf states, Morocco and Turkey. Russia's overall influence in the region is growing in the context of Western retreat. The Russian defense sector has problems, but also demonstrated improvements, learning and flexibility. Undoubtedly, Russia's arms sales to the MENA region will continue to present a challenge for American interests in this region in the coming years.

Introduction

Russia is one of the world's top arms exporters, second only to the United States since at least 1999.[1] In recent years, the Middle East and North Africa (MENA) region emerged as Russia's second most important arms market after Asia. From 2000 to 2016, almost a fifth of Russia's arms exports went to the MENA region.[2] To put this in perspective, in 2009, Moscow sold approximately $9 billion worth of arms to this region. In 2016, it sold $21.4 billion.[3] Many of these sales are upgrades to existing packages.[4] Since 2000, Moscow also diversified from traditional Soviet-era regional clients.

Since officially coming to power in May 2000, if not before, Russian President Vladimir Putin sought to restore Russia's image as a Great Power in the context of zero-sum anti-Westernism— for Russia to win, the West had to lose. His approach to the Middle East is the extension of former Russian prime minister Evgeniy Primakov's vision of a "multipolar world," driven by desire to prevent the West from dominating any region, and curb Western support for democratization efforts in other countries. For the last 17 years, Putin worked to regain political influence and raise Russia to the status of a competitor to the United States by increasing emphasis on Russia's business interests—primarily arms, energy and high-tech goods such as nuclear reactors.[5]

Russia's economy remains over-reliant on raw materials and natural resources, but the defense industry is one technology-intensive sector where Russia holds an international leadership position. Domestically, Russia's defense industry is a major source of employment. Russian President Vladimir Putin renewed his emphasis on modernizing the armed forces, especially the navy, on May 7, 2012, on the same day as he took office as president for a third time.[6] Internationally, the Russian defense industry is a source of important revenue. Thus, Putin lamented in February 2012 about Iraq and countries undergoing the Arab Spring, "Russian companies are losing their decades-long positions in local commercial markets and are being deprived of large commercial contracts."[7] As Sergei Chemezov, chief of the powerful state industrial holding Rostec, said in February 2015, "As for the conflict situation in the Middle East, I do not conceal it, and everyone understands this, the more conflicts there are, the more they [clients] buy weapons from us. Volumes are continuing to grow despite sanctions. Mainly, it is in Latin America and the Middle East."[8]

Yet, arms sales entail far more to the Kremlin than mere financial gains. They are also Moscow's tactical foreign policy tool for wielding political influence and changing power balance dynamics. Indeed, in July 2012, Putin said that arms exports are "an effective instrument for advancing [Moscow's] national interests, both political and economic."[9] In December 2013, Deputy Prime Minister Dmitry Rogozin said that Russia's arms sales are the most important element of Moscow's relations with other countries.[10] And Moscow's chief goal—regime survival, which it hopes to achieve through reduction of Western influence—runs counter to Western interests and values. Thus, in the MENA region, Moscow courts virtually everyone, and competes with the West whenever an opportunity arises. Arms exports are a major component of these efforts.

Measurement Issue

Several obstacles hamper a complete understanding of Russia's arms trade. Rosoboronexport, Russia's arms export agency, does not publicize total annual sales figures. In addition, some companies can sell arms directly to clients, bypassing Rosoboronexport, and may not disclose information. When Moscow does disclose Russia's arms sales figures, the details are generally sparse. Unlike Western countries, Moscow does not provide disaggregated data. The recipient countries in the Middle East are also not consistently forthcoming with details about receiving Russian weaponry.[11]

Theoretically, as Chatham House points out, two measures are available to understand arms trade: military capabilities transfer, which involves estimating the material volume of arms transfer, and the financial value of arms transfers. [12] Both present challenges. For example, some countries pay more than others do for the same weaponry. Also, countries and sources use different definitions of what constitutes an arms transfer, often with substantial variation. These issues hamper a complete understanding of Russia's arms sales, and some, such as the Stockholm International Peace Research Institute (SIPRI), have come up with their own measures to overcome these difficulties.[13] Yet, the available data, though incomplete, is sufficient to gain at least an outline, and occasionally a more complete picture of Russian arms exports.

Why Choose a Russian Weapon?

When countries prefer Russian weaponry over American systems, it is usually for evident reasons. The US will not sell weapons to many of Russia's clients for a variety of reasons. Russian weaponry is relatively inexpensive and, generally speaking, often more robust than comparable American systems. In some areas, Moscow's systems lag severely behind the US in terms of quality and capabilities, but in others, it is a near-peer competitor. For instance, Moscow is quite good at building anti-aircraft missiles, such as the S-300 and S-400 systems, based on lessons-learned from the Kosovo Air War. The American F-35 joint strike fighter can likely currently beat an S-400 (although there is no way to know for sure unless they engage in direct combat). However, Moscow is developing the next generation, the S-

500, whose full capabilities are unknown. Russian current-generation aircraft and ballistic missile defenses are on par with those of the US in terms of defense technology. Some Russian missiles have as long a range as American missiles, a few of them even longer. [14] In addition, the US Foreign Military Sales (FMS) system is very slow, bureaucratic and cumbersome, while Moscow takes less time to deliver after a contract is signed.

Moscow is weak when it comes to follow-up support of sales, and Russian weaponry is not always as technically advanced as America's, but it is good enough for the needs of many markets, and is often far better than what the purchasing countries can build themselves. Russian weaponry is also a good choice for states on a budget. Moscow advertises this fact. For example, in early October 2015, days after Russia's Syria intervention, Moscow fired 26 cruise missiles from primarily small corvettes in the Caspian Sea to hit targets in Syria. [15] Moscow made a public display of the event, not only to demonstrate Russia's own might but also to show other countries they need not purchase a large expensive warship to achieve strong naval capabilities, and that Moscow would be happy to help them achieve this goal.

Another practical consideration is that many local military personnel in the MENA region have trained on Russian weaponry and feel comfortable operating it. As one American source familiar with the situation explained it, "If you have an AK-47, why change to an M-16?" [16] For example, helicopters are especially crucial to Egypt's anti-Islamist campaign; and according to first-hand pilot accounts, Russia' less expensive helicopters fit Egypt's needs well. Overall, Russian attack helicopters are not necessarily superior technologically, but they bring heavy firepower to a fight. They may fare worse in a contested air space, but the Sinai airspace is not contested. The Russian MiG-29 is a highly advanced aircraft, easier to maintain than an American one, and cheaper than an F-22[17] (which the US is currently not even exporting).

Beyond these advantages, Russian weaponry comes with few strings attached, in contrast to arms sales from Washington. Moscow, unlike the US, does not prohibit secondary arms sales. This means, for example, that when the US sells weapons to Egypt, the weapon must stay in Egypt.[18] But in Egypt's context, buying a Russian weapon it can easily resell to someone else for profit may be a preferable option.

Moscow also does not burden arms sales with preconditions, such as mandated improvements of human rights. In addition, many in the MENA find Russia easier to deal with—no one needs to worry about falling afoul of a theoretical Russian equivalent of the US Foreign Corrupt Practices Act, for example. Thus, countries turn to Moscow when they wish to signal to Washington that they have other options if they do not like the United States' pre-conditions. At the same time, some Arab states are genuinely interested in diversifying supplies away from the US. Indeed, after the 1991 Gulf War, several GCC states bought Russian systems. The West should not discount Arab countries making such decisions. Russia, unlike the America, invests effort across the MENA region to sell weapons systems. Western analysts tend to point out Russia could never replace the United States. Nevertheless, such views discount another option: Moscow does not have to replace the US. Other authoritarian leaders can choose to move closer to Russia because the Kremlim offers Arab states different advantages including quicker delivery and better negotiating terms. When it comes to arms sales in the MENA region, Moscow has made major inroads during the Putin era with Iran, Syria, Egypt, Libya and Algeria, and to a lesser extent with Turkey, Iraq, and elsewhere in the Arab Persian Gulf. It is also making small inroads with Tunisia and Morocco.

Iran

Russia and Iran share a complicated and primarily adversarial centuries-long history, but things slowly began to change following the end of the Iran-Iraq war in 1988, the death of Iran's revolutionary leader, Ayatollah Ruhollah Khomeini, and Soviet withdrawal from Afghanistan in 1989. Between 1989 and 1991, the Kremlin signed several arms-supply deals with Tehran worth $5.1 billion, and Iran emerged as one of the Soviet defense industry's biggest clients. When Putin became president, many hardline Russian politicians and generals endorsed improving relations with Iran in anticipation of major arms sales. Soon Moscow began assisting Tehran's nuclear program. In October 2000, another important event took place. Putin publicly repealed the 1995 Gore-Chernomyrdin pact—an agreement that limited Russia's sale of conventional arms to Iran. According to press reports, in practice the agreement actually gave Russia "a free pass to sell conventional weapons to Iran" until 1999.[19] Moreover, the public cancelation of the deal signaled Putin's interest in closer cooperation with Iran.

By 2001, Iran became the third largest foreign buyer of Russian weaponry.[20] The increased arms trade raised Russia-Iran cooperation to a new level, based on mutual interests. Upon Putin's invitation, Iranian president Mohammad Khatami came to Moscow in March 2001—the first high level visit since June 1989, when Iranian Parliament Speaker Ali Akbar Hashemi Rafsanjani traveled to Russian, and the first visit by an Iranian president since the 1979 Islamic Revolution

In December 2005, Tehran signed a billion-dollar arms deal that included 29 Tor-M1 missile-defense systems to protect the Bushehr nuclear power plant. According to press reports, in early 2006, Russia also invested $750 million in energy projects in Iran.[21] The same year, Moscow strongly endorsed the P5+1 format[22] for negotiating with

Tehran on the nuclear issue. This new context gave Russia increased diplomatic leverage, and the Kremlin used it to repeatedly dilute sanctions against Iran and extract concessions from the West in exchange for Russia's cooperation. Indeed, in 2010, the Kremlin extracted an unprecedented concession: Moscow would support some sanctions on Iran in exchange for the US lifting sanctions against the Russian military complex, which would allow Moscow to sell anti-aircraft batteries to Tehran. The same year, under American and Israeli pressure, Moscow froze the sale of S-300 air-defense missiles to Iran.

Several factors explain Moscow's more permissive stance toward Iran's nuclear program. First, Moscow never envisioned the threat of Iran's nuclear program as the West did. For Moscow, a pro-Western Iran would be more threatening than a nuclear Iran. [23] Moscow for decades has been surrounded by nuclear powers and while one more may not be desirable, it is something Moscow feels it could also live with. Soviet and then Russian diplomat on arms-control and non-proliferation issues Victor Mizin wrote in October 2000 that while "certain people in Russia pay lip service to the politically correct notion that proliferation is dangerous," Moscow rejects the Western term "rogue states." Deployed ballistic missiles would not threaten Russian troops stationed abroad as they do American troops, and Russia has no domestic lobbies to pressure the government on such issues as is prevalent in the West. "That is why one always hears very politically correct words from Russian political scientists about concerns that Iran is developing missile capabilities. No one in the Russian political elite is seriously considering the threat of this development."[24]

Second, Moscow wanted to increase trade with Iran, and sanctions hampered these aspirations. In 2013, Russia's and Iran's political interests converged more than ever before. Russia's state-run Atomstroyexport helped Tehran complete the Bushehr nuclear power plant and officially gave Iran control of the facility in September 2013.

In November 2014, Russia's state nuclear corporation Rosatom announced an agreement to build two new reactor units in Iran, possibly to be followed by six more. As nuclear deal negotiations advanced, the Kremlin highlighted Russia's indispensable role in them. He also lifted the freeze on the S-300 sale, and deliveries began in April 2015, despite Israeli concerns. Putin may have lifted the freeze to strengthen Iran's hand as the nuclear negotiations were ending. When the negotiating parties concluded the agreement in July 2015, Putin praised the nuclear deal and emphasized Russian diplomacy in the process. Some might argue Tehran did not obtain the best deal from a commercial perspective—by this time Russia had S-400s and was developing the S-500—but an S-300 is a formidable weapon in its own right, and should not be discounted.

Third, Russia has been trying to expand its military cooperation with the Islamic Republic. In August 2016, Moscow used Iran's Hamadan airbase to bomb targets in Syria. This action surprised not only the world, but many within Iran itself. Not since World War II did a foreign power base itself in Iran. The Iranian public was outraged and Iranian Defense Minister Hossein Dehghan accused Moscow of "ungentlemanly"[25] behavior for publicizing Russia's use of the base—but not for the use of the base itself. Furthermore, Iranian Parliament Speaker Ali Larijani said only days afterwards, "The flights [of Russian warplanes] haven't been suspended. Iran and Russia are allies in the fight against terrorism," though the Hamedan air base, he claimed, was only "used for refueling."[26] The next month, Putin said that it would be "just" if Iran reached the pre-sanction's level of oil production.[27] In November 2016, Putin began discussing a $10 billion arms deal with Tehran.[28] And in August 2017, Germany's *Die Welt* reported that Tehran was transferring weapons to Russia via Syria for maintenance, which violated United Nations Security Council Resolution 2231.[29] Meanwhile, the Tartus naval base, at least theoretically, provides Moscow with another opportunity to arm

Iranian proxy Hezbollah indirectly through Syria if it chooses to do so.

Syria

Damascus is historically not only Moscow's closest ally in the Arab world, but also one of its biggest arms customers. Putin improved bilateral ties further after meeting with President Bashar al-Assad in January 2005. Upon the meeting's conclusion, Moscow announced it would write off most of Syria's $13.4 billion debt and sell arms to Damascus in return for Syria's permission to establish permanent Russian naval facilities in Tartus and Latakia.[30] Soon Russia emerged as Syria's primary weapons supplier. From 2007 through 2010, Russian arms sales to Syria reached $4.7 billion, more than twice the figure for the previous four years.[31] According to SIPRI, Russia accounted for 78 percent of Syria's weapons purchases between 2007 and 2012. And press reports indicate that Russian ships have been involved in several Syria-related incidents in international waters.[32]

When anti-al-Assad protests broke out in Damascus in March 2011, Putin supported the Syrian president unequivocally and in multiple ways—politically, diplomatically and economically. But Moscow's Syria intervention in September 2015 was a game changer that officially returned Russia to the Middle East. The Kremlin had many interests in Syria. While, from an arms sales perspective, it was the perfect advertising arena.

In early October 2015, just days after launching its intervention, Moscow fired 26 cruise missiles from the Caspian Sea Flotilla. The cruise missiles travelled across Iran and Iraq into Syria to strike what Moscow claimed were Islamic State targets. From a military standpoint, it was questionable at best whether strikes from this location were truly necessary.[33] For one thing, Moscow could have easily hit the same targets from Russia's existing assets in Syria. But the advertising benefits for Moscow were clear. The attack displayed formidable capabilities of the relatively new Kalibr cruise missile, which Moscow exports as the shorter-range "Club." Moscow also showed that even Russia's small missile corvettes are quite powerful, and that a country on a budget looking for strong naval capabilities does not need to pay for a large and expensive ship.[34]

During the next two years, Moscow amplified Russia's military presence by expanding the Tartus port and the Khmeimim airbase. These ensured Russia's military presence for the next 49 years, providing Russia with ideal strategic military access to the region while limiting the West's ability to maneuver. Indeed, after Putin announced yet another faux "withdrawal" from Syria in December 2017,[35] he almost immediately called for further expanding Russia's naval presence in Tartus.[36] At the same time, Moscow used Syria to test weaponry and equipment in real battles, advertise these efforts, project power and train the Russian military, especially the pilots. That Moscow went to great lengths to publicize Russia's arms exports shows how important the arms sales element has been for Moscow's Syria campaign.[37]

True, Moscow failed to react to American cruise missiles, which flew well within the orbit of Russia's S-300s and S-400s. The no-show may seem like a missed advertising opportunity to display Russian surface-to-air missiles (SAM), but shooting down a cruise missile would have been a big risk, and could have triggered a major escalation. Shooting down a cruise missile is much harder than an aircraft. Cruise missiles have much smaller radar cross-section and lower flight profile.[38] Second, when the US launched its Tomahawk cruise missiles, Washington, at least by some accounts, first told Moscow about its intent and provided specific locations as part of de-confliction with Russia. Therefore, if Moscow had attempted to intercept an American missile, Washington would have read this action as a direct challenge, rather than give Moscow the benefit of the doubt and consider it a mistake.[39] Moreover, for all of Putin's bluster, he presumably knew the

US far outmatched him in the region. A direct military confrontation is not what he sought—only to create the perception that he might, in order to scare the US into thinking letting him do what he wanted in Syria was the only option to avoid war.

Meanwhile, Moscow's advertising efforts paid off. "This [Russia's Syria operations] is colossal advertising and Russia expects new purchases worth tens of billions of dollars," said Alexander Markov, a political analyst and member of Russia's Council on Foreign and Defense Politics, in April 2016.[40] More recently, Russian Deputy Defense Minister Yuri Borisov said in August 2017, "Customers have started queuing up for the weapons that have proven themselves in Syria."[41] To give one example of such success, Russian Su-34 and Su-35 jets, which Moscow tested and used extensively in Syria, began to sell well.[42] China bought 24 Su-35 jets in November 2015, and Algeria ordered 12 Su-34s in January 2016.[43] The United Arab Emirates began discussion with Russia in February 2017 about purchasing Su-35s.[44]Many other countries have expressed interest, such as India and Indonesia, but also many African countries, including Nigeria, Uganda and Ethiopia.[45] Russian Deputy Defense Minister Alexander Fomin said, in October 2016, "[W]e know that the African continent has a great potential and it [cooperation] can be market-oriented and based on mutual interest."[46] Africa is a region increasingly important to watch for Russia's arms sales as a tactic to enter the Sahel.[47]

North Africa

Speaking at Russia's annual Valdai conference in October 2016, President Putin said Africa "cannot be on the periphery of international relations."[48] Indeed, Moscow is looking at the entire African continent, whose demand for military hardware is growing as GDP rises. In the context of Western sanctions and the Kremlin's desire to boost Russia's global power status, reduce Western influence, and make money to keep the Russian government afloat, Putin has already made strides in much of Africa that are impossible to ignore.[49]

North Africa is a major part of his calculus. According to Russian sources, in 2016 Moscow delivered over $1.5 billion in arms to Algeria and $37 million to Egypt.[50]

Moscow's relationship with Cairo, steadily on the rise in recent years, is most robust in the military sector. In September 2014, Russia and Egypt initialed arms contracts worth $3.5 billion, their largest deal in many years, to be funded by Saudi Arabia and the United Arab Emirates. The contract reportedly stipulates that Russia will supply the Egyptian military with MiG-29 fighter jets, Mi-35 attack helicopters, air-defense missile complexes, ammunition, and other equipment. There is no direct evidence that the transaction has happened yet, although according to some credible reports in July 2016, Russia began building 46 MiG-29M fighter jets as part of a contract worth at least $2 billion. No public information about the recipient is available, but Egypt is probably the leading candidate.[51]

Regardless of whether or not Egypt is indeed the buyer in question, Russian-Egyptian military cooperation is visibly growing. The two countries held their first joint naval drills in June 2015, and other military exercises in October 2016.[52] In September 2017, Cairo finalized negotiations with Moscow to build Egypt's first nuclear power plant, approximately two years after inking a preliminary agreement in February 2015.[53] According to later reports in spring 2016, Moscow will lend Egypt $25 billion for construction.[54] In this context, it is worth recalling that Cairo used to be Washington's partner on energy cooperation as part of the George W. Bush administration's Global Nuclear Energy Partnership (GNEP).[55] President Barack Obama, however, effectively scrapped parts of GNEP in June 2009 [56] and showed little interest in expanding an energy partnership with Egypt. This episode provided a gap for Putin to move in.

In November 2017, Moscow and Cairo began to discuss an agreement to allow Russia and Egypt to access the other's airspace and air bases, perhaps the clearest sign of growing bilateral military cooperation.[57] In March 2017, Moscow deployed special forces to Egypt on the Libyan border, signaling Russia's growing role in that country.[58]

Libya historically is another major Russian arms customer. Following NATO's 2011 intervention, Russia lost billions of dollars' worth of arms contracts in Libya. While the Russian government and analysts typically quantified this loss at $4 billion to $4.5 billion, "the real lost revenue," according to Mikhail Dmitriyev, who heads Russia's Federal Service on Military and Technical Cooperation, "could top tens of billions of dollars."[59] Lost contracts covered a wide range of military equipment, including Su-35 fighters, Yak130 combat and training planes, Project 636 submarines, advanced S-300 systems, Mi-17 transport helicopters, and many others. Importantly, Moscow also lost access to the port of Benghazi. Libya is a good candidate for another potential Moscow intervention under the guise of fighting Islamic terrorism, albeit on a smaller scale than in Syria. As a result of Western disinterest in Libya, Putin has been able to insert himself, both in leaning heavily on General Khalifa Haftar in Libya's oil-rich east, and by establishing contacts with all other major actors on the ground. Putin is now reportedly eyeing Tobruk and other ports for potential berthing agreements.[60] Such a development would entail significant Russian investment, but a permanent naval presence in Libya by Russia as a regional power broker is a serious possibility.

Moscow is also making some headway in Tunisia. In June 2015, Moscow signed a Memorandum of Understanding on nuclear cooperation with Tunisia "[f]or the first time in the history of Russian-Tunisian relations," according to Rosatom, Russia's state nuclear regulatory corporation.[61] In September 2016 the memorandum was expanded into a nuclear cooperation agreement.[62] Morocco is a traditionally Western ally, but reportedly, the country is talking with Moscow about purchasing S-400s.[63] In October 2016, the two countries signed 11 agreements, and Russian Prime Minister Dmitry Medvedev announced Russia's decision to "deliver military equipment" to Morocco, though he did not disclose details.[64]

Algeria has long been in Moscow's camp and remained a top buyer of Russian arms throughout the 2000s. Since 2001, when Russia and Algeria signed a declaration of strategic partnership, bilateral relations have been strongest in the military sector. In 2006, Russia concluded a $7.5 billion arms deal with Algeria, its largest post-Soviet weapons sale, which included a military modernization and training program and cancelation of a $4.7 billion Soviet-era debt. In 2014, the two countries signed a $1 billion arms deal, which a Russian military expert in business-oriented *Vedomosti* described as "possibly the largest export contract for main battle tanks in the world."[65] Weapons sales from Russia in 2010, 2012, 2013 and 2015 provided Algeria with additional military equipment, including helicopters, tanks and submarines. In 2016, Algeria and Russia also began sharing intelligence on terrorist group movement across North Africa, and they announced additional plans for deeper military cooperation.

The Arab Persian Gulf and Turkey

The West traditionally dominates the Gulf arms market, but the Kremlin has always courted this region. For Moscow, it is important to compete with the West. And as an added benefit, Gulf customers are wealthy and can pay full price for Russian weaponry, unlike clients such as Egypt. Indeed, the UAE has been among major buyers of Russian arms in the 1990s and early 2000s.

Russia's relations with this region deteriorated significantly during the Syrian conflict, with Russians and Arabs generally lining up on opposite sides. Despite this, interest in Russian arms among Arab states remains. In February 2017, the UAE signed a letter of intent to purchase the Sukhoi Su-35, as mentioned above.[66] Only China currently buys these jets from Russia. The Emirates has also purchased ground weapons from Russia, such as BMP-3 infantry combat vehicles and Pantsir S1 air-defense systems. In February 2017, the UAE also signed $1.9 billion worth of military contracts, which reportedly includes 5,000 anti-armor missiles, in addition to training and logistic support. The country also started talks with Rostec about the development of a fifth-generation MiG-29 aircraft variant; though experts are skeptical, the UAE can co-produce. Very few countries can produce a fifth-generation fighter aircraft. Theoretically, Russia can, but it only recently began production of fourth-generation Su-34s developed in the 1980s.[67]

Reportedly, Qatar is also talking to Russia about purchasing S-400s, and here the discussion appears more realistic. In October 2017, Moscow and Doha signed a military and technical cooperation Memorandum of Understanding, according to *TASS*,[68] and the Qatari government apparently expressed interest in purchasing the S-400s.[69]

In October 2017, Saudi King Salman bin Abdulaziz Al Saud became the first ever Saudi monarch to visit Russia. The fact that the visit occurred shows how much influence Putin has achieved in the Middle East. Upon the meeting's conclusion, Salman and Putin signed a packet of documents on energy, trade and defense, and they agreed to several billion dollars' worth of joint investment.[70] Reportedly, Saudi Arabia also decided to purchase Russia's S-400 air defense system, making it, after Turkey, the second American ally to do so.[71]

Russia's presence in Iraq is relatively small but important. In 2012, the Kremlin signed a $4 billion arms deal with the Iraqi government—one of the larger arms deals of Putin's tenure. This agreement places Russia as the second largest arms supplier to Iraq after the United States.[72] Reportedly, Moscow began deliveries in October 2013, after a delay due to internal corruption claims in the Iraqi parliament.[73] The same month Putin identified Iraq as an important Middle East partner and announced Russia's readiness, in this context, to help Iraq, including through "military-technical" cooperation.[74]

In the early 2000s the Kremlin began expanding areas of cooperation with Turkey, a NATO member, and these included modest arms contracts.[75] But in September 2017, in the context of deteriorating relations with the West, Turkey signed what many called a landmark $2.5 billion deal, Ankara's first major arms agreement with Russia, to purchase the S-400 missile system.[76] The deal raises several questions. First, the Russian system is not compatible with NATO systems. Second, it is unclear how Turkey intends to use the S-400. Some question whether the deal will go through at all, but the fact of the matter is, the signing alone is significant. It shows how much influence Putin has gained with the NATO ally, who for years now has increasingly turned away from Western democratic values. Nor should analysts dismiss the possibility that the deal will go through either, as Turkey is falling deeper into Moscow's sphere of influence.

Conclusion

Russia's defense industry is not without problems. As mentioned previously, Russian weaponry often lags far behind the United States in terms of effectiveness or technological innovation. China, meanwhile, wields a level of commercial influence Russia cannot compete with; and indeed, some countries, such as Algeria, are increasingly looking toward China, even as Algiers signed its blockbuster deal with Moscow. China is also starting to dominate in high-growth areas such as unmanned aerial vehicles (UAV), where Russia is no match.[77] Another element is Western sanctions on Russian dual-use high-technology imports, especially effective toward Russia's defense industry. Commercially available technologies such as microelectronics and quantum computing have increasingly important modern military applications, but Russia cannot produce them independently. It has tried to resort to import substitution, but so far with poor results. In addition, Russian weapons met no real opposition in Syria. Therefore, despite Moscow's tests and displays, questions about the full extent of these weapons' capabilities remain.

Nonetheless, there is no denying that Putin is making great strides overall in the MENA region since May 2000, and more recently in the defense sector as part of Russia's tactic to use weapons sales to garner closer relations with Arab states at the expense of the US and Europe. Moscow's military reform efforts since 2008 have clearly paid off, and arms sales have been an effective tactical tool in Moscow's foreign policy arsenal. In dollar terms at least, Russian arms sales to the Middle East continue to increase every year. In addition, the advantages Russian arms offer to this region continue to outweigh the disadvantages, both practically and politically. Russia's overall economic trajectory is on a slow and long-term path of deterioration, but still nowhere near a collapse. As a July 2016 NATO Defense College report points out, the West should not confuse Russia's weakness with fragility.[78] Even if Moscow boasts more than it achieves in reality, the Kremlin has been playing a diminishing hand very well. While most US defense experts believe Russia will be unable to produce much next-generation weaponry, Moscow is making significant strides with its existing technology. Russian arms are sufficient for most of Moscow's clients—particularly those who cannot afford top-of-the-line American technology. In the context of US retreat from the region, Moscow has stepped into a vacuum where the Kremlin's efforts generate a multiplier effect of real power. As long as US leadership is absent from the region, Russia's arms sales to the Middle East and North Africa will remain a serious problem for American interests.

ENDNOTES

[1] Christopher Woody, "The US and Russia are dominating the global weapons trade," Business Insider, December 28, 2016, http://www.businessinsider.com/us-russia-global-arms-sales-2016-12.

[2] Richard Connolly and Cecilie Sendstad, *Russia's Role as an Arms Exporter: The Strategic and Economic Importance of Arms Exports for Russia,* Chatham House, p 5, https://www.chathamhouse.org/publication/russias-role-arms-exporter-strategic-and-economic-importance-arms-exports-russia.

[3] Based on data author obtained from IHS Jane's on November 23, 2017.

[4] Author interview with anonymous US aviation source, November 14, 2017, Washington, DC.

[5] Robert O. Freedman, "Russian Policy toward the Middle East under Yeltsin and Putin, Jerusalem Letter/Viewpoints 461 (Jerusalem Center for Public Affairs, September 2, 2001), http://www.jcpa.org/jl/vp461.htm.

[6] Vladimir Putin, Decree, "Realization of the Plans for the Development of the Armed Forces and the Modernization of the Defense Industry," May 7, 2012, http://kremlin.ru/events/president/news/15242.

[7] "Russia and the Changing World," *RT*, February 27, 2012, available at https://www.rt.com/politics/official-word/putin-russia-changing-world-263/.

[8] "Glava 'Rostekha' soobshchil o roste prodazh: 'Chem bol'she konfliktov, tem bol'she u nas pokupayut vooruzheniya'" Newsru.com, February 23, 2015 http://www.newsru.com/russia/23feb2015/chemezov.html.

[9] President of Russia, Meeting of the Commission for military technology cooperation with foreign states," Kremlin.ru, July 2, 2012, http://en.kremlin.ru/events/president/news/15865.

[10] "Rogozin: Russia Ranks Second in the World on Export Supply of Military Goods," Daily News Light, December 11, 2013, http://dailynewslight.ru/?u=11122013868.

[11] Author email exchanges with SPIRI, November 2017.

[12]Richard Connolly and Cecilie Sendstad, *Russia's Role as an Arms Exporter: The Strategic and Economic Importance of Arms Exports for Russia*,Chatham House, p 5, https://www.chathamhouse.org/publication/russias-role-arms-exporter-strategic-and-economic-importance-arms-exports-russia.

[13] SIPRI has developed a system called "trend indicator values" (TIV), rather than actual dollar values. For a more detailed explanation see: SIPRI has developed a unique system to measure the volume of international transfers of major conventional weapons using a common unit, the trend-indicator value (TIV).

[14]Author interview with anonymous US aviation source, November 14, 2017, Washington, DC.

[15] Thomas Gibbons-Neff, "Pentagon: Some Russian cruise missiles crashed in Iran," *The Washington Post*, October 8, 2015, https://www.washingtonpost.com/news/checkpoint/wp/2015/10/07/these-are-the-cruise-missiles-russia-just-sent-into-syria/.

[16] Author interview with anonymous US aviation source, November 14, 2017, Washington, DC.

[17] Ibid.

[18] Unless the US grants special permission.

[19] "Gore's Secret Pact," October 18, 2000 The Wall Street Journal, https://www.wsj.com/articles/SB971819748452949326.

[20] Ariel Cohen and James A. Phillips, "Countering Russian-Iranian Military Cooperation," Backgrounder 1425 on Russia (Heritage Foundation, April 5,

2001),
http://www.heritage.org/research/reports/2001/04/counteringrussian-iranian-military-cooperation.

[21] For example, a recent survey of Syrian refugees in Germany—the first survey of Syrian refugees in Europe—found that approximately 70 percent of Syrian refugees are fleeing Assad. Complete survey results are available at http://washin.st/1RMy3sj. According to the Office of the UN High Commissioner for Refugees (UNHCR), at the end of 2013 the total number of displaced people worldwide, for the first time since World War II, surpassed 51 million, a 6-million-person increase over the previous year. This rise, UNHCR found, is due largely to the Syria crisis. See UNHCR, "World Refugee Day: Global Forced Displacement Tops 50 Million for First Time in Post–World War II Era," June 20, 2014, http://www.unhcr.org/53a155bc6.html.

[22] The five permanent United Nations Security Council members United States, United Kingdom, France, Russia and China, plus Germany.

[23] Indeed, Russian Middle East expert Georgiy Mirsky wrote in his blog on the liberal website *Echo Moskvy* in April 2015, "Several years ago, I heard from the lips of one MIA [Ministry of Internal Affairs] employee such reasoning: 'For us, a pro-American Iran is worse than a nuclear Iran.' "

[24] Quoted in Carnegie Endowment for International Peace, Proliferation Brief, Vol. 3, no. 22, July 25, 2000, Richard Speier, "Iran-Russia Missile Cooperation Richard Speier, Rober Gallucci, Robbie Sabel, Viktor Mizin," section "The Russian View," http://carnegieendowment.org/files/Repairing_12.pdf.

[25] Anne Barnard, Andre E. Kramer, "Iran Revokes Russia's Use of Air Base, Saying Moscow 'Betrayed Trust'" The New York Times, August 22, 2016 https://www.nytimes.com/2017/11/30/world/middleeast/syria-talks-geneva.html?ribbon-ad-idx=3&rref=world/middleeast&module=ArrowsNav&contentCollection=Middle%20East&action=swipe&region=FixedRight&pgtype=article.

[26] Allen Cone, "Russia gets permission to use Iran's Hamadan air base for Syria airstrikes," UPI, November 30, 2016, https://www.upi.com/Top_News/World-News/2016/11/30/Russia-gets-permission-to-use-Irans-Hamadan-air-base-for-Syria-airstrikes/8251480520159/.

[27] " Putin: spravedlivo, yesli Iran dostignet dosanktsionnogo urovnya dobychi nefti," RIA Novosti, September 5, 2016, https://ria.ru/economy/20160905/1476118270.html.

[28] Adam Kredo, "US officials 'concerned' as Iran, Russia plan $10 billion arms deal," November 15, 2016, http://www.foxnews.com/world/2016/11/15/us-officials-concerned-as-iran-russia-plan-10-billion-arms-deal.html.

[29] Von Christina Brause, Julia Smirnova, and Walter Wolowelsk, "Neue Schmuggelroute zwischen Russland und dem Iran," Welt N24 TV (Berlin), August 13, 2017, https://www.welt.de/politik/ausland/article167624550/Neue-Schmuggelroute-zwischen-Russland-und-dem-Iran.html.

[30] Van Hipp, "Russia's Putin Is Making His Moves in Syria and Beyond," Fox News, June 27, 2012, http://www.foxnews.com/opinion/2012/06/27/russia-putin-is-making-his-moves-in-syria-and-beyond.html; Ariel Cohen, "Russia's Troubling Arms Sales," Washington Times, March 19, 2007, http://www.washingtontimes.com/news/2007/mar/19/20070319-0920463099r/print/.

[31] Richard F. Grimmett, "Conventional Arms Transfers to Developing Nations, 2003–2010," Congressional Research Service, September 22, 2011, https://www.fas.org/sgp/crs/weapons/R42017.pdf. See also reference in David M. Herszenhorn, "For Syria, Reliant on Russia for Weapons and Food, Old Bonds Run Deep," New York Times, February 18, 2012, http://www.nytimes.com/2012/02/19/world/middleeast/for-russia-and-syriabonds-are-old-and-deep.html.

[32] See for example the following articles: "A Ship Comes Loaded with Timber...or Weapons?" Utrikesperspektiv, December 12, 2013, http://utrikesperspektiv.se/?p=348.208; "Russia Denies Hijacked Ship Was Carrying Missiles," CNN, September 8, 2009, http://www.cnn.com/2009/WORLD/europe/09/08/russia.missing.ship/index.html?iref=nextin; Luke Harding, Michael Schwirtz, "More Questions about a Hijacked Ship," New York Times, October 10, 2009, http://www.nytimes.com/2009/10/11/world/europe/11arctic.html?_r=0.209; Interfax, "EU Rapporteur Presumes Arctic Sea Transported Russian Missiles," August 19, 2009, https://archive.is/RWW5z.210.

[33] Dave Majumdar, "Cruise Missile Strikes in Syria: Russia's Big Ad Campaign?" The National Interest, October 8, 2015 http://nationalinterest.org/blog/the-buzz/cruise-missile-strikes-syria-russias-big-ad-campaign-14032.

[34] Dave Majumdar, "Cruise Missile Strikes in Syria: Russia's Big Ad Campaign?" The National Interest, October 8, 2015, http://nationalinterest.org/blog/the-buzz/cruise-missile-strikes-syria-russias-big-ad-campaign-14032; Thomas Gibbons-Neff, "Pentagon: Some Russian cruise missiles crashed in Iran," The Washington Post, October 8, 2015, https://www.washingtonpost.com/news/checkpoint/wp/2015/10/07/these-are-the-cruise-missiles-russia-just-sent-into-syria/.

[35] In March 2016, for example, Putin announced a withdrawal of the "main part" of Russia's armed forces in Syria, but in reality Russia's presence continued to grow.

[36] "Putin Asks Lawmakers to Expand Russia's Navy Presence in Syria," The Moscow Times, December 13, 2017, https://themoscowtimes.com/news/patin-asks-lawmakers-to-expand-russias-navy-presence-in-syria-59928?utm_source=push&utm_medium=push&utm_campaign=131217.

[37] Alex Luhn, Russia's campaign in Syria leads to arms sale windfall," The Guardian,

March 29, 2016, https://www.theguardian.com/world/2016/mar/29/russias-campaign-in-syria-leads-to-arms-sale-windfall; Andrew O'Reilly, "Russian sale of fighter jets to UAE highlights shift toward Kremlin amid US hesitancy," Fox News, March 2, 2017, http://www.foxnews.com/politics/2017/03/02/russian-sale-fighter-jets-to-uae-highlights-shift-toward-kremlin-amid-u-s-hesitancy.html; "Going Global: Russian Su-34 on the Way to Become Export Bestseller," Sputnik, June 1, 2016, https://sputniknews.com/military/201601061032735202-russia-su34-bomber-algeria/.

[38] Author email exchange with anonymous US aviation source, December 7–9, 2017.

[39] Author conversation with anonymous US aviation sources, Washington, DC, December 7, 2017.

[40] Mansur Mirovalev, "Syria's war: A showroom for Russian arms sales," Al Jazeera, April 6, 2016, http://www.aljazeera.com/news/2016/04/syria-war-showroom-russian-arms-sales-160406135130398.html.

[41] Vladimir Isachenkov, "Russia hoping to boost arms sales after Syrian usage," DefenseNews.com, August 30, 2017, https://www.defensenews.com/global/asia-pacific/2017/08/30/russia-hoping-to-boost-arms-sales-after-syrian-usage/.

[42] Daniel Brown, "Russia is using Syria as a testing ground for some of its most advanced weapons," Business Insider, May 24, 2017, http://www.businessinsider.com/russia-is-using-syria-testing-ground-some-advanced-weapons-2017-5.

[43] Oscar Nkala Algeria Orders 12 Su-34 'Fullback' Fighter-Bombers from Russia," DefenseNews.com, January 5, 2016, https://www.defensenews.com/home/2016/01/05/algeria-orders-12-su-34-fullback-fighter-bombers-from-russia/.

[44] Giovanni de Briganti "UAE Swings to Russia for Future Combat Aviation," Defense-Aerospace.com, February 21, 2017, http://www.defense-

aerospace.com/articles-view/feature/5/181311/uae-swings-to-russia-for-future-combat-aviation%2C-signs-3-agreements.html.

[45] "Russia Faces High Demand for Su-34, Su-35 Jets After Success in Syria," Sputnik, April 5, 2016, https://sputniknews.com/military/201604051037515495-su-jets-potential-buyers/; "Going Global: Russian Su-34 on the Way to Become Export Bestseller," Sputnik, January 6, 2016, https://sputniknews.com/military/201601061032735202-russia-su34-bomber-algeria/.

[46] "Putin says Russia wants to restore cooperation with African countries," Russia Beyond the Headlines, October 12, 2016, https://www.rbth.com/news/2016/10/12/putin-says-russia-wants-to-restore-cooperation-with-african-countries_638253.

[47] Theodore Karasik and Giorgio Cafiero, "Why does Vladimir Putin see in Sudan?" The Atlantic Council, November 27, 2017, http://www.atlanticcouncil.org/blogs/new-atlanticist/why-does-vladimir-putin-care-about-sudan.

[48] "Putin zayavil, chto Afrika ne mozhet byt' na periferii mezhdunarodnykh otnosheniy," RIA Novosti, October 27, 2016, https://ria.ru/world/20161027/1480166410.html.

[49] For example, The Stockholm International Peace Research Institute announced in December 2011 that Russia supplied 11 percent of major arms to sub-Saharan Africa, as reported in: "Russia eyes Africa to boost arms sales," The Guardian, April 4, 2013, https://www.theguardian.com/world/2013/apr/04/arms-trade-africa; see also; Eugene Steinberg, "Revealed: Russia's Mighty Pivot to Africa," The National Interest, October 14, 2015, http://nationalinterest.org/blog/the-buzz/revealed-russias-mighty-pivot-africa-13585. Sudan is also looking to Russia for assistance in upgrading its armed forces: "Russia to help Sudan upgrade its armed forces," TASS, November 23, 2017, http://tass.com/defense/977087http://tass.com/defense/977087. Sudanese

President Omar al-Bashir visited Moscow that month and asked Moscow for "protection" from the US and Sudan could become "a key to Africa for Russia." The International Criminal Court wants Bashir for a number of crimes, including genocide: see "Sudan's President Visits Russia, Asks for Protection From US," *Voice of America*, November 23, 2017, https://www.voanews.com/a/sudan-president-visits-russia-asks-for-protection-from-us/4131704.html.

[50] Andrei Akulov, "Russia's Arms Sales to Middle East Countries Spike to Record-High Levels," StrategicCulture.org, November 18, 2017, https://www.strategic-culture.org/pview/2017/11/18/russia-arms-sales-middle-east-countries-spike-record-high-levels.html.

[51] Matthew Bodner, "Who Is Russia Secretly Supplying With MiGs?" *The Moscow Times*, July 20, 2016, https://themoscowtimes.com/articles/mig-aircraft-company-finds-savior-in-egypt-54642.

[52] Damien Sharkov, "Russia and Egypt hold first ever joint naval drill," June 12, 2015, http://www.newsweek.com/russia-militaryrussian-navyrussiaegyptkremlin-603690; "Russia, Egypt start first joint military exercise in the desert," October 16, 2016, https://dailynewsegypt.com/2016/10/16/russia-egypt-start-first-joint-military-exercise-desert/.

[53] Associated Press, "Egypt Finalizes Deal With Russia for First Nuclear Plant," *Voice of America*, September 4, 2017, https://www.voanews.com/a/egypt-finalizes-deal-with-russia-for-first-nuclear-plant/4014549.html.

[54] Reuters Staff, "Russia to lend Egypt $25 billion to build nuclear power plant," *Reuters*, May 19, 2016, https://www.reuters.com/article/us-egypt-russia-nuclear/russia-to-lend-egypt-25-billion-to-build-nuclear-power-plant-idUSKCN0YA1G5.

[55] It aimed to create an international partnership, which would advance safe and extensive global expansion of nuclear power through so-called "cradle-to-grave fuel services" within a regulated market for enriched uranium, where several large countries would provide enriched uranium to smaller

countries. This plan aimed to address crucial concerns about nuclear weapons proliferation and waste management, and to eliminate the need for smaller countries to build facilities for uranium processing and disposal in the first place, saving them billions.

[56] Federal Register, Vol. 74, No 123, June 29, 2009, https://energy.gov/sites/prod/files/nepapub/nepa_documents/RedDont/EIS -0396-Cancellation-2009.pdf.

[57] "Russia, Egypt in Talks to Sign Airbase Deal," *The Moscow Times*, November 30, 2017, https://themoscowtimes.com/news/russia-egypt-in-talks-to-sign-airbase- deal-59766.

[58] Phil Stewart, Idrees Ali and Lin Noueihed, "Exclusive: Russia appears to deploy forces in Egypt, eyes on Libya role – sources," *Reuters*, March 13, 2017, https://www.reuters.com/article/us-usa-russia-libya- exclusive/exclusive-russia-appears-to-deploy-forces-in-egypt-eyes-on- libya-role-sources-idUSKBN16K2RY.

[59] Alexei Anishchuk, "Gaddafi Fall Cost Russia Tens of Blns in Arms Deals," Reuters, November 2, 2011, http://www.reuters.com/article/2011/11/02/russia-libya-arms- idUSL5E7M221H20111102.

[60] Theodore Karasik and Jeremy Vaughn, "Middle East Maritime Security: The Growing Role of Regional and Extraregional Navies." Washington Institute Near East Policy, Policy Notes 41, September 2017, http://www.washingtoninstitute.org/policy-analysis/view/middle-east- maritime-security.

[61] "Russia and Tunisia sign nuclear MOU," *World Nuclear News*, June 2, 2015, http://www.world-nuclear-news.org/NP-Russia-and-Tunisia-sign- nuclear-MOU-02061503.html.

[62] Rosatom, "Tunisia and Russia signed an Intergovernmental Agreement on Peaceful Uses of Atomic Energy," September 26, 2016,

http://www.rosatom.ru/en/press-centre/news/tunisia-and-russia-signed-an-intergovernmental-agreement-on-peaceful-uses-of-atomic-energy/.

[63] Christopher Woody, "The US and Russia are dominating the global weapons trade," *Business Insider*, December 28, 2016, http://www.businessinsider.com/us-russia-global-arms-sales-2016-12.

[64] Associated Press, "Russian Prime Minister Strikes Energy Deals in Morocco," *Voice of America*, October 11, 2017, https://www.voanews.com/a/russian-prime-minister-strikes-energy-deals-in-morocco-/4066941.html.

[65] Alexei Nikolskiy, " Zaklyuchen kontrakt po litsenzionnomu proizvodstvu tankov T-90 v Alzhire," *Vedomosti*, February 20, 2015, https://www.vedomosti.ru/newspaper/articles/2015/02/20/tank-alzhirskoi-sborki.

[66] "UAE wants to buy over a squadron of Su-35 advanced fighter jets from Russia," *TASS*, October 3, 2017, http://tass.com/defense/968593.

[67] Author email exchanges with military experts, Washington, DC, November 2017.

[68] "Russia, Qatar sign agreement on military and technical cooperation," *TASS*, October 25, 2017 http://tass.com/defense/972547.

[69] "Qatar turns its back on the US as it looks to Moscow for missiles," *The New Arab*, August 25, 2017, https://www.alaraby.co.uk/english/news/2017/8/25/qatar-interested-in-s-400-missile-deal-with-russia.

[70] Agreements signed upon conclusion of Saudi-Russian negotiations, October 5, 2017, http://kremlin.ru/supplement/5236.

[71] Reuters, "Saudi Arabia to buy S-400 air defense system from Russia," *Haaretz*, October 5, 2017, https://www.haaretz.com/middle-east-news/1.815867.

[72] Russia to Become Iraq's Second-Biggest Arms Supplier," *BBC*, October 9, 2012, http://www.bbc.com/news/world-europe-19881858.
[73] United Press International, "Iraq Gets Russian Arms Shipments under Landmark $4.4B Deal," October 21, 2013, http://washin.st/23s7HzF.

[74] "Presentation of foreign ambassadors' letters of credence," Kremlin.ru, October 23, 2013, http://kremlin.ru/events/president/news/19478.

[75] Robert O. Freedman, "Russia and the Middle East under Putin," Ortadogu Etutleri 2, no. 3 (July 2010): p. 26, http://www.orsam.org.tr/en/enUploads/Article/Files/201082_robertfeedman.orsam.etutler.pdf; "Russia Offers Gas to Turks," *Kommersant*, November 24, 2000, http://www.kommersant.ru/doc/161412; Turkish Ministry of Foreign Affairs, "Turkey's Political Relations with Russian Federation," http://www.mfa.gov.tr/turkey_s-politicalrelations-with-russian-federation.en.mfa.

[76] Fulya Ozerkan, "Turkey Signs Landmark Russian Weapons Deal," September 12, 2017, https://www.military.com/daily-news/2017/09/12/turkey-signs-landmark-russian-weapons-deal.html.

[77] Author telephone interview with Ben Moores, analyst, IHS Jane's, November 23, 2017.

[78] Richard Connolly, *Towards Self Sufficiency? Economics as a Dimension of Russian Security and the National Security Strategy of the Russian Federation to 2020*, NATO Defense College, July 18, 2016, http://www.ndc.nato.int/news/news.php?icode=96432.

9. Russia in the Middle East: Energy Forever?

Rauf Mammadov

Summary

The Middle East and North Africa (MENA) is an obvious target region for Russian energy diplomacy. Unlike Western European states, Russia has never had an imperial presence in the region. During the Cold War, the Soviet Union pursued the policy of supporting Arab socialist movements under the flag of Communist ideology and served as a counter-balance to the United States' influence in the region. Hence, bereft of the burden of an imperialist state and by untangling political concerns from its commercial interests, Russia has embarked on a pivot to the energy industry of the MENA region. Russia's goals can be summarized as:

- Find new markets for its oil and gas.
- Attract investment for an economy whose capital from the West has dried up from sanctions.
- Work with other energy exporters to stabilize international oil prices.
- Undermine Europe's efforts to diversify its natural gas supplies.
- Help Russia deliver more oil and gas to Asia.

A conducive geopolitical environment, coupled with plummeting oil prices, has eased the Kremlin's efforts to build bilateral energy relations with the regional powers. Russia's presence in the region is nascent but quickly growing. But, will Russia be able to maintain its presence in the region? Will Russia or Saudi Arabia be interested in cooperation to extend the volume-cut deal now and in the future? All of it will depend on a number of factors. The resilience of the American shale industry to the low oil price environment as well as the future of the Iran nuclear deal will be among the most significant elements influencing Russia's future in the region. What will happen by 2025 to Russia's energy policy of the Middle East is of critical importance in terms of meeting vision with the reality of energy politics and economics.

Introduction

Russia's foreign policy agenda includes regaining its role as a center of power and persuading other countries that the West's influence is declining.[1] Moscow perceives the West as the main threat to its national security. A plethora of Russian security and foreign policy documents either imply or say straight-out that the unipolar world is over and Russia deserves a more significant role in a new world order.[2] And energy diplomacy is an integral element of this assertive foreign policy Russia has been pursuing in global affairs.

Energy policy will continue to be a major player in global geopolitics. International trade has soared the past 50 years, and energy supplies have been the major element of that growth. At the same time, the glut in the oil and natural gas markets is expected to increase the global share of oil supplied by low-cost producers such as the Middle East and Russia. By 2025, the Middle East, Russia and Australia will be the largest exporters of gas, whereas the share of the Middle East the Organization of the Petroleum Exporting Countries (OPEC), Russia and the United States in global liquids supply will increase to 60 percent, from 56 percent in 2015.[3] The Middle East will also account for a considerable share in demand growth for natural gas, along with China and the US.[4]

As the largest producer of crude oil (including condensate) and the second-largest producer of natural gas in the world, Russia's economy is highly dependent on hydrocarbon exports.[5] Oil and gas revenues constituted more than one-third of its federal budget during the last two years. The economy of Russia has been faltering because of sanctions the West imposed in 2014 for Moscow's seizure of Crimea and for sparking and fueling the war in eastern Ukraine, and because of a global drop in energy prices. Although Russian monetary policy has helped generate a marginal recovery, the Russian Central Bank governor has warned that without a major economic overhaul, the country's gross domestic product (GDP) will grow at less than 2 percent a year, even if oil prices jump to $100 a barrel.[6] Economic experts inside and outside Russia know that the state budget's dependence on oil and gas revenues obliges the Kremlin to embrace policies that guarantee maximizing energy income. Given that energy constitutes about half of all Russian exports, stabilizing volatile oil prices is one of the important challenges of Kremlin energy diplomacy.

Furthermore, energy is indispensable to the growth of the world's two most populated countries, China and India. Most of the projected 28 percent increase in global energy consumption over the next 25 years is expected to come from developing countries. In fact, forecasts suggest that China and India will account for more than half of the world's increase in energy consumption through 2040.[7]

Competition to develop additional oil and gas supplies will become fiercer due to inhospitable locations or complicated geologies in regions such as the Arctic Ocean, the North Sea, and the pre-salt reserves of Brazil. Therefore, countries with ready access to large-scale and low-cost reserves, Including Russia, the United States and the oil-producing states of the Middle East, will lead the supply growth during the upcoming decade. These countries will assert their competitive advantage to capture the largest share of the global oil-production market. In recent years, the oil glut triggered a plunge in oil prices from well over $100 per barrel, down to the mid-$50s, causing shocks to the economies of oil- and gas-exporting countries. It also shifted the power to control supply and prices from OPEC to non-OPEC countries for the first time. An important consequence has been that OPEC producers have had to rethink both their domestic and foreign policies.

The shale ("fracking") revolution, a key contributor to the current oil and gas glut, has so far been largely confined to the United States. This fact has led to even fiercer competition for conventional oil sources. As the world's largest oil producer and second-largest gas producer, Russia knows it can use its influence on energy supply and prices as a geopolitical instrument. So it is important to understand Russia's key security perceptions and foreign policy objectives.

They include:

- Perpetuating the notion of a multipolar world.
- Proving the Kremlin's contention that Russia can play an indispensable role in resolving regional and global problems—the idea that "You break it, we will fix it."
- Continuing to compete for scarce global resources, especially oil and gas.
- Striving to develop new export markets, particularly if/after the West lifts the economic sanctions it imposed on Russia for the latter's heavy role in triggering the Ukraine crisis.
- Looking for financial support from countries outside the West to counter the impact of the sanctions.
- Continuing to support Russia's state-owned oil and gas companies' pursuit of resource replenishment.

- Trying to prevent China from using its Silk Road project to increase its economic and geopolitical clout in Europe.

In addition to flexing its military muscle in Ukraine, Syria and other places, Russia has been exercising its energy muscle to achieve foreign policy goals. The world was shocked at how ruthless Russia could be in using energy as a weapon when it cut off gas to Western Europe in the dead of winter during a gas-pricing dispute with Ukraine a decade ago. The cut-off was intended to prod Europe into forcing Ukraine to capitulate in the dispute. However, Europe saw this as Russia engaging in energy blackmail, compelling it to take steps to reduce its dependence on oil and gas, both in the short term and particularly over the long haul.

Moscow has never apologized to Europe about the heavy-handedness, but it has adjusted its energy policies to the new reality of an oil and gas glut. The adjustments are aimed at maintaining and increasing its oil and gas customer base—since most of its state budget comes from petroleum exports. The new approaches include deepening energy relations with other countries and working with international organizations such as OPEC to help shape energy policy that can help Russia achieve foreign policy goals. An overarching goal is to maintain or expand its energy markets in neighboring Western Europe and China, two of the world's largest oil and gas consumers. By doing so, Russia appears to believe it will stabilize its economy, maximize its budget revenues and continue to re-establish itself as a global power.

Why the Middle East?

The Middle East is among the largest proven crude oil and natural gas rich regions of the world. According to current estimates, 81.5 percent of the world's proven crude oil reserves are located in OPEC member countries, with the bulk of OPEC oil reserves in the Middle East, amounting to 65.5 percent of the OPEC total.[8] Once US shale oil plateaus in the late 2020s and the share of non-OPEC production decreases, the market will become increasingly reliant on the Middle East.[9]

Russia's leaders believe the country's re-ascendancy depends on countering the United States and its European allies in every strategically important part of the world. The MENA is crucial to Russian energy diplomacy for several reasons:

- The countries in the region have more than half of the world's oil and gas reserves.
- They sit on strategic sea-lanes that can move their oil and gas.
- They are close to one of the world's biggest energy markets: Europe.
- Two of Russia's biggest competitors are in the region—Saudi Arabia for oil and Qatar for natural gas.
- The region is Russia's biggest competitor for the lucrative Asian market, particularly China and India.

Russia is pursuing energy diplomacy in the region through bilateral relations with individual countries or international organizations like OPEC and the Gas Exporting Countries Forum (GECF). Collaborating with organizations that have a major impact on global energy markets, especially OPEC, is driven by several factors. For one thing, the Kremlin blames the oil price collapse on a concerted US effort to prevent Russian economic growth. Russian leaders remember all too well that the collapse of oil prices in the late 1980s played a key role in the collapse of the Soviet economy, which in turn led to the disintegration of the Soviet Union. They do not want to see a repeat of this in Russia itself. President Vladimir Putin, who decried the Soviet Union's collapse as the greatest "catastrophe" of the 20th century, has been vehement about safeguarding the Russian Federation from a similar fate. Working with OPEC and similar organizations, the Kremlin believes, could help boost oil prices, thus shoring up the Russian economy.

Because the fall in oil prices has been rooted in a surge in US shale oil production, Moscow sees the shale revolution as a US government–directed conspiracy to weaken Russia's security, not a consequence of the normal market cycles of supply and demand, Moscow has decided that one way to bring oil prices back up and maximize budget revenues is to work with former rivals in the MENA. Russia also believes that working with these countries can help it protect its share of the prime European oil and gas market.

Energy diplomacy methods and tactics that the Russians are employing in the MENA include:

- Partnering in oil and gas exploration and development projects.
- Taking part in energy transportation infrastructure projects, such as oil shipping terminals.
- Signing bilateral energy and foreign-policy agreements with Saudi Arabia, Qatar, Iran and other energy-rich countries in the area.
- Working with OPEC and the GECF on energy price-bolstering mechanisms.
- Using a combination of Russia's and the region's energy export potential as a bargaining chip in relations with the West.

Russia sees the MENA region as its main competitor in the energy markets. The two share geographical proximity to the European continent, and both have access to the maritime routes used to deliver oil and gas to the lucrative Asian market. Russia is competing with Saudi Arabia to supply oil to Europe and China, whereas Qatar and Algeria are its main regional rivals in supplying gas to Europe.

Participating in exploration and development as well as transportation-infrastructure projects in the region will help Russia influence the area's petroleum-product delivery decisions to Russia's traditional delivery markets. The strategy is also aimed at undermining the European Union's energy supply diversification efforts, which have accelerated since Russia invaded Crimea. Despite EU efforts to thwart Gazprom's dominance in its import portfolio, the Russian gas giant has, in fact, managed to increase supplies to Europe by 8.7 percent in 2017.[10] Indeed, Russia supplied a record amount of gas to Europe in 2017 through its state-owned Gazprom, which has been able to avoid Western sanctions. It has traditionally supplied the lion's share of Europe-bound oil and gas through Ukraine, but Moscow and Kyiv had a falling out over prices between 2005 and 2010, which affected Russian gas supplies to Europe. At one point in the dispute, Russia actually cut off gas flowing through Ukrainian pipelines to the continent.

The crisis prompted the European Union to pass legislation and adopt administrative policies to diminish its dependence on Russian energy, especially gas. The Europeans' focus was on alternative supply options such as the Southern Gas Corridor pipeline, new energy-supply connections in Central and Eastern Europe that skirted the Ukrainian pipeline network, and the construction of liquefied natural gas (LNG) terminals on its coasts.

Russia is aware, of course, that the EU is trying to further diversify its energy transit routes and sources of supply. In response, it is building pipelines to Europe that skirt the Ukrainian network—"Nord Stream 2" and "Turk Stream"—to try to maintain its stranglehold on the European market, particularly in the east. And it is taking part in Middle Eastern and North African projects to diversify its export capabilities. This includes participating in the development of the "Zohr" gas field off Egypt and buying oil from Libya and Kurdistan.

Russia believes that putting itself in position to influence decisions on the supply of MENA energy to Europe will make it harder for the continent to weaken the geopolitical influence that Moscow can exert there. This surround-the-continent tactic not only gives Russia an additional bargaining chip in its foreign policy dialogue with the EU but also enables Moscow to create schisms in Trans-Atlantic alliance in respect to energy security policies of the continent.

Russia sees Central Asia and Azerbaijan as competitors in Southeastern Europe and the Mediterranean region. Kazakhstan delivers most of its oil to Europe and beyond through pipelines that run across Russia to the Black Sea. A country with one of the world's biggest gas reserves, Turkmenistan, is eager to send more of it to Europe, but also lacks a pipeline that bypasses Russia. Both landlocked countries support the West's idea of a Trans-Caspian Pipeline that would feed their oil and/or gas to an existing pipeline in Azerbaijan that skirts Russia. By helping MENA producers send more oil and gas to Europe's Mediterranean region, Russia makes the idea of pipelines connecting areas outside the region and Europe less feasible.

A combination of the price-battering oil and gas glut along with Western sanctions over the Crimean annexation and the Kremlin's support for an insurgency in eastern Ukraine left Russia with little choice but to turn toward China and other places in Asia to try to maintain its energy export income. It is also sending LNG to parts of the Middle East. In addition to the Middle East being a place where Russian energy companies can access upstream and midstream energy projects, it sees the area as a place to obtain funding for its oil and gas projects now that sanctions have dried up funding from the West.

Russia also believes that working with MENA countries and energy organizations will not only help it bring stability to global energy markets but also protect its market share in the Far East. A number of factors have contributed to the growing rapprochement between Russia and countries in the region. They include the devastating impact that low oil prices have had on the budgets of oil-exporting

Gulf countries, repercussions of the Arab Revolutions for the MENA states and Russia's military success in Syria. A key message that Russia is trying to convey by repositioning itself in the area is that it is indispensable to resolving both regional conflicts and global conflicts with regional components. Meanwhile, it sees its growing geopolitical role in the region as a springboard to increasing its economic activity in Europe and the Far East as well as short-circuiting China's plan to increase its economic clout in Europe through the Silk Road program.

Russia in North Africa

Traditionally, Moscow has perceived North Africa as an area of rivalry with the United States. And the intensification of Russian engagement in the energy sectors of Algeria, Libya and Egypt is an integral part of its multidimensional global energy diplomacy strategy. Rebuilding its superpower status in the region, utilizing its political privilege gained through assertive relations with state leaders or contenders for power (as in Libya), along with gaining leverage to influence decisions about oil and gas supplies to the European continent are only a fraction of Russia's policy objectives in North Africa.

Russia and Libya

The power struggle in Libya between the UN-backed Government of National Accord (GNA) and The Libyan National Army (LNA) has divided the country into two camps. Criticized for allowing the coalition forces to overthrow Muammar Qaddafi, the Russian leadership has decided to act carefully in choosing sides in Libya's ongoing internal conflict. Russia maintains a pragmatic approach toward both camps by projecting itself as a broker between Libya's rival camps rather than supporting any of them exclusively. Thus, Moscow is playing a wait-and-see game in order to reap the maximum political and economic benefit from the conflict.

From a tactical standpoint, Russia seeks to strengthen its positions in the Mediterranean basin. By gaining ground in a future Libyan government, Russia aims to expand its influence over southern Europe—a major customer for North African oil exports—thus equipping Moscow with additional bargaining tools in its relentless energy dialogues with the EU. Moreover, by continuing its "glorious fight" against international terrorism in Libya, Russia aims to reassert itself as a global player capable of resolving conflicts in the region, as it did in Syria.

From an economic standpoint, the Russian leadership is looking for ways to compensate for the losses it faced following the overthrow of Qaddafi. Russia expects to make $150 million from construction projects, $3 billion from railway construction, $4 billion from arms sales, and up to $3.5 billion from energy deals in Libya.[11]

By being actively involved in Libyan politics and commercial projects, Russia not only substantiates one of its central narratives of becoming a regional and potentially globally important actor, but also lays the groundwork for undermining competitors of Russian oil and gas companies. Increased production from Central Asia and China's expanding influence in the Middle East obliges Russia to take measures to protect its market share in European and Far Eastern oil and gas markets.

Financial, economic and security concerns that have divided Libya since the toppling of Qaddafi in 2011 continue to plague Libya. This turmoil has had negative repercussions on Libyan petroleum exports: Years of violent conflict cost the country $126 billion in lost oil revenues.[12] In 2017, Libya has managed to surpass one million barrels a day for the first time in four years.[13] Libya is currently exempt from the volume-cut deal negotiated by Russia and Saudi Arabia, but attempts to rebound production to pre-war levels are weakened by constant conflicts among tribal leaders, by blockaders, and as a result of the whims of competing political factions and militias.

Before the Libyan revolution, Russian companies such as Gazprom, Lukoil and Tatneft were actively engaged in energy projects in the country. Notably, Gazprom had concluded a partnership with German Wintershall to develop Libyan gas fields, while Tatneft signed a contract with Libyan National Oil Company to develop several offshore oil fields on the Libyan continental shelf.[14] Gazpromneft also signed a production sharing agreement with an Eni-led consortium in 2011.[15] But the implementation of those deals was deferred by the ongoing conflict. Russian officials have so far adhered to the position that the parties to the above agreements are still committed to the contractual obligations signed before the overthrow of Qaddafi. But the Libyan side has yet to express its adherence to the same premise.

In their engagement in Libya, Russian companies are deploying similar, albeit risky, methods to those already successfully tested in other politically unstable resource-rich countries. Early entrance into risky markets is important for Russian companies to expand their activities in regions where Western companies are hesitant to operate. Illustratively, Russian oil giant Rosneft has signed a deal to purchase oil from Libya's National Oil Corp. As part of a yearlong contract, the Russian firm is using a long-term prepayment model for this oil-purchase deal, signed in February 2017.[16] This model has already been successfully deployed in Iraqi Kurdistan and Venezuela. The model distributes the risks between producers and consumers, while Rosneft takes advantage of its access to state money.

Algeria

Russia is also trying to carve out a larger presence in Algeria's oil and gas sectors. Algeria, the second-largest gas supplier to the European market, is perceived as a main threat to Russian natural gas interests on the southern shores of the continent.[17] Algeria is vitally important for the EU, which considers the country one of the most viable alternatives to Russian natural gas dominance on the continent. Thus, it is in the interest of pragmatic Russian leadership to have a presence in Algeria, especially in the country's gas industry, to gain leverage over decisions pertaining to future supplies to the European market. Rosneft and Gazprom already have a presence in Algeria, although both of them would be happy to expand further in the Algerian market.[18] Russia's efforts to capture stronger positions in lucrative Algerian market were hindered by equally ambitious Gulf States who are also interested in building presence in Algeria. Russia particularly faces Qatar as a main competitor in Algerian gas market due the latter's active penetration to the Algerian market.

Egypt

Egypt's market liberalization efforts were jump-started by the reform program agreed with the International Monetary Fund (IMF).[19] Those reforms have opened the door for oil and gas companies to enter the Egyptian market. In particular, by enhancing the flexibility of its gas sector, Egypt now competes with Turkey and Greece to become a major gas hub on Europe's doorstep.[20] Natural gas field discoveries in the Eastern Mediterranean basin, coupled with market liberalization, have only served to bolster Egypt's gas hub aspirations. Notably, a new law enables foreign companies to use Egypt's import and distribution facilities to trade in natural gas.[21] Increasing production from domestic fields and the presence of two largely idle liquefaction plants at Idku and Damietta could enable Egypt to import gas from Israel and Cyprus and export it to Europe and Asia.[22] With increasing domestic production as well as the deployment of renewable and nuclear energy sources for electricity production, Egypt could develop a gas surplus in 2018[23]. Moreover, Egyptian exports could reach at least 20 billion cubic meters (bcm) per year by 2035.[24]

In August 2017, Rosneft delivered its first cargo shipment of liquefied natural gas (129,000 tons) to Egypt. It was reported earlier that Rosneft would supply ten consignments of LNG to Egypt with a total volume of 600,000 tons, and deliveries would be carried out from May to October 2017.[25]

In October 2017, Rosneft acquired the right to export gas to Egypt by purchasing 30 percent of the Eni-operated Zohr field of Egypt. By acquiring shares in the Zohr field, Rosneft has become a participant in exploiting Egypt's largest deep-water gas field. Rosneft CEO Igor Sechin assessed the acquisition as an opportunity to reinforce his company's position in this "promising and strategic region."[26]

Russia acknowledges that the gas market is globalizing and that it will ultimately be impossible to dominate this new market environment by deploying conventional energy diplomacy methods. Hence Russian energy diplomacy is putting increasing emphasis on acquisitions of oil and gas assets in geographically well-positioned locations and diversifying its own gas exports to these regions, including Egypt. The goal for Russia is to become a formidable actor amid growing competition for global energy resources, as well as to obtain access to energy markets and control over transport arteries.

By gaining influence over directing Libyan oil and Egyptian gas supplies to Europe, Russia is trying to undermine Western-backed diversification projects designed to bring Central Asian and Azerbaijani oil and gas supplies to the European market. And by contributing to increasing supplies from Libyan oil fields as well as by bringing more Kirkuk oil to Ceyhan (Turkish Mediterranean port where Azerbaijani oil is delivered), Russia seeks to muscle out supplies from Kazakhstan and, especially, light oil from Azerbaijan shipped to the Mediterranean basin. Moreover, Moscow's activities in North Africa will make any proposed Trans-Caspian oil pipeline project less economically feasible. Similarly, by becoming a formidable player in a future Egyptian gas hub, Russia is undermining the economic rationale for a potential future expansion of the Southern Gas Corridor.

The only alternative pipeline project to supply natural gas to Europe currently under construction is the Southern Gas Corridor (SGC) project, which will strategically deliver gas to traditionally Russian-dominated markets in Southeastern Europe. At its widest, the SGC's designed throughput capacity is 16 bcm per year, which is almost one-tenth of the annual Russian supply to Europe. However, by adding additional pumping stations, the operator could easily double the throughput capacity of the SGC pipeline network. This technical flexibility of the pipeline enables the SGC to potentially bring additional volumes from Central Asia, the Eastern Mediterranean or Northern Iraq. By obtaining control over the direction of additional volumes of Europe-bound natural gas from Northern Africa and the Mediterranean basin, Russia is pursuing the goal of making the expansion of the Southern Gas Corridor and the realization of proposed Trans-Caspian pipeline projects economically less feasible.

Saudi Arabia

The parameters of energy relations between Russia and Saudi Arabia are, in broad terms, defined by the following factors:

- The race for market share in Asian markets.
- Mutual interest in stabilizing energy commodity prices (oil prices).
- Potential Saudi Arabian investments in the Russian economy.
- LNG exports to Saudi Arabia.

The Race for Market Share

As the two largest oil exporters in the world, Russia and Saudi Arabia are natural competitors. However, in addition to competing to capture the largest share of the global oil market, Moscow and Riyadh are also positioned in opposing camps in the Syrian conflict.

Furthermore, Russia has cozy relations with Saudi Arabia's biggest regional foe—Iran. Nevertheless, Moscow and Riyadh have managed to put aside their differences and are currently pursuing a pragmatic approach to economic cooperation. The desperate need to stabilize oil prices and to break the resilience of the US domestic shale oil industry has drawn these traditional competitors into a productive collaboration.

In addition to Syria, oil was the most important agenda item during Saudi King Salman bin Abdulaziz Al Saud's trip to Moscow in 2017—the first such visit by a reigning Saudi monarch since the collapse of the Soviet Union. According to Russian Energy Minister Alexander Novak, the two sides signed deals worth $3 billion, following the visits of King Salman and the subsequent visit of Saudi Energy Minister Khalid al-Falih to Moscow in the second half of 2017.[27] The agreements included Memorandum of Understandings (MoU) on the construction of a $1.1 billion petrochemical plant in Saudi Arabia by Russian firm Sibur, the establishment of a joint $1 billion investment fund for energy and technology development, as well as an agreement between Saudi Aramco and Gazpromneft on drilling technology.[28] Unconfirmed reports also pointed to apparent talks regarding investment by Saudi Arabia in the largest oil-drilling contractor of Russia, Eurasia Drilling Co., and Novatek's proposed Arctic LNG 2 project.[29]

Russia is interested in selling LNG to Saudi Arabia. On December 8, 2017, Saudi Energy Minister al-Falih attended a ceremony dedicated to the first loading of liquefied natural gas from Russia's Yamal LNG project in the Arctic. President Putin's message to Minister al-Falih's government was straightforward: "Buy our gas, you will save your oil." On this issue, the two countries' interests are complementary: The Kingdom is interested in decreasing the dependence of its domestic power sector on crude oil, while Russia is desperately searching for markets for its LNG volumes.[30]

The Russia-OPEC Deal

The Russian state budget's dependence on oil and gas revenues obliges the Kremlin to embrace policies that maximize the income from energy exports. Since energy constitutes about half of all Russian exports, stabilizing volatile oil prices is one of the most important challenges of Kremlin energy diplomacy. Saudi Arabia has now also abandoned generous production levels. That policy was aimed at keeping prices low to hammer shale oil companies, whose costs were higher than traditional producers. But shale producers displayed unexpected resilience by improving their technology and efficiency so they could remain profitable even when oil prices were low. This meant that production-volume cuts were inevitable. And with these cuts came shifts in oil exporters' foreign policies. Notably, OPEC and non-OPEC exporters, led by Saudi Arabia and Russia, decided, on November 30, 2017, to extend a volume-cut deal for another nine months.[31] Russia has been instrumental in achieving the deal and then successfully extending despite hesitation demonstrated by parts of the leadership in Moscow. An important lesson from the negotiating process is that Saudi Arabia can no longer single-handedly dictate global oil price policy. The Saudis needed Russian support to achieve the cut they wanted. This development leaves the Kingdom vulnerable to the Kremlin's whims. Thus, Russia has gained formidable leverage by making its major competitor dependent on Russian energy diplomacy through international institutions. Moreover, Moscow's new ability to influence international production cut deals, and thus oil prices, is likely alarming for Riyadh. The Kremlin has become the power behind OPEC's command. Saudi Arabia had to face the new reality that without Russia the deal would collapse.

Qatar

Qatar is currently the world's largest LNG exporter and the second-largest gas exporter after Russia. [32] Although the LNG market is currently oversupplied due to new volumes from the United States, Australia and West Africa, according to the consulting firm McKinsey & Company, this oversupply will continue merely until 2022–2025.[33]

Economic cooperation between Qatar and Russia started with the visit of Emir of Qatar Tamim bin Hamad Al Thani to Moscow in February 2016.[34] What started with routine intergovernmental agreements and mutual declaration of intentions to bolster political and economic cooperation soon yielded concrete results. In the beginning of December, the consortium of Qatar's sovereign wealth fund and commodities trader Glencore purchased 19.5 percent of shares in Rosneft for $11.3 billion.[35] At that point, the Russian state, which owns 50 percent of Rosneft, was still struggling to narrow its budget gap resulting from low oil prices. Thus, the deal came as a relief for the Russian leadership. The shares purchase by the Qatari sovereign wealth fun also carried political connotations. By selling almost 20 percent of a state-owned oil company to an international consortium, Russia demonstrated that its companies could still conclude deals with foreign partners despite Western sanctions. In fact, Glencore and Qatar's sovereign wealth fund became the first investors in a Russian oil company following the passage of economic sanctions by the US and the EU. In September 2017, the consortium sold 14.2 percent of the Rosneft shares purchased year earlier to China Energy Company Limited (CEFC).[36]

Besides cultivating bilateral relations with Qatar, Russia is also trying to use the Gas Exporting Countries Forum as a platform for tightening cooperation with its major Middle Eastern natural gas rival. During their meeting in Moscow, both Russian President Vladimir Putin and Qatari Emir Hamad Al Thani emphasized the need to strengthen the coordination between the two states within the framework of the Forum, which was established in Tehran, but is currently headquartered in Doha and chaired by the representative of Russia. Although not as effective as its oil-sector analogue, the GECF, through its members, own 67 percent of the world's gas reserves and supplies 42 percent of global consumption.[37] By building coordination within the framework of the GECF, Russia is seeking to avoid conflicts with one of its main competitors and aims to divide up the international natural gas market based on mutually agreed mechanisms.

Iraq

Russian oil and gas companies actively participated in a re-division of Iraqi oil reserves following the toppling of Saddam Hussein. In 2009, Lukoil became a shareholder in West Qurna-2, one of the largest oil fields in the world.[38] Gazprom affiliate Gazpromneft also won the contract as a part of a larger consortium to develop Badra field, located in eastern Iraq. Moreover, Gazpromneft holds a participating interest in several blocks located in Kurdistan region.[39] Rosneft's engagement in Iraq's oil industry started with the acquisition of the controlling stake of another Russian oil company, Bashneft, which had previously secured the right to operate inside Iraq. Importantly, Rosneft agreed to take control of Iraqi Kurdistan's main oil pipeline during the political crisis triggered by the Kurdish vote for independence, held in September 2017.[40] Rosneft's investment in the project was expected to be around $1.8 billion on top of $1.2 billion already lent to Kurdistan in the first of months of 2017[41] Kurdistan is planning to repay the loan with future oil sales. Northern Iraqi oil volumes are important for Rosneft from a tactical standpoint. Along with cementing Russia's economic and political presence in northern Iraq, oil from the Kurdistan region could be supplied to German refineries owned by the company. By investing in production increases in Kurdistan and pledging to increase the throughput capacity of the Erbil pipeline, Rosneft will be able to deliver oil volumes from Kurdistan region to its refineries in Germany. By doing so, Rosneft will be able to divert its Ural's blend volumes to Asian markets in order to capture more share vacated by Saudi Arabia as a result of the Russian-OPEC volume-cut deal.

Syria

Syria is not a major oil and natural gas producer, although it does have considerable gas reserves (240 bcm). However, plans to develop these fields, either independently or in joint cooperation with foreign investors, were thwarted by the internal war.[42]

At the moment, Syria is more important as a potential energy transit country. Both Russia and Iran have shown interest in Syria's transit capacity before the civil war broke. Gazprom is engaged in several infrastructure and refining projects in Syria via its subsidiary Stroytransgaz. In 2008, this firm, controlled by Gennadiy Timchenko, started talks with the Ministry of Oil of Iraq and Iraq's North Oil Company regarding the renovation of the major oil pipeline connecting Kirkuk to the Syrian port of Banias.[43] Stroytransgaz also completed a stretch of The Arab Pipeline from the Jordanian border to the Homs in Syria.[44]

In 2009, Syrian President Bashar al-Assad rejected the proposal of Qatar to lay a gas pipeline from to its North Field to Turkey and to the EU citing its long-standing friendly relations with Russia and Gazprom.[45] In 2010, Gazprom reiterated its interest in participating in development of the Syrian oil and gas industry. Sergei Prikhodko, then an assistant to the president of the Russian Federation, made a statement in support of Gazprom's efforts to participate in a gas pipeline project connecting Syria to Lebanon.[46] And in July 2011, the governments of Iran, Iraq and Syria signed a pipeline deal to bring natural gas from the South Pars field to Damascus, via Iraq.[47] However, the ongoing civil war obstructed the implementation of these projects. Russian upstream company Soyuzneftegas, run by Yuri Shafrannik, the former energy minister of Russia, signed the first ever offshore oil deal in the Mediterranean basin in the Syrian sector, in December 2013, but later abandoned plans to develop this project.[48]

In February 2015, Gazprom CEO Alexander Miller met with the Syrian ambassador to Moscow in order to discuss cooperation in the oil and gas industry.[49] Additionally, the CEO of Gazprom's subsidiary Stroytransgaz visited Damascus in September to meet with Prime Minister of Syria Wael Nader al-Halki to reinstate his company's activities in Syria.[50] Syrian Foreign Minister Walid Muallem stated in November 2015 that Syria is hoping to see not merely Russian military vessels but also offshore drilling platforms. Soyuzneftegaz reinstated the construction of North Gas Processing Plant, nearby Raqqa, in December 2017, following the liberation of the city from the Islamic State.[51]

It is still far from clear how the political map of war-torn Syria will ultimately be shaped. The country's importance as a transit route connecting the energy-rich Gulf region with Mediterranean ports and Turkey will be a key element of this process. By providing political and military support to al-Assad, Russia not only aims to reopen Syrian markets to Russian energy companies, but also attempts to become an indispensable player in pipeline geopolitics within the region.

Conclusion

A number of cataclysms have enveloped the MENA in the past decade. The Arab Spring revolts against a number of regimes in the region began in 2010. They led to several overthrows and civil wars that continue in some countries. Terrorist groups, such as the Islamic State, which emerged from the ruins of failed states, worsened the tumult. Seizing on the opportunity to fill the vacuum created by the United States' largely non-interventionist foreign policy in the region over the past few years, the Kremlin sent military forces to try to shore up the area's security. Its success in Syria in particular helped Moscow institute the active energy diplomacy it is pursuing there now.

Moscow has embarked on a more vigorous foreign policy in the region to:

- Find new markets for its oil and gas.
- Attract investment for an economy whose capital from the West has dried up because of sanctions.
- Work with other energy exporters to stabilize international oil prices.
- Undermine Europe's efforts to diversify its natural gas supplies.
- Help Russia deliver more oil and gas to Asia.

Disagreements between traditional allies in the region have helped Russia become a player there. By building economic ties with its energy rivals in the area, and working with international organizations such as OPEC to pursue its goal, the Kremlin is doing what it has always excelled at: divide and conquer. Russia has tried to use its energy diplomacy in MENA both to bring the region to its area of influence and to drive a wedge between the United States and its traditional allies, especially in Gulf region.

In its more muscular role in the MENA, Russia has been putting pragmatic energy policies above political differences. A key question is whether it can continue cooperating with regional energy players while disregarding its geopolitical differences with them. In other words, how sustainable will Russia's energy diplomacy in the region be? And how will international oil prices affect Russia's relations with energy-exporting countries in the area over the long term?

The United States has become far less dependent on oil imports and even less dependent on Middle Eastern oil than just a decade ago. But the global nature of energy markets exposes the US economy to oil and gas price fluctuations. Both a recent explosion at a natural gas terminal in Baumgarten, Austria, and China's decision to slash its coal production roiled global energy markets, underscoring how interdependent they are. Washington must ensure that Russia does not outmaneuver it to increase its influence over global energy policy, and thus prices. This means the United States must keep a close eye on relations between its most important allies in the Gulf as well as its rival Russia. Gulf countries, especially Saudi Arabia and Qatar, will remain among the world's biggest energy exporters for many decades to come. And American oil companies are still major oil and gas producers in the region. The United States needs to keep lines of communication with Middle Eastern oil producers given region's indispensability to global energy industry. Russia is keen to further expand its energy cooperation in MENA region to prevent volatility in energy commodity markets in order to maximize revenues gained from the exports of hydrocarbons.

ENDNOTES

[1] Foreign Policy Concept of the Russian Federation, http://www.mid.ru/en/foreign_policy/official_documents/-/asset_publisher/CptICkB6BZ29/content/id/122186.

[2] National Economic Security Strategy of Russian Federation until 2030, Threats and Challenges. http://www.kremlin.ru/acts/bank/41921.

[3] BP Energy Outlook 2035, https://www.bp.com/content/dam/bp/pdf/energy-economics/energy-outlook-2017/bp-energy-outlook-2017-region-insight-middle-east.pdf.

[4] International Energy Agency, https://www.iea.org/topics/naturalgas/.

[5] Energy Information Agency, https://www.eia.gov/beta/international/analysis.cfm?iso=RUS.

[6] Anna Adrianova, "Russia feels growth limits again after short-lived acceleration," *Bloomberg*, November 2017, https://www.bloomberg.com/news/articles/2017-11-12/russia-feels-growth-limits-again-as-economic-rebound-seen-slower.

[7] Energy Information Agency, https://www.eia.gov/outlooks/ieo/.

[8] OPEC official web site,
http://www.opec.org/opec_web/en/data_graphs/330.htm.

[9] International Energy Agency, https://www.iea.org/weo2017/.

[10] Gazprom Press Release,
http://www.gazprom.com/press/news/2017/june/article335990/.

[11] Lincoln Pigman, Kyle Orton, "Inside Putin's Libyan Power Play," *Foreign Policy*, September 2014 http://foreignpolicy.com/2017/09/14/inside-putins-libyan-power-play/.

[12] Anjli Raval, "Libya's oil guardian coaxes ravaged industry into recovery," *Financial Times*, November 13, 2017,
https://www.ft.com/content/f8d6f892-c85c-11e7-ab18-7a9fb7d6163e.

[13] "Update 1-Libya's oil output tops one million barrels per day," *Reuters*, June 30, 2017, https://www.reuters.com/article/libya-oil/update-1-libyas-oil-output-tops-one-million-barrels-per-day-idUSL8N1JR2BT.

[14] Wintershall Official Website, Tatneft Official Website Press release,
http://www.tatneft.ru/press-center/press-releases/more/1725/?lang=en.

[15] Gazprom Official Website Press Release,
http://www.gazprom.com/press/news/2011/february/article109011/.

[16] National Oil Corporation of Libya Official Website Press Release,
https://noc.ly/index.php/en/new-4/2095-noc-and-rosneft-sign-cooperation-framework-agreement-at-london-ip-week.

[17] Energy Information Agency, Country Analysis,
https://www.eia.gov/beta/international/analysis.cfm?iso=DZA.

[18] Gazprom press release,
http://www.gazprom.com/press/news/2015/february/article218247/;

Rosneft Official Website, https://www.rosneft.com/business/Upstream/exploration/Prospective_proj ects/245_s_algeria/.

[19] Nadine Abou el Atta, "The Complete Guide to the New Gas Regulatory Authority and Market Liberalization," *Egypt Oil & Gas Newspaper*, September 6, 2017, http://egyptoil-gas.com/features/the-complete-guide-to-the-new-gas-regulatory-authority-and-market-liberalization/9096/.

[20] Salma El Wardany, Mirette Magdy & Tamim Elyan, "Egypt Moves to end state monopoly of natural gas market," *World Oil*, August 8, 2017, http://www.worldoil.com/news/2017/8/8/egypt-moves-to-end-state-monopoly-of-natural-gas-market.

[21] Nadine Abou el Atta, "The Complete Guide to the New Gas Regulatory Authority and Market Liberalization. (See note 19.)

[22] Eran Azran, "Egypt Starts talk with Cyprus," *Haaretz News Agency*, November 2017 https://www.haaretz.com/israel-news/business/1.824498.

[23] Salma El Wardany & Trace Alloway, "Eni's Giant Gas Field Prompts Egypt to End LNG Imports in 2018," *Bloomberg*, November 14, 2017, https://www.bloomberg.com/news/articles/2017-11-14/eni-s-giant-gas-field-prompts-egypt-to-end-lng-imports-in-2018.

[24] Charles Ellinas, "Egypt's law opens gas market," *Natural Gas World*, September 2017, https://store.naturalgasworld.com/ngw-magazine-egypts-law-opens-gas-market-54786.

[25] "Rosneft delivers 129000 tonnes of LNG to Egypt," *TASS Russian News Agency*, September 2017, http://tass.com/economy/959129.

[26] Rosneft official website, https://www.rosneft.com/press/today/item/188235/.

[27] Ed Chow and Andrew Stanley, "Russia-Saudi Arabia New Oil bromance" *Global Trade Magazine*, December 2017

http://www.globaltrademag.com/global-trade-daily/russia-saudi-arabia-new-oil-bromance.

[28] Oliver Carrol, "Saudi Arabia and Russia sign $3bn arms deal," *Independent*, October 2017, http://www.independent.co.uk/news/world/europe/russia-king-salman-visit-saudi-arabia-moscow-vladimir-putin-a7985161.html.

[29] Wael Mahdi, Elena Mazneva & Ilya Arkhipov, "Saudi Arabia weighs Russia Deals," *Bloomberg*, October 2017, https://www.bloomberg.com/news/articles/2017-10-03/saudi-arabia-is-said-to-plan-russia-deals-deepening-energy-ties.

[30] "Putin to Saudi minister: Buy our gas, save your oil," *Reuters*, December 2017, https://www.reuters.com/article/us-russia-saudi-lng-oil/putin-to-saudi-energy-minister-buy-our-gas-save-your-oil-ifx-idUSKBN1E221P.

[31] OPEC Official Website Press release, http://www.opec.org/opec_web/en/press_room/4696.htm.

[32]Qatar National Bank Official Website, https://www.qnb.com/cs/Satellite?blobcol=urldata&blobheader=application%2Fpdf&blobkey=id&blobtable=MungoBlobs&blobwhere=1355571894690&ssbinary=true.

[33] McKinsey & Company, "Global Natural Gas and LNG Outlook," *McKinsey & Company*, August 2017, https://www.mckinseyenergyinsights.com/services/market-intelligence/reports/global-gas-and-lng-outlook/.

[34] Official website of Russian President http://en.kremlin.ru/events/president/news/51177.

[35]Rosneft Annual Report 2016, https://www.rosneft.com/upload/site2/document_file/a_report_2016_eng.pdf.

[36] "Glencore sells down stake in Russia's Rosneft," *Telegraph*, September 2017, http://www.telegraph.co.uk/business/2017/09/08/glencore-sells-stake-russias-rosneft/.

[37] Gas Exporting Countries Forum Official Website, https://www.gecf.org/countries/country-list.aspx.

[38] Lukoil Official Website, http://www.lukoil.com/Business/Upstream/Overseas/WestQurna-2.

[39] Gazprom official Website, http://www.gazprom.com/about/production/projects/deposits/iraq/.

[40] Rosneft Official Website, https://www.rosneft.com/search/?q=kurdistan.

[41]Sroytansgaz Official Website. http://www.stroytransgaz.ru/en/activity/services/oilgas_engineering/?sphrase_id=46123.

[42] Energy Information Agency, International Analysis, https://www.eia.gov/beta/international/analysis.cfm?iso=SYR.

[43]Stroytransgaz Official Website . Projects http://www.stroytransgaz.ru/en/activity/services/oilgas_engineering/?sphrase_id=46123.

[44] Stroytransgaz Official Website, "Projects," http://www.stroytransgaz.ru/en/activity/services/oilgas_engineering/?sphrase_id=46123.

[45] Hurriyet, "Moscow rejects Saudi Offer to drop Assad for arms deal" *Hurriyet Newspaper*, August 2013 http://www.hurriyetdailynews.com/moscow-rejects-saudi-offer-to-drop-assad-for-arms-deal-52245.

[46] "Gazprom is ready to evaluate the opportunities to transport gas from Syria to Lebanon," *RIA Novosti*, May 2010, https://ria.ru/economy/20100510/232498178.html.

[47] Olgu Okumush, "Some reasons to materials Iran-Iraq-Syria pipeline," *Natural Gas World*, February 2013, https://www.naturalgasworld.com/iran-iraq-and-syria-gas-pipeline.

[48] Oil Price, "Syria Sings first ever offshore oil deal with Russia," *Oil Price*, December 2013, https://oilprice.com/Energy/Energy-General/Syria-Signs-First-Ever-Offshore-Oil-Deal-with-Russia.html.

[49] "A.Miller discussed cooperation in oil and gas sphere with Syrian Ambassador," *Neftegaz*, 2016 https://neftegaz.ru/news/view/145945-A.-Miller-obsudil-s-chrezvychaynym-poslom-Sirii-R.-Haddada-sotrudnichestvo-v-neftegazovoy-sfere.

[50] "Russia and Syria discussed cooperation in oil and gas industry," *Neftegaz*, February 2016, https://neftegaz.ru/news/view/141522-Rossiya-i-Siriya-obsudili-sotrudnichestvo-v-neftegazovoy-otrasli.

[51] Evgeny Kalyukov, "G.Timchenko's company to complete the construction of the gas refinery in Syria," *RBK*, February 2017, https://www.rbc.ru/business/20/12/2017/5a3a1c4a9a79472cf27f7602.

10. Russia's Financial Tactics in the Middle East

Theodore Karasik

Summary

Russia's strategy to build a greater presence in the Middle East and North Africa (MENA) region, and specifically the Persian Gulf, by using finance to influence geopolitics has become an integral part of Putin's foreign policy.

Since 2007, Russia has increasingly focused on financial tactics to achieve its strategic policy goals in the Middle East. This "soft power" links Russia to the Middle East in new and creative ways, a trend that has continued without letup since Russian President Vladimir Putin visited the region twice 10 years ago. These financial ties are both formal and informal: public transactions but also gray zones of monetary interaction between Russia and Arab states that are illustrative of a far more robust set of monetary connections than recognized by policymakers and analysts.

Middle Eastern states are an attractive market for Russian state-owned and private companies, such as Stroitransgaz, Rosneft, LUKOIL Overseas Holding Ltd., Russian Railways, Magnitogorsk Metallurgical Factory, Hydromashservice, Technopromexport, KAMAZ and Russian Helicopters. ROSTEC and other defense and aviation companies are also making inroads. It should be noted that Russian small and medium enterprises, too, contribute to trade and economic cooperation with many of the MENA countries. Russia's industrial giants are able to compete for project tenders at reasonable prices against other competitors despite Russia's flagging economic performance and increasingly strong Western sanctions against Moscow that may or, may not, be working.

Since 2007, these Russian tactics are:

- Creating a "north–south" corridor of economic connections based on a confluence of Russia's historical and cultural drive to achieve a rightful place in the Middle East;
- Pushing connectivity through soft power instruments such as "Roadshows" but also through Russian business councils activity;
- Signing Russia-Arab finance agreements, especially between Sovereign Wealth Funds (SWFs) and other Gulf Arab government–owned investment vehicles;
- Printing currency for distribution in Middle East war zones.

Russia's ability to use finance as a tactic is new to the Kremlin's arsenal, with most of the financial activity occurring in the Persian Gulf states. The Russian goal is to build greater ties between the Middle East and Russia-dominated Eurasia, despite a history of some bad deals during the global financial crisis. Russia sees the utility in being contractually tied to Arab funds given that the Russian SWF's parent, Vnesheconombank (VEB), has been under US sanctions since 2015.[1] Russia's financial tactics in the Middle East undermine US foreign policy by manipulating local economies with the aim of winning the hearts and minds of civil servants, soldiers and state employees in Arab lands supported by Moscow.

Thus, Russia's desire to have a greater presence in the MENA region and specifically the Gulf is a critical part of Putin's foreign policy in terms of finance and influencing geopolitics.

Introduction

Russia's characterization of the West as immoral and corrupt as well as its dismissals of Western styles of democracy resonate with Arab leaders, who see Russia's approach as correct since they believe strong governance is required in today's Middle East. Thus, Russia's moral vision involving "spiritual sovereignty," great national wealth in strategic minerals and energy, plus Moscow's relationship with China and the rest of the Far East appeal to Arab authorities and businessmen.[2]

The Russian Federation is building robust financial ties with key Arab states, and probing others for future investment opportunities. Russia's goal is to build on the goodwill of the Gulf States in various business sectors, thereby building geopolitical advantage that elicits Arab cooperation, for Russia to enter into other areas of the Middle East as a strategic partner.[3] The development of a "north–south corridor" based on finance and politics, initiated by Putin in 2007 and since grown, plays an important part in linking the two regions.[4] The north–south corridor is a strategic reality that allows Russia's relationship with Arab states to serve as a jumping off point for Russian economic initiatives in Africa and the global South.[5] Despite Russia's domestic economic woes, the Kremlin's financial tactics aimed at the Middle East seem well grounded.

On the flip side, Arab Sovereign Wealth Funds (SWF) are engaged in receiving their own political dividends from Russia that appear to be tied directly to the immediate future of the Levant and other warzones. Gulf SWFs are looking for help from Moscow to power the region's reconstruction. A "Grozny Plan" or an "Arab Marshall Plan" to rebuild the region's shattered cities would join Russia with Middle East states in ways that would encourage new geostrategic realities.[6]

Russia's Emerging Financial Approach to the Persian Gulf

In 2007, two drivers were noticeable between Russia and the Persian Gulf states. The driver is the north–south corridor between the Gulf and Russia. This is historical in nature—going back through the Soviet era to Imperial Russia—and has implications for the current and future relations between the regions. The second driver is in the political and economic sphere. When Vladimir Putin visited Saudi Arabia, Qatar and Jordan in early 2007, it was the first visit of a Russian president to these countries.

In a second trip to the region in September 2007, Putin, accompanied by the heads of Rosoboronexport, Aeroflot and Roskosmos, visited the United Arab Emirates (UAE), where economic, cultural, and military deals were signed—including for Arab access to Russia's space launch facilities in Kazakhstan—and a foundation stone was laid for the Arabian Peninsula's first Russian Orthodox church in Sharjah.[7] The establishment of a Russian Orthodox Church in the conservative emirate holds special significance for the current status of Russo-Islamic relations by building on Emirati concepts of tolerance. A second Russian Orthodox Church is now open in Abu Dhabi. The collection of alms is part of church operations and is allowed by UAE authorities.

Putin's visits in 2007 were a masterstroke for Russia. His trip to the UAE accelerated Moscow's interest in bidding for—and winning—energy projects. For example, in July 2008, Stroytransgaz won a $418 million contract to build a gas pipeline from Abu Dhabi to Fujairah. And the traffic is two-way. At the time, UAE investments in Russia totaled about $3.5 billion dollars, mostly equity in state and private companies, but several businesses in the UAE are investigating further ventures in Russia. Dubai World, for instance, is looking at ports, logistics and infrastructure investments, while Limitless, Dubai World's real estate arm, is building more than 150,000 homes in Russia.[8] Russia was moving from a bilateral relationship with the UAE based solely on shuttle trade and tourism to inter-state relations at the highest levels of government.

In the wake of Putin's visit to the Gulf region in 2007, Russia began to use its financial might to launch two different, successive tactics for Russian investment into the Gulf States.[9]

A key tool used by Russia to build local connections was "The Roadshow." The Roadshow concept brought Russian business leaders to the Gulf, and specifically to the UAE. These events attracted wealthy Russian investors into the Dubai property market, which at that time was valued at $1.5 billion.[10] One result of interactions in Russia's Roadshow concept was Russia becoming active in Iraq's oil sector through the training of Iraqi technicians.[11]

The Roadshow was augmented by meetings of the Russia-Arab Business Council (RABC) and the Russia Business Council, Dubai (RBC-Dubai). The RABC—naturally—was founded by Yevgeny Primakov when he served as chairman of the Russian Chamber of Commerce and Industry (CCI) a few years prior to the Roadshow effort, with up to 12 individual councils across MENA. Primakov's vision for the MENA region is instituted in the RABC's mission as part of a soft power outreach to major UAE and other GCC authorities.[12] Both the RABC and the RBC-Dubai held key meetings of business leaders not only in the UAE but also in Iraq, Egypt and other MENA countries. At these meetings, discussion involved ways to improve the investment climate between Russia and MENA in areas such as commercial aviation, real estate, banking, and general trade. Moscow-based officials from the Ministry of Trade frequently visited these meetings specifically to float ideas about how Russia and Arab states can cooperate better together. Support for the RABC and the RBC-Dubai came from a combination of sources, including respective Russian embassies but also local Russian expatriates. Gulf businessmen were interested in opportunities in Russia with favorable conditions guaranteed for easy market entry.[13]

The onset of the global economic crisis led to a retreat for Russia's push in MENA. Russian Railways' bid to be part of Saudi Arabia's "land-bridge" project failed but succeeded in having a Lukoil subsidiary operating in the eastern province. Moscow also wanted to discuss a gas suppliers' equivalent of OPEC—a "Gaspec"—between Qatar, Russia and Iran. However, the idea failed due to a number of political and economic factors, including the fact that all parties did not trust each other.

Russian businesses were eager to benefit from the innovative opportunities available in the Gulf—where infrastructure and industrial projects are estimated to be worth more than $2 trillion by 2020. Again, Moscow was set back by economic conditions globally but also in Russia itself. A preliminary deal was to have Dubai's SWF, Dubai World,[14] invest up to $5 billion in the Russian energy concern OGK-1. But the deal broke down due to poor market conditions, according to Russia Direct Investment Fund (RDIF), Russia's SWF.[15] The opportunity for an SWF purchase of a Russian energy operation was premature.

Russia and Gulf States Move Into Sovereign Wealth Funds

The OGK-1 case represents what later became one of Russia's primary approaches to large-scale financial investment deals between the Gulf States and the RDIF. Despite the low price of oil, both Russia and wealthy Arab states with sovereign monies, are beginning to seek new, unique, large-scale, high return investments for political purposes. These emerging relationships are opening a new chapter in to the conduct of countries with large sovereign national assets as a tool to gain access to other markets that were unreachable just a few years ago.

Russia's development of ties with Middle East states based on interactions with their SWFs has become an important part of the Kremlin's tool box. SWFs, besides being state-owned entities, are used as a political tool by their governments to achieve geopolitical and strategic advances. The activities of Saudi Arabia's Public Investment Fund (PIF), the Qatar Investment Authority (QIA), and the UAE's Abu Dhabi Investment Authority (ADIA) investment vehicle, Mubadala, all serve as good examples of this.[16]

Now, the Gulf states are using their economic strength to flex their political muscle, in order to invest in Russia at a time when Moscow's embattled economy is struggling with low oil prices. Investments by Saudi Arabia, the UAE and Qatar into the RDIF reaches well into the tens of billions of dollars, although the actual amount of money delivered via Memorandums of Intent (MoI) vs Memorandums of Understanding (MoU) is unknown; the distinctions are important in terms of any payments to lock in terms.[17] All three GCC states are using investments as a political tool to gain leverage over Moscow by investing in Russia through their SWFs.[18]

Qatar

Qatar's SWF activity is probably the most advanced of any Arab state, a function of Doha's craftiness and Russia's requirements to influence Gulf politics. Doha is using its financial muscle to woo Moscow in a bid to regain lost political influence in the Syrian conflict and the broader Middle East.[19] Qatar's Emir Sheikh Tamim bin Hamad al-Thani visited Russia in January 2017 to address Middle Eastern geopolitics and energy issues. Tamim stated, "Russia plays a leading role in stability in the world," while Putin said, "Qatar is an important component of the situation in the Middle East and the Gulf." Tamim's visit was to achieve an equilibrium between actions in the Levant and

Qatar's energy influence via its liquefied natural gas (LNG) exports, while Putin knew that Doha was ready to negotiate on the outcome of several regional conflicts.

From Doha's point of view, the Qataris are attempting to leverage their investment portfolio with Moscow by flexing their country's wealth. Qatar is a useful partner for Russia regarding alternative sources of financing and investment, and has used its large SWF to obtain political influence with the Kremlin by investing in Russia. The Qatari Investment Authority (QIA) is worth $335 billion in global assets, as of the June 2017 Qatar crisis, making it the 14th largest in the world.[20] Through three main investments, the QIA now has over $2.5 billion worth of assets in Russia.[21]

In 2013, the QIA purchased a $500 million stake in VTB, a Russian bank sanctioned by the West.[22] That year, the QIA's CEO, Hamad bin Jassim bin Jaber al-Thani, became a board member of the RDIF. In October 2016, the QIA made its second Russian investment to become a 25 percent stakeholder in St. Petersburg's Pulkovo airport.[23]

Factors driving Qatari investment in Russia sought political leverage in the regional geopolitical environment. Doha saw Russia as a way to voice unhappiness about Bashar al-Assad while supporting various groups in the jihadist opposition.[24] The Qataris recognized that Doha's network of Syrian rebels is unable to achieve its objective. As the Syrian Civil War draws to a close, Doha needs Moscow more than ever due to the Qatar Crisis. Doha is finding itself thrust into the Russia/Iran/Turkey camp on Syria by Saudi/UAE actions via the Anti-Terrorism Quartet (ATQ) made up of Bahrain, Egypt, Kuwait, Saudi Arabia, and the UAE. This development is a net positive because the reconstruction of Syria is set to be a lucrative and politically-charged process.

Thus, Qatar's deals with Moscow through investments in Rosneft give Doha a better bargaining position across the Arab world as the Emirate's political investments in Cairo and in Field Marshall Khalifa Haftar's Libya have produced diminishing returns.[25] Now, Qatar is employing the unique political tool that is its SWF to influence the Syrian endgame. Qatar is hoping its SWF activity will achieve positive results on the ground in Syria, which Doha has thus far failed to secure during the civil war.

Saudi Arabia

Until 2013, the RDIF had established partnerships with Western sovereign funds. But Russia's political stand-off with the West over Ukraine has made US and European funds cautious about teaming up with a Russian state-backed entity that may eventually be sanctioned. Since then, the Russian fund's new partnerships have been dominated by entities in Asia and the Middle East.

With the war raging in Syria, Saudi Arabia's sovereign wealth fund agreed to invest $10 billion in Russia in 2015, in a powerful sign of the rapprochement between Moscow and Riyadh to discuss regional issues.[26] The passing of King Abdullah and the accession to the throne of King Salman in January 2015 opened a new relationship between the Kremlin and the Kingdom.

Then–Deputy Crown Prince Mohammed bin Salman (widely referred to as MBS) traveled to the St. Petersburg Economic Forum, where discussion over investment ideas were first broached between the Kingdom and the Kremlin. The RDIF CEO Kirill Dmitriev said that, "The first seven projects have received preliminary approval, and we expect to close ten deals before the end of the year," apparently in reference to infrastructure and food security projects.[27] Importantly, the RDIF's campaign to attract Saudi investment began in 2014, illustrating Russia's persistent determination to convince Saudi Arabia to give Moscow $10 billion.

With King Salman's visit to Moscow in 2017, the links between the RDIF and Saudi Arabia's SWF—the Public Investment Fund (PIF)—became clearer. Russia and Saudi Arabia established a $1 billion fund to invest in technology and innovation and another $1 billion fund to invest in energy projects, including Saudi investment in Russian toll roads that are coming out of the PIF fund too. The Russians are to invest in Saudi projects linked to infrastructure, retail, logistics and agriculture over a period of up to five years, and the Saudi investment vehicle would invest together with other foreign sovereign wealth funds mostly from Asia, including the Russia-China Investment Fund, a two-billion-dollar vehicle backed by the China Investment Corporation and the RDIF.[28] The Russian sovereign fund also agreed to invest jointly with the Saudi Arabian General Investment Authority (SAGIA) in projects in Saudi Arabia and other Middle Eastern countries. The PIF's commitment adds to earlier pledges from Asian and Middle Eastern sovereign wealth funds to invest in Russia.

A key goal is to open the Arctic to PIF investment. Saudi Arabia sees Arctic resources as a necessary potential strategic and economic opportunity. Security factors are also in play: Riyadh is concerned about what will happen next in what can be termed a "pivot to the north policy" over Arctic energy extraction and transit as part of a hedging strategy. To be sure, the PIF's actions in Russia cannot be taken as an isolated event. Arab Gulf States have opportunities for their SWFs to invest in the Arctic region. Forward-leaning SWFs, such as the UAE's Mubadala, already work with Russia and Norway. The QIA is investing in Rosneft and the RDIF for Arctic projects. It serves the Arab Gulf states interests to make investments in Arctic countries, which have contributed both resources and guidance to the Arabian Peninsula states across a number of spheres from finance to security.[29]

Both the PIF and the RDIF agreed to collaborate on two new platforms to invest in Russian energy services and technology sectors.[30] The RDIF's Dmitriev said, "Thanks to the team at Saudi Aramco, the world's largest oil producer, the platform will be able to help portfolio companies enter new markets. Our Saudi partners highly value the development potential of leading Russian energy companies, and the Russian energy sector can benefit from their expertise to further cooperate in the Middle East."[31] In addition, the PIF and the RDIF are to focus on IT-sector opportunities, including big data, digital infrastructure and e-commerce. The two funds are also evaluating investment prospects in retail, real estate, transportation and logistics infrastructure. The intent, from the Russian point of view as articulated by the RDIF's CEO, is for Russian high-tech companies to deliver to the Kingdom innovative solutions specifically designed for Saudi Arabia's efforts to achieve fourth industrial revolution status.[32]

From the Russian side, the RDIF is supporting the Russian Export Center (REC). Headed by Petr Fradkov, the ambitious son of former foreign intelligence (SVR) chief and current CEO of Almaz-Antei Corporation Mikhail Fradkov, the REC is working with the PIF to coordinate the entry of Russian companies into the Saudi market in energy and strategic minerals; two dozen such companies have already establishing their presence in the Kingdom.[33] Fradkov's REC operations throughout the MENA region are facilitating the entry of Russian high-end products in IT and communications, in addition to supply chain support.[34]

MBS's determination to bring Saudi Arabia into a new era is attracting Russian investment. Russia's interest in Saudi Arabia's NEOM Project—a planned futuristic transnational free trade zone based on Artificial Intelligence (AI) and robotics—is a case in point. In October 2017, Saudi Arabia's PIF, hosted the Future Investment Initiative, at which MBS unveiled his country's plans to build a 10,230-square-mile business and industrial zone that would link with Jordan and Egypt through energy and water, biotechnology, food, advanced manufacturing and entertainment industries. The project is to be the first trans-boundary free trade zone, which will represent new opportunities for both Egypt and Jordan, two of Russia's partners in the region.[35] The NEOM project will be backed by more than $500 billion from the Saudi government, the PIF, and local and international investors. RDIF CEO Dimitriev immediately pledged "several billion dollars" to the project.[36] NEOM is ambitious, transformative and potentially lucrative.

Saudi Arabia sees Russia's SWF as a way to bring Moscow into a relationship that helps to make the Kremlin a partner in areas necessary to the joint interests of both countries in terms of security, energy and innovation. In turn, the Kremlin sees Saudi Arabia as the key to its planting deep roots in the Kingdom's Vision 2030 strategic development plan.

UAE

In 2013, Abu Dhabi established with the RDIF a $3 billion fund to develop infrastructure in Russia's south, with Mubadala investing in Russia's agricultural sector.[37] Simultaneously, Russia seeks to build an air hub in the UAE to deliver aid and knowledge transfer to Africa. This facility is to act as a bridge to Africa, where Russia, with its extensive air cargo-carrying capabilities, can help develop infrastructure and provide health services in areas affected by conflict and famine.[38] It is interesting to note that Russia and the UAE, through Mubadala, are cooperating to build a $750 million airport in Cuba, as well as redeveloping a port and building a railway line in the Caribbean country.[39] Ties between the UAE and Russia are robust thanks to inter-SWF investment and well-developed in terms of geopolitical and economic engagement. These look to continue, with many plans for productive collaboration.[40]

In the UAE case, Russia's SWF is making agreements in Abu Dhabi's defense sector. The RDIF has formed a consortium with Abu Dhabi to finalize a deal to acquire a minority stake in Russian Helicopters, which is part of the Rostec State Corporation.[41] Rostec is a Russian company created in 2007 to promote development, production, and export of high-tech industrial products for civil and military purposes. It is comprised of over 700 organizations, and its portfolio includes brands such as the Russian car-maker Avtovaz, the truck-maker Kamaz, the arms manufacturer Kalashnikov Concern, Russian Helicopters, and the world's largest titanium producer, VSMPO-Avisma, among others.[42]

The transaction consists of two stages.[43] The first involves the sale of a 12 percent stake and an investment of $300 million, as well as an agreed-upon subsequent potential increase to $600 million.[44] The deal will help the company to implement its strategy and business plan, including the development of new types of helicopters. The company's range of helicopters includes light-lift models such as the Ansat GMSU 2 and the Ka-226T.[45]

Russia's military offerings to the UAE include the Mi-28 rotor-wing attack aircraft. RFID CEO Dmitriev said, "The RDIF consortium's investment in Russian Helicopters will enable the company to continue its expansion into new markets, particularly in the Middle East, thanks to the participation of our partners from the region."[46] Sergei Chemezov, chief executive of Rostec, said the company's value is estimated at more than $2 billion: "Today we have agreed with the [RFID] and Middle East investors, on the final parameters of the deal and signed documents for the sale of a minority stake in Russian Helicopters, based on the valuation of the company at $2.35 billion."[47]

At the time, the UAE launched an alternative investment approach to Russia's. Under the Abu Dhabi Investment Authority (ADIA), the UAE's parent SWF, there are dozens of multi-billion dollar companies, including International Golden Group (IGG) and Royal Group. These companies conduct UAE foreign policy in what can be called "a backchannel."[48] Both IGG and Royal Group made substantial investments in Chechnya during the reconstruction phase of the Russian republic, "and thanks to Emirati generosity, [the Chechen capital of] Grozny now looks like Dubai," according to a senior Emirati official's remarks to the author in 2015.[49]

Out of all the Gulf states, the UAE sees a special utility in investing in Chechnya, which is now helping out in Syria and Libya with counterterrorism and constabulary responsibilities in the former and negotiations with the city of Misrata for an overall Libyan settlement in the latter.[50] Thus, the political dividend from an SWF investment is fully revealed. In the early days of the Arab Spring, the Royal Group, a subsidiary of the ADIA, began to invest in Grozny.[51] Chechen President Ramzan Kadyrov and the president of Royal Group, Sheikh Tahnoon Bin Zayed Al Nahyan, meet on a regular basis.[52] Chechnya also receives sizable payments annually from UAE foundations such as the President Khalifa Foundation, which donates to construction projects in Grozny.[53] For the Emiratis, the Moscow-Grozny relationship represents a good opportunity. For the Russians, the Abu Dhabi–Dubai relationship gives a menu of options for Moscow, which is quite familiar with the UAE's internal politics and financial sector.

Russia's relationship with Dubai is different than with Abu Dhabi. Dubai has a number investment vehicles investing in Russia tied to the emirate's core sovereign fund, Dubai Holdings. Under this entity, DP World is now investing in Vladivostok to enhance the port's capacity, and Dubai Multi Commodities Centre (DMCC) is exploring investing in strategic minerals extraction for export from Russia through this key Pacific Ocean maritime outlet.[54] Russia, as a major player in the strategic minerals market, uses diamond and gold markets effectively for leverage in other political arenas, specifically in Israeli and South Africa.[55] Russian and Emirati interests converge from the Arctic to Africa in the growth of global requirements for strategic minerals.[56] In December 2017, REC CEO Petr Frolov established a Skolkovo Foundation IT cluster in Dubai. Seven Russian hi-tech companies working in areas including infrastructure security, cybersecurity, artificial intelligence, 3D modeling and automated industry have already committed to having a permanent presence at the hub. Frolov's relationship with Dubai government officials related to innovation and fourth industrial revolution technologies helps to marry Russia's tech industry with Dubai's innovation hub concept and financial backing.[57]

Both Abu Dhabi and Dubai have interests that are complimentary and competitive through their use of SWFs. For Russia, the competition is welcomed, given the boost the UAE's investments provide for current and future bilateral financial relations. Moscow sees Abu Dhabi as a gateway to achieve Russia's strategic plans in the region. Notably, Russia's relationship with the UAE has allowed for Chechnya's growing role in the Levant and Libya. Chechen President Ramzan Kadyrov's strong relationship with Gulf monarchs, specifically with the UAE, plays an important role in bringing Moscow closer to Arab states as a result of UAE SWF activity.

Russia's Currency Tactics

Russia's tactic of printing currency for the region's warzones helps to establish Moscow not only as a reliable partner with the receiver but also links Russia to that country's future economy. Undoubtedly, Russia seeks to prop up governments in times of state failure.

GOZNAK Joint Stock Company, which is owned 100 percent by the Russian government, prints these currencies.[58] GOZNAK also prints money for Lebanon Guatemala, Rwanda and Angola, among others. Russia's printing money for Middle Eastern governments under duress allows additional political and military influence in the countries in question. GOZNAK operates under Russia's Ministry of Finance (MINFIN).[59] Thus Russia's MINFIN plays an important foreign policy role in MENA, using currency as a tool.

Russia is printing money for Syria, Libya and Yemen to achieve a solid presence on the ground in these complex civil wars. In each case,

Russia plays a critical role in introducing new currency into war theaters. These currencies are difficult to duplicate and launder due to the high quality of security (thread, banding) in GOZNAK's products.

In Syria, Russia began to print currency for the al-Assad regime in 2012 in order to pay Damascus' two million civil servants.[60] The currency, according to Syrian bankers, entered circulation because the civil war interrupted traditional government revenues.[61] Under Russian Ministry of Finance supervision, the production of currency from GOZNAK went through a logistic chain of both Syrian and Russian cargo carriers that transported over 200 tons of currency in a ten-week period to the Syrian government with a continuous flow of currency as needed to prop up the Syrian economy.[62] It should be noted that US and European sanctions forbid the printing of Syrian currency, and thus Damascus turned to Russia and GOZNAK for its currency requirements.[63] Syrian Deputy Prime Minister for Economic Affairs Qadr Jamil called the currency deal with Russia a "triumph" over sanctions.[64]

In Libya, Russia's GOZNAK is providing Libyan Marshal Khalifa Haftar as well as the government in Tobruk (the House of Representatives, HOR), with fresh Libyan banknotes.[65] Less than two years ago, GOZNAK printed 20- and 40-dinar denominations for circulation in Libya, which were transported by Russian cargo craft. However, with the complex civil war in Libya, the government in Tripoli, did not recognize the validity of the over 4 billion dinar Russian-made banknotes.[66] This fact led to a financial dichotomy in Libya that helped to boost the morale of Tobruk at the expense of Tripoli, which prints its money in Britain thereby making it subject to London's jurisdiction.

The fresh banknotes from Russia are intended to support Haftar and the Tobruk government. Additional deliveries from Russia to the Labraq Airbase of 20-dinar notes occurred on several occasions.[67]

Interestingly, the banknotes helped to break the jihadist financial networks in and around Benghazi and Sirte by reducing the ability of extremists to use cash transactions as Jihadists were using older dominations.[68] In addition, the banknotes also became a useful tool for winning hearts and minds in Libya's east and south, when fresh dinars were distributed before Islamic holidays, especially Ramadan.[69] In this manner, Russia is able to use currency as a tool to build influence with Libya's Tobruk government.

Yemen is beset by a severe shortage of cash since the internationally recognized government relocated the headquarters of the Central Bank to Aden in September 2016 in order to stop the Houthis in Saana from plundering the bank's reserves.[70] The first cargo carrier to bring GOZNAK-minted royals arrived in June 2017.[71] Russia's GOZNAK is supplying the Aden government with 400 billion Yemeni royals to pay salaries for the army and security forces.[72] Yemen's internationally recognized leader, President Abd Rabbuh Mansur Hadi, is an old friend of Moscow's, dating to Hadi's history in the country's south when Yemen was two states, one supported by the Soviet Union. Hadi, who is beholden to Saudi Arabia and the UAE, is seeking a solution to the country's complicated civil war. Just as in Syria, Russia is gaining leverage in Aden by coming to Hadi's rescue, which is under sanctions by both Riyadh and Abu Dhabi.[73]

Overall, whether in Syria, Libya or in Yemen, Russia provides currency for these governments to stay afloat and to continue financing their respective efforts at governance and security. Russia uses currency as a tool to influence local economic conditions, curry favor with local elites, and win the hearts of minds of locals who see hope when receiving salaries or gifts of shiny new banknotes.

Conclusion

For Russia, the Kremlin sees its historical mission coming to fruition in the MENA region, where it is using financial tools that are helping to guide these states firmly within Moscow's orbit and influence. The Kremlin's move is smart and timely. The status and prospects for Arab-Russian bilateral relationships are growing, and both the Arab states and the Kremlin are expanding their financial connectivity. The United States needs to pay closer attention to Russia's financial tactics in the Middle East in order to gauge Moscow's successes and failures over the coming years.

The growing financial cooperation and interconnectivity between Russia and Arab Middle East states raises a number of troubling questions. To what extent are Arabian Peninsula states enabling Russian foreign objectives? What is the impact of Russia's financial tactics on the interests of American allies in the Middle East? How do these activities affect their relations with the US? How do Asian countries, and specifically their SWFs, interact with Arab SWFs that conduct business with Moscow? Is there a triangulation effect ongoing that shifts the geo-economic center of global economics eastward?

Russia's ability to use finance as a tactic is new to the Kremlin's arsenal, with most of the financial activity seen in the Persian Gulf states. The goal is to build greater ties between the two regions. Arab states that are open to and engaging with Russia's financial tactics are enabling Moscow to further cement itself in Middle Eastern affairs. America's Gulf allies are conducting business with Russia, a country that sees itself on a historical mission.

Overall, Russia's financial tactics in the Middle East undermine US foreign policy and are contributing to an unhealthy financial environment for the United States by manipulating local economies in order to win the hearts and minds of civilians but also of the civil servants, soldiers and employees of the states supported by Moscow in the region. Russia's use of finance to build a presence in the MENA region and specifically the Gulf is a critical part of Putin's foreign policy. The US would be wise to track these developments and assess their implications for Washington's foreign security strategy.

ENDNOTES

[1] "US Treasury Sanctions Russian Direct Investment Fund," undated, https://www.swfinstitute.org/swf-news/u-s-treasury-sanctions-russian-direct-investment-fund/.

[2] *Shehab Al-Makahleh* "The Arab View of Russia's Role in the MENA: Changing Arab Perceptions of Russia, and the Implications for US Policy," The Jamestown Foundation, October 2017, https://jamestown.org/program/arab-view-russias-role-mena-changing-arab-perceptions-russia-implications-us-policy/.

[3] Theodore Karasik, "Russia looks to strengthen its links with the Gulf," *The National*, November 13, 2008, https://www.thenational.ae/russia-looks-to-strengthen-its-links-with-the-gulf-1.504200.

[4] Interviews with Russian Embassy–Abu Dhabi and participation in the Dubai-based UAE-Russia Business Council functions and events, 2012–2016. It should be noted that a major theme for several meetings was how BRICS fits into the UAE hub strategy for supply chain trade. The focus of BRICS was on strategic minerals and energy given the interests of each member of the trans-regional economic bloc.

[5] Russia is to set up a logistics hub in Al-Ain, in the UAE, for cargo going to Africa and South Asia, according to the Russian Embassy in the UAE. Interviews in UAE, 2015–2016. In addition, Russia's ability to sign mil-mil and energy contracts with Nigeria, Niger, Chad and Sudan in October–November 2017 shows how quickly Moscow is moving into key areas of African instability. See Theodore Karasik and Gorgio Cafiero, "Why does Vladimir Putin Care about Sudan?" *The New Atlanticist*, November 27, 2017, http://www.atlanticcouncil.org/blogs/new-atlanticist/why-does-vladimir-putin-care-about-sudan.

[6] Bethany Allen-Ebrahimian, "Syrian Reconstruction Spells Juicy Contracts for Russian, Iranian Firms" *Foreign Policy*, October 20, 2017, http://foreignpolicy.com/2017/10/20/syrian-reconstruction-spells-juicy-contracts-for-russian-iranian-firms-china-civil-war/.

[7] "Russian Orthodox Church Opens in Sharjah," via https://www.unian.info/world/532159-russian-orthodox-church-opened-in-uae.html.

[8] Karasik, op. cit.

[9] Ibid.

[10] Ibid.

[11] Interviews, Abu Dhabi, 2009.

[12] Russia-Arab Business Council website, http://www.russarabbc.ru/en/about/.

[13] Observations by the author while in the UAE, 2004–2008.

[14] Dubai World Offers $5.34 Billion for OGK-1, June 30, 2008, https://dealbook.nytimes.com/2008/06/30/dubai-world-offers-534-billion-for-ogk-1/.

[15] Simon Shuster, "Russia's OGK-1 says Dubai World not only bidder," *Reuters*, August, 7, 2008, https://www.reuters.com/article/us-ogk1-buyer/russias-ogk-1-says-dubai-world-not-only-bidder-idUSL0727371020080707.

[16] Leone Lakhani, "Russia-Gulf States Relationship of Convenience," *The Cipher Brief*, March 7, 2017, https://www.thecipherbrief.com/russia-gulf-arab-states-a-relationship-of-convenience.

[17] Interviews with Abu Dhabi and Dubai officials, 2016–2017.

[18] Ibid.

[19] Theodore Karasik, "Why is Qatar Investing so much in Russia?" Middle East Institute, March 8, 2017, http://www.mei.edu/content/article/why-qatar-investing-so-much-russia.

[20] Mohammed Sergie, "The Tiny Gulf Country With a $335 Billion Global Empire," *Bloomberg*, January 11, 2017, https://www.bloomberg.com/news/articles/2017-01-11/qatar-sovereign-wealth-fund-s-335-global-empire.

[21] "Qatar Investment Authority said to seek further $2bn deal with Russia," *Arabian Business*, January 26, 2017, http://www.arabianbusiness.com/qatar-investment-authority-said-seek-further-2bn-deal-with-russia-660984.html.

[22] "Mezhgosudarstvennyye otnosheniya Rossii i Katara," *RIA Novosti*, January 18, 2016, https://ria.ru/spravka/20160118/1360222882.html.

[23] "Qatar Investment Authority Completes Largest Single Privatization Sale in Russian Federation History," January 6, 2017, https://www.clearygottlieb.com/news-and-insights/news-listing/qatar-investment-authority-completes-largest-single-privatization-sale-in-russian-federation-history.

[24] Aurangzeb Qureshi, "The Qatar-Russia energy deal that might lead the way to peace in Syria," Middle East Eye, December 22, 2016, http://www.middleeasteye.net/columns/can-qatar-russia-energy-ties-translate-peace-syria-1234735369.

[25] Ibid.

[26] Kathrin Hill, "Saudi sovereign fund to invest $10bn in Russia," *Financial Times*, July 6, 2015, https://www.ft.com/content/0205a0d6-2412-11e5-bd83-71cb60e8f08c.

[27] Ibid.

[28] Ibid.

[29] Theodore Karasik and Alexander Murinson, "The Pivot to the Arctic: Implications for the Gulf Cooperation Counci,l" *Syria Deeply*, March 27, 2017, https://www.newsdeeply.com/arctic/community/2017/03/27/the-pivot-to-the-arctic-implications-for-the-gulf-cooperation-council.

[30] Sophie Baker, "Russia, Saudi Arabia sovereign wealth funds create fund to invest in Russian energy, technology," October 5, 2017, http://www.pionline.com/article/20171005/ONLINE/171009872/russia-saudi-arabia-sovereign-wealth-funds-create-fund-to-invest-in-russian-energy-technology.

[31] Ibid.

[32] Ibid.

[33] "REC will help Russian companies to localize production in Saudi Arabia," October 25, 2017, https://chelorg.com/2017/10/25/rec-will-help-russian-companies-to-localize-production-in-saudi-arabia/.

[34] "Petr Fradkov Speech to GITEX 2017," October 2017, http://gitex2017.expocentr.ru/en/about/welcome/fradkov/.

[35] "Saudi Arabia Just Announced Plans to Build a Mega City That Will Cost $500 Billion," *Bloomberg*, October 24, 2017.

[36] "Russia to Invest Billions of Dollars in Saudi Arabia's Future Megacity," Russia Today, October 26, 2017.

[37] Karasik, op cit (The National)

[38] Ibid.

[39] Ibid.

[40] Ibid.

[41] Chris Nelson, "Idex 2017: Middle East backers to buy stake in Russian Helicopters," *The National*, February 27, 2017, https://www.thenational.ae/business/idex-2017-middle-east-backers-to-buy-stake-in-russian-helicopters-1.28075.

[42] Ibid.

[43] Ibid.

[44] Ibid.

[45] Ibid.

[46] Ibid.

[47] Ibid.

[48] Observations and discussions, Abu Dhabi and Dubai, 2010–2017.

[49] Interviews, Abu Dhabi and Dubai, 2010–2017.

[50] This Chechen activity has been ongoing for over two years. See Theodore Karasik, "Chechnya in the Shadow of Russia's Middle East Strategy," *Al-Arabiya*, October 19, 2015, https://english.alarabiya.net/en/views/news/middle-east/2015/10/19/Chechnya-in-the-shadow-of-Russia-s-Mideast-strategies.html.

[51] Henry Meyer, Zainab Fattah and Ilya Arkhipov, "Royal Group to Invest in Chechnya as Putin Pushes Rebuild" *Bloomberg*, February 21, 2011, https://www.bloomberg.com/news/articles/2011-02-21/abu-dhabi-royal-to-invest-in-chechnya-as-putin-pushes-rebuild.

[52] "'Royal Group' intends to continue to invest in Chechnya," November 26, 2014, http://vestnikkavkaza.net/news/politics/62615.html.

[53] "Fond Chechni i OAE razvivayet islamskoye partnerskoye finansirovaniye," November 23, 2017 https://t.co/5hkWb8sGPJ.

[54] "DP World aims to expand in Russian Far East"JOC.com, December 3, 2017, https://www.joc.com/port-news/international-ports/dp-world-aims-expand-russian-far-east_20170925.html.

[55] This topic is another avenue of Russian financial tactics that deserves additional attention into its implications for US foreign policy. Interviews, Abu Dhabi and Dubai, 2010–2018. See, also, forthcoming, Adam Ereli and Theodore Karasik, "Sovereign Wealth Fund Decision Making: The Influence of Politics and the Dangers of Liability" 2018.

[56] Author observations of relevant planning meetings in UAE, 2012–2016.

[57] Shura Collinson, "Skolkovo and Russian Export Centre to set up innovations hub in UAE," December 4, 2017, http://sk.ru/news/b/news/archive/2017/12/04/skolkovo-and-russian-export-centre-to-set-up-innovations-hub-in-uae.aspx.

[58] Madina Turava, "Unique Manufacturer of Security Printing Products" *Manufacturing Journal*, Vol 4/10, 2015, pp. 15–20, http://www.murgesi.com/murgesi-incorso/images/File/press/ManufacturingJournal.pdf.

[59] Ibid.

[60] Michael B. Kelly, "Russia is printing money for Syria to pay government expenses," *Business Insider*, June 13, 2012, http://www.businessinsider.com/russia-is-printing-money-for-syria-to-pay-government-expenses-2012-6.

[61] Suleiman Al Khalidi, "Exclusive: Syria prints new money as deficit grows: bankers," *Reuters*, June 13, 2012, http://www.reuters.com/article/us-syria-economy-money/exclusive-syria-prints-new-money-as-deficit-grows-bankers-idUSBRE85C0CL20120613?feedType=RSS&feedName=topNews&utm_source=feedburner&utm_medium=feed&utm_campaign=Feed%3A+reuters%2FtopNews+%28News+%2F+US+%2F+Top+News%29.

[62] "Syrian Flight Manifests" via
https://www.documentcloud.org/documents/522212-syrian-flight-manifests.

[63] At the time, Syria's currency was being minted by Oesterreichische Banknoten-und Sicherheitsdruck GmbH, a subsidiary of Austria's Central Bank. See "EU Imposes Sanctions on Iran, Syria," *Los Angeles Times*, October 15, 2012, http://latimesblogs.latimes.com/world_now/2012/10/eu-new-sanctions-iran-syria.html.

[64] Dafna Linzer, Jeff Larson and Michael Grabell "Flight Records Say Russia Sent Syria Tons of Cash," *Pro Publica*, November 26, 2012, https://www.propublica.org/article/flight-records-list-russia-sending-tons-of-cash-to-syria.

[65] "Libya's parallel central bank issues banknotes printed in Russia," May 26, 2014, https://www.rt.com/business/344475-libya-prints-banknotes-russia/.

[66] Ibid.

[67] Ibid.

[68] Interviews in Malta, March–April 2016.

[69] Ibid.

[70] "The arrival of a new batch of printed currency in Russia to Aden," June 1, 2017, http://www.yemenpress.org/yemen/the-arrival-of-a-new-batch-of-printed-currency-in-russia-to-aden.html.

[71] Ibid.

[72] "'Awraq naqdiat matbueat fi rusia tasilu alyaman," *RT Arabic*, September 24, 2017, https://arabic.rt.com/business/900751--سيا-روال-أمو-جديدة-دفقة-وصول/اليمن.

[73] Interviews, Abu Dhabi, 2016–2017.

11. Russia in the Middle East: A New Front in the Information War?

Donald N. Jensen

Summary

Russia uses its information warfare capability as a tactic, especially its *RT Arabic* and *Sputnik* news services, to advance its foreign policy goals in the Middle East: become a great power in the region; reduce the role of the United States; prop up allies such as Bashir al- Assad in Syria, and fight terrorism. Evidence suggests that while Russian media narratives are disseminated broadly in the region by traditional means and online, outside of Syria its impact has been limited. The ability of regional authoritarian governments to control the information their societies receive, cross cutting political pressures, the lack of longstanding ethnic and cultural ties with Russia, and widespread doubts about Russian intentions will make it difficult for Moscow to use information operations as an effective tool should it decide to maintain an enhanced permanent presence in the region.

Introduction

Russian assessments of the international system make it clear that the Kremlin considers the country to be engaged in full-scale information warfare. This is reflected in Russia's latest military doctrine, approved December 2014, comments by public officials, and Moscow's aggressive use of influence operations.[1] The current Russian practice of information warfare combines a number of tried and tested tools of influence with a new embrace of modern technology and capabilities such as the Internet. Some underlying objectives, guiding principles and state activity are broadly recognizable as reinvigorated aspects of subversion campaigns from the Cold War era and earlier. But Russia also has invested hugely in updating the principles of subversion. These new investments cover three main areas: internally and externally focused media with a substantial online presence (RT and Sputnik are the best known); use of social media (especially online discussion boards and comment pages) as a force multiplier to ensure Russian narratives achieve broad reach and penetration, and language skills in order to engage with target audiences on a wide front. The result is a presence in many countries acting in coordination with Moscow-backed media and the Kremlin itself.[2]

Western media organizations were entirely unprepared for a targeted and consistent hostile disinformation campaign organized and resourced at state level. The result was Western shock and awe at the initial Russian approach in the Crimea operation in 2014 and the initial stages of the war in eastern Ukraine. Reports from journalists on the ground there identifying Russian troops did not reach mainstream audiences because editors in their newsrooms were baffled by inexplicable Russian denials. Months later, Western media outlets were still faithfully reporting Russian disinformation as fact, but the realization that they had been subjected to a concerted campaign of subversion was beginning to filter into reporting.

In subsequent months, it became apparent that that the Kremlin was using information operations on a far broader front than just Ukraine. The Kremlin saw information warfare as but one weapon in a wide-ranging arsenal including energy, money, cultural ties, and the Russian Orthodox Church, to be used to serve its foreign policy objectives elsewhere, especially against the United States and its European allies.[3] These goals included reducing the role of the United

States on the continent, weakening NATO and the European Union, disrupting the political processes of the Western democracies, and strengthening Russia's influence in the states along its periphery, often by claiming a "responsibility to protect" ethnic Russians outside the Russian Federation. Although a coordinated strategy to push back has not emerged in the West—either through a multilateral response or by most individual states—there is broad agreement that Moscow's information campaign threatens to undermine open, democratic societies. Western governments and private think tanks have created impressive centers of expertise to examine Russian narratives, the networks by which they are spread, and their impact on target audiences.

Outside Europe and the United States, however, the Kremlin's use of information operations to achieve its foreign policy objectives—especially in Turkey and the Middle East—has scarcely been discussed. The questions such operations raise are vital: do such they resemble such activity elsewhere? What are the differences? What impact have the Kremlin's information activities had on the states in the region? Does Moscow's use of information operations in the Syria conflict resemble those in Ukraine? Relying primarily on extensive Russian- and Arabic-language sources, this paper will argue that Kremlin information activity has played a significant role in consolidating Russia's role as a major player in the region, especially in Syria, but that longstanding geopolitical, cultural and other factors have ensured that the impact of that activity is limited.

Russia's Strategy in the Middle East

In the two years since Moscow's intervention in Syria, the statements of Russian officials suggest the Kremlin intends to be a major player in the region for the foreseeable future. Russia does not appear to have a clear regional strategy, but Moscow's actions indicate it is constantly seeking to improve its short-term economic, military, and political advantages while reducing the short-term advantages of competitors, especially the United States. Nevertheless, the Middle East is less important than Europe and Asia to the Kremlin's national security strategy, as stated in the 2013 and 2016 Russian Ministry of Foreign Affairs Foreign Policy Concept Papers. In both versions, the Middle East is listed near the end of the section on "Regional Priorities," illustrating its relative lower priority in Moscow's worldview.[4]

While the longstanding drivers of Russian policy are constant— prestige, trade and stability—the Kremlin has broadened its interests in recent years. First, Russia promotes its ability to interact with many state and non-state actors in the Middle East.[5] Second, Russia is making a concerted effort to reclaim its role as the arms supplier of choice for Arab governments. Third, the Kremlin seeks to stop the spread of international terrorism into Russia. A reported 3,200 Russian nationals have traveled to Syria or Iraq since 2014, and leaders in Moscow worry about foreign fighter returnees as well as Russians who may have been radicalized by Islamic State propaganda. Finally, Russia seeks to support existing state structures and governments against both external intervention and internal insurrection. Russia equates status quo preservation in the Middle East with reduced terrorist threats, increased transactional opportunities with autocratic states, and reduced US sociocultural influence across the region.[6] Moscow blames the West for the current crisis in the region, a view that aligns with Russian leaders' concerns about "color revolutions" in former Soviet countries and Moscow's global reluctance to accept any potentially unfavorable changes to the status quo. In Syria, Russia has helped President Bashir al-Assad maintain his rule. Although Moscow's military intervention there was an exceptional post–Cold War escalation by Russia that goes against its traditional preference to avoid direct engagement, the intervention is consistent with Russian support for a long-standing ally and Russia's stance against regime change. It also reflects Russia's concern about international terrorism and the defense and expansion of its naval and air bases in Latakia and

Tartus, which are the only significant Russian power projection facilities in the eastern Mediterranean and Middle East.[7]

Despite its successes in the region, several factors work to limit Russian influence, at least for the long term. First, Russia potentially lacks the economic and military power to sustain a long-term strategy. Its economic position also only worsened since the start of the Arab Spring.

In addition to the limitations on what Russia itself can achieve, the Middle East states have the greatest power and agency to determine the viability of any Russian strategy. Those states determine the depth of their relationship with Russia, either enabling or limiting Russian action. Finally, Russia's own contradictory behavior undermines its effectiveness in the region. Although it presents itself as a conservative power in the Middle East, in the near abroad, Russia is disruptive. It has intervened in Ukraine and seeks to destabilize other parts of Europe. These activities undermine the Kremlin's narrative about the importance of state sovereignty and nonintervention. Moscow also cooperate works with Iran, which has intervened across the region, and Russia is cultivating relations with opposition groups in Libya.[8]

Tools of Russian Information Warfare

In order to pursue these objectives, Russia makes extensive used of information operations. It has identified a rich source of material with which to criticize the West, while cultivating sympathetic regional audiences. As with many international broadcasters, the Kremlin supplements news stories produced by a central news operation inside Russia with contributions of local journalists from target states. This programming is disseminated via television, radio and online. Social media's open approach to content—on YouTube and Facebook, for example—has enabled unreliable and highly partisan material to reach large audiences.[9] Limited evidence suggests, however, that in contrast to information operations against the West, the number of attacks by Moscow's troll farms and Russia-sponsored bots in MENA are relatively small.

The Kremlin disseminates news to the Middle East through two prime channels: *RT Arabic* and the *Sputnik News Service.*

RT Arabic, formerly known as *Rusiya Al-Yaum* (Arabic: روسيا اليوم, meaning *Russia Today*, also called Россия сегодня *Rossiya segodnya* in Russian) is a Russian TV news channel broadcasting in Arabic and headquartered in Moscow. *RT Arabic* started broadcasting on May 4, 2007. It has steadily increased in importance to official Moscow since the Arab Spring and Russia's intervention in Syria in 2015. The channel covers a wide variety of events worldwide from the point of view of the Russian government. It features interviews, debates and stories about cultural life in Russia, as well as developments in the Arab world. At present, people from the Middle East, North Africa and Europe have open access to the satellite signal of the channel. The channel can also be watched on the Internet all over the world. As of November 2012, it also became available on myTV, a technology platform that streams Arabic-language *TV* channels to North/South America and Australia. RT Arabic has correspondents in Lebanon, Palestine, Iraq, Egypt, Israel, the United Kingdom and the United States.

RT Arabic Programs include:

- **Panorama**, a weekly round-table discussion, where various topics are covered;
- **Person**, a 26-minute prime-time program that features interesting people with unique knowledge, experience and qualifications in the political, cultural and other fields;

- *Zoom*, a weekly edition covering current or unusual events, featuring public personalities or ordinary people in extraordinary situations;
- *Weekly Report*—26-minute news and analysis program that covers main political events over the previous seven days;
- *Press Review*—3-minute feature, four times a day, which introduces Arab viewers to interesting items in the Russian and foreign press, with special attention paid to Russian-Arab relations;
- *Documentaries*, a selection of documentaries designed to open new horizons and bring viewers facts about Russia.
- *RT Online*, a new interactive project that will provide live news to social networks users.[10]

The newer **Sputnik Arabic News Service** provides coverage of "the most important international events and opinions that many other media sources do not report," by email, FTP-server and though its online news terminal. Sputnik's correspondent network includes over 80 journalists in more than 50 countries around the world. Its newswriters are native Arabic speakers. The newswire is operated from two locations—Moscow and Cairo. News coverage is 24 hours/day, 7 days/week. Content includes breaking news, analysis and interviews.[11]

A War of Narrative

Russian narratives on these two media—in the Russian, Arabic and English languages—reflect Russia's foreign policy line and use the full range of Moscow's disinformation techniques (See **Appendix I**, page 281). They emphasize that the US and its European allies are responsible for the instability in the Middle East. Although the channel broadcasts statements by Russian officials who stress the need for cooperation with the US in countering the Islamic State, it also gives significant coverage to material critical of Washington, such as the Russian charge that the US is supporting terrorist organizations, including al-Nusra. Another frequent theme is the value of Russia's regional partnerships with Turkey and Iran. Russian officials are prominently featured.

The war in Syria—at least the version offered by the Kremlin—is a major theme on both *RT Arabic* and *Sputnik*. Beginning with the Russian military intervention in Syria in 2015, propaganda and the Russian narratives have focused on the idea that all massacres are carried out by the "extremist" opposition, with no links made to the Syrian regime or Russian forces. Russian media have insisted on exaggerating and distorting false claims, rebroadcasting them in different formats on different sites loyal to Russian policy.[12]

This propaganda messaging was especially evident in coverage of the Khan Sheykhun massacre in April 2017 that killed at least 87 civilians, including 31 children, in a chemical weapons attack. On *RT* and *Sputnik*, there was no mention of the testimonies of survivors, nor reports about Abdul Hamid Youssef, the Syrian father who lost his twin babies and 20 members of his family. There was also no mention of the documented history of massacres, bombings, and chemical attacks by the Syrian regime, mentioned in international reports. After the event, Russian media, particularly *RT* and *Sputnik*, broadcast content almost daily that questioned the root of the massacre or attributed the killing to the armed opposition. For example, *RT* posted reports attributed to Russian military analysts claiming that images of the town did not feature evidence of the use of live bombs containing chemical materials.[13] It also carried an analytical piece about the timing of the bombing, and why such a bombing does not benefit Bashar al-Assad.[14] The actual identities of the "experts" cited were not given, nor did the reporting include the evidence upon which *RT* based its views. Similarly, *Sputnik* broadcast a report on one channel that claimed the bases of the Syrian regime targeted by US missile strikes did not contain chemical agents.[15] Again, there was no mention of evidence, nor was credible analysis presented.

One alternative version of events presented by Russian media was a broadcast by *Sputnik* that claimed that the children who died in the Khan Shekhun massacre were not killed by chemical weapons launched by the Syrian regime, but rather were killed by the civil defense volunteers known as the White Helmets. The news was based on reports falsely attributed to Swedish doctors alleged to have said, according to a Russian site, that they "uncovered the deceit of the White Helmets." Russian media, through *Sputnik* and *RT*, spread this fake news extensively across all social media outlets and other media sources backing the Syrian regime, from *Al-Alam* to *Al-Manar* to *Al-Maydan*. All described the chemical massacre as an "act" produced by the White Helmets who, according to the Russian narrative, "did not rescue Syrian children but instead killed them in order to produce media images and videos that look more realistic." Some sites that translated the news, such as the English site South Front are registered in Moscow.[16]

Russian media spread other disinformation on a daily basis:

- An op-ed on *Sputnik*, on September 28, 2017, argues that US forces are illegally deployed in Syria, maintain control of the oil fields east of the Euphrates River and continue to destabilize the liberated parts of Syria.[17]
- On September 29, *Sputnik* published an article with the title, "Guardian of the World," claiming that, thanks to Russia, the course of the war has changed, "a ray of hope for the restoration of peaceful life in the republic is shining brighter than ever."[18]
- An *RT* article on September 30, 2017, stated that the Trump administration had increased the risk of an armed conflict with Russia by its direct confrontation between US and Syrian government troops.[19]
- On September 30, *Sputnik* commemorated the second anniversary of the Russian intervention in Syria by

attempting to delegitimize the efforts of the non-Russian allied international coalition to settle the Syrian civil war.[20]

Broad Reach

Measuring who pays attention to these *RT Arabic* and *Sputnik* narratives, however, is difficult.[21] Although recent data on viewership of *RT Arabic* is not available, a February 2015 survey, seven months before the start of the Russian intervention in Syria, found that *RT Arabic* was among the top three most watched news channels in six Arabic countries. Anecdotal evidence suggests the rate today may be even higher. The channel had a bigger higher daily audience in six MENA countries than the UK's *BBC Arabic* and *Sky News Arabia*, the US *Al Hurra* and China's *CCTV* in Arabic. In Egypt, Morocco, Saudi Arabia, Jordan, the UAE and Iraq, *RT Arabic* was watched by 6.7 million viewers every day.[22]

- Eighteen percent of all residents in these six countries watched *RT* at least once, according to the poll, total of 18.2 million people.
- Approximately 11.5 million of those—11 percent—are estimated to have watched the channel during the previous month. This level puts *RT* ahead of *Deutsche Welle Arabic, CCTV Arabic, France 24 Arabic, Al Alam News* and *Sky News Arabia.*
- Among the surveyed countries, *RT* demonstrated the best performance in Iraq: its daily viewership there made up about 44 percent of the country's population. There, *RT* was also ahead of *BBC Arabic, Sky News, France 24, Deutsche Welle, CCTV, Al Hurra* and *Al Alam News.*
- *RT*'s audience in Iraq is also the most loyal compared to all competing channels: 98 percent of weekly viewers watch the channel daily, vs. 93 percent for *Al Arabiya*, 85 percent for *Al Jazeera*, 66 percent for *Al Hurrah*. Remarkably, of all the

Iraqis who have ever watched *RT*, 100 percent watched it over the past month.

- *RT* ranks number one in terms of viewer trust. Only 3 percent of those, who are aware of the channel, but do not watch it, cited mistrust of *RT's* news reports as a reason for not viewing the channel. This rate was 30 percent for *Al Jazeera*, 9 percent for *Al Arabiya*, 6 percent for the *BBC Arabic*, 8 percent for *Al Hurra*, and 6 percent for *Sky News Arabia.*

- According to the study, 30 percent of *RT Arabic's* monthly audience in Egypt like the channel for its "relevant and reliable news reports," while 20 percent in the UAE and 14 percent in Saudi Arabia like it for its "alternative opinions," and being "distinct from other networks."

- Fifty-nine percent of *RT Arabic's* audience watch it for more than an hour a day on weekdays, while 38 percent of its viewers watch the channel for more than an hour a day on weekends. *RT* is similarly ahead of all its competitors in the region by its daily-to-weekly viewership conversion ratio: 74 percent of *RT's* weekly audience watched the channel in the previous day.[23]

The study also showed a mostly white-collar audience. Fifty-seven percent of *RT's* monthly audience in the six surveyed counties were either top managers, mid-level or junior executives, and other professionals and office workers. Here *RT* also led the competition. Those kinds of viewers made up 56 percent of the audience of *Sky News*, 54 percent of *Al Alam News* and 45 percent of *CCTV*. *RT* also boasted the largest share of audience between the ages of 25 and 34— 30 percent.[24]

Despite these impressive numbers, *RT* may be exaggerating size of its audience. A 2015 investigation by the *Daily Beast* found that the channel aggressively oversells its success in the West, writing that the site is "pretending that it has had a far bigger impact in the Western media sphere than it has, particularly online." (These findings were based on documents leaked by former employees at *RIA Novosti*, a separate and rival Russian state-funded media venture that was defunded in 2015.) The same investigation found that the channel lied in claiming its English-, Spanish- and Arabic-language broadcasts reached 630 million people worldwide. "In reality, that number is just the theoretical geographical scope of the audience," the *Daily Beast* wrote.[25]

When *RT* does get attention—mostly through its viral video hits online—it is not for its political coverage. *RT's* biggest hits are clips of bizarre patterns and people doing crazy things. Those videos, according to the *Daily Beast*, receive "far more traffic than any videos on Russian or Western politics or those featuring Vladimir Putin." As the *Daily Beast* writes:

> Of the top 100 most watched over five years, 81 percent—344 million views—went to videos of natural disasters, accidents, crime and natural phenomena. *RT's* political news videos, featuring the content by which it seeks to shape Western opinion and thus justify its existence, accounted for a mere 1 percent of its total YouTube exposure, with fewer than 4 million views. [...] RT Documentary, cited as one of the brand's least popular YouTube channels, got an average of 200 to 300 views per video in 2013. The Daily Beast found that now, only about 100 of RT Documentary's videos have had more than 10,000 views. Many of the most-watched are part of a graphic birthing series called "newborn Russia."[26]

Geographic Variation

RT Arabic satellite television is carried throughout the Middle East, Africa, and Europe is widely available because it is free. However, Russian-media consumption varies considerably by country. The perception of Russian influence and its media generally is driven by whether a government tilts toward Iran, a Russian partner in the region, or Saudi Arabia, a longtime adversary. Since an overwhelming amount of news in the Middle East is consumed through television, smart phones and radios, and since many of these outlets are controlled or restricted by the state, it is difficult for Russia to propagate narratives that the host government does not approve.[27]

Utilizing the MEMRI project's TV database, we can access popular and state-broadcast TV programs that provide insight into how Russia is discussed, received or if disinformation is being broadcast in individual countries.[28] This data shows that Iran, al-Assad in Syria and Iraq generally are positive toward the Kremlin and its policies. Whereas, Saudi Arabia, Jordan, Kuwait and Syrian opposition movements are openly critical of Putin and Russia's involvement in the region.[29]

The media in **Saudi Arabia** is privately owned but heavily subsidized and regulated by the government; the media in the **UAE** is government-owned. *RT* and *Sputnik* stories do not appear in either Saudi/UAE newspapers or television, including Saudi-owned satellite television that is broadcast throughout the Middle East (*Rotana* and *Middle East Broadcasting Center*, based in Dubai), and *Orbit Showtime* (Bahrein). Since Saudi Arabia is well of aware of the threat to stability posed by Russian propaganda, it works to counter its influence.

- *Al Alam*, Iran's Arabic news channel, is broadcast throughout the Middle East and is available in Iraq without a satellite receiver. *Al Alam* regularly uses *RT* and *Sputnik* as the source for news articles.
- Qatari-owned *Al Jazeera* attempts to maintain neutrality, but is becoming increasingly pro-Iran and pro-Russia.

Perception of Russia appears to be improving in **Iraq**. In 2017, Iraqi member of parliament (MP) Kadhim Al-Sayadi stated on air that Iraq should cancel its "Strategic Framework Agreement" with the United States and instead join a coalition with Russia and Iran.[30] Al-Sayadi's opinions on Russia may not be unique: Abu Mahdi Al-Muhandis, deputy commander of the Popular Mobilization Units, shared in another interview that there is political cooperation occurring between Russia and the Iraqi government. He stated as well that should the government in Baghdad choose to work closer with Russia, he and his militias will as well.[31]

The media in **Jordan** maintains a very negative outlook on Russia, especially the state-run media. In 2017, the *Jordan Times* published a piece by former UK MP Robert Harvey warning against the security threat from Russia. The article explicitly claimed that under Putin, the country is reverting to Cold War tactics against domestic institutions and foreign targets, that Russia's elections are not free, that Russia it is conducting illegal land grabs in Europe, and that in 17 years Putin has shown himself to be a violent and venal leader who has benefited from oil booms to enrich himself and his friends. The article also mentions that it will only be a short time before jihadist attention shifts from the West to focus on Russia following its destructive involvement in the region.[32]

In **Lebanon,** the Russian ambassador, Alexander Zasypkin, is uniquely active on the media. Much of the footage available from the last two years is centered around Zasypkin defending Russian interests in Syria, especially Moscow's involvement in fighting terrorism and supporting al-Assad. Additionally, he makes several appearances in which he works to separate modern Russia from the Union of Soviet Socialist Republics (USSR) and to paint Putin as a new kind of global leader. Zasypkin also supports the narrative that Russia is the savior for the Middle East.[33]

In war-torn **Syria,** the Kremlin is making the most progress. There, Moscow is s leveraging its military intervention to cement its influence, but using its information machine to talk directly to Syrians: Arabic-language broadcasting by *RT* and *Sputnik* appears to be securing a growing audience in government-held territory, helping Russia gain a powerful hold on Syrian hearts and minds. *RT* has been able to operate remarkably freely in a country that ranks lower on media freedom indexes even than Russia. The Syrian government helps *RT* reporters obtain swift access to frontline locations and other stories they want to cover.[34]

This Syrian government's support has helped *RT's* Arabic channel vault ahead of the regional heavyweights, Qatar-funded *Al Jazeera* and Saudi-funded *Al Arabiya*, when it comes to reaching Syrian audiences, since Russian forces intervened in the civil war. As of 2016, it has been joined by *Sputnik*, which produces a daily, live one-hour show for *Sham FM*, one of Syria's most popular radio stations. Broadcast from Moscow each day at 6 p.m., the program features a mix of news and features and studio discussion, as well as a 20-minute "Military Monitor" segment, covering the latest frontline developments, with an emphasis on Russian actions. The aim of the show, according to a Syrian media report, is to translate the popular and official Russian position to the Syrian people and global public opinion." It is hard to find exact figures, but there is no doubt *Sham FM* reaches a wide audience in Syria, both on radio and via its Facebook page. Not all Syrians in government-controlled areas, however, are happy with Russia's intervention. Some raise questions about its legitimacy and the long-term price the country will have to pay for becoming so dependent on Moscow for its security. [35]

Conclusion

The projection of Russian power into the Middle East in recent years has been accompanied by an impressive Kremlin information warfare effort intended to advance Moscow's foreign policy objectives. The media tactic is an important tool in Russia's arsenal. This campaign was been somewhat successful across the region, especially in Syria. But the effectiveness of that effort is undermined by several factors.

- First, government censorship in the Middle East is much more prevalent than in more open media areas such as Eastern Europe, where we have seen Kremlin disinformation campaigns be effective. This fact allows host governments to block Russian messaging they oppose.
- Second, Russia in general receives a mixed basket of popular praise and disapproval. Research by Pew finds that 35 percent of those polled in the Middle East see Russia as a threat; 35 percent have a favorable view of Russia. These findings, moreover, have been consistent over the last few years.
- Third, there are few cultural, linguistic, historical or other ties between Russia and the peoples of the Arab world. In no country are there ethnic-Russian communities large enough to be mobilized by Kremlin information activities.
- Finally, Russia is geographically distant from MENA, making its messaging harder to sustain.[36]

Appendix I: The Kremlin's Disinformation Techniques

Russia disinformation and new propaganda can take many forms—from the use of false visuals or misleading headlines, to social media techniques that create an impression that the "majority" understands an issue in a certain way. In the echo chamber of the modern information space, the spreading of disinformation is as easy as a "like," "tweet" or a "share." The following are some of the Kremlin's most commonly used techniques for spreading false stories and disinformation:

Ping pong – The coordinated use of complementary websites to springboard a story into mainstream circulation.

Wolf cries wolf – The vilification of an individual or institution for something you also do.

Misleading title – Facts or statements in the article are correct, or mostly correct, but the title is misleading.

No proof – Facts or statements that are not backed up with proof or sources.

Card stacking – Facts or statements are partially true. This occurs when information is correct, but it is offered selectively, or key facts are omitted. The Kremlin typically uses this technique to guide audiences to a conclusion that fits into a pre-fabricated or false narrative.

False facts – Facts or statements are false. For example, an interview mentioned in an article that never took place, or an event or incident featured in a news story that did not actually occur.

False visuals – A variant of false facts, this technique employs the use of fake or manipulated provocative visual material. Its purpose is to lend extra credibility to a false fact or narrative.

Denying facts – A variant of "false facts," this occurs when real facts are denied or wrongly undermined. The facts of an event might be reported, but an attempt is made to discredit their veracity. Alternatively, the facts may be re-interpreted to achieve the same effect: to establish doubt among an audience over the validity of a story or narrative.

Exaggeration and over-generalization – This method dramatizes, raises false alarms or uses a particular premise to shape a conclusion. A related technique is *totum pro parte.*

Totum pro parte – The "whole for a part." An example: portraying the views of a single journalist or expert as the official view or position of a government.

Changing the quotation, source or context – Facts and statements are reported from other sources, but they are now different than the original or do not account for the latest editorial changes. For example, a quotation is correct, but the person to whom it is attributed has changed, or a quote's context is altered so as to change its meaning or significance in the original story.

Loaded words or metaphors – Using expressions and metaphors to support a false narrative or hide a true one; for example, using a term like "mysterious death" instead of "poisoning" or "murder" to describe the facts of a story.

Ridiculing, discrediting, diminution – Marginalizing facts, statements or people through mockery, name-calling (i.e. *argumentum ad hominem*), or by undermining their authority. This includes using traditional and new media humor, in order to discredit on non-substantive merits.

Whataboutism – Using false comparisons to support a pre-fabricated narrative or justify deeds and policies; i.e., "We may be bad, but others are just as bad" or, "The annexation of Crimea was just like the invasion of Iraq." This technique is often accompanied by an *ad hominem* attack.

Narrative laundering – Concealing and cleaning the provenance of a source or claim. When a so-called expert of dubious integrity presents false facts or narratives as the truth. Often, this happens when propaganda outlets mimic the format of mainstream media. A common technique is to feature a guest "expert" or "scholar" on a TV program whose false fact or narrative can then be repackaged for wider distribution. For example, "Austrian media writes that…" or "A well-known German political expert says that…"

Exploiting balance – This happens when otherwise mainstream media outlets try to "balance" their reporting by featuring professional propagandists or faux journalists and experts. The effect is to inject an otherwise legitimate news story or debate with false facts and narratives. This technique is common in televised formats, which feature point-counterpoint debates. Propagandists subsequently hijack a good-faith exchange of opposing views.

Presenting opinion as facts (and vice-versa) – An opinion is presented as a fact in order to advance or discredit a narrative.

Conspiracy theories – Employing rumors, myths or claims of conspiracy to distract or dismay an audience. Examples include: "NATO wants to invade Russia"; "The United States created the Zika virus"; "Secret Baltic agencies are infecting Russian computers with viruses"; or "Latvia wants to send its Russian population to concentration camps." A variation of this technique is conspiracy in reverse—attempting to discredit a factual news story by labeling it a conspiracy.

Joining the bandwagon – Creating the impression that the "majority" prefers or understands an issue in a certain way. The majority's presumed wisdom lends credence to a conclusion or false narrative: e.g., "People are asking..," "People want…" or "People know best."

False dilemma – Forcing audiences into a false binary choice, typically "us" vs. "them."

Drowning facts with emotion – A form of the "appeal to emotion" fallacy, this is when a story is presented in such an emotional way that facts lose their importance. An example is the "Lisa case," in which Muslim immigrants in Germany were falsely reported to have sexually assaulted a Russian girl. While the event was entirely fabricated, its appeal to emotion distracted audiences from the absence of facts. Common variants of this method evoke post-Soviet nostalgia across Central and Eastern Europe, or stoke public fear of nuclear war.

Creating a context – Most commonly found on broadcast news programs, it creates the context for a pre-fabricated narrative by preceding and following a news story in such a way that it changes the meaning of the news itself. For example, in order to send the message that recent terrorist attacks in Europe were the result of EU member states not working with Russia—which is helping to fight ISIS in Syria—commentary broadcast before the news on the March 2016 Brussels attacks described Russia's success in Syria and its ability to fight ISIS effectively.

Source: Center for European Policy Analysis
http://infowar.cepa.org/Techniques

ENDNOTES

[1] Ministry of Defense of the Russian Federation, *Military Doctrine of the Russian Federation*, http://news.kremlin.ru/media/events/files/41d527556bec8deb3530.pdf.

[2] Keir Giles, "Russia's Toolkit," in Keir Giles, et al. *The Russian Challenge*, Chatham House, June 2015, https://www.chathamhouse.org/sites/files/chathamhouse/field/field_docum ent/20150605RussianChallengeGilesHansonLyneNixeySherrWoodUpdate. pdf, 47.

[3] Atlantic Council, *The Kremlin's Trojan Horses*, http://www.atlanticcouncil.org/images/publications/The_Kremlins_Trojan _Horses_web_0228_third_edition.pdf, November 16, 2016.

[4] Ministry of Foreign Affairs of the Russian Federation, *Foreign Policy Concept of the Russian Federation*, 2013, paragraph 88; and Ministry of Foreign Affairs of the Russian Federation, *Foreign Policy Concept of the Russian Federation*, 2016, paragraph 92.

[5] "Russia's Policy in the Middle East: 'We Have Crossed the Rubicon'," Middle East Research Institute, Special Dispatch No. 7171, November 9, 2017.

[6] Sladden, et al. *Russian Strategy in the Middle East*, RAND Corp., 2017, https://www.rand.org/pubs/perspectives/PE236.html.

[7] Sladden, 2017.

[8] Ibid.

[9] Jack Nicas, "Russia State News Outlet RT Thrives on YouTube," Wall Street Journal, October 23, 2017, https://www.wsj.com/articles/russia-state-news-outlet-rt-thrives-on-youtube-facebook-1508808937.

[10] "RT Arabic," in Wikipedia, https://en.wikipedia.org/wiki/RT_Arabic. https://arabic.rt.com/.

[11] Sputnik Arabic News Service, https://arabic.sputniknews.com/. https://sputniknews.com/docs/products/sns_arabic.html.

[12] Diana Moukalled, "Propaganda, lies and videos: Russian media and the Khan Sheikhun massacre," *Arab News,* April 18 2017, http://www.arabnews.com/node/1086131/media.

[13] للتفكــــــــــير معطيـــات بالكيميـــــــــــائي؟ شـــيخون خان الســوري الطـــيران قصـــف هل., *RT Arabic,* May 4 2017, https://arabic.rt.com/middle_east/871737-%D9%84%D9%88-%D8%A7%D8%B3%D8%AA%D8%AE%D8%AF%D9%85-%D8%A7%D9%84%D8%AC%D9%8A%D8%B4-%D8%A7%D9%84%D8%B3%D9%88%D8%B1%D9%8A-%D9%82%D9%86%D8%A8%D9%84%D8%A9-%D9%83%D9%8A%D9%85%D9%8A%D8%A7%D8%A6%D9%8A%D8%A9-%D9%81%D9%8A-%D8%AE%D8%A7%D9%86-%D8%B4%D9%8A%D8%AE%D9%88%D9%86-%D9%81%D8%B9%D9%84%D8%A7/.

[14] John Wight, "Chemical Weapons Attack on Idlib: Why Questions Need to Be Asked,"May 4, 2017, *Sputnik Arab News Service,* https://sputniknews.com/analysis/201704051052330649-syria-chemical-attack-idlib/.

[15] الغامضـــة لحاويـــات: لـم يكـــن لـم أي أسـلحة كيماويـــة فــي مطار الشـــعيرات (فيـــــديو)., Sputnik Arab News Service, September 4, 2017, https://arabic.sputniknews.com/arab_world/201704091023354931-%D9%85%D8%B7%D8%A7%D8%B1-%D8%A7%D9%84%D8%B4%D8%B9%D9%8A%D8%B1%D8%A7%D8%AA-%D8%A7%D9%84%D8%AD%D8%A7%D9%88%D9%8A%D8%A7%D8%AA-%D8%A7%D9%84%D8%B3%D8%A7%D9%85%D8%A9/.

[16] Ekaterina, Blinova, "White Lies: 'Syria Civil Defense' Caught Faking Rescues, Doctoring Dead Children," *Sputnik,* April 10, 2017.

https://sputniknews.com/middleeast/201704101052484101-sweden-syria-white-helmets/.

[17] Ekaterina, Blinova"US' Plan B? From Alleged Evacuation of Daesh to the Murder of Russian General," *Sputnik*, October 13, 2017. https://sputniknews.com/analysis/201709281057790173-us-syria-daesh-alnusra/.

[18] "Guardian of the World," September 30, 2017. *Sputnik*, https://sputniknews.com/cartoons/201709291057820772-russia-syria-operation-two-years/.

[19] "2 years of Russia in Syria: ISIS shrinking, Iran & Turkey linking, conflict risk with US lurking," *RT*, September 30, 2017, https://www.rt.com/news/405098-russian-campaign-syria-anniversary/.

[20] "Two Years Of Russia's Military Operation in Syria," *Sputnik* , September 30, 2017, https://sputniknews.com/world/201709291057818987-russia-military-operation-syria-two-years/.

[21] Amanda Erickson, "If Russia Today is Moscow's propaganda arm, it's not very good at its job," *Washington Post,* January 12, 2017, https://www.washingtonpost.com/news/worldviews/wp/2017/01/12/if-russia-today-is-moscows-propaganda-arm-its-not-very-good-at-its-job/?utm_term=.f2ed02f37f7b.

[23] "RT Arabic Is Among Top-3 Most Watched News Channels In 6 Arabic Countries," *RT,* February 19, 2015. https://www.rt.com/about-us/press-releases/rt-arabic-top-3/.

[24] Ibid.

[25] Katie Zavadsky, "Putin's Propaganda TV Lies about it Popularity," *The Daily Beast*, February 19, 2015, https://www.thedailybeast.com/putins-propaganda-tv-lies-about-its-popularity.

[26] Katie Zavadsky," Putin's Propaganda TV Lies about it Popularity," *The Daily Beast* , February 19, 2015, https://www.thedailybeast.com/putins-propaganda-tv-lies-about-its-popularity.

[27] Everette E. Dennis and Robb Wood, "Media in the Middle East: A new study shows how the Arab world gets and shares digital news, September 19, 2017, *Neiman Lab,* http://www.niemanlab.org/2017/09/media-in-the-middle-east-a-new-study-shows-how-the-arab-world-gets-and-shares-digital-news/.

[28] "Abd Al-Jalil Said, Former Press Secretary for the Syrian Mufti: Russians and Russian Interests Will Become a Target for the Free Army in Syria," *MEMRI TV*, February 7, 2012, https://www.memri.org/tv/abd-al-jalil-said-former-press-secretary-syrian-mufti-russians-and-russian-interests-will-become/transcript.

[29] Bruce Stokes, "Russia, Putin Held in Low Regard around the World," *Pew Research Service,* August 5, 2015, http://www.pewglobal.org/2015/08/05/russia-putin-held-in-low-regard-around-the-world/.

[30] "Iraqi MP Kadhim Al-Sayadi: We Should Cancel the Strategic Framework Agreement with the U.S., Sign Another Sponsored by Russia and Iran," *MEMRI TV,* January 7, 2017, https://www.memri.org/tv/iraqi-mp-kadhim-al-sayadi-we-should-cancel-strategic-framework-agreement-us-sign-another/transcript.

[31] "Abu Mahdi Al-Muhandis, Deputy Commander of the Popular Mobilization Units: Optimism over Liberation of Mosul Was Exaggerated; No Objection to Russian Military Intervention in Syria; After Mosul, We Will Enter Syria; Hizbullah Trained Us against the Americans after 2003," *MEMRI TV* , January 2, 2017, https://www.memri.org/tv/abu-mahdi-al-muhandis-deputy-commander-popular-mobilization-units-optimism-over-liberation-mosul/transcript.

[32] Robert Harvey, "How Dangerous is Putin?" *Jordan Times*, March 12, 2017, http://jordantimes.com/opinion/robert-harvey/how-dangerous-putin.

[33] "Russian Ambassador to Lebanon: Withdrawing Our Troops from Syria Encouraged the Opposition to Come to the Negotiating Table," *MEMRI TV,* March 15, 2016, https://www.memri.org/tv/russian-ambassador-lebanon-withdrawing-our-troops-syria-encouraged-opposition-come-negotiating.

[34] "The Russian Offensive in Syria You Haven't Heard About ," *Coda,* https://codastory.com/disinformation-crisis/armed-conflict/the-russian-offensive-in-syria-you-haven-t-heard-about.

[35] يســـــتهدف إعلامي تعـــاون فـــي إم أف شـــام عـــبر ســـوريا داخل تبـــــث ســـــبوتنيك الشـــارع الســـوري, *Sputnik Arab News Service,* July10, 2016, http://hawaalsham.com/2016/01/%D8%B3%D8%A8%D9%88%D8%AA%D9%86%D9%8A%D9%83-%D8%AA%D8%A8%D8%AB-%D8%AF%D8%A7%D8%AE%D9%84-%D8%B3%D9%88%D8%B1%D9%8A%D8%A7-%D8%B9%D8%A8%D8%B1-%D8%B4%D8%A7%D9%85-%D8%A3%D9%81-%D8%A5%D9%85-%D9%81%D9%8A/.

[36] Margaret Vice, "Publics Worldwide Unfavorable Toward Putin, Russia," August 16, 2017, *Pew Research Center,* http://www.pewglobal.org/2017/08/16/publics-worldwide-unfavorable-toward-putin-russia/.

12. 'Continuing War by Other Means': The Case of Wagner, Russia's Premier Private Military Company in the Middle East

Sergey Sukhankin

Summary

The Wagner Group is a Russian private military company that has been active in Ukraine and Syria. In early 2018, reports of the combat deaths of over 200 Wagner personnel in eastern Syria shed an important light on the gray zone of Russian military operations in which such paramilitary forces are deployed. Meanwhile, Wagner's ongoing expansion across the globe is providing key lessons for understanding the evolution and likely transformation of this type of organization in the future. Given Moscow's reliance on non-linear means of warfare and the frequent desire to maintain "plausible deniability" in its operations abroad, exploring and analyzing the Wagner Group offers a deeper insight into Russia's role and modus operandi in conflicts across the world, especially when using Private Military Companies (PMC).

Introduction

The decimation of the Wagner Group PMC near Deir el-Zour (a city in eastern Syria, some 450 kilometers from Damascus) in early February 2018,[1] has highlighted the role Russian mercenaries play in the Kremlin's foreign policy. But the broader phenomenon of Russian PMCs, including the Wagner Group, is highly complex, as exemplified by the nervous and incoherent official reaction to the deadly Deir el-Zour clash;[2] the re-initiation of a highly contradictory debate on the legalization of PMCs in Russia by all key ministries/institutions/fractions (including the *siloviki*, or security services personnel); as well as the alleged assassination (officially identified as a suicide), in April 2018, of Maxim Borodin, a Russian journalist who had been investigating Wagner. The sense of confusion surrounding the activities and roles played by Wagner in Syria was further increased by the ensuing comments of prominent Russian conservative military officers. For instance, Colonel General (ret.) Leonid Ivashov, currently serving as the president of the Academy for Geopolitical Problems (and well-known for his anti-Western posture), claimed that the official version of the deaths of Wagner fighters at Deir el-Zour was a "purposeful distortion" by the Russian media and the Ministry for Foreign Affairs.[3] Similarly, authoritative Russian media started to question whether the Wagner Group may have been "set up."[4]

This article aims to analyze the activities of Russian PMCs in the Middle East, with specific emphasis on the Wagner Group. The following will:

- Provide a general framework for explaining the historical context behind the development of PMCs in Russia and the evolution of their functions;

- Analyze the background of the Wagner Group, its main stages of development, the geographical scope of operations and the main tasks/functions performed;

- Examine the nature of the Wagner Group through the lens of its alleged ties with the Kremlin and key Russian ministries;

- Outline the composition, organizational structure as well as the command-and-control (C2) system of the Wagner Group; as well as

- Reflect upon this organization's prospective future activities, both within the region and beyond.

Mercenaries, 'Tourists,' and 'Volunteers': Russian PMCs in a Historical Context

The use of private military forces by the state for achieving specific geopolitical and strategic objectives was an integral part of the pre-1917 Imperial Russian state. Examples include:

- The employment of Carsten Rohde by Ivan the Terrible during the Livonian War (1558–1583) to conduct both military operations and propagate economic contacts in the Baltic Sea region;

- The expedition of Yermak Timofeyevich (1582–1584), organized and handsomely financed by the powerful Stroganov family, which paved the way for the Russian conquest of Siberia; and

- The "volunteer army" assembled by Prince Dmitry Pozharsky and Kuzma Minin, which ultimately managed to expel the forces of the Polish-Lithuanian Commonwealth.

The employment of mercenary forces also included extensive reliance on non-Russians (for example, the Nogais); and these formations often performed as "private armies."[5] Furthermore, "asymmetric actions" featured the use of partisan movements that could effectively target the over-extended communication lines of an invading adversary. The backbone of such partisan units was formed out of experienced military forces. This idea gained such popularity in 19th-century Russia that, in the aftermath of the Patriotic War of 1812, infamous Russian soldier-poet Denis Davydov implicitly suggested granting partisan forces the status of a separate branch within the Russian Armed Forces.[6]

In effect, Russia's vast landmass, harsh climactic conditions and lack of proper infrastructure historically had a profound impact on Russian military strategists. On several major occasions (such as those mentioned above), these materialist factors generated a reliance on the principle of asymmetry, including the employment of irregular military formations. In those instances, Imperial Russia's military behavior thus somewhat came to resemble the mercenary raiding tactics used by the Scythians against the Persians around 513 BCE.[7]

In the Soviet period, Moscow's overarching Communist ideology ushered in a new pattern in the state's use of asymmetric activities. Notably, the Cold War was marked by numerous regional conflicts in the so-called "Third World" that the two superpowers became involved in either overtly or covertly. And aside from offering economic support in those instances, the Soviets also regularly sent in "military advisors." The Middle East, in particular, presents one of the best examples for how Soviet military advisors grew into an important instrument of Moscow's foreign policy. In Egypt alone, between 1967 and 1973, the numbers of Russian military personnel rotated into and out of the conflict reached a staggering 30,000–50,000.[8] However, the death of Gamal Nasser (1970), the somewhat more moderate approach taken by the new president, Anwar el-Sadat (1970–1981), as well as dramatic developments in Syria shifted Moscow away from viewing Egypt as a "vanguard" of anti-Western forces in the Middle East.

After the "loss of Egypt," and following the military coup in Damascus led by Hafez al-Assad (the father of current Syrian President Bashar al-Assad), Soviet attention shifted toward Syria. The latter country began receiving substantial economic and military assistance from Moscow directly coordinated by the Soviet Ministry of Defense. However, Soviet soldiers and military instructors were being transported to the Middle East as "tourists"; and their subsequent deaths in the Arab-Israeli wars (a.k.a. the "Wars of Attrition, 1967–1974) as well as the civil war in Lebanon (particularly in the late 1970s) were kept quiet.[9] This mode of operation highlighted Moscow's concern over maintaining a level of deniability in regional conflicts across the Middle East. Illustratively, Marshal of the Soviet Union Andrei Grechko declared, in 1970, "should any of you [Soviet soldiers furtively sent to the region] be shot down near the Suez channel, we do not know you… get out of this mess by yourselves."[10]

Similarly, during the Angolan civil war and its most intense period of fighting (1975–1991), Moscow sent Soviet military advisors (their number likely exceeded 10,000 men) clandestinely to Africa as non-military personnel. These soldiers ended up playing a decisive role in the conflict. This focus on ensuring Moscow's ability to deny the presence of Russian mercenary forces deployed abroad was honed during the Soviet period at the highest levels of government. Additionally, the Soviet Union approved the use of Cuban "military advisors" throughout Africa as heralds of the Socialist cause.

While the institution of "military advisors" formed the security pillar of Soviet methods of non-linear warfare against the West, the Soviet period also witnessed the simultaneous use of so-called "ideological diversions" as one of the main tools of Moscow's information-psychological warfare against the "capitalist world."[11] This combination sharply contrasted with the patterns established during the antecedent period of Russian warfare. In the pre-1917 period, Russia did not wage a permanent ideological struggle against the West—irregular forms of warfare were either used on an *ad hoc* basis (during military conflicts, such as the War of 1812), or for achieving geo-strategic objectives (including the conquest of Siberia). But under Communist rule (especially after 1945), irregular warfare primarily became a tool used by the Soviet side to achieve geopolitical objectives within its broader ideological confrontation with the West.

The dissolution of the Union of Soviet Socialist Republics (USSR) witnessed a number of regional conflicts that broke out on the margins of the former USSR. And these clashes notably featured the introduction of Russian mercenaries. So as not to lose its influence over the newly independent republics on its periphery, Moscow was keen to use illegal military formations, in addition to other strategies, to secure Russia's participation in those regional conflicts without becoming directly or overtly involved. This experience, however, was undermined by several important failures, including inside Russia's borders. For instance, prior to the First Battle of Grozny (1994–1995), Russian special services (allegedly the Federal Counterintelligence Service) organized an attack by recruits without any military insignia to force then–Chechen President Dzhokhar Dudayev from power. However, after the humiliating collapse of this campaign, the Russian soldiers who had "volunteered" for the operation were disavowed by the authorities; notably, Defense Minister Pavel Grachev labeled them "mercenaries."[12]

Russia also used irregular forces in other strategically important theaters beyond the former Soviet Union, namely in Yugoslavia in the early 1990s. Russian "volunteers" (up to several hundred people) began arriving to the region in small groups to perform reconnaissance-subversive tasks between 1992 and 1995. Specifically, in the city of Višegrad, in 1993, the first Cossack unit (*sotnia*) numbering 70 persons was deployed. According to various sources, the unit consisted of Russians from Rostov Oblast and the Volga Region of southern Russia; they were later joined by members from St. Petersburg and Siberia. Most likely, these first groups were assembled as volunteers. In time, effort was made to set up a more institutionalized, contractual process that could move beyond an *ad hoc* system of attracting mercenaries. Evidence suggests that at this later stage, the decisive role in terms of formation and organization was played by the St. Petersburg–based security company "Rubikon," which was said to have been coordinated by the Federal Security Service (FSB).[13]

Rubikon was the first attempt to create a Russian PMC for specific geopolitical objectives. At the same time, Rubikon signified the growing interests of the *siloviki* in monetizing the mercenary business. In July 2007, the Russian Duma and the Federation Council (the lower and the upper chambers of the Russian parliament, respectively) voiced their support for a piece of legislation[14] that allowed such "strategically important enterprises" as Joint Stock Company Transneft and Gazprom to "employ arms and *special means for securing production procured by the state* [author's emphasis]."[15] This move by the Russian government granted the security services permission to create businesses and enterprises involved in the extraction and the transportation of hydrocarbons, their status and ownership rights. The Ministry of Internal Affairs stood to profit from the Russian legislation by contributing to the effort.[16]

It is thus worth mentioning that between 1997 and 2013, Russia PMCs (or groups roughly falling within this definition) went through an interesting transformation in both quantity and quality: Their overall number increased dramatically, and some important structural changes ensued. Among the most well-known companies, one could mention the RSB-Group, MAR, Antiterror, Moran Security Group, E.N.O.T. Corp., Tigr Top-Rent Security, and Slavonic Corps

Limited.[17] Furthermore, the *siloviki* started to play increasingly important role in terms of composition of these groups.

In this regard, an important point should be made: Russian PMCs started as a force tasked with solving narrow geopolitical objectives but then began taking on broader economic (mainly energy) issues. The ongoing Ukrainian crisis, which witnessed Russia's employment of non-linear warfare means in Crimea and the Donbas region, also triggered further dramatic changes in the domain of Russian PMCs.[18] It is crucial to acknowledge that the Wagner Group and its predecessor, the Slavonic Corps (the surviving parts of which were turned into and rebranded as Wagner), were a living embodiment of these transformations.

Russian Conceptualization of PMCs: War, Politics and Business

Over time, Russian writers and military theoreticians developed an understanding of PMCs that pointedly differs from the Western perspective. In contrast to Western views, for Russia, PMCs occupy an equal position with regular army units in the battle space and play an increasingly important role in a conflict zone. Moreover, given the fact that the state is the *de facto* main stakeholder and a coordinator of PMC activities, these companies are "not 'private,' " writes Valeriy Boval, adding, they "are some sort of governmental structures, and a tool of the state's foreign policy."[19]

Major General Sergey Kanchukov, the former head of Siberian Military District intelligence and a veteran of the military intelligence service (GRU), implies that a combination of advanced technical equipment and high professional skills, directly controlled by the state, allows Russian PMCs to take on tasks usually performed by regular Russian army forces. Furthermore, he argues that unlike the regular Armed Forces, these structures are free to choose any means to achieve their specific objectives.[20]

Other Russian writers take a broader prospective: they deem PMCs to be a backbone of the so-called "power economy" (*silovya ekonomika*). Professor Alexandr Ageev, a member of the Russian Academy of Natural Sciences, defines the power economy as a state-controlled system of coercion (including a reliance on limited-scale military conflicts, if necessary) aimed at realizing economic goals.[21] This important aspect envisages the convergence of geopolitical and geostrategic/economic objectives that are to be attained by PMCs operating under the umbrella of the government. That arrangement, importantly, allows the state to avoid being implicated in *de facto* illegal activities (plausible deniability).

The outbreak of the Ukrainian crisis and the Syrian civil war give new impetus to the development of Russian PMCs under the principle of "asymmetry"—particularly as "non-linear conflict" reenters Russian military-strategic parlance.[22] Importantly, Russian writers, including Igor Panarin, Alexander Dugin, Sergey Moshkin and others, have been quoting classical Russian/Soviet military strategists such as Alexander Svechin (Soviet military thinker and professor at the Academy of General Staff) and Marshal of the Soviet Union and Chief of the General Staff of the USSR (1977–1984) Nikolai Ogarkov. Both of those men, during separate periods, envisioned non-conventional forms of warfare as a backbone of future conflicts.[23] The fact that current Russian military theorists are quoting Svechin and Ogarkov is highly significant as it points to increasing emphasis on "the necessity to develop their own theories, forms and types of employment of military forces—not to follow Western principles." This is particularly notable given the necessity, according to Russian military analysts and intellectuals, to plan and provide asymmetric forms of response (*asymmetrichny otvet*).[24]

The continuity between the Soviet and Russian periods of PMC development appears to reflect traditional Russian models of using proxies. Perhaps the best example of such continuity was expressed by the Russian chief of the General Staff, Army General Valery

Gerasimov, who has emphasized a direct connection between "guerrilla and subversive methods" and "color revolutions." This fact, according to Gerasimov, requires maintaining a balance between a "high-technology component" and the necessity to prepare the Russian Armed Forces for actions in "non-traditional circumstances" during color revolutions sponsored by the West.[25] This objective is to be achieved through anti-asymmetric forms of warfare, the ability to nullify the high-tech capabilities of the enemy, and the reintegration of Russia's own experience of partisan/guerrilla fighters of the Great Patriotic War (1941–1945).[26] Gerasimov primarily referred to the above-mentioned classic military thinkers and their stress on off-the-beaten-path ways of thinking. He also called for taking a fresh look at works of the Soviet military theorist Georgy Isserson (1898–1976) and reconsider the principle of mobilization and concentration of armed forces *prior* to the outbreak of military conflict.

In this context, Gerasimov is making a clear reference to aligning traditional and non-conventional forms of warfare, relying on Russian historical strengths in employing PMCs. Importantly, the ability to effectively fight partisan/guerrilla warfare has traditionally been seen as one of the most important means to achieve Russian military victory.

In this regard, Russia's PMCs are explicitly a force capable of both economic and geopolitical functions. And as such, Russian PMCs have both a broader range of tasks and employ different tactics in comparison with standard PMCs, particularly in the West. Consequently, Russia's PMCs regularly assume control over "gray zones" in order to create "zones of artificial stability." The purpose of this PMC mission is "exploitation of natural resources and assuming partial political control over an area(s), with the existing political regime still remaining 'in charge' to preserve the legitimacy of the territory."[27] Again, this factor allows the Russian side to bolster plausible deniability and ward off accusations while at the same time remaining a *de facto* party to the conflict. Moreover the government is relieved of the burden of supporting these proxy forces. The case study of the Wagner Group provides the most salient example of a Russian PMC in action utilizing the above-described conceptual notions articulated by Russian military theorists.

Who Is Who in Wagner?

A key question boils down to identification of actors in the Wagner saga. It is essential to look into the personalities and factors that make-up the Wagner Group.

The Leader

The Wagner Group is headed by former GRU Lieutenant General (ret.) Dmitry Utkin. Initially employed by the Moran Security Group, Utkin later took part in the Syrian campaign with the Slavonic Corps. Known for his sympathies toward ultra-conservative ideologies—one Ukrainian report suggested that Russian neo-Nazis joined the Wagner Group first in Ukraine and subsequently in Syria to serve the higher purpose of achieving a "Russian World," or *Russkiy Mir*, beyond Russia's actual borders[28]—Utkin demonstrated loyalty and devotion to the Kremlin's *Russkiy Mir* idea. His valuable experience serving within Russia's elite military forces, combined with relatively deep knowledge of the Syrian environment (despite the poor performance of the Slavonic Corps in Syria), made him one of the most experienced and charismatic PMC leaders in Russia. His success as the commander of the Wagner Group in Ukraine and Syria elevated Utkin to such an extent that he and his colleagues were invited to the Kremlin on December 9, 2016. Utkin's picture, standing alongside Vladimir Putin, was circulated in the Russian media, and he was awarded the Order of Courage (*Orden Muzhestva*).[29]

Training Techniques

Wagner's training center is located in Molkino, Krasnodar Krai. The facility belongs to the GRU's 10th special forces brigade. Notably, the site's recent modernization was funded by the Russian Ministry of Defense, which spent some 41.7 million rubles ($675,000) on these improvements.[30] All this points to the close ties between the group and both the GRU and the defense ministry. Specifically, the Wagner Group has access to the training techniques and resources used by elite Russian military formations, which made it superior to other Russian PMCs as well as their adversaries in Syria.

Arms and Equipment

Various sources have identified Wagner personnel to be armed with advanced small arms and light weapons. In addition, during the period of this PMC's greatest combat successes, news reports have noted the Wagner Group's employment of, *inter alia*, T-72 main battle tanks, BM-21 Grad multiple rocket launchers, as well as D-30 122-millimeter howitzers. Routine training involves constant shooting practice with different types of arms. And, importantly, before deployment to the theater, Wagner personnel go through a preparatory stage that includes comprehensive training for up to two months at the Molkino base[31].

Command and Control

The Wagner Group maintains a clear and well-developed C2 system. Out of the 2,349 personnel reportedly deployed to Syria during 2016–2017, Wagner's command structure was organized into an upper level, consisting of the commander-in-chief and a managing director, as well as a middle level of command. The latter includes the administrative group (388 personnel), the general staff (19 persons), and the control group (36 persons).[32] On top of that, Wagner places special emphasis on coordination of the "military part" of the group, where the key role is ascribed to the Department of Military Preparation. Various subunits within the Department of Military Preparation are responsible for firearm training (*ognevaja podgotovka*), engineer training (*inzhenernaja podgotovka*), tank and infantry fighting vehicle crews (*ekipazi tankov y BMP*), tactical training (*takticheskaja podgotovka*), as well as artillery and anti-aerial defense (*artilleria y PVO*).

Importantly, the Wagner Group's clear division of functions and responsibilities as well as its well-established C2 system follow a template drawn from the structure of the Russian Armed Forces. This structure allows Wagner and other Russian PMCs to carry out offensive missions or operations usually performed by the regular Armed Forces. This aspect has meant that the Wagner Group could conduct operations against forces deemed to be unfriendly to the Russian and Syrian regimes, independent of Syrian forces, and even sometimes instead of Bashar al-Assad's regular military.

Finances

After 2014, Russia experienced a visible economic downturn, with both living standards and real wages rapidly falling. These trends have been particularly painful for Russians living in the remote parts of the country (*glubinka*). Private interviews and investigative reporting revealed that many middle-aged Russian men (35–50), especially those with a former military background who could not adjust to the reality of civilian life, with dependents and/or families (on many occasions burdened with financial troubles), have sought employment with Russian PMCs.

Wagner's finances are difficult to ascertain, but there is clearly a robust flow of cash into this firm. It needs to be stated that information on the "financial side" of participation in Wagner is rather contradictory (different sources present various details); yet, on the basis of the available data, it is possible to provide some basic figures. Prior to deployment to Ukraine or Syria, members of the group could expect to receive 80,000 rubles ($1,300) per month during preparations at Molkino; 20,000 rubles ($1,900) monthly once in Ukraine; and 180,000 rubles ($2,900) each month for "installing order" on the territory of the "Luhansk People's Republic" (LPR—the occupied, separatist portion of Ukraine's Luhansk region).

In addition to the salary, 60,000 rubles ($960) per week was guaranteed while serving in action. Compensation for death to the family varied from 2,000,000 to 3,000,000 rubles ($32,000–$48,000). In comparison, the "insurgents" from the Donetsk and Luhansk "People's Republics" were making approximately 15,000 rubles ($240) per month.[33] The income differential was a persuasive argument for joining the conflict in eastern Ukraine as a member of a PMC.

The Syrian experience, on the other hand, consisted of two parts. From 2015 to 2016, the salary earned by Wagner employees (on average) may have reached 240,000 rubles per month ($3,800). Whereas, at the height of Russia's Syrian campaign (as of early 2017), Russian sources suggest that the monthly wages may have been as high as 500,000 rubles ($8,000). This figure, however, was contradicted by other sources, which suggested salaries of 250,000–300,000 rubles ($4,000–$4,800) per month.[34] Death in combat reportedly resulted in up to 5,000,000 rubles ($80,000) in compensation for the family,[35] which is notably the standard compensation for the death of a Russian contract soldier.

Logistics

Another essential aspect for the Wagner Group's success has been Russia's commitment to provide it with the logistical resources of the entire Southern Federal District (SFD). At this juncture, it is also imperative to underline strategic role of Rostov-on-Don in terms of the development and functioning of Wagner. The city located in the southern part of the SFD, which effectively makes it one of the key logistical venues in southern Russia. The Rostov Oblast plays a pivotal function in the eastern Ukrainian conflict, serving as the main artery for technical-material support for the Donbas separatist forces. At the same time, the city of Rostov has been allocated the primary role in terms of transferring Russian servicemen (both privates and contract soldiers) to Syria via the Cham Wings air company (which also flies civilian Airbus A320s).[36] Most likely, members of the Wagner Group were transferred to Syria via the same scheme, using the Platov International Airport (also in Rostov Oblast).

Ownership Structure

The perception of Wagner as the private army of Kremlin-connected Russian billionaire Yevgeny Prigozhin (popularly known as "Putin's chef") has indeed gained much popularity, especially in light of a May 2017 energy-related deal, which granted Prigozhin a sizable 25 percent share of Syria's oil and natural gas extraction business. This assessment is also supported by an argument that Wagner took part in the takeover and subsequent protection of oil and gas fields in Syria. This argument, however, raises the issue of how one tycoon (close to Putin, yet by no means the most influential one) would be allowed to singlehandedly play such an important role in the Syrian conflict.

Here, it is noteworthy to recall the proposed March 27, 2018, bill in the State Duma that was supposed to legalize PMCs in Russia (PMCs are technically illegal in the Russian Federation). Despite the potential profitability of the measure, the initiative suffered a sound defeat after being unanimously rejected by the Ministry of Defense, the Ministry of Foreign Affairs, the Russian National Guard (Rosgvardia), the Federal Security Service (FSB), the Foreign Intelligence Service (SVR) and the Federal Guard Service of the Russian Federation (FSO).[37] The sense of controversy was amplified by the fact that, on previous occasions, such key figures as Foreign Minister Sergei Lavrov, former deputy prime minister for defense and space industry Dmitry Rogozin, prominent members of the *siloviki* faction (such as Colonel General Vladimir Shamanov) and even President Vladimir Putin himself had argued in favor of legalizing PMCs.

The above leads to three suppositions that could explain Russia's unwillingness to legally sanction PMCs despite a clear expansion of these types of groups. First, Russian officials might be preoccupied with issues of licensing and potential constitutional amendments, the unpredictability of PMCs' performance, and/or the forfeiture of deniability by the state—these, rather superficial arguments are most commonly floated in the Russian official media. Second, the performance of Wagner in Syria was ultimately so poor that the potential legalization of PMCs would cast a shadow on the military skills of Russian forces engaged abroad. This argument was voiced by Leonid Ivashov who asserted, "[W]e have attained success against poorly armed terrorist formations; yet, against the US, we have no argument other than our strategic nuclear forces, which are not present in Syria."[38] Third, thanks to its legally ambiguous status, Wagner Group is a much-sought-after instrument for performing tasks that regular armed forces could not be implicated in (such as seizing control over gas/oil fields and critical infrastructure).

These calculations do not, however, rule out a fourth option that could represent a combination of the aforementioned arguments. Namely, interested parties can currently use private military companies to accomplish specific economic objectives, while principles of asymmetric warfare can simultaneously be tested in conditions of real-time warfare. Incidentally, this option does naturally reflect the thinking of leading Russian writers and analysis on the role and nature of Russian PMCs.

The Ukrainian Chapter and Its Effects

The Wagner Group can originally be traced back to the so-called Slavonic Corps, registered in Hong Kong by Vadim Gusev and Yevgeniy Sidorov from the Moran Security Group.[39] Elements of this earlier PMC eventually formed the backbone of Wagner. The Wagner Group first conducted combat operations in southeastern Ukraine, in 2014. Russian investigative journalist Ruslan Leviev has reported that the Wagner Group took an active part in Russia's illegal annexation of Crimea.[40] At that time, the Wagner Group consisted of a patchwork of various elements, ranging from the remnants of the Slavonic Corps to local volunteers with personal motives. However, Russian sources denied the fact that at this stage the group included "volunteers."[41] In any event, while in Ukraine, the group primarily operated on the territory of the self-proclaimed Luhansk People's Republic, with Wagner remaining one of the least known units due to the fact that it was inactive on social media and on no occasions was it mentioned by the local authorities.[42] Its high level of competency in this hot spot signaled that Wagner was being run, organized and equipped by the GRU.[43] Russian and Ukrainian sources note that the Wagner Group performed operations on the territory of the LPR that required a high level of military proficiency. For example, Wagner personnel were responsible for the assassination of LPR's "minister of defense," Alexander Bednov; the killing of Aleksey Mozgovoy, the leader of the Prizrak Brigade; the disarmament of the "Odessa" mechanized brigade; and of wide-scale repressions against Russian Cossacks who had previously served in Luhansk Oblast but, with the collapse of the Moscow-backed "Novorossiya" ("New Russia") project for southeastern Ukraine, grew more "independent" of the Kremlin.[44]

The "Ukrainian chapter" of Wagner's history demonstrated the ability of the group to solve tasks of relatively high complexity in a discreet manner. This aspect allowed it take on increasingly sophisticated tasks and responsibilities as well as an expanded geographic area of operations.

The 'Syrian Chapter': From Triumph to the 'Russian Ilovaysk'

Wagner's performance in Syria is a story of success followed by failure, at least as of mid-2018. During the retaking of Palmyra from the Islamic State (in spring 2016), the main forward advance into the ancient Syrian city was conducted by the Wagner Group. This fact was implicitly acknowledged by the commander of the Russian Armed Forces in Syria, Colonel General Aleksandr Dvornikov, who noted the presence of certain "forces of special operations [...] tasked with various special missions."[45] Moreover, it was reported that, near Latakia and Aleppo, members of the Wagner Group (and presumably members of others PMCs, such as ENOT) were coordinated by the GRU and the FSB for various duties. Arguably, at this preliminary stage, when Wagner played an important role in terms of enabling pro-al-Assad forces to re-gain parts of the country, military successes were to a greater extent stipulated by the weakness of the opponent rather than the inherent strength and invincibility of the Russian PMC itself. As rightfully pointed out by Colonel General Ivashov, the main adversaries Wagner faced in Syria at that time were poorly organized and inadequately trained, lacking experience, coordination and proper C2. At the same time, Wagner by no means performed the role of a standard PMC in the Western sense: both the nature of its operations and the mode of actions suggest that the group carried out purely military functions—not supporting tasks Western PMCs are normally tasked with as part of their corporate mission.[46]

The Wagner Group's massacre at Deir ez-Zor, where the group was deploying to seize oil and gas fields in early 2018, illustrated the collapse of deception tactics (*maskirovka*), including the use of Russian mercenaries in conjuction with Syrian forces in conditions of the desert. Approximately, 200 Wagner personnel were killed in a battle with joint US-Kurdish forces.

The 'Russian Ilovaysk': What Went Wrong at Deir ez-Zor?

The decimation of the Wagner Group near Deir ez-Zor—an incident sometimes referred to as the "Russian Ilovaysk, in reference to the huge losses suffered by Ukrainian forces in August 2014, at the hands of regular Russian military units—can be attributed to a combination of factors:[47]

Lower quality of training and equipment. In spite of the Wagner Group's initially excellent training and equipment, the fighting quality of its personnel deployed to Syria subsequently began to drop. Namely, regular shooting practice was abandoned, and both the quality and quantity of arms and munitions stagnated. Furthermore, the lack of any aerial support (one of the key factors behind this PMC's tragic rout in 2018) left Wagner somewhere in between being a regular armed force and a guerrilla/partisan formation, thus profoundly restricting its operational capabilities and decreasing the group's effectiveness.

Lower quality of personnel. Prior to 2017, with a very minor exception (the *"Karpaty"* unit, headed by Russian Lieutenant Colonel Oleg Demianenko), the group consisted of Russian citizens with some level of primary military background. But this policy subsequently underwent changes. Namely, in 2017, the Spring Brigade (*Vesna*), consisting predominantly of ethnic Ukrainians (numbering 100–150) with no proven record of military experience, was formed.[48] Furthermore, the Conflict Intelligence Team (CIT), which investigates Russia's participation in conflicts around the world, has highlighted the lack of elite special forces present among the Wagner Group's casualties in Syria and Ukraine.[49] Other known examples also suggest that the quality of personnel has been gradually decreasing, particularly since 2017.

New payment policy. As of 2017, financing (the nature of which remains blurred by frequently contradictory information) of the

Wagner Group has allegedly become the sole responsibility of the Syrian government, which has led to "constant delays in payment and altercations over the promised amount."[50] Only top-notch specialists were given the highest possible monthly wages, equaling 240,000 rubles ($3,300); whereas lower ranks were paid $2,200 per month. These changes have had a profound influence on both the training and equipment available. At the same time, it has resulted in a lower quality of new recruits. Changes in the payment policy still remain unclear and subject to debate and speculation. These changes are frequently attributed to a struggle between Prigozin and Shoigu for influence and redistribution of economic means,[51] although the lack of precise data does provide conclusive answers on the matter.

The above-indicated factors undoubtedly played a primary role in Wagner's dramatic defeat in early 2018. However, the following factors may have also contributed:

Comparatively poor level of preparation. When clashing with militant groups, the Wagner Group could boast superior fighting skills; yet, the US military represented a foe wielding superior weaponry and at least equally if not better trained personnel. Indeed, its lack of aerial support, aged arms and munitions (including older motorized vehicles), and lack of access to air defense made Wagner an easy target for an assault.

Surprise effect. The majority of available accounts point to the fact that the Wagner Group units were not expecting an aerial attack of such scope and decisiveness—though, explanations vary as to why not. The group was marching in an open space without having taken any precautions; and the US-led attack clearly took them by surprise. Consequently, the idea that the Wagner forces were somehow "betrayed" has gained some popularity among certain Russian experts.[52]

Particularities of the "Russian style" of non-linear warfare. Historically, Russia has waged successful partisan or guerrilla warfare against a strong(er) opponent defensively (meaning on Russian territory) and in a friendly natural landscape (forests and mashes). In Syria, neither of these two elements were available.

And yet, despite the Wagner Group's deficiencies and ensuing military defeat in Syria, recent evidence suggests that Russia has not abandoned the idea of using Wagner as a geopolitical tool of confrontation against the West.

Life After Death: Future Prospects

The loss of life suffered by Wagner in Syria notwithstanding, the Russian PMC has continued to expand. For instance, some analysts have pointed to Russia's growing presence in other zones of instability, such as the Central African Republic (CAR) and Sudan, where the Wagner Group is being deployed.[53] Furthermore, the Ukrainian investigative media outlet *Information Resistance* has presented information on the Wagner Group not only altering its name to Liga (while retaining its former leaders), but also adopting some C2 changes to its structure with the introduction of four new categories of specialists. The nature of those collective changes suggests parts of Wagner could eventually be redeployed to the Donbas region.[54]

It also appears that the main base of preparation for Wagner personnel might be moved from Molkino (which has now been compromised) to other regions. The most logical options seem to be Tajikistan, Transnistria, Karabakh and/or Abkhazia—although other locations cannot be ruled out. Wagner (or its analogue) requires facilities to train in if the group wants to remain relevant, especially as its missions seem to be expanding (such as in Africa).

One way or another, utilizing PMCs is almost certain to remain an essential part of the Russian military-strategic agenda. This doctrinal aspect is supported by the following:

First, the issue of deniability and Moscow's "we are not there" behavior and rhetoric profoundly enhances the maneuverability of the Russian side. This aspect is assisted by the murkiness regarding the actual military losses suffered by Russia in local military conflicts, since PMC personnel deaths are generally not included in regular casualty lists. Such obfuscation is an important element of the propaganda disseminated by the Russian state-sponsored media, which aims to present the image of the Russian Armed Forces as invincible and superior to other militaries.

Second, the presence of PMCs on the battlefield offers both flexibility and auxiliary functions. These structures could thus be used at virtually any stage of a New Type (or hybrid/non-linear) conflict, as identified by Gerasimov.[55]

Third, is the growing profitability of war. Oleg Krinitsyn, the president of RSB-Grupp, another Russian PMC, noted in 2013, "[T]he era of local and corporate wars is approaching, and services of PMCs will be sought after to even greater extent." Notably, however, Krinitsyn added that he did not envisage "a bright future for Russian PMCs" in terms of their upcoming legalization.[56] Additional evidence, both direct and implicit, points to the fact that various segments of the Russian ruling elites remain preoccupied with the idea of using these sorts of corporate organizations to accomplish specific power economy objectives. RSB-Grupp, for instance, is concerned with intelligence gathering, legal and military consulting and training, as well as the protection of sea vessels.

Fourth, the issue will in part be driven by the level of public reaction to Moscow's military campaigns abroad. Wagner body bags do not have the same effect as images of killed regular Russian military personnel coming home. Thus, the death of Russian citizens in Syria, presented by the Russian media either as an invention of US information warfare, or, if partly acknowledged, explained away as "mercenaries" dying for economic gain, may not preoccupy the Russian population, thereby insulating the Kremlin from growing public discontent.

Fifth, the proliferation of PMC fighters on the front lines offers Russia a deep source of "cannon fodder" (*pushechnoye miaso*). Poor living conditions, widespread criminality and various difficulties that prevent Russian soldiers from adjusting to civilian life have created a huge pool of recruits (especially middle-aged men) willing to take part in regional conflicts. Interestingly enough, some informed sources have argued that "the structure [i.e., the Wagner Group] has been eradicated at least five times" due to repeated losses of personnel.[57]

Conclusion

In the final analysis, by cultivating a growing number of PMCs like the Wagner Group, Russia has created both a powerful and convenient weapon of non-linear warfare as well as a tool for the Russian elites to achieve their own geo-economic goals. From a military point of view, Wagner's operations in Donbas and Syria appear to have, in part, been designed to test its ability to "control the territory," a concept strongly emphasized by Gerasimov and the Russian General Staff. Importantly, PMCs offer Moscow deniability and conceal its responsibility for deaths of Russian soldiers in operations abroad. Additionally, Russian PMCs and especially Wagner allow for the potential integration of foreigners (from impoverished parts of the post-Soviet space), which provides the Kremlin with another powerful tool of influence to use overseas. Undoubtedly, the Wagner model is here to stay.

ENDNOTES

[1] Sergey Sukhankin, "War, Business and 'Hybrid' Warfare: The Case of the Wagner Private Military Company (Part One)," *Eurasia Daily Monitor*, Volume: 15 Issue: 60 (April 19, 2018), https://jamestown.org/program/war-business-and-hybrid-warfare-the-case-of-the-wagner-private-military-company-part-one/; Sergey Sukhankin, "War, Business and 'Hybrid' Warfare: The Case of the Wagner Private Military Company (Part Two)," *Eurasia Daily Monitor*, Volume: 15 Issue: 61 (April 23, 2018), https://jamestown.org/program/war-business-and-hybrid-warfare-the-case-of-the-wagner-private-military-company-part-two/.

[2] "'Klassicheskaya dezinformatsiya': Zakharova pro soobshcheniya o gibeli soten rossiyskikh grazhdan v Sirii," *RT*, February 15, 2018, https://russian.rt.com/world/article/481891-mariya-zaharova-brifing.

[3] "Kak pogibali 'vagnerovtsy' v Sirii," *Youtube*, published: February 17, 2018, https://www.youtube.com/watch?v=uxdr--B_-HA.

[4] Vladimir Shcherbakov, "Boynya pod Deyr-ez-Zorom — izmena ili samonadeyannost?" *Nezavisimoe Voennoe Obozrenie*, February 22, 2018, http://nvo.ng.ru/wars/2018-02-22/1_985_siria.html.

[5] Sergey Kanchukov, "Chastnye voennye kompanii — pomoshch ili obuza dlya Rossii?" *Informatsionnoe agentstvo REX*, August 22, 2012, http://www.iarex.ru/articles/28444.html.

[6] Denis Davydov, "Dnevnik partizanskih dejstwij". Biblioteka Internet proyekta 1812. 2001, http://www.museum.ru/museum/1812/Library/davidov1/index.html#c1.

[7] The Scythians were famously sought after as mercenaries for various settled state armies.

[8] Igor Eliseev, Aleksey Tikhonov, "V teni piramid," *Rossiyskaya Gazeta*, №5300 (221), September 30, 2010, https://rg.ru/2010/09/30/taina.html.

[9] Leonid Mlechin, "Pogib, zasshchishchaya Siriyu," *Novaya Gazeta*, September 18, 2015, https://www.novayagazeta.ru/articles/2015/09/18/65656-171-pogib-zaschischaya-siriyu-187-8212.

[10] Sergey Kravchuk, "Pozor Rossii," *Snob*, February 16, 2018, https://snob.ru/profile/31374/blog/134437.

[11] Leonid Barinov, "Ideologicheskie diversii — chast psikhologicheskoy voyny," *Voyna i Mir*, June 23, 2008, http://www.warandpeace.ru/ru/article/view/24331/.

[12] "Zagovor. Chechenskiy kapkan," 1 seriya, *Youtube*, published: October 23, 2011, https://www.youtube.com/watch?v=P4XwVSmNT2k.

[13] "Chastnye voennye kompanii Rossii: vypolnyaya prestupnye prikazy Kremlya," *Informnapalm*, accessed June 2, 2018, http://informnapalm.rocks/chastnye-voennye-kompanii-rossii-vypolnjaja-prestupnye-prikazy-kremlja.

[14] *Federalny zakon o vnesenii izmeneniy v v federalny zakon "O postavkah produktsyy dlya federalnykh gosudarstvennyh nuzhd" I statyu 12 federalnogo zakona "Ob oruzhyi,"* July 24, 2007, Moscow, Kremlin. Available at: https://gkrfkod.ru/zakonodatelstvo/Federalnyy-zakon-ot-24.07.2007-N-222-FZ/.

[15] Ivan Rodin, "'Gazprom' i 'Transneft' vooruzhayutsya," *Nezavisimaya Gazeta*, March 2, 2007, http://www.ng.ru/politics/2007-03-02/3_transneft.html.

[16] Konovalov I, Valetsky O, *Evolyutsyya chastnykh voennykh kompaniy* (Pushkino: Tsentr strategicheskoy konyuktury, 2013), 47.

[17] "Pervye chastnye voennye kompanii v Rossii," *Chastnaya voennaya kompaniya MAR*, December 26, 2014, http://chvk-mar.ru/novosti/pervye-chastnye-voennye-kompanii-v-rossii.

[18] This issue will be explored in greater detail in subsequent sections of this piece. It is, however, important to acknowledge that both the Syrian civil war and the Ukrainian crisis have had a profound impact on trajectory of development of Russian PMCs and their evolution.

[19] Valeriy Boval, "Soldaty udachi, 'dikie lebedi', 'psy voyny'… Naemniki — kto oni?" *Voennoe Obozrenie,* January 28, 2013, https://topwar.ru/23484-soldaty-udachi-dikie-lebedi-psy-voyny-naemniki-kto-oni.html.

[20] Sergey Kanchukov, "Chastnye voennye kompanii Rossii," *Armeyskiy Vestnik,* August 30, 2012, http://army-news.ru/2012/08/chastnye-voennye-kompanii-rossii/.

[21] Aleksandr Ageev, "Silovaya ekonomika I smena mirovogo gegemona," *Strategicheskie prioritety* no. 2 (6) (2015): 27–48.

[22] Sergey Sukhankin, "'Syrian Lessons' and Russia's 'Asymmetric Response' to the US," *Eurasia Daily Monitor,* Volume: 14 Issue: 118, (September 26, 2017), https://jamestown.org/program/syrian-lessons-and-russias-asymmetric-response-to-the-us/.

[23] Aleksandr Svechin, *Strategiya,* (M.: Voenny vestnik, 1927), 29–30.

[24] Vasily Mikryukov, "Mertvye petli strategii — chast I," *Voenno-Promyshlennyi Kurier,* February 13, 2018, https://vpk-news.ru/articles/41236.

[25] Valeriy Gerasimov, "Po opytu Sirrii," *Voenno-Promyshlennyi Kurier,* March 7, 2016, https://vpk-news.ru/articles/29579.

[26] The Great Patriotic War (1941–1945) is how World War II is referred to in Russia.

[27] Pavel Shashkin, "Politicheskie aspekty naemnichestva," *Gumanitarnye nauki. Vestnik Finansovogo Universiteta,no.* no.5 (29) (2017): 47-55, https://cyberleninka.ru/article/n/politicheskie-aspekty-naemnichestva.

[28] "Rossiyskie neofashysty na sluzhbe Rossii pod prikrytiem CHVK 'Vagnera'," *Informnapalm*, June 1, 2018, https://informnapalm.org/43865-rossijskie-neofashisty-na-sluzhbe-rossii-pod-prikrytiem-chvk-vagnera/.

[29] Denis Korotkov, "Vagner v Kremle," *Fontanka.ru*, December 12, 2016, https://www.fontanka.ru/2016/12/12/064/.

[30] Denis Korotkov, "Spisok Vagnera," *Fontanka.ru*, August 21, 2017, http://www.fontanka.ru/2017/08/18/075/.

[31] Ibid.

[32] Ibid.

[33] Denis Korotkov, "'Slavyanskiy korpus' vozvrashchaetsya v Siriyu," *Fontanka.ru*, October 16, 2015, https://www.fontanka.ru/2015/10/16/118/.

[34] Ilya Rozhdestvensky, Anton Baev, Polina Rusyaeva, "Prizraki voyny: kak v Sirii poyavilas rossiyskaya chastnaya armiya," *RBK*, August 25, 2016, https://www.rbc.ru/magazine/2016/09/57bac4309a79476d978e850d.

[35] Ilya Rozhdestvensky, Anton Baev, Polina Rusyaeva, "Vagner, Molkino, CHVK — spekulyatsiya infopovodom," *Soldat.pro*, August 28, 2016, https://soldat.pro/2016/08/28/vagner-molkovo-chvk-spekulyaciya-infopovodom/.

[36] "Reuters vyjasnilo taynyy sposob dostavki v Siriyu naemnikov iz Rossii," *Radio Svoboda*, April 6, 2018, https://www.svoboda.org/a/29150044.html.

[37] "Pravitelstvo RFne podderzhalo zakonoproekt o chastnykh voennykh kompaniyakh," *Interfax*, March 27, 2018, http://www.interfax.ru/russia/605539.

[38] Leonid Ivashov, "My rano stali prazdnovat pobedu," *Izborskiy klub*, March 8, 2018, https://izborsk-club.ru/14888.

[39] "Posledniy boy 'Slavyanskogo korpusa'," *Fontanka.ru*, November 14, 2013, https://www.fontanka.ru/2013/11/14/060/.

[40] Andrey Sharogradsky, Aleksandr Gostev, Mark Krutov, "Siriyskie poteri 'Slavyanskogo korpusa'," *Radio Svoboda*, December 13, 2016, https://www.svoboda.org/a/27642396.html.

[41] Mikhail Zhyrokhov, "Landsknekhty Putina na Donbasse," *Begemot*, accessed June 1, 2018, https://begemot.media/power/landsknehty-putina-na-donbasse/.

[42] Denis Korotkov, "'Slavyanskiy korpus' vozvrashchaetsya v Siriyu," *Fontanka.ru*, October 16, 2010, https://www.fontanka.ru/2015/10/16/118/.

[43] Ilya Rozhdestvensky, Anton Baev, Polina Rusyaeva, "Prizraki voyny: kak v Sirii poyavilas rossiyskaya chastnaya armiya," *RBK*, August 25, 2016, https://www.rbc.ru/magazine/2016/09/57bac4309a79476d978e850d.

[44] Denis Korotkov, "'Slavyanskiy korpus' vozvrashchaetsya v Siriyu," *Fontanka.ru*, October 16, 2010, https://www.fontanka.ru/2015/10/16/118/.

[45] Yuriy Gavrilov, "Siriya: russkiy grom," *Rossiyskaya Gazeta*, no.6929 (61), March 23, 2016, https://rg.ru/2016/03/23/aleksandr-dvornikov-dejstviia-rf-v-korne-perelomili-situaciiu-v-sirii.html.

[46] Aleksey Makarkin, "Rossiyskie CHVK v Sirii," *Polit.ru*, February 13, 2018, http://polit.ru/article/2018/02/13/syria/.

[47] Denis Korotkov, "Spisok Vagnera," *Fontanka.ru*, August 21, 2017, http://www.fontanka.ru/2017/08/18/075/.

[48] "'Chastnaya armiya Putina': SBU naschitala v gruppe 'Vagnera' bolee 50 ukraintsev-naemnikov," *Rakurs*, May 7, 2018, http://racurs.ua/n104746-chastnaya-armiya-putina-sbu-naschitala-v-gruppe-vagnera-bolce-50-ukraincev-naemnikov.

[49] Ilya Rozhdestvensky, Anton Baev, Mikhail Rubin, "Sosluzhyvtsy soobshchili o gibeli v Sirii shestogo rossiyskogo voennogo," *RBK*, March 23, 2016, https://www.rbc.ru/politics/23/03/2016/56f007d59a794704531f9229.

[50] Anastasiya Yakoreva, Svetlana Reyter, "'Restorator Putina' perestal byt lyubimym podryadchikom Minoborony," *The Bell*, March 2, 2018, https://thebell.io/restorator-putina-perestal-byt-lyubimym-podryadchikom-minoborony/.

[51] Vsevolod Nepogodin, "Shoygu protiv Prigozhyna. Razborki na voennoy kukhne," *Ukrainsko-Rossiyskoe Obozrenie*, January 30, 2018, https://politua.org/2018/01/30/34785/.

[52] Vladimir Shcherbakov, "Bojnia pod Deir-el-Zorom izmena ili samonadejannost?" *Nezavisimoye Voennoye Obozreniye*, February 2, 2018, http://nvo.ng.ru/wars/2018-02-22/1_985_siria.html.

[53] Sergey Sukhankin, "Beyond Syria and Ukraine: Wagner PMC Expands Its Operations to Africa," *Eurasia Daily Monitor*, Volume: 15 Issue: 65 (2018), https://jamestown.org/program/beyond-syria-and-ukraine-wagner-pmc-expands-its-operations-to-africa/.

[54] Dmitry Tymchuk, "Koordinator IS: CHVK Vagnera menyaet nazvanie I organizatsyonnuyu strukturu," *Informatsyonnoe Soprotivlenie*, May 24, 2018, http://sprotyv.info/ru/news/kiev/koordinator-chvk-vagnera-menyaet-nazvanie-i-organizacionnuyu-strukturu.

[55] Valeriy Gerasimov, "Tsennost nauki v predvidenii," *Voenno-Promyshlennyi Kurier,* February 26, 2013, https://vpk-news.ru/articles/14632.

[56] Pavel Aristarkhov, "Trudnyi debyut russkih CHVK," *Segodnya.ru*, May 1, 2015, http://www.segodnia.ru/content/159810.

[57] "CHVK Vagnera. Dey-ez-Zor," *Youtube*, published: April 6, 2018, https://www.youtube.com/watch?v=-_8p-v5frPs.

13. Demography's Pull on Russian Mideast Policy

Ilan Berman

Summary

Demography is among the most underappreciated drivers of contemporary Russian policy in the Middle East. Yet Russia's ongoing population decline—and the expansion of Russia's own Muslim minority—has exerted significant influence over Moscow's attitudes and activities in the region in recent years. Most immediately and prominently, the growth and radicalization of "Muslim Russia" has helped propel the Kremlin into a leading role in the Syrian civil war since 2015. This same constituency will play an important role in shaping Russia's objectives in the Middle East in the years to come, as Moscow seeks to deepen and expand its strategic and political footprint in the region.

Introduction

What propels Russia's current policy toward the Middle East, and what will determine its trajectory in the future? Most contemporary analysis of Russia's return to the region in the past decade has focused on a number of conventional factors.

The first is geopolitics and the long-standing Russian aim of "multipolarity." This notion, popularized by former premier Yevgeny Primakov during the 1990s, was seen as a way of "ensuring the country's security under the conditions of a resource deficit" through the development of "strategic relations" with a range of international partners in the immediate aftermath of the Soviet collapse.[1] Since then, the strategy has been perpetuated by President Vladimir Putin as a method of denying global primacy to the country that the Kremlin still views as its "main enemy": the United States.[2] In the process, the Middle East has become a critical zone of strategic competition between Moscow and Washington.

Second, and related, is a resurgence of imperial ambition on the part of Russia's leaders. The collapse of the Soviet Union remains a deeply traumatic event for Russian elites and ordinary Russians alike, all of whom had grown accustomed to their country's superpower status. Not surprisingly, a broad political consensus persists within the country regarding the reestablishment of national greatness and the reclamation of former holdings. This sentiment, which former Russian finance minister Alexei Kudrin has described as an "imperial syndrome,"[3] has shaped Moscow's covetous attitude toward the countries of its "Near Abroad" and steadily driven it back into the Middle East.

In these efforts, Russia has been greatly aided by the retraction of US power and strategic influence. During its time in office, the Barack Obama administration made a concerted decision to reduce Washington's strategic footprint and influence in the region. This "right-sizing" of US Mideast policy[4] was driven by a range of considerations, not least a desire to disengage from a problematic region in favor of the comparatively more stable (at least at the time) Asian theater. But its practical result was to create empty political space that external powers such as Russia were quick to exploit.

Commercial opportunities have attracted Russia to the region as well. Historically, the Middle East and North Africa have cumulatively served as a key arms market for the Kremlin. But, as Anna Borshchevskaya of the Washington Institute for Near East Policy has documented, US disengagement during the Obama era allowed Moscow to recapture a growing share of the regional arms trade, with annual sales rising from $9 billion in 2009 to $21.4 billion in 2016.[5] So the situation has remained. Russia has recently concluded major new contracts with regional states such as Saudi Arabia, Bahrain, Egypt, and Morocco—ensuring that the greater Middle East will remain an area of intense commercial focus for the Kremlin for the foreseeable future.[6]

However, there is yet another, purely domestic driver that has propelled Russia back into the Middle East: the country's burgeoning Muslim population. While largely overlooked as a factor in the Kremlin's strategic calculus, the changing size and nature of this constituency has played a significant role in shaping official Russian attitudes regarding policy toward, and engagement with, the countries of the region.

The Rise of Muslim Russia

The growing importance of Russia's Muslims to the Kremlin's dealings with the Middle East finds its roots in the country's ongoing—and extensive—demographic decline.

At their core, Russia's population problems are neither new nor unexpected. For decades, the Soviet Union (and subsequently Russia) grappled with deeply negative demography. In stark contrast to the positive official predictions of Soviet authorities throughout the decades of the Cold War,[7] a significant demographic downturn was already apparent in the USSR by the 1960s. By the following decade, total fertility had dropped to below two children per woman in almost all of the Soviet Union's European republics.[8] With the Soviet collapse, the USSR's successor state, the Russian Federation, entered a protracted period of demographic decline driven by a range of societal factors, from poor health standards to rampant drug addiction to extensive abortion practices.[9]

This situation remains largely unchanged today. The last official Russian census, taken in 2010, tallied the national population at 142.9 million.[10] That figure represented an overall decline of nearly 3 percent over the preceding decade.[11] Since then, Russia's population has expanded slightly; the annexation, in 2014, of the Crimean Peninsula as a result of Russia's ongoing conflict with Ukraine added two million new citizens, most of them Slavs, to the population rolls. This modest growth, however, is artificial in nature, insofar as it does not reflect a meaningful alteration of Russia's overall trajectory of population decline. As official figures released in May 2017 by the country's state statistics agency, ROSSTAT, reflect, Russia's demographic downturn (temporarily ameliorated by a range of social programs), has returned with a vengeance, with the country experiencing nearly 70,000 fewer births during the first four months of 2017 than it did a year earlier.[12] Thus, despite the triumphalist narrative propounded by the Kremlin (which argues that strong leadership and shrewd investments have allowed Russia to decisively turn a demographic corner), it is clear that the decline of Russia's population is actually accelerating.[13]

The most recent official data confirms this conclusion. Statistics issued by ROSSTAT in January 2018 indicate that Russia experienced a drop of more than 10 percent in births between 2016 and 2017, bringing the national birth rate down to its lowest point in a decade.[14] Moreover, experts expect this decline to stretch into the foreseeable future, as the number of women of child-bearing age in Russia continues to dwindle.[15]

Russia's population downturn is not taking place in uniform fashion, however. While the country's demographic base is constricting as a whole, certain segments of the population are faring considerably better than others, with Russia's Muslims prominent among them. Indeed, a key feature of Russia's demographic transition is what could be termed "the rise of Muslim Russia."

According to Russia's 2002 census, while the country's overall population declined by nearly four percent between 1989 and 2002, the number of Russian Muslims grew by 20 percent.[16] This imbalance still exists. Today, although Russia's Muslims remain a distinct minority (less than 15 percent of the country's overall population in the wake of the annexation of Crimea), differences in communal behavior—including fewer divorces, less alcoholism and a greater rate of reproduction—have given them a more robust long-term demographic profile than their ethnic Russian counterparts. As the United Nations has noted, the fertility of Russia's Muslims, at 2.3, is significantly higher than the overall Russian national fertility rate of 1.7.[17] Other estimates peg the reproductive rate of Russia's Muslims higher still.[18]

The effects of this disparity are both cumulative and far-reaching. While estimates of the projected growth of Russia's Muslim minority vary,[19] it is clear that this expanding constituency has begun to impact both Russian domestic politics and the country's foreign policy priorities.

Russia's Muslims on the March

The growing size and prominence of Russia's Muslim population is significant in and of itself. But it is all the more so given its fraught relationship with what is perceived to be an increasingly distant and unaccountable federal state under Vladimir Putin.

Since taking power in 1999, Russia's president has steadily incubated nationalist sentiment throughout the country via a variety of organizations (among them *Nashi* and the Young Guard), and simultaneously sought to harness nationalist ideas for his own ends.[20] The resulting rise of xenophobia and race-related violence within Russia has made Muslims, both native-born and labor migrants from Central Asia, a primary target of aggression. Simultaneously, Putin's government has fundamentally altered the relationship between Russia's regions and the "federal center," robbing the country's federal subjects of their historic autonomy and making them increasingly subservient to the Kremlin's "power vertical." The cumulative effect of these dynamics has been to exclude Russia's Muslims from contemporary Russian politics and society—and to leave them vulnerable to the lure of alternative ideologies.

Islamist groups have been notable beneficiaries of this trend.[21] Indeed, since the Kremlin's formal intervention in the Syrian civil war in September 2015 there has been a marked uptick in Islamist activity within the Russian Federation. This has included a transformation of a significant portion of the country's most prominent *jihadist* organization, the Caucasus Emirate, into a formal affiliate of the Islamic State, as well as an extensive mobilization and migration of Islamist cadres to the Middle East.[22] The Soufan Group, a leading Washington, DC, counterterrorism consultancy, has documented that Russia now represents the single largest contributor of foreign fighters to the *jihad* in Syria.[23] In fact, while the number of Islamic extremists who have joined the Islamic State originating from countries such as Saudi Arabia and Tunisia has declined appreciably since 2015, those from Russia has risen. In all, nearly 3,500 Russian nationals are believed to have joined the Islamic State to date—an increase of 40 percent from the 2,400 Russian nationals that were estimated to have affiliated with the group as of 2015.[24] Cumulatively, extremists from Russia and the countries of Central Asia now account for nearly 10 percent of the roughly 40,000 radicals estimated to have joined the "caliphate."[25] In turn, Russian was estimated to be the third most frequently spoken language among fighters of the Islamic State until its collapse in late 2017.[26]

For its part, the Kremlin has sought to manage this dynamic in a variety of ways. Russia's various security services have facilitated the departure of terrorists from within the Russian Federation, essentially seeking to "externalize" the country's *jihadist* problem.[27] Simultaneously, the Kremlin has passed new and increasingly draconian counter-terrorism measures designed to constrict the domestic room available for political maneuver to Russia's Islamists— and to nudge them toward going abroad. Prominent among these has been the "Yarovaya Packet," a series of laws passed in 2016 which, among other things, expand the definition of "extremism" and allow the criminalization of a highly subjective range of acts, as well as expanding official oversight over the Internet domain.[28] In 2016, Russia also created a new super-security service known as the National Guard, ostensibly to help the Kremlin better fight terrorism and organized crime.[29] Finally, the Kremlin has launched an expansive—and open-ended—version of its own "war on terror" abroad. Most concretely, this has been manifested in Russia's ongoing military campaign in Syria, which is intended—at least in part—to target Russian-origin *jihadists* and neutralize them before they have a chance to return home.

The Shape of Russia's Mideast Strategy

The rise and radicalization of Russia's Muslim minority has played a significant (if often overlooked) role in shaping the Kremlin's strategic thinking about its current and future priorities in the Middle East. Today, that influence can be seen in at least three distinct initiatives.

A Persistent Presence in Syria

In early December 2017, Russian Chief of Staff General Valery Gerasimov formally announced that "[a]ll armed IS [Islamic State] groups on Syrian territory have been destroyed, and the territory itself has been liberated."[30] During his subsequent surprise visit to Syria, President Vladimir Putin himself said much the same thing, announcing that—as a result of these successes—Russia was beginning the withdrawal of a "significant part" of its Syrian contingent.[31]

Despite these pronouncements, however, Russia does not appear to be eyeing an exit from the Syrian theater any time in the foreseeable future. To the contrary, the Kremlin has mapped out plans for a long-term military presence in the country. These include an open-ended naval basing arrangement concluded with the Syrian regime in mid-2017,[32] as well as upgrades—underway as of this writing—to that facility and to the new airbase at Khmeimim, north of Damascus, that will make both installations capable of hosting expanded numbers of Russian forces and materiel.[33] Simultaneously, the Kremlin has begun a significant reconfiguration of the nature of its deployed forces in Syria to better achieve its strategic objectives.[34] These include not only strengthening the Syrian regime and maintaining military freedom of action in the Levant, but also maintaining a forward presence that allows the Kremlin to carry out anti-terrorist operations at a distance.

New Fronts for Strategic Operations

Over the past year, the US-led Global Coalition to Defeat ISIS has made major strategic gains against the Islamic State terrorist group. At the height of its power, in late 2014 and early 2015, the territory of the Islamic State covered 81,000 square miles—a geographical expanse roughly equivalent to the size of the United Kingdom[35]—and held sway over some eight million civilians, a population on par with that of Switzerland.[36] It likewise generated annual revenue of nearly

$2 billion, making it the best-funded terrorist group in recorded history.[37]

Today, however, the Islamic State had contracted considerably, both in terms of territory and resources. As a result of coordinated military action by the Coalition, as of late 2017 the group had lost nearly 90 percent of the territory it once held and some 6.5 million people had been liberated from its control.[38] But as IS has declined in its "core" caliphate of Iraq and Syria, the organization has begun to migrate to other strategic theaters. In particular, the group has come to view Libya, in the throes of a protracted civil war since the 2011 death of former leader Muammar Qaddafi, as an important "second front" where it can regroup and from which it can continue to stage regional and international attacks.[39] And, like they were in Syria/Iraq, Russian Islamists can be expected to be actively represented in this new IS theater of operations.

The Kremlin, for its part, has mapped out plans to follow these radicals as they disperse from the Syrian theater. Thus, in December 2017, the Russian government made clear that it plans to become more involved in the conflict in Libya, where it is "prepared to work with all parties" in order to stabilize the political and security situation in the country.[40] Moscow has also initiated discussions with a number of other existing and potential regional partners (including Algeria, Tunisia and Morocco) about the possibility of an expanded strategic presence in those places.[41] This activism is driven, at least in part, by the same dynamic of proactive counter-terrorism that propelled Russia into Syria—and which is likely to lead the Kremlin to further expand its political presence and military activities in North Africa in the future.

Engaging the Sunni World

For years, Russia has pursued what could be termed an "accidentally Shia" policy in the Middle East. Although the overwhelming majority of its Muslim population is Sunni, Russia's principal strategic partners in the region have long been Shia: the Islamic Republic of Iran and the regime of Bashar al-Assad in Syria. This feature of Russia's regional policy, long a matter of resentment for regional states and among Russia's own Muslims, made the Kremlin the focal point for considerable Sunni anger following its entry into the Syrian civil war in the fall of 2015. In October of that year, dozens of Saudi clerics issued a public letter urging Sunni militants to travel to Syria to join the fight against the "Crusader/Shiite alliance" of Russia and Iran.[42] More directly, the Russian government's intervention into the Syrian civil war has made the country itself the target of various extremist groups. Jabhat al-Nusra (since renamed Jabhat Fateh al-Sham), al-Qaeda's Syrian affiliate, called for terrorist attacks within Russia as a retaliatory measure following Russia's involvement in the Syrian conflict.[43] So, too, did the Islamic State, which released a video through its various social media feeds that warned "[w]e will take through battle the lands of yours we wish," and predicted that "[the] Kremlin will be ours."[44]

None of this, however, means that Russia is prepared to abandon its strategic partnership with Iran. To the contrary, the ties between Moscow and Tehran appear more robust than ever.[45] Strategically, Iran has come to be seen in Moscow as a dependable proxy in the Middle East—and a force multiplier for Russia's regional initiatives there. Commercially, meanwhile, the economic windfall received by Iran as a result of the 2015 Joint Comprehensive Plan of Action has made Tehran once again a major arms client of the Russian Federation, placing orders for billions of dollars in new military materiel.[46] Russia, now squeezed by multiple rounds of international sanctions as a result of its conduct in Ukraine, can ill afford to forego this business. At the same time, Iran—like Russia—has become a major stakeholder in Syria, and one that Moscow must accommodate in order to preserve a long-term presence in the country. Finally, both Iran and Russia retain a shared interest in curtailing the operations and capabilities of the Islamic State, albeit for different reasons.

Nevertheless, the Kremlin is now under pressure to "balance" its strategic partnership with the Iranian regime. Officials in Moscow are acutely aware that Russo-Iranian ties serve as an irritant to the country's (Sunni) Muslim population. As a result, Russia can be expected to offset its ties to the Islamic Republic through heightened interaction with an array of Sunni states, the Sunni Gulf kingdoms prominent among them, in the years ahead as a way of conducting what would be considered a more representative foreign policy in the region.

The Russian government has already begun to do so on a number of fronts. Politically, the past year has seen a concerted effort by the Russian government to expand its diplomatic engagement with, and activism among, the countries of the Middle East and North Africa.[47] Russia has likewise started, however tentatively, to deepen its interaction with the region in the religious sphere. To this end, Russia concluded a memorandum of understanding with Morocco in March 2016 under which the Kingdom would begin to train Russian imams—an initiative that reflects a growing official awareness of the need to instill moderate religious teachings among the country's expanding Muslim minority.[48]

The Nexus of Demography and Ideology

Can Russia be a reliable partner in the Middle East? Ever since the terrorist attacks of September 11, 2001, that question has preoccupied policymakers in Washington. The answer that has emerged so far as a result of Kremlin conduct is decidedly mixed.

President Putin's early *laissez faire* attitude toward US and Coalition operations against al-Qaeda and the Taliban in the immediate aftermath of the 9/11 attacks greatly aided the early stages of the "War on Terror." Gradually, however, this cooperation dissipated as Russia once again sought to compete strategically with the United States, both in the "Near Abroad" of Central Asia and the Caucasus and beyond.[49]

Today, Russian policy can be said to be one of "selective counter-terrorism," in which Moscow plays both sides in the struggle against radical Islam, providing support to a range of extremist actors in the region (including Afghanistan's Taliban and the Palestinian Hamas movement) even as it battles others. As Svante Cornell of the American Foreign Policy Council's Central Asia–Caucasus Institute has noted, this strategy is informed by the Russian view of "insurgency and terrorism as forces to be manipulated for the purpose of weakening America's position in the world, undermine U.S. allies, and maximize Russian influence in world affairs."[50] Thus, "[w]hile the United States may need to work with Russia on a case-by-case basis, it must understand that Russia views all its instruments of statecraft as interconnected, serving a common purpose; and that Russia's aims are seldom, if ever, compatible with those of the United States."[51]

Yet even those cases may become fewer and farther between as, over time, Russia's changing demography fundamentally alters its engagement with the Middle East, and the Muslim World more broadly. As the country's demographic transition progresses, Russia's involvement in the politics of the region can be expected to increase, even as its potential to serve as a reliable partner of the United States there will continue to diminish. Fundamentally, Russian policy in the Middle East (and toward the Muslim World more broadly) is already competitive, seeking to assert Russia as a counterpoint to US alliances and interests. The demographic pressures exerted by Russia's swelling Muslim minority are likely to reinforce these tendencies over the next several years. In the process, they will make Moscow's already unconstructive, zero sum approach to the Middle East all the more so.

ENDNOTES

[1] Yevgeny Primakov, "Russia and the Outside World," *International Affairs* 3, 1998: 7–13.

[2] Stephen Blank, "The Foundations of Russian Policy in the Middle East," Jamestown Foundation, October 5, 2017, https://jamestown.org/program/foundations-russian-policy-middle-east/.

[3] "Former Finance Minister Alexei Kudrin: 'We Have To Take A Chance with More Democracy,'" *Der Spiegel* (Hamburg), January 23, 2013, http://www.spiegel.de/international/world/interview-with-putin-ally-alexei-kudrin-on-democracy-in-russia-a-878873.html.

[4] See, for example, Marc Lynch, "Right-Sizing America's Mideast Role," *Foreign Policy*, January 11, 2013, http://foreignpolicy.com/2013/01/11/right-sizing-americas-mideast-role/.

[5] Anna Borshchevskaya, "The Tactical Side of Russia's Arms Sales to the Middle East," Jamestown Foundation, December 20, 2017, https://jamestown.org/program/tactical-side-russias-arms-sales-middle-east/.

[6] "Russia has $8Bln Worth of Weapon Orders From Arab Countries," *Sputnik*, November 15, 2017, https://sputniknews.com/military/201711151059127900-russia-weapons-orders-arab/.

[7] Perhaps the most striking was the estimate issued in early 1991, just months before the Soviet collapse, by the prestigious Soviet Academy of Sciences, predicting that and the number of ethnic Russians within the USSR would grow by as much as two million over the following half-

decade, and that ethnic Russians would number 158 million by 2015. As recounted in Venyamin A. Baslachev, *Demografiya: Russkie Proriv. Nezavisimoye Isledovanie* (Demography: the Russian chasm. An independent investigation) (Moscow: Beluy Albii, 2006), 6.

[8] Stephan Sievert, Sergey Zakharov and Reiner Klingholz, *The Waning World Power: The Demographic Future of Russia and the Other Soviet Successor States* (Berlin Institute for Population and Development, April 2011), http://www.berlin-institut.org/publications/studies/the-waning-world-power.html.

[9] For a detailed review of these drivers, see Ilan Berman, *Implosion: The End of Russia and What It Means for America* (Regnery Publishing, 2013).

[10] *Vserosiiskii Perepis Naselenie 2010*, http://www.perepis-2010.ru/.

[11] Ibid.

[12] Government of Russia, Federal Service of Government Statistics, "Natural movement of the population in the section of subjects of the Russian Federation," May 30, 2017, http://www.gks.ru/free_doc/2017/demo/edn04-17.htm.

[13] This is a view shared by observers of Russia's overall demographic trajectory. See, for example, "The Extinction of Russians has Accelerated," *NewsLand*, May 31, 2017, https://newsland.com/community/5325/content/vymiranie-russkikh-uskorilos/5853964.

[14] "Birth Rate Hits 10-Year Low in Russia," *The Moscow Times*, January 29, 2018, https://themoscowtimes.com/news/birth-rate-hits-10-year-low-russia-60321.
[15] Ibid.

[16] *Vserossiyskaya Perepis Naseleniya 2002a Goda*, www.perepis2002.ru.

[17] Pew Forum on Religion and Public Life, "The Future of the Global Muslim Population: Projections for 2010–2030," January 27, 2011,

http://www.pewforum.org/future-of-the-global-muslim-population-russia.aspx.

[18] "Muslim Birthrate Worries Russia," *Washington Times*, November 20, 2006, http://www.washingtontimes.com/news/2006/nov/20/20061120-115904-9135r/?page=all.

[19] Based upon then-prevailing trendlines, experts estimated a decade ago that Russia's Muslims will make up one-fifth of the entire population by the end of the that decade. See Jonah Hull, "Russia Sees Muslim Population Boom," *Al-Jazeera* (Doha), January 13, 2007, http://english.aljazeera.net/news/europe/2007/01/2008525144630794963.html. Some of the more extreme estimates at the time predicted that the Russian Federation will become majority Muslim by mid-century. See "Cherez polveka Musulmani v Rossii Mogut Stat Bolshenstvom – Posol MID RF [In Half a Century, Muslims in Russia Could Become the Majority – Russia's OIC Ambassador]," Interfax (Moscow), October 10, 2007, http://www.interfax-religion.ru/islam/print.php?act=news&id=20767. More modest growth rates on the part of Russia's Muslims over the past several years have revised these projections downward.

[20] Charles Clover, "'Managed Nationalism' Turns Nasty for Putin," *Financial Times*, December 23, 2010, http://www.ft.com/intl/cms/s/0/046a3e30-0ec9-11e0-9ec3-00144feabdc0.html#axzz2KtFLqYoI; Owen Matthews and Anna Nemtsova, "Fascist Russia?" *Newsweek*, August 7, 2011, http://www.thedailybeast.com/newsweek/2011/08/07/why-the-kremlin-aids-the-rise-of-russia-s-far-right-hate-groups.html.

[21] Alexei Malashenko, "The Dynamics of Russian Islam," Carnegie Moscow Center. February1, 2013, http://carnegie.ru/2013/02/01/dynamics-of-russian-islam/f890; David M. Herszenhorn, "Russia Sees a Threat in Its Converts to Islam," *New York Times*, July 1, 2015, https://www.nytimes.com/2015/07/02/world/russia-sees-a-threat-in-its-converts-to-islam.html.

[22] For a detailed summary of the contemporary state of Islamism in Russia, see the Russia chapter in the American Foreign Policy Council's *World Almanac of Islamism 2017*, available online at http://almanac.afpc.org/russia.

[23] Richard Barrett, *Beyond The Caliphate: Foreign Fighters and the Threat of Returnees* (The Soufan Center, October 2017), http://thesoufancenter.org/wp-content/uploads/2017/10/Beyond-the-Caliphate-Foreign-Fighters-and-the-Threat-of-Returnees-TSC-Report-October-2017-v2.pdf.

[24] Ibid.

[25] Ibidem.

[26] Interview with Evgenia Albats, *Ekho Moskvy*, November 17, 2015, http://echo.msk.ru/programs/personalno/1659708-echo/.

[27] See, for example, Michael Weiss, "Russia is Sending Jihadis to Join ISIS," *The Daily Beast*, August 23, 2015, http://www.thedailybeast.com/articles/2015/08/23/russia-s-playing-a-double-game-with-islamic-terror0.html.

[28] Russian Federation, *Federal Law #1039149-6 on Changing Legislative Acts of the Russian Federation and Establishing Extra Counter-Terrorism Measures and Public Safety Guarantees*, March 6, 2016.

[29] Russian Federation, *Federal Order on Questions of Federal Service of a National Guard*, April 5, 2016, http://kremlin.ru/acts/news/51648; Mark Galeotti, "Putin's New National Guard," *In Moscow's Shadows*, April 5, 2016, https://inmoscowsshadows.wordpress.com/2016/04/05/putins-new-national-guard-what-does-it-say-when-you-need-your-own-personal-army/.

[30] "Russia's Defense Ministry Says Syria '100% Free of Islamic State,'" *The Moscow Times*, December 7, 2017, https://themoscowtimes.com/news/syria-100-percent-free-from-islamic-state-says-russias-defense-ministry-59846.

[31] Matti Suomenaro and Jackson Danbeck, "Back To The West: Russia Shifts Its Air Campaign In Syria," Institute for the Study of War, December 12, 2017, http://iswresearch.blogspot.com/2017/12/back-to-west-russia-shifts-its-air.html.

[32] "Putin Signs Deal Cementing Russia's Long-Term Military Presence in Syria," *Radio Free Europe/Radio Liberty*, July 27, 2017, https://www.rferl.org/a/putin-hmeimim-air-base-syria-deal/28643519.html. The deal is said to give Russia rights to use the facility cost-free for a period of 49 years—after which the lease can be renewed for another quarter-century. The agreement is also said to permit 11 Russian vessels to concurrently dock at the facility, and provide diplomatic immunity to base personnel and their families throughout the entirety of Syrian soil. See Taha Abed Al Wahed, "Russia's Kremlin Speeds Up Tartus Base Expansion," *ASharq Al-Awsat* (London), December 20, 2017, https://aawsat.com/english/home/article/1118856/russia%E2%80%99s-kremlin-speeds-tartus-base-expansion.

[33] "Russia Begins Development of Syrian Bases to Host Nuclear Warships & Warplanes," RT, December 26, 2017, https://www.rt.com/news/414261-russia-permament-bases-syria-nuclear/.

[34] Suomenaro and Danbeck, "Back to the West: Russia Shifts its Air Campaign in Syria."

[35] Rick Noack, "How The Islamic State Compares With Real States," *Washington Post*, September 12, 2014, https://www.washingtonpost.com/news/worldviews/wp/2014/09/12/heres-how- the-islamic-state- compares-to- real-states/.

[36] "In ISIL-Controlled Territory, 8 Million Civilians Living In 'State Of Fear' - UN Expert," un.org, July 31, 2015, http://www.un.org/apps/news/story.asp?NewsID=51542#.WDZYsKIrKYU.

[37] Stefan Heissner et al., *Caliphate in Decline: An Estimate of Islamic State's Financial Fortunes* (London: ICSR, 2017), http://icsr.info/wp-

content/uploads/2017/02/ICSR-Report-Caliphate- in-Decline-An-
Estimate- of-Islamic- States-Financial- Fortunes.pdf.

[38] "ISIS Lost Nearly 90% of Territory Seized on 2014: US-led Coalition,"
NDTV, October 17, 2017, https://www.ndtv.com/world-news/isis-lost-
nearly-90-of-territory-seized-on-2014-us-led-coalition-1764206.

[39] See, for example, Mustafa Fetouri, "How Islamic State is Undermining
Peace Prospects in Libya," *Al-Monitor*, September 4, 2017, https://www.al-
monitor.com/pulse/originals/2017/09/libya-peace-isis-political-solution-
threats-conflict-war.html.

[40] Tom O'Connor, "Russia Claims Victory in Syria War, now Moscow has
its Eyes on Libya Crisis," *Newsweek*, December 12, 2017,
http://www.newsweek.com/russia-claim-victory-syria-war-moscow-has-
eye-libya-crisis-746069.

[41] See, for example, Anna Borshchevskaya, "From Moscow to Marrakech:
Russia is Turning its Eyes to Africa," *The Hill*, September 21, 2017,
http://thehill.com/opinion/international/351584-from-moscow-to-
marrakech-russia-is-turning-to-africa.

[42] "Saudi Clerics Call for Jihad Against Iran and Russia in Syria," Reuters
and *VICE News*, October 5, 2015, https://news.vice.com/article/saudi-
clerics-call-for-jihad-against-iran-and-russia-in-syria.

[43] Martin Chulov, "Syrian War's Al-Qaida Affiliate Calls for Terror Attacks
in Russia," *Guardian* (London), October 13, 2015,
https://www.theguardian.com/world/2015/oct/13/syria-al-qaida-group-
jabhat-al-nusra-terror-attacksrussia.

[44] Malia Zimmerman, "ISIS Coming for the Kremlin, New Video Warns,"
Fox News, November 12, 2015,
http://www.foxnews.com/world/2015/11/12/new-isis-video-says-jihadis-
coming-for-kremlin/.

[45] See, for example, Ilan Berman, "Why Russia Won't Help Trump On
Iran," *Foreign Affairs*, February 10, 2017,

https://www.foreignaffairs.com/articles/united-states/2017-02-10/why-russia-wont-help-trump-iran?cid=int-lea&pgtype=hpg.

[46] Roland Oliphant, "Russia may sell Iran $10 Billion Worth of Tanks and Jets in New Arms Deal," *Telegraph* (London), November 14, 2016, http://www.telegraph.co.uk/news/2016/11/14/russia-may-sell-iran-10-billion-worth-of-tanks-and-jets-in-new-a/.

[47] See, for instance, Patrick Wintour, "Saudi King's Visit to Russia Heralds Shift in Global Power Structures," *Guardian* (London), October 5, 2017, https://www.theguardian.com/world/2017/oct/05/saudi-russia-visit-putin-oil-middle-east; See also Ali Younes, "Sergei Lavrov Calls for Dialogue to Resolve Gulf Crisis," *Al-Jazeera* (Doha), August 30, 2017, http://www.aljazeera.com/news/2017/08/sergey-lavrov-calls-dialogue-resolve-gulf-crisis-170830113114395.html.

[48] Larbi Arbaoui, "Morocco to Train Russian Imams," *Morocco World News*, March 19, 2016, https://www.moroccoworldnews.com/2016/03/182434/182434/.

[49] For a detailed description of Russian policy post-9/11, see Ilan Berman, "The New Battleground: Central Asia and the Caucasus," *The Washington Quarterly*, Winter 2004–2005, http://www.ilanberman.com/6002/the-new-battleground-central-asia-and-the-caucasus.

[50] Svante Cornell, Testimony before the House of Representatives Foreign Affairs Committee Subcommittee on Terrorism, Nonproliferation, and Trade, November 7, 2017, http://docs.house.gov/meetings/FA/FA18/20171107/106596/HHRG-115-FA18-Wstate-CornellS-20171107.pdf.

[51] Ibid.

14. Russia in the Middle East Until 2024: From Hard Power to Sustainable Influence

Yuri Barmin

Summary

Russia's campaign in Syria has allowed Russia to re-emerge as a leading actor in the Middle East thanks, to a large extent, to the use of hard power and coercive diplomacy. As Vladimir Putin eyes reelection as president in 2018, he will rely on his victories on the Middle East front in his campaign rhetoric; but he will also need to plan his strategy toward the region for his next term in office. As Moscow looks to solidify its presence in the region, it will need to capitalize on the military foothold in Syria that it has established in order to project more political influence in the Middle East and the Mediterranean. As the Syrian war comes to an end, Russia will also need to look beyond weapons in order to be recognized as a trusted partner among Sunni Arab states and might see its positioning toward existing partners, particularly Iran, readjusted. In the post–Syrian war Middle East, Russia may choose to act in a way that would distance it from conflicting parties, as it does in Libya, in order to be recognized as a regional referee.

Introduction

Vladimir Putin's return to power in Russia in 2012 signified a dramatic change in the country's foreign policy and military strategy. Scrapping the achievements of the Dmitry Medvedev era in the Kremlin, which was characterized by a thaw in relations with the West, Vladimir Putin opted for a more aggressive approach toward positioning the country in the international arena. Experts still argue what prompted this review of the country's foreign policy strategy, but the developments that likely had a major impact on Vladimir Putin's policy planning in 2012 included the war with Georgia in 2008, the Arab Spring protests, and the North Atlantic Treaty Organization's (NATO) infamous military campaign in Libya, which brought down Russia's long-time ally Muammar Qaddafi.

Contours of the new policy approach to the region started to emerge when Russia updated two of its key documents, the Foreign Policy Concept of the Russian Federation and the Military Doctrine of the Russian Federation, in 2013 and 2014, respectively.[1] The documents pronounced strategies based on protecting Russian national interests abroad, including militarily if need be, and increasing Moscow's role in maintaining global security.

Quite notably, a more recent edition of the Foreign Policy Concept of the Russian Federation, signed by President Putin in November 2016, has a specific focus on the Middle East and names foreign meddling there as one of the causes of instability and extremism in the region that directly affect Russia.[2] The statement that serves as *de facto* justification for the Russian military campaign in Syria became the first official document to elucidate the country's ambition to play a bigger role in the Middle East and North Africa. In the three years that divide the two concepts, Vladimir Putin's approach to foreign policy experienced an evolution and increasing securitization (the word "terrorism" figures 15 times in the 2013 Concept and 35 in its 2016 edition). The Foreign Policy Concept also spells out the Russian president's growing ambition to deal with instability where it originates before it reaches Russian borders.

The rationale behind Russia's re-emergence as one of the leading powers in the Middle East was of a defensive nature and largely reactionary. The Arab Spring movement in the region was a painful reminder of the Color Revolutions that broke out across several post-Soviet states in the first half of the 2000s and, according to the Kremlin, led to the 2014 EuroMaidan revolution in Ukraine. Vladimir Putin himself is of the belief that that the Arab Spring is a continuation of those Color Revolutions and that both are foreign-instigated.[3] Coupled with a forced revolution in Libya and the removal of Qaddafi in what Russia declared was a violation of international law, this episode is often cited as a watershed in Vladimir Putin's foreign policy thinking.[4] A wave of revolutions across Eurasia convinced the Russian leadership that the apparent domino effect of regime change would eventually target Russia. It is not a coincidence that the Russian president likens Color Revolutions and the Arab Spring protests to each other and often makes no distinction between them. Commenting on anti-corruption protests in Russia in March 2017, he went as far as to call them "an instrument of the Arab Spring."[5]

Vladimir Putin sees Russia as a legitimate actor in designing a new power balance in the Middle East and as its integral part since security challenges originating in the region reverberate across the former Soviet space as well as in Russia. The United States, on the other hand, is an outsider in this region in the view of Russian officials. Criticism of the White House over its "destructive" role in the Middle East is a central theme of many of Vladimir Putin's speeches, including the one he delivered at the UN General Assembly prior to launching his military campaign in Syria in September 2015. In those remarks, the Russian president accused the United States of being the source of problems in the Middle East.[6]

A gradual withdrawal of the United States from the Middle East under Barack Obama among other things meant that the region's "policeman" was no longer interested in maintaining order there, which arguably presented Moscow with numerous security challenges. Russia's re-emergence in the Middle East to a large extent happened to fill some of the void left by the retreating Obama administration. In some cases it happened effortlessly, such as in Egypt, where the US decision to cut aid to Cairo in 2013 led to the emergence of a budding Russia-Egypt alliance. In other contexts, most prominently in Syria, Russia had to invest significant diplomatic and military resources to marginalize the US in the war and in the peace process. What started out as an attempt to replace the United States where it was no longer interested in playing a leading role later transformed into an ambition to challenge the US even where it had no intention of retreating, for instance in the Gulf region.

Russia's return to the Middle East differs from the Soviet experience: Today, Moscow is extending its reach without the baggage of Soviet ideology. The idea of using its arms exports to the Middle East in the ideological struggle against the West evaporated as soon as the Union of Soviet Socialist Republics (USSR) disintegrated and was replaced with the idea of making a profit for the cash-strapped budget. The Kremlin is looking to support its geopolitical claims with a strong pragmatic dimension.

In the Middle East, Moscow to reinforce its influence there as well as offset the burden upon the Russian federal budget associated with the expenses of the Syrian campaign. Following in the footsteps of the Soviet Union, Russia has used arms deals to reach out to Cold War–era allies in Egypt, Iraq, Libya and Syria to consolidate a new power balance. During the Cold War, Wynfred Joshua and Stephen P. Gilbert wrote that as more countries became recipients of Soviet military aid programs, there was a tendency for these countries to become greater political allies of the Soviet Union.[7] And it seems that this argument is increasingly relevant today. According to SIPRI, in 2015 $5.5 billion in Russian arms exports were destined for clients in the Middle East, which was ten times more than all Russian experts to the region for all of the 1990s.[8]

With Vladimir Putin declaring victory over the Islamic State during his December 2017 visit to Syria, Russia is faced with a number of opportunities as well as challenges. Its military operation in Syria may have put Russia back on the radar in the Middle East; but in all certainty, it essentially solidified its position in the region. As Vladimir Putin is eyeing re-election as president in March 2018, foreign policy achievements, chiefly in the Middle East and North Africa, figure prominently in his election campaign rhetoric.

One of the effects of Russia's assertive foreign policy has become an expectation from regional partners and opponents alike that Moscow will be active in the Middle East. However, the hard power that brought Russia to prominence in the region will not be a helpful tool to support long-term influence there and could, in fact, produce a negative impact for Russia's international standing. As a result, during his next term in office, Vladimir Putin will be faced with a challenge to depart from hard power, his preferred *modus operandi*, to embrace a spectrum of other tools in order to make Russia's presence in the region lasting and sustainable.

From Status Quo Disruptor to Status Quo Creator

New Military Positioning

In the next few years, due to Russia's gains in Syria, Moscow will be recalibrating its military position in the wider region. The most significant of its gains has to do with the establishment of permanent military bases in Syria. In December 2017, the Russian parliament approved the agreements with the Syrian government leasing the Tartus and Hmeymim bases to Russia for 49 years with an automatic

25-year prolongation.[9] The Tartus naval base, which is about to be upgraded, will be able to host up to 15 warships as well as submarines.[10]

The establishment of a permanent military presence in Syria fits with the Russian strategy to acquire air and naval supremacy in the Black Sea and the Eastern Mediterranean and signals the restoration of the Soviet strategy toward the region. From 1967 up until the collapse of the USSR, the Soviet 5th Squadron operated in the Mediterranean despite Moscow having no permanent bases in the region. In 2013, the Russian President made a decision to revive a perpetual naval presence there and ordered the establishment of the Mediterranean Task Force (MTF) within the Black Sea Fleet.[11] The establishment of permanent bases in Syria will allow Russia to overcome the shortcomings of the Soviet experience in the Mediterranean when warships had at times to use ad hoc supply lines to refuel and restock food and water. Remarkably, commenting on the setting up of the MTF, Vladimir Putin said in 2013 that Russia may use these warships for operations in the Atlantic and the Indian Ocean, if such a need emerges.[12]

Russia has essentially developed what some analysts call an anti-access, area denial (A2/AD) strategy in the Mediterranean. Along with the deployment of the S-400 air-defense system to Syria, in November 2015 (and to Crimea, in August 2016), the Russian naval group in the Eastern Mediterranean is equipped with Kalibr cruise missiles and P-800 Onyx anti-ship missiles, which create an added advantage against a potential enemy.[13] By returning to the Mediterranean, Russia challenges NATO's freedom of action there as well as parts of the Middle East. This was demonstrated by the de facto no-fly zone that Russian air-defense systems established over parts of Syria, Turkey as well as the Eastern Mediterranean.

Expanding its naval infrastructure will likely become a priority for Russia in the Mediterranean for years to come as it will be looking for ways to support the MTF, expand its operations and make them more autonomous. A temporary diplomatic conflict between Russia and Turkey in 2015–2016, following the shoot-down of a Russian Su-24, demonstrated that the position of the Russian naval group in the Mediterranean is quite vulnerable: the MTF is entirely dependent on Turkey since virtually all the supply lines pass through the Turkish-controlled Bosporus.

Additionally, North Africa is increasingly playing a more prominent role in the Russian military expansion in the Mediterranean. Illustratively, speaking at the Valdai Club Conference in 2016, Vladimir Putin said that "Africa cannot be on the periphery of international relations"[14] given its security problems, which affect all of the international community.

Russia is increasing its military cooperation with Cairo, a partner with which Moscow had a strong partnership under Gamal Abd'el Nasir and more recently with President Abdel Fatah El Sisi. Military-technical cooperation between the two countries is on the rise. But even more importantly, this cooperation now extends to annual joint naval drills[15] and military exercises[16] as Russia looks for additional access to Egypt's military infrastructure. Moreover, in order to simultaneously boost its Libya portfolio, Russia reportedly boosted the frequency of its use of Egyptian facilities at the border with Libya, including the port of Marsa Matrouh and the base at Sidi Barrani, once used by the Soviet Union.[17]

It is too early to conclude what Russia's endgame in Libya is. Yet, notably, apart from lucrative arms and energy deals that Moscow had with Muammar Qaddafi—but which were erased by the revolution in the country—the Russian military has long mulled using Libyan naval infrastructure for its operations in the Mediterranean. Indeed, during the early 2000s, Qaddafi even reportedly granted Russia access to the port of Benghazi for its fleet in an attempt to use the Russian military as a deterrent against Western incursion.[18] Moscow may now wish to try to revive and perhaps further expand this type of relationship.

At the same time, Russia increasingly looking at warm-water ports in Algeria, Tunisia and Morocco in the 2000s. Moscow has significantly stepped up diplomatic engagement with each of these actors over the past twenty years since the Soviet collapse.[19] Algeria has been Moscow's most committed partner since 1963 despite firmly remaining in the Western camp. In 2001, during the visit of Algerian President Abdelaziz Bouteflika to Russia, the two countries signed a declaration of strategic partnership, which became a milestone in the expansion of bilateral relations. Moscow continues to export its weapons to the country: 91 percent of Algerian arms are purchased in Russia.[20] Moreover, in 2006, the two governments signed Algeria's largest post–Cold War arms deal, which amounted to $7.5 billion.[21] Despite having a more stable relationship than that with Egypt, Russia's ties with Algeria usually are opaque. However, Moscow's ambition to play a role in the resolution of the Libyan crisis, combined with threats emanating from terrorist groups that find refuge in Mali, Niger and Chad, have motivated Russia to expand its security cooperation with the country. As far back as 2010, Moscow has asked Algeria for access to the Mers el-Kebir naval base, near Oran with negotiations, at least publicly, still ongoing.[22] Moreover, the two countries signed an agreement on counter-terrorist cooperation in 2016, and have already held two rounds of consultations on stepping up joint countering violent extremism in North Africa as well as set up regular exchanges of intelligence on extremist groups.[23]

The October 2017 visit of Prime Minister Dmitry Medvedev to Algeria is also remarkable in that it finally demonstrated that the Maghreb is again on Moscow's radar. Besides regular arms deals talks, the two sides reportedly discussed an agreement on a potential purchase of Russian S-400 missile systems, which Moscow only exports to select clients. If implemented, such an arms sale would symbolize a new strategic era in Russian-Algerian relations.

In Putin's calculus, Morocco also plays a crucial role, despite the fact that this country's military-technical cooperation with Russia is meager compared to Algeria's. Morocco's location, however, provides access both to the Mediterranean and the Atlantic, something Russia has always sought to acquire in order to link the operations of its Black Sea and Northern Fleets. To that end, Moscow has taken steps to indicate interest in the resolution of the Western Sahara issue, a sensitive matter for Rabat. Russian officials hosted the Polisario Front, an independence movement from Western Sahara, in Moscow in 2017, which clearly unnerved Morocco.[24] The issue of Western Sahara is the kind of political leverage that Russia could use in order to position itself as a go-to mediator for Morocco.

Military presence in the Mediterranean may only be a first step in Moscow's ambitious naval expansion. With the MTF deployed to the Mediterranean in 2013, Russia also started demonstrating a keen interest in the Red Sea, sending its warships there for drills as well as to project power.[25] In 2017, Russian ambitions regarding the Red Sea took an entirely different form when Sudan's Omar al-Bashir expressed willingness to host a Russian naval base just across the sea from Saudi Arabia and next to Djibouti, which already hosts US and Chinese bases.[26] It is yet to be seen how Russia feels about setting up such a base so soon after acquiring a permanent military foothold in the Mediterranean. But proposals like this are already indicative of how local powers perceive Russia's growing role in the Middle East.

It is in Russia's long-term interest to continue building up its military capabilities in the Mediterranean to support existing bases in Syria, linking its Northern and Black Sea Fleets' operations in the Atlantic, as well as to obtain more leverage against NATO. Given failed Soviet attempts to set up a military presence in Egypt and Libya, Russia may finally revisit this idea.

Channeling Growing Military Clout Toward Political Sustainability

The key challenges facing Russia in the next few years concern how to convert gains made in Syria into sustainable political influence in the wider region. Military power projected by Moscow in the Syrian conflict and, by extension, its political clout have allowed it to be recognized as a leading external power in the Middle East. Once the fighting dies down, however, Moscow will have a hard time maintaining its relevance in the region at the same level.

Without ways to project political power in the Middle East, Russian military forces there will be irrelevant. The bottom line is that hard power is a crisis management tool but not an agenda setting one. Moscow's military clout in the region has reached the level at which it guarantees Russia presence in the Middle East, but what it does not guarantee is long-term political influence.

For Russia to replace the United States as the guarantor of security in the Middle East, it needs to show a long-term commitment to the region. But if Vladimir Putin looks to preserve his country's influence in the Middle East, he will need to come up with ways to engage partners that would convince them of Russia's resolve. With the Middle East not being the most strategically important region to Moscow, Putin will need to decide exactly how much influence he actually wants to project in the region. Maintaining the image of a great power in the Middle East will require Russia to invest diplomatically and financially in the resolution of other crises, such as the Libyan war and the Israeli-Palestinian conflict. However, these investments will chiefly concern maintaining stability in the region and will not yield fast returns.

Russia will finally need to set a long-term agenda for the Middle East. Short-termism has so far prevailed in Moscow's Middle Eastern strategy because its actions were largely reactionary and most decisions were ad hoc. This was evidenced by the fact that Russia's bid on Iran's ground forces as the main fighting force in Syria later led to multiple attempts by Tehran to hijack international agreements on the ground and undermine Moscow's mediation attempts.[27] While hard-power projection is unlikely to be at the center of Putin's regional agenda, certain contours of his post-Syria policy can already be named.

The Russian government as well as Russian intellectuals and Middle East experts have been flirting with the idea of a regional system of collective—an idea that has been pitched to governments in the region on many occasions in the past. Igor Ivanov, a former minister of foreign affairs of the Russian Federation and the president of the Russian International Affairs Council, notably laid out a vision for such a regional security system in a February 2016 article.[28] According to him, the mechanism should include the Arab countries as well as Turkey, Iran and Israel. The collective security system must consist of three tracks or "baskets": security, economy and humanitarian cooperation. Disarmament in the Middle East should become a starting point for the discussion on the regional security system. The first steps in this direction could be the creation of demilitarized zones, the prohibition of destabilizing accumulations of conventional weapons (including anti-missile weapons), as well as a balanced reduction of armed forces by the main military powers in the region and neighboring countries.

Speaking before the United Nations General Assembly, on September 28, 2015, when he announced the beginning of the Russian military operation in Syria, Vladimir Putin proposed creating a global anti–Islamic State coalition "similar to the anti-Hitler" alliance.[29] He reiterated this idea at the G-20 meeting in Turkey, in November of that year.[30] This proposal, which he has voiced several times in the course of the Russian operation in Syria, pointedly feeds into the idea of creating a regional security system. The viability of a regional anti–Islamic State alliance was demonstrated when Turkey, Iran and Russia partnered to implement de-escalation zones in Syria. Egypt and Jordan played a distinct role in the negotiation process on the creation of de-escalation zones and their implementation, and Vladimir Putin may try to institutionalize what already looks a lot like a regional anti-extremist alliance. An anti-terrorist alliance that could later transform into a collective security system seems to be one of the few areas in which Russia is willing to commit resources, based both on Russia's domestic security concerns as well as its foreign policy calculations.

Old and New Partners

With Russia's military position gradually readjusting as a result of the Syrian conflict, its partnerships night also eventually undergo a broader rethink. Russia will need to find a way to reach out to Sunni Arab powers and win their trust, which was undermined as a result of Russia's perceived alliance with the Shia in the Syrian conflict. According to Pew Research, as of mid-2017, only 28 percent of people in the Middle East expressed confidence in Russia and Vladimir Putin's foreign policy and only 35 percent had a favorable view of Russia.[31]

The Syria campaign has demonstrated that Russia's relations with regional powers are extremely fluid, as was demonstrated by a temporary break-up with Turkey, a surprising thaw with Saudi Arabia and a growing mistrust with Iran. Once the Syrian conflict is over, Russia will need to reassess its relations with partners and opponents, but nonetheless they might remain transactional and be based on short-term political, military and economic gains.

As the Syrian conflict gradually draws to an end, confrontational tendencies in relations with Iran might become more visible. Moscow and Tehran will likely come to realize that their relationship is much bigger than Syria. The number of outstanding problems plaguing the alliance is already multiplying (militarization of the Caspian Sea, competition for the European gas market, Iran's growing influence in Central Asia) while both make a bid on their partnership in Syria as a unifying element. Even in Syria, however, Russia and Iran increasingly find it difficult to sustain their alliance. Moscow finds it hard accepting Iran's view of the future of Syria that essentially solidifies the sectarian split in the country and often looks beyond its existing alliance to garner the support of the Sunni population.[32] The process of reconstruction in Syria also means that Russia and Iran will have to shoulder a heavy financial burden if they want to continue to play a leading political role in the country; neither, however, is capable of doing that. Consequently, Russia has asked world powers,[33] as well as the Sunni monarchies of the Gulf,[34] to chip in, which will require a significant drawdown in Iran's political role in Syria.

While Russia's relationship with Iran is set to become rockier, there is no guarantee that Moscow's ties with Sunni powers, specifically with Saudi Arabia, will transform into a real partnership. The visit of the Saudi King to Moscow in October 2017 may have been indicative of a positive dynamic in bilateral relations, but it was largely prompted by the Saudi domestic dynamic rather than a genuine desire to reach out to Moscow. The biggest achievement that Moscow and Riyadh can boast about is that they managed to compartmentalize their relations, as was demonstrated by the oil deal reached by Russia and the Organization of the Petroleum Exporting Countries (OPEC), in November 2016, despite the ongoing Syria crisis.

Dichotomy Between Stability and Managed Democracy

Experts who had argued that authoritarianism in the Middle East would maintain stability and keep extremism at bay were proven wrong by the events of the Arab Spring.[35] The Russian leadership, however, still projects its vision of "autocratic stability" onto the region. And even though Moscow repeatedly insists that it is up to the Syrian people to decide through a presidential election who will lead the nation into the post-war period, the Russian government is unlikely to become a supporter of democracy movements in the Middle East. After all, elections have been a crucial legitimization tool of Russia's own "managed democracy."

The consolidation of power in the hands of the national leader as well as the securitization of the political agenda have characterized the Russian political system throughout the last 17 years Vladimir Putin has been in power. And they continue to guide him in how he sees regimes in the Middle East. Some of these authoritarian Arab regimes share a long history with Russia: during the Cold War, they proved their ability to maintain order for longer than any democratic regime could sustain it, not least due to Moscow's financial and military support.

The fact that Bashar al-Assad survived throughout the bloody Syrian conflict, to a large extent due to Russia's aid, solidifies the idea that authoritarianism in the Middle East guarantees stability and puts a cap on "toxic" democratic values imposed from the outside. In Moscow's view, authoritarian tendencies are indigenous to the region, much like they are to Russia, which is why they need not be battled but rather be correctly managed.

Russia's idea of "authoritarian stability" in the Middle East may find a potential supporter in Donald Trump, who notoriously dropped America's agenda for promoting democracy in the Middle East. The distinct security focus of Donald Trump's strategy toward the region has emboldened his allies, Saudi Arabia and Israel, and convinced them that the regional policeman will no longer restrain their geopolitical ambitions.

The position of both Russia and the United States is, thus, likely to resonate with many governments in the region that previously had to put on airs of civil society engagement and liberalization just to have international political and diplomatic backing. Egypt and Turkey are the two cases in point: the 2017 Human Rights Watch World Report specifically points to them to illustrate how the tide of new authoritarianism is sweeping through the Middle East.[36]

In Turkey, the attempted coup in July 2016 was used by President Recep Tayyip Erdoğan and his Justice and Development Party (AKP) as an excuse to crack down not only on suspected plotters but also on wider circles critical of the government's policies. Western powers sharply rebuked Erdoğan over his suspension of the rule of law in the country and mass detentions—but Russia pointedly did not. Putin was the one world leader who gave a call to Erdoğan to tell him Moscow supports his campaign to root out dissent, which the Turkish president described as "anti-constitutional."[37] Furthermore Putin hosted his Turkish counterpart in St. Petersburg less than a month after the failed coup, during which Erdoğan explained that Vladimir Putin's call to him was an important move, "a kind of moral support and display of Russia-Turkey solidarity," as the Turkish president described the situation.[38] All this occurred just weeks after Erdoğan's late June apology to Russia for the November 2015 downing of a Russian Su-24 jet over Syria; and it goes to show how masterfully Vladimir Putin uses authoritarian movements to his own political benefit.

Egypt is going through a similar wave of authoritarianism, with President Abdel Fattah El Sisi cracking down on dissent that is not necessarily associated with the Muslim Brotherhood. That government campaign is happening against the backdrop of economic instability, currency devaluation and increased poverty rates. However, the army's grip on power and full control over the public sphere give a semblance of stability in the country. Sisi's fight to eradicate extremism in the Sinai as well as his crackdown on dissent find support in Moscow, which is reflected in official statements coming from the Kremlin. Egypt reemerged as Russia's key partner in the Middle East, including in crucial spheres of military-technical cooperation. The two countries signed a protocol on military cooperation in March 2015, significantly ramped up joint military exercises, and are looking to green light an agreement that would allow Russian military aircraft to use Egyptian airspace and infrastructure.[39] With the turmoil and regular attacks in the Sinai Peninsula, counter-terrorism cooperation has become a distinct characteristic of the bilateral relationship. A security-heavy agenda acts as a glue between Moscow and Cairo, not least due to the military and security background of the political elites of the two countries.

Both Russians and Egyptians will head to the polls in March 2018 to elect their respective heads of state, while presidential elections in Turkey are to take place in November 2019. The outcome is already known in all three countries; Putin, Sisi and Erdoğan will almost certainly serve out their next terms into the first half of the 2020s, meaning that we are unlikely to witness a disruption in the security-comes-first policy employed by Moscow in its bilateral relations with both Cairo and Ankara.

The cases of Egypt and Turkey illustrate that Vladimir Putin is likely to encourage authoritarian "stability" across the region through skewed security-heavy policies. Putin's support for autocratic tendencies will hardly find any resistance among other powers in the region and will almost certainly be embraced. Syria's recovery from the seven-year war is unlikely to happen through the emergence of democratic institutions and freedom, but will probably lead to the creation of a strong regime with an inflated security apparatus to shield a fragile government and keep extremist tendencies at bay. Iraq's increasingly sectarian policies hint at a similar trend. And as Libya's internationally recognized government fails to establish control over much of the country's territory, Libyan National Army Field Marshall Khalifa Haftar represents the type of leader the Kremlin would presumably like to see for a post–civil war Libya.

If Russia's Syria policy is any indication, a highly centralized system will be Moscow's remedy for extremism throughout the wider region. The fear of a new wave of extremism will push many regimes to seek more control over the population, and a lack of incentives to democratize may bring about new repressive regimes. In other words Russia's leadership in the Middle East may significantly lengthen and reinforce the era of authoritarianism there.

New Positioning Vis-à-Vis Conflicts

The Syrian war became the first armed conflict in which Russia openly took part after the collapse of the Soviet Union. Its support for the al-Assad government and recorded Russian bombings of civilian infrastructure in Syria painted Moscow as a proponent of violence. Despite its undeniable contribution to devising de-escalation zones and its attempts to balance Iran's influence in Syria, Russia is seen as a power broker by key Arab states. But Vladimir Putin did not go to Syria to be equally distant from the government and the opposition playing the role of a referee. He noted on many occasions that the Syrian President asked Russia for military aid and that was the grounds upon which Moscow made the decision to intervene.[40]

A combination of factors bolstered Russia's commitment to intervention in Syria. First, geopolitically, the fall of Bashar al-Assad meant humiliation for Russia, his main global ally, and would deprive Moscow of a springboard to the rest of the Middle East. Second, from the pragmatic standpoint, Syria's proximity to Russia, coupled with the fact that it was becoming a training camp for jihadists from the former Soviet Union, meant that the civil war there was becoming a national security issue for Moscow. Hence, Vladimir Putin undertook this risky affair with no guaranteed outcome.

Syria, however, gives one a skewed idea as to how Russia's strategy toward the region may look in the future. The military campaign in Syria cost Russia $484 million, according to the Russian president,[41] or up to $1 billion annually, according to independent estimates.[42] These costs have been offset by returns on arms contracts and the existing budget for drills. This sum is manageable for the federal budget, even despite low oil prices. Russia's defense spending has been continuously growing from 2010, its share in the GDP increased from 3.2 percent to 4.4 percent in 2016[43]. The recession, however, is taking a toll on the budget of the Russian Ministry of Defense resulting in its 6 percent contraction in 2017.[44] Syria was the reason why the Ministry of Defense managed to secure a larger budget until 2016, but it is also the reason why Moscow now looks for ways to cut the overinflated defense expenses. This only goes to show that the Syria operation is an exceptional affair that Russia is unlikely to repeat elsewhere in the Middle East due to geopolitical risks as well as financial costs that are already too high.

With the focus previously exclusively on Syria, the Russian foreign policy agenda toward the Middle East appears highly securitized to observers. Meanwhile the military and intelligence circles took charge over the policy making towards the region. Despite a wide range of goals that Moscow pursues in Syria, the distinct focus on security issues stoked fears over Russia seeking a military foothold in the Middle East by US officials.[45]

While Syria is a special case, Libya might provide more insight into how Russia will position itself vis-à-vis conflicts in the Middle East for years to come. Following the fall of its partner Muammar Qaddafi in Libya, Moscow did not show much interest in the Libyan conflict, essentially leaving it to NATO to deal with the crisis. At the same time, Libya was a convenient case to go back to lambaste the West each time Russia felt its interests in the Middle East were ignored.

Russia re-emerged on the Libya scene, if not accidentally, pronouncing no specific agenda and making incoherent statements about the desired endgame there as the Libyan civil war erupted. Back in 2016, following the visit of General Khalifa Haftar to Moscow, the international community was convinced that the Kremlin was looking at Libya within the context of where it would continue to project military power once the conflict in Syria is over. The Russian ambassador to Libya, Ivan Molotkov, publicly spoke of a possible delivery of Russian weapons to the government in Tobruq.[46] Russia's informal backing of Haftar sent a clear signal to parties to the Libyan conflict as well as to the international community that Russia was following its traditional strategy of siding with the secular force with significant military power. These signals emboldened Haftar and prompted him to vow to gain full control over Libya and set up his capital in Tripoli, the formal seat of the UN-backed government.[47] Many experts predicted a Russian military operation in the country and looked for signs of a military build-up; but that were continuously off the mark.[48]

Haftar took note of the Russian policy in Syria and capitalized on it. While the Kremlin was attempting to turn the army leader into a politician and looked to restart talks on the Libyan Political Agreement, Haftar was undermining these attempts by expanding his military operations. Russia's narrative on Libya changed significantly in 2017, as Moscow realized that its policy was undermining its goals for the country by actually enabling more violence; thus, it gradually distanced itself from Haftar. The Ministry of Foreign Affairs and the Russian Duma set up a special ad hoc body, "the Russian contact group on the intra-Libyan settlement," tasked with developing a network of contacts in Libya to help Moscow engage all relevant political forces in the country and offset the negative impact of being associated with Khalifa Haftar.[49]

This approach did in fact work, and Russia became a go-to power for various parties to the Libyan conflict. Moscow hosted representatives of the Tripoli government as well as representatives from Misrata, the two major power centers in Libya. Even more importantly, Russia facilitated direct talks between Tripoli and the Touareg and Tobu tribes in November 2017, the first such talks between these parties given the fact that the tribes have not sided with any party to the Libyan conflict yet.[50]

The head of the ad hoc contact group, Lev Dengov, describes Russia's position vis-à-vis the Libyan warring factions the following way: "Russian Foreign Minister Sergei Lavrov has repeatedly explained that Russia is equidistant from all sides of the conflict and does not support either side to a greater or lesser degree than the other."[51] This marks the emergence of a fundamentally new approach to conflict resolution in Russia. Hypothetically, Russian military aid and diplomatic support for Haftar could have resulted in the capture of Tripoli by the Libyan National Army, marking the end of the Libyan Political Agreement. Moscow, however, made a U-turn away from Haftar and opted for a more balanced position toward the settlement of the conflict, which helped it be recognized as a key power broker by all sides in this conflict.

The "strategic equidistance" approach that Russia has adopted in Libya is something Vladimir Putin might explore further in the future. And signs abound that Russia will attempt to become a referee and power broker in other contexts in the Middle East as well. One particular example is the Israeli-Palestinian conflict. Following the US decision to recognize Jerusalem as the capital of Israel, Russia did not come out with harsh criticism of either the United States or Israel. The Russian Foreign Ministry limited its response to expressing "serious concern."[52] Likewise, Vladimir Putin did not directly condemn Donald Trump's decision, only noting that it was "counterproductive."[53]

Russia's relatively calm reaction to Trump's move and Israel's policies toward Palestine can be explained by Moscow's growing ambition to play a bigger role in the settlement of the Israeli-Palestinian conflict. Russia intensified its diplomacy with Israel and Palestine in 2016, when Russian Prime Minister Dmitry Medvedev visited both in an attempt to bridge the differences between them. Later, in January 2017, Russia hosted all major Palestinian political organizations,[54] including Fatah, Hamas and the Palestinian Islamic Jihad, for direct talks among them in an attempt to facilitate the formation of a coherent position for talks with Israel. Russia recognized that the US-led process of reconciliation had not led to a breakthrough.

With the US recognition of Jerusalem as the capital of Israel, Washington's leadership role in the Israeli-Palestinian talks is no longer acceptable to Palestine, and it seems the Middle East Quartet (the United Nations, United States, European Union and Russia) is no longer relevant. This presents a unique opportunity for Moscow to position itself as a new power broker in the conflict, one that does not favor one of the two sides. Russian diplomats have already participated in a flurry of meetings with Israeli and Palestinian officials following Trump's announcement, and each time they engage both parties.

Other contexts in the region seem to support the idea that Russia will be looking to remain equidistant from all conflicting sides in the Middle East, which does not necessarily mean remaining inactive. The GCC crisis that broke out in June 2017 is another example of how Russia creates a certain distance between itself and conflicting sides and tries to put itself above the dispute. Both sides made numerous attempts to win Putin's diplomatic support following the crisis. Doha is historically wary of Russia's role in the Middle East; yet, it engaged Russian diplomats at various levels and even canceled visas for Russian citizens[55]. Saudi Arabia went on a similar charm offensive, which culminated in King Salman's visit to Russia.

Conclusion

As Syria gradually falls from the top of Russia's political agenda in the Middle East over the coming years, Moscow will be looking for new ways to stay relevant in the region. Russia's permanent military bases in Syria have the potential to change the power balance in the Mediterranean. Moscow has created a heavily guarded perimeter in the Eastern Mediterranean by deploying air-defense capabilities to Syria, which complemented its permanent naval force in these waters. Together, these deployments and growing capabilities will become a challenge for NATO as Moscow spreads its presence into the Alliance's naval underbelly in the Mediterranean. Down the line, Russia is managing to expand military cooperation with Egypt and the future government in Libya, and is expanding its naval presence in the Red Sea.

Politically, however, hard power will produce fewer benefits for Moscow, at higher costs, which is why the Russian government will need to discover new ways to remain relevant in the regional arena. Having used Syria to rebuild its image as a regional power, Russia is faced with the challenge of how to balance its relations with Saudi Arabia and Iran, neither of neither of which is a true ally for Moscow. In order to forge stronger regional alliances, Vladimir Putin might revisit the idea of a global anti-terrorist coalition, which feeds into the concept of a regional system of collective security widely discussed by Russian policymakers.

Trying to insert itself in regional politics in the post-Syria era, Russia is likely to rebrand its image in the Middle East and position itself as a regional referee in an attempt to offset the negative impact of the Syrian conflict on its profile. Being a regional referee, however, does not necessarily translate into being a supporter of democracy. The legacy of the Arab Spring and Russia's own experience with democratic movements led Putin to believe that authoritarian stability may help the Middle East overcome its security problems. And Russia's military campaign in Syria has further crystallized this notion for the Kremlin.

ENDNOTES

[1] Voennaya Doctrina Rossiyskoy Federatsii (Military Strategy of the Russian Federation), Signed by the President of the Russian Federation Vladimir Putin on December 25, 2014, http://static.kremlin.ru/media/events/files/41d527556bec8deb3530.pdf; Konceptsiya Vneshney Politiki Rossiyskoy Federatsii (Foreign Policy Concept of the Russian Federation), Signed by the President of the Russian Federation Vladimir Putin on February 12, 2013, http://www.mid.ru/foreign_policy/official_documents/-/asset_publisher/CptICkB6BZ29/content/id/122186.

[2] Foreign Policy Concept of the Russian Federation, Approved by the President of the Russian Federation Vladimir Putin on November 30, 2016. http://www.mid.ru/foreign_policy/news/-/asset_publisher/cKNonkJE02Bw/content/id/2542248.

[3] Alina Malik, Putin Recognized the Negative Impact of Trump, gazeta.ru, April 14, 2017, https://www.gazeta.ru/politics/2017/04/12_a_10623461.shtml.

[4] In his widely acclaimed book *All the Kremlin's Men* insider into the workings of Vlaimir Putin's inner circle Mikhail Zygar argues that Putin absorbed the death of Qaddafi as a lesson: weakness and compromise were impermissible. "When he [Gaddafi] was a pariah, no one touched him," Zygar wrote. "But as soon as he opened up he was not only overthrown but killed in the street like a mangy old cur."

[5] Some political goals use this for promotion in the political arena, Znak, March 30, 2017, https://www.znak.com/2017-03-30/vladimir_putin_nazval_mitingi_protiv_korrupcii_instrumentom_arabskoy_vesny.

[6] Putin's UN General Assembly Speech, Washington Post, September 28, 2015, https://www.washingtonpost.com/news/worldviews/wp/2015/09/28/read-putins-u-n-general-assembly-speech/?utm_term=.c9837439bf3d.

[7] Wynfred Joshua and Stephen P. Gilbert, Arms for the Third World: Soviet Military Aid Diplomacy, Baltimore: The Johns Hopkins Press, 1969, p. 147.

[8] Nikolay Kozhanov, Arms Exports Add to Russia's Tools of Influence in Middle East, Chatham House, July 20, 2016, https://www.chathamhouse.org/expert/comment/arms-exports-add-russia-s-tools-influence-middle-east#sthash.JYHR0jTz.dpuf.

[9] Committee of the Federation Council on Defense approved the agreement on the Navy base in Tartus. RIA, December 25, 2017, https://ria.ru/syria/20171225/1511640481.html.

[10] Veliky Novgorod and Kolpino Submarines Fired the Kalibr Cruise Missiles from Submerged Position Against ISIS Critical Objects in Syria, Russian Ministry of Defense, September 14, 2017, http://eng.mil.ru/en/news_page/country/more.htm?id=12142271@egNews.

[11] Three years ago, the operational command of the permanent operational unit of the Russian Navy in the Mediterranean Sea was formed, Russian Ministry of Defense, September 22, 2017, https://function.mil.ru/news_page/country/more.htm?id=12096837@egNews#txt.

[12] Putin: Ships in the Mediterranean are not "saber-rattling", RIA, June 6, 2013, https://ria.ru/defense_safety/20130606/941878268.html.

[13] Andrea Beccaro, Anna Sophie Maass, The Russian Web in the Mediterranean Region, ISPI, Analysis No. 308, February 2017, P. 3.

[14] "Putin said that Africa cannot be on the periphery of international relations," RIA, October 27, 2016, https://ria.ru/world/20161027/1480166410.html.

[15] Egypt and Russia plan to conduct joint exercises in the Mediterranean Sea annually, Voeenoye Obozreniye, June 15, 2015, https://topwar.ru/76978-egipet-i-rossiya-planiruyut-provodit-sovmestnye-ucheniya-v-sredizemnom-more-ezhegodno.html.

[16] Russia and Egypt will hold joint military exercises "Defenders of Friendship", Kommersant, January 6, 2018, https://www.kommersant.ru/doc/3514496

[17] Phil Stewart, Idrees Ali, Lin Noueihed, Russia appears to deploy forces in Egypt, eyes on Libya role - sources, Reuters, March 14, 2017, https://www.reuters.com/article/us-usa-russia-libya-exclusive/exclusive-russia-appears-to-deploy-forces-in-egypt-eyes-on-libya-role-sources-idUSKBN16K2RY.

[18] Tom Parfitt, Gadafy offers Russia a naval base in Libya, The Guardian, November 1, 2008, https://www.theguardian.com/world/2008/nov/01/libya-russia-gadafy-united-states.

[19] Anna Borschevskaya, From Moscow to Marrakech: Russia is turning its eyes to Africa, The Hill, September 21, 2017, http://thehill.com/opinion/international/351684-from-moscow-to-marrakech-russia-is-turning-to-africa.

[20] Mansouria Mokhefi: "Algeria seeks to reaffirm the primacy of its relations with Russia", Jeune Afrique, April 27, 2016, http://www.jeuneafrique.com/321456/politique/mansouria-mokhefi-algerie-cherche-a-reaffirmer-primaute-de-relations-russie/.

[21] Algeria in Russian weapons deal, BBC, March 11, 2006, http://news.bbc.co.uk/2/hi/africa/4796382.stm.

[22] Malek Bachir, Russia's secret plan to back Haftar in Libya, Middle East Eye, January 30, 2017, http://www.middleeasteye.net/news/exclusive-russias-secret-plan-libya-2129027228.

[23] Algiers to host Algeria-Russia counter-terrorism consultations, The North Africa Post, April 18, 2017, http://northafricapost.com/17412-algiers-host-algeria-russia-counter-terrorism-consultations.html.

[24] Habibulah Mohamed Lamin, How Polisario Front hopes to partner with Russia in Western Sahara, Al Monitor, April 11, 2017, http://www.al-

monitor.com/pulse/originals/2017/04/western-sahara-polisario-sell-russia-moscow-visit.html#ixzz55OoQalcn.

25 Russian large anti-submarine warfare ship calls at Egyptian port, TASS, October 19, 2017, http://tass.com/defense/971516.

26 Bashir Discusses with Russia Setting up Military Base on Red Sea, Asharq Al Awsat, November 26, 2017, https://aawsat.com/english/home/article/1095236/bashir-discusses-russia-setting-military-base-red-sea.

27 Anton Mardasov, Russia re-examines relationship with Iran, Al Monitor, August 14, 2017, https://www.al-monitor.com/pulse/originals/2017/08/russia-relationship-iran-syria-military-situation-moscow.html.

28 Igor Ivanov, Three Baskets for the Middle East, Russian International Affairs Council, February 1, 2016, http://russiancouncil.ru/analytics-and-comments/analytics/tri-korziny-dlya-blizhnego-vostoka/?sphrase_id=4717562.

29 Putin: Russia suggests creating a broad anti-terrorist coalition, RIA, September 28, 2015, https://ria.ru/world/20150928/1288414410.html?inj=1.

30 Putin is Calling for the Creation of an Anti-ISIS Front, Gazeta, November 16, 2015, https://www.gazeta.ru/politics/2015/11/16_a_7895243.shtml.

31 Margaret Vice, Publics Worldwide Unfavorable Toward Putin, Russia, Pew Research, August 16, 2017, http://www.pewglobal.org/2017/08/16/publics-worldwide-unfavorable-toward-putin-russia/.

32 Anton Mardasov, Russia re-examines relationship with Iran, Al Monitor, August 14, 2017, https://www.al-monitor.com/pulse/originals/2017/08/russia-relationship-iran-syria-military-situation-moscow.html.

33 Kathrin Hille, Russia asks world powers to pay for Syria reconstruction, FT, February 23, 2017, https://www.ft.com/content/47933554-f847-11e6-9516-2d969e0d3b65.

34 Saudi Arabia sets conditions to role in Syria reconstruction, The Arab Weekly, October 15, 2017, http://www.thearabweekly.com/Gulf/9440/Saudi-Arabia-sets-conditions-to-role-in-Syria-reconstruction.

35 F. Gregory Gause III, Why Middle East Studies Missed the Arab Spring: The Myth of Authoritarian Stability, Foreign Affairs, Vol. 90, No. 4 (JULY/AUGUST 2011), pp. 81–84, 85–90.

36 World Report 2017, Human Rights Watch, P. 7, https://www.hrw.org/sites/default/files/world_report_download/wr2017-web.pdf.

37 Telephone conversation with President of Turkey Recep Tayyip Erdogan, July 17, 2016, http://en.kremlin.ru/events/president/news/52529.

38 News conference following talks with President of Turkey Recep Tayyip Erdogan, August 9, 2016, http://en.kremlin.ru/catalog/countries/TR/events/52673.

39 Polina Khamshiashvili, A foothold in North Africa: Why does Russia need Egyptian military airfields, RBC, November 20, 2017, https://www.rbc.ru/politics/30/11/2017/5a2009699a794757097c2299.

40 Meeting with Syrian President Bashar Assad, October 21, 2015, http://kremlin.ru/catalog/countries/SY/events/50533.

41 Cost of Russia's Syrian Campaign Revealed as $480 Million, The Moscow Times, March 17, 2016, https://themoscowtimes.com/articles/cost-of-russias-syrian-campaign-revealed-as-480-million-52199.

42 Anton Bayev, A Year in Syria: How Much the Military Operation Cost Russia, RBC, September 30, 2016, https://www.rbc.ru/politics/30/09/2016/57ebb7199a7947db5bb2b309#xtor=AL-%5Binternal_traffic%5D--%5Brss.rbc.ru%5D-

%5Btop_stories_brief_news%5D.

[43] Kudrin estimated the damage to Russia from the growth of defense spending, Lenta, October 5, 2017, https://lenta.ru/news/2017/10/05/wane/.

[44] Alexander Sharkovskiy, The Budget of the Defense Ministry Will be Cut by 100 billion, Nezavisimaya Gazeta, December 19, 2016.

[45] Eric Schmitt, Russian Moves in Syria Widen Role in Mideast, The New York Times, September 14, 2015, https://www.nytimes.com/2015/09/15/world/middleeast/russian-moves-in-syria-widen-role-in-mideast.html.

[46] Russian Ambassador: Commander-in-Chief of the Libyan army discussed delivery of arms in Moscow, RIA, June 28, 2016, https://ria.ru/defense_safety/20160628/1453677993.html.

[47] West reaffirms support for Presidency Council "as the sole legitimate government of Libya", says military must be under civilian control, Libya Herald, December 24, 2016, https://www.libyaherald.com/2016/12/24/west-reaffirms-support-for-presidency-council-as-the-sole-legitimate-government-of-libya-says-military-must-be-under-civilian-control/.

[48] Alec Luhn, Russian special forces sent to back renegade Libyan general – reports, The Guardian, March 14, 2017, https://www.theguardian.com/world/2017/mar/14/russian-special-forces-deployed-in-egypt-near-libyan-border-report.

[49] Maxim Suchkov, Russia seeks well-rounded relations with Libyan factions, Al Monitor, December 15, 2017, https://www.al-monitor.com/pulse/originals/2017/12/russia-well-round-relations-libya-lev-dengov.html.

[50] The head of the contact group of the Russian Federation: it's too early to talk about the specific date of the elections in Libya, TASS, December 3, 2017, http://tass.ru/politika/4779828.

[51] Ibid.

[52] Comment by the Information and Press Department on US recognition of Jerusalem as the capital of Israel, Ministry of Foreign Affairs, December 7, 2017, http://www.mid.ru/en/diverse/-/asset_publisher/zwI2FuDbhJx9/content/kommentarij-departamenta-informacii-i-pecati-mid-rossii-v-svazi-s-priznaniem-ssa-ierusalima-stolicej-izraila?_101_INSTANCE_zwI2FuDbhJx9_redirect=http%3A%2F%2Fwww.mid.ru%2Fen%2Fdiverse%3Fp.

[53] Putin commented on Trump's decision to recognize Jerusalem as the capital of Israel, RIA, December 11, 2017, https://ria.ru/world/20171211/1510673229.html.

[54] Vasily Kuznetsov, Moscow offers stage for Palestinian talks, Al Monitor, January 31, 2017, http://www.al-monitor.com/pulse/originals/2017/01/moscow-russia-palestine-israel-peace-process-talks.html#ixzz54r06VJRU.

[55] On a new procedure for obtaining short-term tourist visas to the State of Qatar for citizens of the Russian Federation, Ministry of Foreign Affairs, June 23, 2017, http://www.mid.ru/ru/maps/qa/-/asset_publisher/629HIryvPTwo/content/id/2796326.

15. Russia's Middle Eastern Position in 2025

Stephen Blank

Summary

Through 2025, Russia will continue to enjoy the prominence it now possesses in the Middle East and can be expected to succeed in this quest because it has strategically built and deployed the instruments of power necessary to sustain such a position, all things being equal. Those instruments comprise diplomatic, military and economic elements of power as well as the fact that Russia has leveraged its position in Syria to obtain partners and even enablers for itself who now have and will continue to have over time a serious stake in the success of Russian regional policies. Moreover, Russia is eagerly building up military sinews to retain power projection capabilities throughout the Middle East and Africa for the period up to and even beyond 2025.

Introduction

Forecasting events and trends in the Middle East is an inherently precarious enterprise. But from the vantage point of mid-2018, we must consider what Russia's posture and the scope of its presence in the Middle East will be in 2025 and why. Compelling reasons exist for doing so today, and not only because 2025 is a little over six years from now.

More importantly, it is clear that Moscow, by its own strategic prowess, has seized an ascending position in the Middle East that goes far beyond Syria. That position enables it to be a major actor in the region for years to come—as it has long intended to be. All this underscores the fact that Russian actions, for all their tactical adaptation to a kaleidoscopic reality and flexibility, appear to be part of a larger strategy.

In other words, despite the incessant writing of American and even some Russian writers that Putin has no strategy, he is a strategist, and we are confronting a strategic plan that, like any sound blueprint for action, permits tactical adaptation and flexibility in the face of unforeseen events.[1] Moreover, by employing that strategy, Putin has maneuvered through the storm of events to bring Russia to an unprecedented level of prominence in the Middle East. And in so doing he has created mechanisms that will likely ensure retention of that position until 2025, barring some major unforeseen catastrophe.

Without arguing over the merits of Putin's ability as a strategist in general (and we do not need to do so by merely noting there is a strategy), we can say with confidence that in Syria and the broader Middle East (in no small measure thanks to the victory in Syria), Russia has produced a winning military-political strategy. That strategy has allowed it to expand its regional position since the intervention in Syria. The economic, diplomatic, political, and military mechanisms that Putin has created and fostered, as well as the outcomes they have generated, create the momentum and impetus that will boost Russia's position as a major player in the Middle East through 2025, compared to its current role—again, barring any unforeseen catastrophe. While Moscow must now convert that military victory into the legitimacy of a functioning Syrian authority that commands popular support, there is no *a priori* reason to assume, in the absence of other contending forces, that Russian policy will fail to bring about that outcome in the future.

Instead, there is abundant evidence that Moscow is steadily gaining traction across the entire Middle East thanks to its multi-dimensional strategy. Failing to recognize that fact by the United States and much of the West is an act of willful blindness. Despite the region's inherent volatility, by 2025 Moscow will probably enjoy a position similar in nature but greater in substance compared to today. We can also expect that it will not willingly yield its gains except in return for massive Western political and strategic payoffs, which are unlikely to occur between now and then; there are no visible regional or other forces ready to undertake such an arduous task. Meanwhile, Russia has substantially enhanced its arsenal and therefore its overall capabilities and regional presence for defending and advancing those interests. It is highly unlikely that anyone can currently muster sufficient military forces to evict Russia from the Middle East.

Already Moscow is the acknowledged arbiter between Syria and Jordan.[2] Russia is also maintaining or attempting to maintain the equilibrium between Israel and Iran. One account even likens Russia to being a ringmaster between them.[3] In that capacity the Kremlin now has Military Police and observers stationed in the Golan Heights.[4] Moscow has also enmeshed Ankara. For example, Turkey is now dependent on Russia to be able achieve its objectives with respect to domestic Kurds and those residing in Syria. Moreover, Russia provides 60–70 percent of Turkish natural gas supplies. Similarly, already in 2016, Turkey had to ultimately surrender to Russian economic pressure following the period of chilly bilateral relations caused by the November 2015 incident involving a Russian jet shot down by Turkey over the Syrian-Turkish border. So despite Turkish claims that it is not excessively dependent on Russia, contradictory proof certainly exists.

Furthermore, the closeness of Russia's economic, political, and military ties with Turkey is well known and may grow given the crisis into which Ankara has plunged US-Turkish relations by having incarcerating Pastor Andrew Brunson and buying S-400 air defenses from Russia. The long-standing complex strategic rivalry with Russia in the Black Sea, Caucasus, and now Syria is unlikely to reverse those trends of ever closer Russian-Turkish links.[5]

In the Gulf, Russia and Saudi Arabia alone have essentially set the bar for current energy prices, reducing OPEC to a shadow of its past self. Moreover, Russia is now discussing bringing Iran into the Eurasian Economic Union, clearly cementing its economic ties to the Islamic Republic even as it restricts Iranian policies against Israel.[6] Finally, Moscow is, in fact, effectively supplanting Washington's former leadership role in the region. Russia has been able to regionally come out on top in this way thanks to, *inter alia*, the totality of Turco-Russian relations, Russia's cooperation with Iran and Turkey in Syria's civil war, diverse Russian energy and investment deals with the Gulf states, its ties with Israel, its push into the Sahel and Sub-Saharan Africa based on its accomplishments in the Middle East, as well as Moscow's proliferating relationships across North Africa. Those relationships along the southern coast of the Mediterranean, in fact, could well lead to a ring of naval and airbases there.[7] Therefore we have every reason to believe that Moscow will fight to retain and augment this status as we approach 2025.

As the Helsinki summit showed, Putin apparently believes he can compel the US into reaching an agreement on Syria that reflects more of Moscow's interests than Washington's.[8] In addition Russia has learned a great deal since 1990 and in many ways behaves differently than did the USSR, even if a certain level of continuity between the two regimes is apparent. Thus, the Russian state and military's ability to learn and then shift gears accordingly represent a growing challenge to the United States. Pointedly, Moscow has avoided becoming entrapped in intra-Arab or Arab-Iranian rivalries and is free to make deals with everyone in the Middle East, whether they be Sunni, Shia or Israeli.

Moscow and Its Enablers

Due to its strategic military and political successes across the Middle East, Moscow has attracted numerous local partners and enablers who facilitate its policies and help it advance its interests along with their own objectives. This represents a triumph of Russian diplomacy and overall strategy and is one of the principal mechanisms or factors that will make it possible for Moscow to play a major Middle Eastern role until and probably beyond 2025. For example, Russia's regional successes have led the United Arab Emirates' (UAE) Crown Prince Mohammad Bin Zaid to say that both governments share open communication channels on all issues of international affairs and will form a strategic partnership to promote their relationship.[9] And thanks to their economic and political partnership, the UAE is helping Russia penetrate Africa as well.[10] Presumably, as the UAE visibly increases its capabilities for projecting influence abroad, it will likely bring Russia into at least some of those arenas, like Africa.[11] In the long term, Russia can expect to benefit from the UAE's sharing of economic and political resources to help cement Moscow's own quest for great power standing in the Middle East.

Indeed, success across the entire Middle East and North Africa has, in many ways, facilitated an expansion of Russian activities and quest for leverage in the Sahel and Sub-Saharan Africa, an area that it clearly believes to be of growing interest to Moscow.[12] And its growing presence across the African continent enhances the strategic importance of the Middle East to Russia as a springboard for future activities there. This is another reason why Moscow will be loath to yield its position in the region before 2025 and may seek to strengthen it instead, particularly given its expanding portfolio of interests in Africa and partnerships with states like the UAE further out to 2030.

Nor is the UAE Russia's sole regional partner. Iran and Iraq are clearly engaged deeply with Russia in Syria and over energy and arms sales.[13] Saudi Arabia's partnership with Moscow in the energy sphere is sufficiently well known to suggest that their collusion has either effectively supplanted OPEC's role as a price setter for oil and gas or has greatly weakened that organization's role in this process. Egypt works with Russia not only to acquire a nuclear reactor, but also offers it bases and cooperates with Moscow against Libyan rebels.[14] And Sudan has offered Moscow a base in return for arms sales to prevail against its rebels.[15] The above examples do not even exhaust the inherent future prospects in these partnerships, which continue to progress two steps forward for every step back.

Moscow's ability to forge partnerships is partly based on its disregard for the domestic political character of its interlocutors and partly driven out of sheer necessity given the structural weaknesses of post-Soviet Russia. That approach has allowed the Russian government to even enhance its ties and develop partner-like relations with states directly opposed to Russia's preexisting partners like the UAE: Qatar is a prime example here.[16] This capability has been and will likely remain one of the most important reasons for Moscow's enduring presence in the Middle East. As many commentators and Foreign Minister Sergei Lavrov have argued, this "network diplomacy" of dealing with everyone while remaining above the fray has long since become a characteristic hallmark of Russian diplomacy across the board.[17] The British analyst Bobo Lo calls it a penchant for multilateralism (with Russia in the lead).[18] Because this *modus operandi* has paid off handsomely for Moscow, there is no reason to assume that Putin or subsequent regimes will forego that practice. As such, Russia in 2025 can be strongly expected to enjoy approximately the same level of standing and power in the Middle East that it now enjoys if not a higher one, absent radical changes.

Russia's ability to work with everyone also helps it become or aspire to become an arbiter between rivals, as is now occurring with regard to Israel and Iran as well as between the UAE and Saudi Arabia on the one hand and Iran on the other. Moscow also mediates among the rivals for power inside Libya and is doing the same thing in Sub-Saharan Africa.[19] This helps Moscow coordinate with every player in the Middle East and also highlights the tactical flexibility of Russian policy. For example, even as Russia consorts with Sunni Gulf monarchies and Israel to restrain Iran, Moscow is negotiating with Tehran to draw it into the Eurasian Economic Union (EEU—the centerpiece Russian-led integrationist organization within the former Soviet space).[20] Doing so softens the blow of its collaboration with Israel, helps rescue Iran from the crushing pressure of United Nations sanctions and creates a new, enduring basis for Iranian dependency upon Russia. In turn that flexibility bolsters Russia's long-term ability to enhance its current position in the Middle East until 2025, if not later.

This tactic predates the intervention in Syria but has continued there and elsewhere since then.[21] Not only has Moscow forged ties with partners and enablers, in the Middle East it executes the same policy it conducts elsewhere, namely an effort to regulate conflicts among regional actors to enhance its interests and control those wars' potential for escalation.[22] Consequently, to the degree that Russia can enforce "escalation control" on local crises via its ability to straddle all sides in these conflicts, its standing in the Middle East grows. Moscow has taken a similar approach with regard to its standing in the Commonwealth of Independent States (CIS) and the wider Eurasia. As Dmitry Adamsky has observed,

> Apparently, three strategic principles, unwritten and implicit, drove Moscow's regional conduct towards and following the intervention. First, the Kremlin seeks to preserve controlled tensions in the region. This enables it to promote its goals through

power brokerage in the regional conflicts. Ideally, it seeks to keep political- military confrontations between the parties high enough to sustain the prospects for Moscow's indispensability but not so high that they lead to a counterproductive escalation endangering its regional interests and assets. Consequently, Moscow seeks to act as mediator and dependence amplifier.

In all regional conflicts Moscow cultivates equal access to all parties—a clear competitive advantage vis-à-vis the U.S. Being at once part of the problem and part of the solution provides it with an ability to escalate or deescalate confrontations. It prefers the actors involved not to be too strong and not too weak, and in any political-military development it seeks to demonstrate to them the limits of their power and their dependence on the Kremlin's brokerage.[23]

These enabling partnerships and capacity for controlling escalation strengthen Moscow's presence and reach across the Middle East. Moreover, they are now being replicated in Africa, where Russia has even been asked to mediate a number of local civil wars.[24] Because Moscow can and does make deals with everyone, each state has a stake in its continued ability to uphold and sustain those deals—and thus, each of these actors has an incentive in Russia preserving its long-term regional presence. Given that context, any diminution of Moscow's regional standing, voluntarily or otherwise, will reverberate throughout the Middle East and affect its partners in ways that they will likely perceive as negative. Therefore, Russian partners are likely to resist such negative trends, thereby strengthening Moscow's regional posture and helping it sustain its policies there. This factor marks another way in which Russia, by pursuing a productive strategy, is supplanting the US.

Russia's regional partnerships and those partners' own actions enable Moscow in various ways. For example, Russian deals with Arab sovereign funds and energy firms—such as the business agreements between Rosneft and the Qatar Investment Authority and Glencore—have enriched Russia and Rosneft, all while circumventing Western sanctions.[25] Moscow has also cemented long-lasting ties to economic and political elites that should continue well into the next decade thanks to investments in Russia by Arab sovereign funds.[26] These relationships not only grant Moscow access to most, if not all, Middle Eastern governments, they also strongly reinforce the economic-political foundations of Russian policy in the Middle East because those policies are now ever more entwined with the interests and policies of local and regional elites. Expanding vested interests and affiliations facilitate long-term, mutually beneficial working partnerships. Beyond economic-political gains, these partnerships also help Russia magnify its military presence in the Middle East and Africa.

Arms Sales

Arms sales—which involve military, political and economic policy considerations—represent one of the most successful ways Russia has enhanced its cooperation with military, economic, and political elites in the Middle East and elsewhere. Moreover, they are a traditional method of inserting or augmenting Russian influence on the political, economic, and military sectors of host countries. Indeed, arguably the primary mission of arms sales, or at least one equal to the task of financing the defense-industrial sector, is to increase Moscow's political standing around the globe.[27] President Putin himself stated unambiguously, "We see active military technical cooperation [the official term for military exports] as an effective instrument for advancing our national interests, both political and economic."[28] Many states, to be sure, hold this view; but Russian officials follow Putin in openly articulating it as a rationale for arms exports, which they see as a means of directly influencing another state's ability to deter and defend itself and its interests. Then–Deputy Prime Minister Dmitri Rogozin stated in late 2013, "The FSVTS [Russia's arms selling agency] at the moment is, it can be said, the country's second foreign policy agency, a second MID (Ministry of Foreign affairs), a second Smolensk square, because it strengthens what the diplomats do today, not just in political terms, but rather authenticated in metal, treaty relations, contracts, maintenance services, equipment repair, and its maintenance in a suitable state."[29] From Russia's perspective, when it seeks military export contracts, it is not simply searching for a consumer with a need, but is quite literally inserting weaponry, military personnel, technicians, and military technologies into a region to gain or increase its influence there. Rogozin indicated that this is Russia's stance when he said, "They [the FSVTS] trade arms only with friends and partners."[30] Arms sales are therefore critical tools for building relationships in regions where Moscow has interests. This is especially the case because arms exports are one of the few areas, including energy sales and related services, where Russia has any kind of comparative advantage relative to other arms sellers.

In a 2007 cable later released by Wikileaks, US Ambassador William Burns analyzed the motivations for Russian arms sales to countries in the Middle East:

A second factor driving the Russian arms export policy is the desire to enhance Russia's standing, as a "player" in areas where Russia has a strategic interest, like the Middle East. Russian officials believe that building a defense relationship provides ingress and influence, and their terms are not constrained by conditionality. Exports to Syria and Iran are part of a broader strategy of distinguishing Russian policy from that of the United States, and strengthening Russian influence in international arenas such as the Quartet[31] or within the Security Council. With respect to Syria Russian officials believe that that Bashar [al-Assad]'s regime is better than the perceived alternative of instability or an Islamist government, and argue against a U.S. policy of isolation. Russia has concluded that its arms sales are too insignificant to threaten Israel, or to disturb growing Israeli-

Russian diplomatic engagement, but sufficient to maintain "special" relations with Damascus. Likewise, arms sales to Iran are part of a deep and multilayered bilateral relationship that serves to distinguish Moscow from Washington, and to provide Russian officials with a bargaining chip both with the Ahmadinejad regime and its P5+1 partners.[32] While, as a matter of practice, Russian arms sales have declined as international frustration has mounted over the Iranian regime, as a matter of policy, Russia does not support what it perceives as U.S. efforts to build an anti-Iranian coalition.[33]

Russia exports military systems to the Middle East to purposefully achieve the following national security objectives: 1) to support its image as a global power, 2) to maintain a foreign policy independent of Western power and pressure, 3) to expand its influence in these regions, 4) to obtain resource extraction rights, 5) to initiate and strengthen defense relations, and 6) to secure military basing rights. Moreover arms sales everywhere link up with energy deals and Russia's quest for military bases as component parts of a coordinated multi-dimensional policy to advance Russian interests.[34]

Arms sales and natural gas deals are frequently correlated. For example, Russian arms sales to Algeria and other Middle Eastern and North African states are linked not just to Russia's unremitting efforts to regain its former place in the Middle East but also to the Russian strategy to become the world's dominant gas exporter and to gain decisive leverage upon Europe through its access to Middle Eastern and African energy sources.[35] Thus Russian arms sales to Turkey and Gulf states have strengthened Russia's ties with those governments and created lasting bonds between members of both countries' political and military elites.

But these enhanced relationships between Moscow and Middle Eastern governments also owe much to the widely observed failure of

US strategy under the present and preceding administrations as well as the sense of a US withdrawal or failure to grasp or accept regional governments' interests. This certainly is the case with Turkey, where threats of US sanctions have only stimulated Ankara's further defiance of Washington.[36] Consequently, we run the risk of a lasting long-term estrangement of Turkey if we impose sanctions upon it for buying Russian arms, even though Ankara knows full well the value of its alliance with Washington and membership within NATO.

Certainly, Russian arms sales have been successful in forging effective working relationships with Middle Eastern states and their militaries by answering those governments' perceived defense needs. Yet, as importantly, selling weapons has also translated into obtaining basing rights in perpetuity. Syria, not surprisingly, has asked Russia to keep its forces there for a long time, which was ultimately legally codified in a bilateral treaty allowing for long-term basing.[37] Sudan has also requested Russian arms for use in its conflict with South Sudan, and it offered Moscow a base on its coast in return.[38] And beyond Sudan, as shown below, other countries are permitting Russian bases as well.

The Learning State: Moscow's Clinic on Clausewitz

Indeed, apart from exploiting US policy failures throughout the Middle East, Russia's accomplishments since 2015 demonstrate the fatuity of earlier US assumptions that Moscow neither wanted to nor could displace Washington in the Middle East and that it lacked any power projection capability. Moreover, it punctured the belief in US policy circles that Russia had limited material and other means to influence Middle Eastern trends.[39] Indeed, Syria has not proven to be, at least as of now, the quagmire for Russia that President Barack Obama predicted it might become.[40] Instead, it has provided a springboard for boosting Russian power, influence and leverage across the entire region, largely at US expense, since perhaps as early as 2007. Meanwhile, the US' strategic accomplishments and vision in the Middle East for arguably the last decade have been meager, inconsistent, and self-defeating. Indeed, it is still difficult, if not impossible to ascertain what US objectives in Syria are, other than fighting against the Islamic State.

In contrast, Russia has displayed an impressive ability to learn from its past failures and from the study of contemporary war. It has used those lessons to avoid the trap the US has fallen into: of inconclusive, protracted, militarily indecisive wars that disseminate threats beyond their actual theater and elude escalation control. And importantly, the Russian government and military have learned many of the harsh lessons of contemporary warfare even as they are conducting operations in Syria. Indeed, the Russian system has been set up there to enable Moscow to do just that.[41] Yet, in so doing, the Russian government and military, has also built on past traditions of Russian Middle East policy and the factors that drove it.

Beyond the impressive accomplishments of Russian arms, military strategy, and statecraft in the Middle East, there are enduring domestic imperatives that have historically impelled Moscow to seek prominence if not hegemony in the Middle East. And those factors today and until 2025 are no less important than they were in the past. For example, a 1984 report by CIA analyst Fritz Ermarth observed that,

> The future of the Soviet Union as a superpower, the East-West power balance, and the chance of a major US-Soviet conflict in the next two decades are likely to be determined, more than anywhere else, in the region south of Soviet borders stretching from India to the Eastern Mediterranean. The Southern Theater is by far the most important major region of the Third World to the Soviets, rivaling the strategic status of East Asia and even Europe in some ways.[42]

Ermarth further argued that while Moscow coveted access to regional waterways and energy resources, it also had good reason to fear the power of Islam that threatened to "undermine essential parts of the Soviet system at home if the Soviets do not eventually control it."[43]

Although the course of the Cold War did not go as Ermarth predicted, the importance of the Middle East to Moscow is still based on its role in the superpower competition and the primacy of its anti-American drive (and Moscow still thinks of itself as a global superpower).[44] To an extent that few Western analysts want to acknowledge, Moscow sees itself as being a foreordained global superpower; otherwise, it becomes the object of others' policies, a mere modern appanage princedom like medieval Russia. Thus, the drive to restore superpower status is paramount and has been the mainspring of Putin's policy since he became president.[45] Russian elites and policy analysts openly express both their aspiration to regain that status and the anti-Americanism associated with it. Konstantin Zatulin, first deputy chairman of the Duma's committee for relations with the CIS and Russians nationals abroad, told an interviewer that, Russia seeks larger influence over international affairs: "If by the restoration of the Russian empire, one means restoring the big role that the Russian empire or the Soviet Union played in international life, then we would of course be happy to have such a role today."[46]

And Ambassador Extraordinaire and former deputy Foreign Minister Nikolai Spassky has similarly written,

> At the same time, there is no greater joy for a Russian intellectual than to speculate about a decline of America. The problem is that the Russians still do not see any other worthy role for their country in the 21st century than the role of a superpower, as a state that realizes itself primarily through influence on global processes. Characteristically, such sentiments are widespread not only among the elites, but also among the public at large. This is true for people in their 40s–50s who remember the Soviet Union

fairly well, and for young people who never saw the superpower that actually destroyed itself in the late 1980s. And there are no signs of an alternative vision of Russia—as a country for itself and for its citizens.[47]

In this context, it also bears noticing that Spassky has additionally written, "There is no greater joy for a Russian intellectual than to speculate about a decline of America."[48]

The attraction of controlling or at least gaining access to Middle Eastern energy in order to insert Russia into regional politics and gain leverage on both local regimes and European energy supplies has become, if anything, more important given the paramount role of energy in Russia's economy and politics. As the Russian economy stagnates while energy behemoths like Rosneft appear to prosper, the Middle East's energy holdings become all the more strategically tempting to Moscow.[49] At the same time, the threat from Islamic terrorism has been a prominent justification for Putin's national security policy since its inception. Moreover the historic attraction of Russian power that has sought dominance or at least bases in the Middle East and the Mediterranean since Catherine the Great's time serves as a compelling memory and motive for Russia to project itself as a military superpower again throughout the region.

Even before the intervention into Syria, Russia was significantly enhancing its standing and presence in the area despite the misplaced complacency of the Obama administration and the numerous observers who dismissed the idea that Russia could become a Middle East actor.[50] Thus, history, the domestic imperatives of great power politics and standing for purposes of regime consolidation at home, and the necessity to challenge Washington if not the entire West while also resisting and defanging Islam all have driven and will continue to drive Russian policy for the foreseeable future. And beyond those considerations, Russian spokesmen have frequently justified Russia's

Middle Eastern policies by referencing the fact that Russia is an increasingly Muslim country whose Islamic population is the most dynamic factor in Russian demography.[51]

Therefore, both the internal and external factors driving Russia to intervene militarily and in many other ways across the Middle East will lose none of their salience between now and 2025. And Moscow has enhanced its capabilities to meet those challenges, particularly, though not exclusively, the external ones. This insight applies to military policies, energy policies and domestic affairs as well as to the dissemination of information warfare by Russia as part of its Middle Eastern strategy.[52]

In Syria, Moscow has conducted a clinic on Clausewitz that revealed it to be both a learning government and a learning military, something Washington has conspicuously failed to do. Thus, as was the case in Iraq, Washington has no adequate political vehicle capable of ruling Syria to complement its military presence there. This is the same mistake the US made in Vietnam and, apparently, also in Afghanistan. In contrast, Russia's military operations in Syria represent a classic successful manifestation of Clausewitz's dictum that war is an act (or acts) of force intended to compel the enemy to do our (i.e., in this case, Moscow's) will. Surprisingly, this banal observation evidently comes as a surprise to many Russia observers as if it were conceivable that Putin would use force for no discernible strategic or policy purpose.[53] As Dmitry Adamsky has shown, Russia understood from the outset the need to tailor military capability to the objectives it had postulated at the level of the principle of reasonable or rational sufficiency (*Razumnaia Dostatochnost'*)—that is, using the minimum amount of force needed to secure those objectives.[54] Such thinking prevented Moscow from overshooting its "culminating point." In turn, that allowed it to focus on attaining its political goals rather than on being seduced by purely tactical or operational objectives. Moscow's lessons and newly created systems of battle management will come in handy for it in future conflicts, whatever their provenance. Thus Moscow's or anyone else's "intervention" in a third party civil war like Syria, for that matter, is an act of war to compel one or more side to do the "intervener's" will. Equally, if not more importantly, Russia's intervention and subsequent operations there carry important lessons for us about war in general, contemporary combat operations as well as about Russia itself. We must learn or ignore these lessons at our own peril. But beyond those cases of strategic learning, Adamsky highlights numerous examples of operational and other strategic learning that show careful attention to the requirements of the theater and a willingness to absorb lessons that will prove useful in future conflicts in the Middle East if not elsewhere.[55]

This Syrian clinic on Clausewitz's teachings about war can also serve as a textbook example of how to use limited forces to attain strategic, political objectives or, as Clausewitz would say, to use war successfully as an instrument to achieve the goals of policy or politics (the word *Politik* in German means both things) by other means. And from today's vantage point, clearly the greatest of those objectives is the entrenchment of Russia as a permanent and widely accepted Middle Eastern power broker and great power. Beyond this point, Syria has provided the world with an object demonstration of the improvements in Russia's war fighting, battle management, and strategy-making capabilities that it will continue to refine through 2025. Thus, Syria has been and will remain, until completely "pacified," a laboratory for the execution of Russian military operations and strategy as well as a test-bed for its weapons systems— the latter being a point that Russian military and civilian leaders have repeatedly reiterated.[56] And because of the fact that Russian weapons have been showcased in Syria to good effect, this battleground has become proof of performance for new arms sales that further enrich Moscow's coffers, sustain its military capabilities, and enrich the defense industrial complex while also reinforcing ties with consumers in and beyond the Middle East.[57]

Moscow also learned to innovate in other ways, namely the creation of private military companies (PMC), like Wagner Group. Sergey Sukhankin traces much of the innovative aspect of this creative adaptation of both Russian tradition and the contemporary Western example of mercenary forces.[58] But he is hardly alone in underscoring the importance of Moscow's ability to create diverse "special" or private forces of diverse provenances to promote its objectives in Syria if not also in Ukraine. [59] Like Adamsky, Sarah Fainberg has found that Moscow's "boosted use of "special operations forces" and "special purpose forces" also illustrates the Russian shift toward a new warfare economy: the use of limited or minimal military means that can generate a maximum military and diplomatic effect."[60]

Fainberg also agrees with other analysts that,

> As a result of its new military doctrine and the reorganization of Russia's Armed Forces, Moscow's new involvement mode, as implemented and honed on the Syrian frontlines, is liable to improve the country's operational capacities and military power, both offensive and deterrent, whether in Russia's "near abroad" or in any potential operation beyond its immediate zone of influence.[61]

But as we now see from events in Africa, Moscow is expanding the use of this innovative force into Russian national security policy. And as regards the Middle East,

> ...one may imagine two models of their activation. In postwar Syria, they could be used as a security force in the energy and critical infrastructure installations. If the situation on the ground deteriorates, they can act as a rapid reaction force, before major reinforcements arrive. Another *modus operandi* might be deploying them elsewhere in the region, in conjunction with Russian needs. In this case, they will be a reconnaissance by force of sorts—they can explore operational configurations in the

theater, gather intelligence and prepare a bridgehead for the main assault force. In both cases, however, given their relatively limited logistical capabilities, coordination and cooperation with the local hosts will be needed.[62]

Thus the use of both regular and private or irregular forces, or anything in between, as shown in Syria, Ukraine, the Balkans and Africa, has opened up a new range of opportunities for Moscow to demonstrate its military prowess and the capabilities of these forces to interested onlookers and to dispose of an especially flexible "proxy war" instrument for use in conflicts in and beyond the Middle East at minimum cost to the government. Therefore, Moscow need not commit regular forces abroad in future conflicts if it feels that option to be disadvantageous. But Moscow can reap the benefit of support for clients and partners by dispatching these groups, as in Africa. As such, Russia has added a highly flexible military capability to Moscow's repertoire in a highly volatile zone that will probably allow it to use those kinds of forces in conflicts occurring between now and 2025.

Beyond being a showcase for foreign arms sales, the Syrian experience also imparts new tactical, operational and strategic lessons to Russia's military and "irregular" or private forces. Syria has given those forces both the reputation and proven capability of intervening in and managing, if not terminating, potential conflicts on behalf of one side or another. This factor clearly is attractive to governments in Egypt, Sudan and the Central African Republic.

Thus, to the extent that Moscow can pacify Syria, that success will enhance its attractiveness in providing help to allies or partners who are or feel at risk. Beyond that, the success of Russian arms in Syria will go far to making Russia a real, not just a potential arbiter of potential future conflicts. Illustratively, Moscow now wants to mediate Israel-Palestinian relations, Jordan-Syria and Israel-Iran, to list only a few. So it can fulfill the functions cited above by Adamsky of being a conflict regulator if not preventer and thus a regional security manager in the future.[63]

The Naval Dimension

However, the military factors that make for Russia's robust military presence in the Middle East by 2025 do not end here. Thanks to its wars in Ukraine and Syria, Moscow has obtained control or maybe even command of the Black Sea. Moreover, today, its navy can deploy permanently in the Eastern Mediterranean and is busily obtaining a network of bases, plus the capability to build another anti-access, area denial (A2/AD) zone there—in this case both maritime and aerial denial against NATO forces. Finally, its armed forces in Syria now have an unprecedented veto over what Israel can do with its air power in Syria and the Levant. These strategic outcomes and their implications have not been sufficiently explored in the West. Nevertheless, the capabilities Moscow has developed and will develop promise to make it an even more formidable obstacle to Western interests in Europe, Africa, and the Middle East by 2025. Furthermore, those capabilities and outcomes make Russia both more attractive and more intimidating to many Middle Eastern governments and will incentivize them to facilitate Russian military plans through 2025.

Even though the navy has traditionally been and most likely will be the overlooked stepchild of the new Russian military procurement plan through 2027, programs now in force demonstrate Moscow's intention of striking at Western navies or restricting their access to critical waterways significant for European security. This program is particularly visible in the Eastern Mediterranean, Middle East and all the way to Central Asia. If fully consummated, it could put much of European energy supplies along with Western navies under permanent Russian threat. Indeed, if and when the grand design is realized, Russia will have achieved something the Soviet Navy sought but could not sustain or realize with incomparably greater conventional firepower.

The first step was the conversion of the Black Sea into a *Mare Clausus* (closed sea) after 2014. As this writer and others have observed, since 2014 a sustained buildup of Russian forces in Crimea and the Black Sea have gone far toward creating a layered A2/AD zone in that sea, although NATO has begun to react to the threat and exercise forces there.[64] That layered defense consists of a combined arms (air, land and sea) integrated air-defense system (IADS) and powerful anti-ship missiles deliverable from each of those forces. Moscow has also moved nuclear-capable forces to Crimea and the Black Sea to further display its determination to keep NATO. Additionally, Russia aims to use the umbrella it has created as the basis for an even more expansive strategy (resembling that used by the Egyptian Army in the Yom Kippur War of 1973) from which it can project power further out into the Levant and deny new areas to NATO or at least threaten the North Atlantic Alliance with heavy costs.[65]

Certainly, Russia regards any presence in the Black Sea as illegitimate and a threat. And true to the Catherinian dictum that it can only defend its lands by expanding them, the defense of the Black Sea inevitably entails excluding NATO from the Eastern Mediterranean and Aegean Seas, if possible. Bases and a functioning A2/AD network throughout the Levant are a perfect answer for this strategic mission. For example, in response to talk of NATO exercises, Andrei Kelin, a spokesperson for the Russian Ministry of Foreign Affairs, labeled such exercises destabilizing and further added that, "This is not NATO's maritime space and it has no relation to the alliance."[66] The Russian defense establishment has announced that "Kalibr" (SS-N-27) ship-based missiles will be "permanently based" in the Eastern Mediterranean, thus providing a capable and reliable reach for Moscow's forces in the region.[67] Such missiles, with a range of up to 300 kilometers, give even older Russian vessels a sufficient offensive as well as defensive counter-punch to strike at naval or even shore-based targets.

Having poured these weapons systems into the Black Sea and having strengthened the Mediterranean Squadron, Russia has created a permanent force in being in the Eastern Mediterranean. Moreover, Moscow is seeking to make good on the request stated by Defense Minister Shoigu on February 26, 2014 (as the Ukraine invasion was beginning) for a global chain of air and naval bases. Shoigu announced then that Russia had made progress in talks with eight governments to establish a global network of airbases to extend the reach of Russia's long-range maritime and strategic aviation assets and thus increase Russia's global military preseence. Shoigu stated, "We are working actively with the Seychelles, Singapore, Algeria, Cyprus, Nicaragua, Venezuela and even in some other countries. We are in talks and close to a result." Shoigu cited Russia's need for refueling bases near the equator and asserted that, "It is imperative that our navy has the opportunities for replenishment."[68]

In August 2014, responding to NATO's heightened naval presence in the Black Sea due to the Ukrainian crisis, Shoigu demanded a new naval modernization plan to "improve the operational readiness of Russian naval forces in locations providing the greatest strategic threat."[69] Indeed, in June 2014, Russian ships even deployed for the first time west of the Straits of Messina.[70] These moves show why dominating the Black Sea is critical for Russia's power projection into the Mediterranean and Middle East.[71]

However, the Mediterranean Squadron may be as much a response to previously declining NATO deployments that created a strategic vacuum there, as it is a conscious strategy.[72] Since 2014, Moscow has moved to reinforce the Black Sea Fleet to use it as a platform for denying NATO access to Russia, Ukraine, and the Caucasus and to serve as a platform for power projection into the Mediterranean and Middle East.[73] And since the intervention in Syria, Moscow has started to fortify the missile, air-defense and submarine component of its Mediterranean Eskadra (Squadron) to impart to it an A2/AD capability against NATO fleets in the Mediterranean. What is thus emerging is Moscow's sea denial strategy against the Alliance and other fleets in the area just as in the Black Sea and other maritime theaters.[74] And by May 2016, US intelligence confirmed that Moscow was building an army base at Palmyra.[75]

But matters do not end there. Western military analysts have described Russia's efforts to build its IADS, anti-ship, and overall A2/AD networks in terms of "bubbles" at certain "nodal points," namely in the Baltic Sea, around the Black Sea, and around Syria. They also include the Caucasus. Just as Moscow has delivered Iskander-M missiles to Kaliningrad—a move that garnered much attention—it has also deployed them in Armenia, ostensibly, though not actually, under Armenian control. Indeed, it is virtually inconceivable that Moscow would grant Yerevan operational as well as physical control over those missiles, which are dual-capable and could take out any target in Azerbaijan within a radius of 500 kilometers (if not more), i.e. including parts of Turkey. Air and air-defense deployments at Moscow's Gyumri base in Armenia thus provide coverage of the entire Caucasus and eastern Turkey. Those deployments in Armenia have received virtually no publicity in the West. But they have vital strategic significance far beyond Azerbaijan and Georgia.

Coupled with the emerging IADS and A2AD networks that Russia is building in and around Syria and the Black Sea, as well as the base in Hamdan, Iran, which Moscow used in 2016, Russia is constructing an elaborate network of air and naval defenses. This not only interdicts foreign intervention in Syria's civil war; it also places the entire Caucasus region beyond the easy reach of NATO and Western air or military power. Additionally, it surrounds Turkey from the north, east and south with Russian forces and capabilities that can inhibit any Western effort to come to Turkey's aid, should another conflict—

however unlikely at this point—flare up between Moscow and Ankara. These capabilities also include the naval and A2AD capacity in the Caspian and the deployment of Russian ships with Kalibr or other cruise missiles there, as well as the possibility of introducing nuclear-capable systems like the Iskander into the Baltic—an already highly volatile theater—if not also the Black Sea.

Indeed, in 2017 this net further tightened. First, Moscow began construction of a new naval base at Kaspiisk, in Dagestan, to control the Caspian Sea. It will accommodate all of the Caspian Flotilla's guided-missile vessels and ensure rapid deployment for use of high-precision strike assets. This base is supposed to become the most advanced of all Russian bases, compared to those in the Arctic, Black, and Baltic Seas. Clearly, this move by Moscow is the latest example of Russia's consistent strategy to dominate not only the former USSR but also to project long-range military power into the Middle East as well. Indeed, we have seen the previous use of Caspian Flotilla ships to launch the deadly Kalibr sea-launched cruise missile into Syria.[76] Russian expert Sergei Mikheyev openly stated the reasons for this base: "The region is of growing interest for third countries. It is rich in oil and gas. Besides, an alternative corridor from Central Asia to the West via post-Soviet Transcaucasia [South Caucasus] can go through it. The idea is promoted by the Americans and the Europeans, but Russia and Iran are against it."[77]

We can and probably should also expect that Moscow will soon announce an accompanying air-defense network to add to this base and to the other air- and ship-defense "bubbles" that encase the so-called southern tier of the Black Sea, Caucasus and Central Asia. These bubbles comprise the land-, air-, and ship-based anti-air defenses at Gyumri in Armenia, the Black Sea and around Ukraine and in Syria. Indeed, it already is the case that, for all practical purposes, Russian forces encircle Turkey to its north, east and south—in the Black Sea, Caucasus and Syria. The new base will only increase that encirclement.

Similarly, this new base expresses Moscow's ongoing determination to project long-term and long-range military power into the Middle East and even close to the Persian Gulf. The Russian Ministry of Defense has long since proclaimed its desire for this regional network of naval bases, and experts are no less candid in explaining the strategic justification for this policy. Thus, defense analyst Mikheyev also said the Caspian Sea is a valuable asset for the Russian military as it is located close to the Middle East and directly borders on Central Asia. "The Syrian operation showed that the Caspian Sea is a safe launching pad for cruise missiles. It can accommodate our warships armed with high-precision weapons. The sea is out of reach for potential adversaries and third-country navies," he noted.[78] Also in this vein, the Russian newspaper *Gazeta.ru* cited an anonymous high-ranking defense ministry official, on November 21, 2017, who declared, "The Russian military presence in the Eastern Mediterranean is necessary for keeping the balance of power and the interests that we lost after the USSR's [Union of Soviet Socialist Republics] disintegration 25 years ago."[79]

Beyond this development, Russia has, for some time, showed this intention with prior statements and actions to ensure a network of bases from Cyprus and Syria to Egypt and Libya, where we can expect a request for a base once that country is stabilized. In Yemen, where Russia is aiding the Iranian-backed Houthis, Moscow announced an interest in a base as early as 2009.[80] Indeed, already in 2008, Admiral Ivan Kapitanets (ret.), a former first deputy commander-in-chief of the Soviet and Russian Fleets, stated that Russia needs ports anchorages and access to bases in the Mediterranean—and specifically in Libya.[81] Mattia Toaldo, a Libya expert and senior fellow at the European Council on Foreign Relations in London, has commented that, "Russia could get a foothold in Libya that could be helpful in strengthening its overall position in the Mediterranean," adding, "There is increasing talk of a Russian base or even just docking rights in Benghazi. Coupled with Syria and in view of the rising ties with Egypt, this would allow Russia to have a much stronger position in this part of the world."[82]

Meanwhile in Yemen's case, Moscow has dramatically upgraded its political profile in that country's civil war. Russia's deepened commitment to ensuring a cease-fire in Yemen can be explained by a mixture of strategic considerations and broader geopolitical aspirations. From a strategic standpoint, a cessation of hostilities could allow Russia to construct a naval base on Yemeni soil. Indeed, a Russian military official told *ITAR-TASS* back in 2009 that establishing a naval base presence in Yemen was a medium-term strategic objective. A Yemeni base would have significant strategic value for Russia, as it would increase Moscow's access to Red Sea shipping lanes and the Bab el-Mandeb Strait, which links the Red Sea to the Gulf of Aden.[83]

A Russian naval base in Yemen—presumably at or near Socotra, where the Soviet Union had such a facility—would give Moscow significant monitoring and power-projection capabilities over the Gulf of Suez, the Suez Canal, the Red Sea, Bab-El Mandab, the Arabian Sea and the Western reaches of the Indian Ocean, possibly including the Persian Gulf. The implications for Middle Eastern and European energy transports are obvious. Another interesting fact about the apparent quest for bases in Yemen is that it is apparently tied to Russia's effort to position itself as a mediator in the Yemeni civil war. In that case, we would see the confluence of its diplomatic tactic of inserting itself into a conflictual relationship and engaging both sides in return for a lasting strategic foothold in a key spot, in this case a naval base overlooking the Red Sea and Indian Ocean.[84]

Nor do reports of Russian interests in bases in the Middle East, the Mediterranean and the Red Sea stop here. In 2014, Foreign Minister Lavrov openly stated that Russia wanted a base in Alexandria, Egypt: "The naval base is certain, and I say it loudly," he replied. "We want to have a presence in the Mediterranean because it is important for Russia to understand what is happening there and to enhance our position." He said that the Syrian port of Tartus will be the fuel base for Russia's Mediterranean Fleet."[85]

In April 2018, local media reports from Somaliland indicted that Russia had requested a small naval and air facility, housing no more than 1,500 personnel, outside the city of Zeila." The naval facility should serve two destroyer sized ships, four frigate-class ships, and two large submarine pens. The air facility will include two airstrips and will be able to host up to "six heavy aircraft and fifteen fighter jets as well as space for fuel, ammunition, and base defenses." In return, Moscow is allegedly promising to assist Somaliland in obtaining international recognition and "is willing to send more military advisors, both tactical and strategic, to assist the emerging Somaliland military.[86]

Finally, toward the end of 2017, Moscow pulled off what might be its greatest coup. The Egyptian government agreed to host a Russian airbase and allow Russia freedom to use its air space (undoubtedly to fight Russian-backed forces in Libya). Furthermore, Sudanese President Omar al-Bashir announced he was seeking Russian protection and arms against the United States and discussed with President Putin the idea of a Russian naval base on the Sudanese coast.[87] Additionally, at the end of 2017, Russia announced that its Syrian naval facility at Tartus will be upgraded to the full status of a naval base and will be under Russian control for 49 years, along with the Khmeinim airbase. The strategic implications of these Russian moves are enormous. Moscow will undoubtedly utilize its Egyptian airbase to strike at anti-Russian and pro-Western factions in Libya. It also now has acquired for the first time direct reconnaissance over Israeli airspace and increasing leverage through its Egyptian and Syrian airbases, something Israel had sought to reject since its inception as a state in 1947. And in addition to the projected base in

Sudan, it now has the capability to strike at Saudi targets as well. Lastly, as shown above, these bases are tied to long-term political and military relationships—either in the form of mediation of civil wars or intervention on behalf of one or another side, or long-term programs of military training and reinforcement. All such approaches have a pedigree that dates back to the Soviet advisors in Egypt and Syria in the 1960s and 1970s.[88]

But the dimensions of Moscow's achievement actually go much further. These bases showcase Russian military and political influence throughout the region. Moscow will now have potential strike and/or intelligence, surveillance, reconnaissance (ISR) capabilities across the entire Middle East. In practical terms, this means that Russian bases in Syria, Egypt (and probably in Iran)—along with its additional bases inside Russia, including in Crimea, as well as in Armenia—give Moscow the capability to project power across the entire breadth and length of the Middle East, much if not all of the Eastern Mediterranean, the Suez Canal, and the Red Sea. Bases in Libya, Cyprus (which it has also sought), Yemen and Sudan would further extend that range to the Central Mediterranean, including Italy and parts of the Balkans, the Arabian Sea, Indian Ocean and the Persian Gulf. Closer to home, Moscow would have secluded the Caucasus and Central Asia from Western power-projection capability, drawn a cordon around Turkey, and attained the capability to threaten Israel in ways Soviet leaders could have only dreamed about. [89]

Meanwhile, Russia will probably deploy its fire-strike weapons and integrated air defenses across these bases. Moscow is likely to outfit those naval and airbases with long-range cruise missiles, UAVs, unmanned combat aerial vehicles (UCAV), unmanned underwater vehicles (UUV), as well as EW and intelligence, surveillance, target acquisition and reconnaissance (ISTAR) capabilities. In that case, Russia could then thoroughly contest Western aerospace superiority over these areas. In other words, given the bases already acquired and those that Moscow still seeks—a naval base in Alexandria and bases in

Libya and Cyprus—Moscow would be able to contest the entire Eastern Mediterranean. And given its strong ties with Algeria we should not rule out the possibility it is seeking a deal along these lines with that government as well. With the ability to contest the entire Mediterranean, Russia will be able to place NATO land, air, and/or naval forces further at risk.

The acquisition of the above-mentioned regional bases will enable Moscow to integrate its deployed long-range strike capabilities and air-defenses into a single overarching network with coverage of the Mediterranean, Black Sea, Caucasus, Central Asia and the Gulf, thus making Western operations in any of those theaters extremely hazardous and costly. Given Russia's existing bases in the Black Sea, Caucasus and the Levant, Turkey is already almost totally surrounded by Russian forces; and the Balkan states and Italy could be vulnerable as well. Arguably Russia is attempting to create what Soviet Marshal Nikolai Ogarkov called a reconnaissance-strike complex across the Mediterranean, Red Sea, Suez Canal, Caucasus, Central Asia and the Persian Gulf by integrating its ISR and fire-strike capabilities from these naval and airbases. This is not only an issue of challenging the West's reliance on an aerospace precision-fire strike—and thus Western and US air superiority—in the first days of any war. These Russian capabilities also threaten international energy supplies because Moscow can then use the threat of its naval and/or air power in the Persian Gulf, Red Sea, Suez Canal, and Mediterranean to interdict or curtail energy supplies that traverse these waterways.

The completion of this network of naval and airbases will challenge Western aerospace superiority, naval assets and lines of communications, and key NATO or Western allies. But additionally, these foreign bases will consolidate Russia as a key regional arbiter and also as an arbiter within each host country's politics—e.g., Syria, Libya, Yemen and Sudan. Moscow also stands to gain enormous leverage over Middle Eastern energy supplies to Europe because it will have gained coverage of both defense threats and international energy trade routes. Undoubtedly, Russia will then take advantage of all these situations and assets to attempt to free itself from sanctions by pressuring Middle Eastern countries (as it is already doing) or by pressuring European states to repudiate the sanctions.[90]

Meanwhile, Moscow's main interest in the Middle East is not peace but the controlled or managed chaos of so-called controlled conflict. Since "power projection activities are an input into the world order," Russian force deployments into the greater Middle East and economic-political actions to gain access, influence and power there represent competitive and profound, attempts at engendering a long-term restructuring of the regional strategic order.[91] Ultimately, Moscow is clearly not content merely to dominate the Caspian and Black Seas and their littorals. In other words, Russia is maneuvering Turkey, as well as Georgia and Azerbaijan, into its orbit through combined economic, ethnic, military and political pressures to ensure that these countries will be placed behind an air-defense umbrella. The completion of that umbrella would then allow the Russian army and/or navy to advance into foreign territories, much as the Egyptian army regained Sinai during the Yom Kippur War in 1973—a war that featured precisely this kind of offensive and that led to far-reaching strategic implications for all concerned. Russian military units would likely be able to move with impunity since Western forces would be deterred by the likely high rate of casualties they would incur. Indeed, when this system is complete, Moscow will not need to invade but only threaten to undermine the sovereignty or integrity of these countries or their pro-Western affiliations and economic-political ties.

But beyond the Caucasus and Central Asia, Moscow also wants to project lasting and long-range military power into the Middle East and connect those forces to the installations it is now building in the Caucasus, Central Asia and the Black Sea. So while Russian naval operations and undersea threats to the sea lanes of communication

(SLOC) in the Atlantic and Mediterranean are formidable and important threats that merit constant and close scrutiny, they are only part of a grander naval and maritime design that goes back at least to 2008–2009, as we have seen. Moscow's naval probes in the southern tier, therefore, merit no less careful and constant scrutiny by NATO and its Middle Eastern allies. If we remember that the cardinal point of the post–Cold War settlement was the indivisibility of European security and understand how imbricated European and Middle Eastern security issues are, then we can see this naval grand design as an element of Moscow's professed desire to overturn that very post–Cold War settlement.

Domestic Politics, Economics and Energy

Apart from the factors listed above that relate to diplomacy and so-called "hard power," there are compelling domestic and "soft power" factors driving Russia's overall Middle Eastern policies. It has utilized them to fashion durable modalities for prolonging and reinforcing its regional presence. First, Russia's quest under Putin has been to reaffirm strongly that Moscow is an Islamic country by virtue of its large and growing Muslim population. Virtually everyone who has studied the demographic issue agrees that a rising overall Muslim segment of the Russian Federation's population will impel the government to take Muslim interests more seriously at home and abroad and to strengthen its presence in the Middle East as well. Moscow's goal is to prevent the influence of extremist, Salafist, and terrorist ideologies from penetrating Russia.[92]

Already in 2003, Putin conceived of an ambitious project to define Russia as an Islamic country and to join the Organization of Islamic Countries (OIC). He has sought to establish Russia as a bridge between Europe and the Islamic world and to "do everything to promote the idea of the similarity of the Russian and 'Islamic' approaches to many international issues."[93] Everything since then has only reinforced elite opinion that Russia must persevere along this course for its own security against terrorism and due to its particular demographic profile.[94] And as that demographic profile becomes more skewed or weighted toward a large Muslim influence in Russian politics and the danger of internal terrorism, Russia will have little choice but to pursue a proactive course in the Middle East, not unlike what it has been doing for several years.

Economic factors also weigh heavily here and may well have moved Russia toward a closer engagement with the Middle East and Asia, particularly as regards energy. This reorientation likely would have occurred even without the post-Ukraine sanctions due to the nature of the energy economy and Western reactions to Russia's predatory energy policies in Europe and Eurasia.[95] Indeed, even before the Syrian intervention in 2015, Moscow was adroitly combining its ability to play both sides in conflict-ridden areas that possess large energy deposits. In Iraq, Russia employed the lure of arms sales to gain enduring leverage upon Baghdad and the Iraqi Kurds.

Yet, Russia's actions in Iraq cannot be abstracted from its objectives in the Middle East as a whole. Certainly the deals with Iraq combined with Russia's efforts to enter Iran, Israel, Cyprus and Turkey confirm that for Moscow, if not for other major actors, "Geopolitical power is less about the projection of military prowess and more about access and control of resources and infrastructure."[96] Russia's energy deals in the Middle East, if not elsewhere, also demonstrates the fundamentally strategic and political motives behind its overall energy policy.

For Russia, energy security means "weaponizing" energy. It is not a philosophy that aims at some future self-sufficient "clean energy" paradise. It is a doctrine for today, which takes the world as it is, vulnerable and addicted to "dirty energy" such as natural gas, oil and coal, and exploits that dependence to make Russia stronger. With this cynical way of looking at the world, much akin to the way Colombian drug lords regard cocaine addicts, Russia pursues energy deals in a way that is quite alien to what most Americans dreamily think it to be.[97]

Additionally, the linkage of energy and arms deals represents another important factor in Russian policy toward Iraq and throughout the Middle East as well as North and Sub-Saharan Africa. Increasingly, it appears that the actual sequence of deals does not matter. So it does not matter whether energy or arms sales come first. But they are certainly more and more often linked. Whatever benefits they bring to the host state, they have been correlated to Russian foreign policy for some time. It was already clear by 2009 that arms sales and gas deals shaped Russia's policies toward Algeria and Libya, for example.

Thus, the subsequent deals chronicled above—which are also explored in the papers by Rauf Mammadov and Theodore Karasik— build on a pre-existing foundation that predated the intervention in Syria and are essential to Russia's multi-dimensional strategy. Today and into the future, the pressure of sanctions, the location of Russia's newest oil and gas fields, and the general evolution of the global economy and its energy component to where Asia is the most dynamic factor will impel Moscow to make more deals with Middle Eastern energy holders and/or consumers in the future.[98] And these collocated energy deals and arms sales, together with the performance of the Russian military and Russian diplomacy, enable Moscow to repeat on a grander scale in the Middle East what it did with Iraq, the Kurds and Turkey in 2012–2015, when it combined energy deals and arms sales to gain lasting leverage on all three of them. Moscow will hunt with the Iraqi hounds and simultaneously run with the Kurdish hare, all while also trying try to prevent Turkey from reducing its excessive dependence on Russian energy.[99]

Indeed, one of the reasons it has supported Syria is also that Syria opposed a Qatari gas pipeline to Europe that would have cut into

Moscow's ability to dominate Southeastern and Central European gas markets through an alternative Iranian-proposed pipeline.[100] While that is still the case and despite the Saudi-UAE pressure against Qatar, Qatar and Russia are discussing arms deals and arms sales, further testimony to Russia's flexibility, and the benefits that confers upon Moscow.[101] Nor do the examples of Russian energy deals in the Levant and wider Middle East presented here exhaust the full scope of Moscow's regional energy interests. After all, Russia has long been interested in gaining entrée to the Eastern Mediterranean gas finds in Egypt, Israel and Cyprus, as well as Algerian gas. And Russia's dominance in the Turkish gas market, where it supplies 60–70 percent of domestic gas, is well known and a clear source of Russian leverage upon Turkey.

Conclusions

The foregoing narrative spotlights the coordinated interaction of all of Russia's instruments of power, save for information. Yet, Donald Jensen's paper shows that Moscow has not neglected that vital component of its foreign and defense policy in the Middle East.[102] This permanent interaction among all these instruments and tactics of Russian power, diplomacy, information, military and economic instruments belies any idea that Moscow is merely a regional power or that Russian policy is essentially improvisatory and lacking in strategy. Indeed, and as this and other papers in this project have shown, Russian objectives in the Middle East and the policies to reach them are long-standing and have deep roots in Russian and Soviet thinking if not the 1990s, when Russia was counted out as a Middle Eastern player.[103]

Precisely because Moscow has combined an impressive learning capacity with a focus on long-standing goals and flexibility in meeting them, it has been able to take advantage of the United States' continuing failure to articulate a coherent or sustainable strategy for the Middle East. US writers already argue that Moscow has supplanted

Washington as the "go to" power in the Middle East.[104] Moreover, as the foregoing assessment shows, Russia has built upon these deep roots of its policy and is constantly strengthening its capability to take advantage of opportunities, not only in the Middle East but in nearby Africa. Consequently, there is no reason to believe, all things being equal, that Russia in 2025 will enjoy a markedly weaker position in the Middle East or would barter away its hard-won gains for anything less than massive American concessions (which Moscow appears to think will come inevitably due to US decline).

Fedor Lukyanov, the editor of *Russia in Global Affairs*, has contended that the Arab Spring showed Russia up to that point was not a key player in the Middle East. But it also shows that Russia is trying to create a situation whereby if it does not participate in or support the resolution of a major issue—e.g., Syria's civil war or the Kurdish issue in Iraq—it will not be possible for anyone else to seriously influence the course of events there. Thus, Moscow, as it has aspired to be since Yevgeny Primakov's tenure as foreign minister and prime minister, still seeks to play the role of a great equalizer against the US and any other potential rivals in the Middle East.[105] Not only has it succeeded in achieving that outcome in Syria, but its triumphs in Syria (amidst US fecklessness) have ensured that it is replicating and extending that victory throughout the region, both spatially and temporally. The idea that Moscow cannot sustain or bear the costs of its Middle Eastern projects are clearly illusory. Indeed, its policies aim to force others to share in those costs as well as the benefits, thereby extending and deepening its presence. Thus, if we are to understand Russia's policies in the Middle East in order to be able to counter them, the first thing the US will need to do is embrace Samuel Johnson's admonition to "clear our minds of can't."

ENDNOTES

[1] Ekaterina Stepanova, "Russia In the Middle East: Back To a Grand Strategy" – Or Enforcing Multilateralism," *Politique Etrangere*, No. 2, 2016, pp. 1–14; Fiona Hill and Clifford Gaddy, *Mr. Putin Operative In the Kremlin: Geopolitics in the 21st Century*, Washington, D.C.: Brookings Institution Press, 2015, Revised Edition, 2015, pp. 339–340.

[2] Osama Al-Sharif, "Russia Key To Reset Of Jordanian-Syrian ties," www.al-moonitor.com, July 23, 2018.

[3] Nikolay Kozhanov, "As Ringmaster: Russia Runs Israel-Iran Balancing Act In Syria," www.al-monitor.com, August 6, 2018; Stephen Blank, "Russia In Syria: Between US-Turkey Dealings and an Iran-Israel Conflict," August 1, 2018, https://www.cgpolicy.org/articles/russia-in-syria-between-u-s-turkey-dealings-an-israel-iran-conflict/.

[4] "Russia To Deploy Military Police On Golan Heights," www.reuters.com, August 2, 2018.

[5] Pavel K. Baev and Kemal Kirisci, *An Ambiguous Partnership: The Serpentine Trajectory of Turkish-Russian Relations in the era of Erdoğan and Putin*, Turkish Policy Project Paper No. 13, https://www.brookings.edu/wp-content/uploads/2017/09/pavel-and-kirisci-turkey-and-russia.pdf, 2017.

[6] "Iran In Talks To Join Eurasian Customs Union, Official Says," www.azernews.az, August 4, 2018.

[7] Jessica Tuchman Matthews, "Russia Replaces America As the Power Player In the Middle East," www.carnegieendowment.org, March 6, 2018; "US Sidelined As Russia Steers New Regional Course In Syria," November 26, 2017.

[8] "Press-Konferentsiia Po Itogam Peregovorov Prezidentov Rossii I SShA," Helsinki, July 16, 2018," http://kremlin.ru/events/president/news/58017.

[9] Theodore Karasik and Giorgio Caflero, "Russia and the UAE: Friends With Benefits," https://intpolicydigest.org/2017/04/26/russia-uae-friends-benefits/, April 26, 2017.

[10] Stephen Blank, "Russia Returns To Africa," Forthcoming, https://www.gisreportsonline.com/.

[11] Camille Lons, "Battle Of the Ports: Emirates Sea Power Spreads From Persian Gulf To Africa," www.newsweek.com, August 6, 2018; "UAE Ready To Take On Greater Security Burden In Middle East, Minister," www.reuters.com, July 28, 2018.

[12] Blank, "Russia Returns to Africa."

[13] Stephen Blank," Energy and Russia's High-Stakes Game in Iraq," EGS Working Paper 2015-2-1, Center for Energy Governance and Security, Hanyang University, 2015.

[14] "Russian Nuclear Energy deals With Egypt Reach Almost $60bn," https://www.rt.com/business/424343-rosatom-russia-egypt-contracts/, April 17, 2018; "Russia Deploys Special Forces on Libyan-Egyptian Border, Reuters Reports, https://www.libyanexpress.com/russia-deploys-special-forces-on-libyan-egyptian-border-reuters-reports/, March 14, 2017; David D. Kirkpatrick, "In Snub To U.S., Russia and Egypt Move Toward Deal On Air Bases," www.nytimes.com, November 30, 2017; "Egypt 'Ready To Agree' New Russian Air Base On Coast," Middle East Eye, October 11, 2016, https://www.middleeasteye.net/news/egypt-ready-agree-new-russian-air-base-coast-reports-1845388280.

[15] Stephen Blank, "From Sochi To the Sahel: Russia's Expanding Footprint," Eurasia Daily Monitor, November 29, 2017, https://jamestown.org/program/sochi-sahel-russias-expanding-footprint/; Real Clear Defense, November 30, 2017, https://www.realcleardefense.com/articles/2017/11/30/russias_expanding_footprint_from_sochi_to_the_sahel_112703.html.

[16] Kirill Semenov, "Russia, Qatar Explore Partnership Potential," www.al-monitor.com, March 28, 2018.

[17] Stefanie Ortmann, "The Russian Network State As A Great Power," Arkady Moshes and Vadim Kononenko, Eds., *Rusisa As a Network State: What Works* in Russia When State Institutions Do Not,? New York and London: Palgrave Macmillan, 20–11, pp. 139–164; Article of Russian Foreign Minister Sergey Lavrov, "Russia's Foreign Policy Philosophy" Published in the magazine "International Affairs" of March 2013 http://www.ieee.es/en/Galerias/fichero/OtrasPublicaciones/Internacional/Article_of_Russian_Foreign_Minister_Sergey_Lavrov.pdf.

[18] Bobo Lo, *Chujtzpah and Realism: Vladimir Putin and the Making Of Russian Foreign Policy*, Russie. NEI, No. 109, Institut Francais des Relations Internationales, www.ifri.org, June, 2018, pp. 10–13.

[19] Press Review: Moscow Mediates Libyan Crisis and Ukrainians Bypass Russian Social Media Ban," http://tass.com/pressreview/975718, November 15, 2017; Blank, "Russia Returns To Africa."

[20] "Iran In Talks To Join Eurasian Customs Union, Official Says."
[21] Samuel Charap, "Is Russia An Outside Power In the Gulf,?" *Survival*, LVII, No. 1, February 2015, p. 154.

[22] Stephen Blank, "Russia, Iran, and the Middle East: What comes Next,?" *Eurasia Daily Monitor*, July 18, 2018, www.jamestown.org; Remarks of Dmitry Adamsky at, the conference, Russia in the Middle East: A View from Israel, Kennan Institute of Advanced Russian Studies, Washington, D.C., June 27, 2018.

[23] Dmitry Adamsky, *Moscow's Syria Campaign Russian Lessons for the Art of Strategy*, Russie. NEI, No. 109, Institut Francais des Relations Internationales, www.ifri.org, July, 2018, p. 8.

[24] Blank, "Russia Returns To Africa."

[25] "Russia Signs Rosneft Deal With Qatar, Glencore," www.retuers.com, December 10, 2016.

[26] Rauf Mammadov," Russia in the Middle East: Energy Forever?" https://jamestown.org/program/russia-middle-east-energy-forever/, March 8, 2018;
Theodore Karasik, "Russia's Financial Tactics in the Middle East," https://jamestown.org/program/russias-financial-tactics-middle-east/, December 20, 2017.

[27] Ibid.

[28] Vladimir Putin, President of Russia, "Meeting of the Commission for Military Technology Cooperation with Foreign States," accessed March 12, 2014, http://eng.kremlin.ru/news/4121.

[29] "Rogozin discusses Glonass, Defense Order, Exports" Interfax-AVN Online, Moscow, Dec 11, 2013.

[30] Ibid.

[31] The Quartet on the Middle East (also referred to as the Madrid Quartet) is a grouping of countries and international entities established to lead mediation in the Israeli-Palestinian peace process. The members of the Quartet are the United States, European Union, United Nations and Russia.

[32] P5+1 is the common shorthand for the five Permanent Members of the UN Security Council plus Germany, who negotiated the Joint Cooperative Plan of Action (JCPOA) with Iran in 2015.

[33] William J. Burns, Addressing Russian Arms Sales," Wikileaks Public Library of US Diplomacy NO. 07 Moscow 5154a.

[34] Stephen Blank, Younkyoo Kim, "Russia and Latin America: The New Frontier for Geopolitics Arms Sales, and Energy," Problems of Post-Communism, LXII, NO. 3, May–June, 2015, pp. 159–173; Stephen Blank, "Russia's New Greek Project: the Balkans in Russian Policy," Margarita

Assenova and Zaur Shiriyev, Eds., *Azerbaijan and the New Energy Geopolitics of Southeastern Europe,* Washington, D.C., Jamestown Foundation, 2015, pp. 121–176.

[35] Stephen Blank, "Russia's Mideast Role," *Perspectives,* XVIII, No. 3, May, 2008.

[36] Constantine Courcoulas, Benjamin Harvey, Onur Ant, and Inci Ozbek, "Erdogan Defiant While Turkey Slips Toward Financial Crisis," https://www.bloomberg.com/news/articles/2018-08-11/with-turkey-crisis-erupting-bankers-gather-for-emergency-talks, August 11, 2018.

[37] "Syria's Assad Says Russia Military Needed In Syria Long Term: Agencies," www.reuters.com, July 26, 2018.

[38] Blank, "Russia Returns To Africa"; Blank, "From Sochi To the Sahel: Russia's Expanding Footprint."

[39] Charap, pp. 153–166

[40] Liz Slay, "No Sign of Obama's Predicted 'Quagmire' As Russia's Engagement in Syria Escalates," www.washingtonpost.com, September 30, 2016.

[41] Adamsky, *Passim.*

[42] Quoted in Paul Thomas Chamberlin, *The Cold War's Killing Fields: Rethinking the Long Peace,* New York: Harper Collins, 2018, pp. 492–493.

[43] *Ibid.,* p. 493.

[44] Zvi Magen, "Russia and the Middle East: Policy challenges," Memorandum NO. 127, Institute for National Security Studies, Tel-Aviv University, 2013.

[45] *Ibid.*

[46] Dmitri Alexander Simes, "A Russian Perspective On Foreign Affairs: An Interview with Konstantin Zatulin," https://nationalinterest.org/feature/russian-perspective-foreign-affairs-interview-konstantin-zatulin-27302, July 30, 2018.

[47] Nikolai Spassky, "Can Russia Become a Superpower Again – And Does It Really Need It,"? *Russia In Global Affairs*, http://eng.globalaffairs.ru.

[48.] N. Spassky, "The Island of Russia," *Russia in Global Affairs*, No. 2, 2011, http://eng.globalaffairs.ru.

[49] "Russia's Rosneft More Than Triples Q2 Net Profit, Shares Hit Record," www.reuters.com. August 7, 2018.

[50] John W. Parker, *Understanding Putin Through a Middle Eastern Looking Glass*, Institute for National Strategic Studies, National Defense University, Fort Leslie McNair, Washington, D.C, 2015 John W. Parker, *Putin's Syrian Gambit: Sharper Elbows, Bigger Footprint, Stickier Wicket*, http://inss.ndu.edu/Portals/68/Documents/stratperspective/inss/Strategic-Perspectives-25.pdf, 2017.

[51] Ilan Berman, "Demography's Pull on Russian Mideast Policy," https://jamestown.org/program/demographys-pull-russian-mideast-policy/, March 8, 2018.

[52] Donald N. Jensen, "Russia In the Middle East: A New Front In the Information War,?" https://jamestown.org/program/russia-middle-east-new-front-information/, December 20, 2017.

[53] Samuel Charap, "Russia's Use of Military Force as a Foreign Policy Tool: Is There a Logic.?" http://www.ponarseurasia.org/sites/default/files/policy-memos-pdf/Pepm443_Charap_Oct2016_4.pdf.

[54] Adamsky, *Moscow's Syria Campaign Russian Lessons for the Art of Strategy*, p. 9.

[55] *Ibid. Passim.*

[56] Anton Lavrov, "Russia In Syria: A Military Analysis," Stanislav Secrieriu and Nicu Popescu Eds., *Russia's Return to the Middle East: Building Sandcastles?* Chaillot Paper No. 146 Institute for Security Studies, European Union, July 2018, https://www.iss.europa.eu/content/russia%E2%80%99s-return-middle-east-building-sandcastles, pp. 47–57.

[57] Anna Borshchevskaya, "The Tactical Side Of Russia's Arms Sales To the Middle East," https://jamestown.org/program/tactical-side-russias-arms-sales-middle-east/, December 20, 2017.

[58] Sergey Sukhankin, "'Continuing War by Other Means': The Case of Wagner, Russia's Premier Private Military Company in the Middle East," https://jamestown.org/program/continuing-war-by-other-means-the-case-of-wagner-russias-premier-private-military-company-in-the-middle-east/, July 13, 2018.

[59] Sarah Fainberg, *Russian Spetsnaz, Contractors, and Volunteers In the Syrian Conflict*, Russie. NEI, No. 105, Institut Francais des Relations Internationales, www.ifri.org, July 2018.

[60] *Ibid.,* p. 8.

[61] *Ibid.,* p. 21.

[62] Adamsky, *Moscow's Syria Campaign Russian Lessons for the Art of Strategy*, p. 31.

[63] *Ibid.,* p. 8.

[64] Stephen Blank, "The Black Sea and Beyond," *Proceedings of the US Naval Institute*, October, 2015, pp. 36-41; "NATO Military Exercises Begin In Black Sea," http://www.bbc.com/news/av/world-europe-31828111/nato-military-exercises-begin-in-black-sea, March 11, 2015; Alex Gorka; "Exercise Sea Shield-2017: NATO Provokes Russia in Black Sea Before Defense Ministers' Meeting," https://www.strategic-culture.org/news/2017/02/10/exercise-sea-2017-nato-provokes-russia-

black-sea-defense-ministers-meeting.html, February 10, 2017; Damien Sharkov, "NATO To Strengthen in Black Sea Region Despite Russian Warning," *Newsweek*, June 15, 2016, http://www.newsweek.com/nato-strengthen-black-sea-despite-russia-warning-470717.

[65] Blank, "The Black Sea and Beyond," pp. 36–41.

[66] Sharkov, "NATO To Strengthen in Black Sea Region Despite Russian Warning."

[67] "Korabli s 'Kalibrami' otpravyatsya na postoyannuyu vakhtu v Sredizemnoye more," *Izvestia*, May 16, 2018, https://iz.ru/744028/2018-05-16/korabli-s-kalibrami-otpraviatsia-na-postoiannuiu-vakhtu-v-sredizemnoe-more.

[68] Bruce Jones "Russia searches for strategic airbase partner" IHS Jane's Defense Weekly. March 4, 2014, http://www.janes.com/article/34916/russia-searches-for-strategic-airbase-partners.

[69] "Russian Defense Minister Vows to Strengthen Navy," Agence France Presse, August 19, 2014, www.defensenews.com.

[70] Moscow, Interfax, in English, June 20, 2014, *FBIS SOV*, June 20, 2014.

[71] Moscow, Interfax, in English, May 20, 2014, *FBIS SOV*, May 20, 2014; Stephen Blank, "Russian Strategy and Policy in the Middle East," *Israel Journal of Foreign Relations*, VIII, NO. 2, May 2014, pp. 9–25.

[72] Captain Thomas S. Fedyszyn, USN, "The Russian Navy 'Rebalances' to the Mediterranean," *Proceedings of the US Naval Institute*, December 2013, www.usni.org

[73] Stephen Blank, "The Black Sea and Beyond," pp. 36–41.

[74] Stephen Blank, "The Meaning of Russia's Naval Deployments in the Mediterranean," *Eurasia Daily Monitor*, March 4, 2016, www.jamestown.org.

75 Bassem Mroue, "Russia Builds Military Camp Near Ancient Site in Palmyra," Associated Press, May 17, 2016, http://www.cbs46.com/story/31990649/russians-building-army-base-at-syrias-palmyra-site.

76 Huseyn Panahov, "Where Does the Caspian Sea Figure in Russia's Strategic Calculus,?" *Eurasia Insight*, www.eurasianet.org, October 23, 2015.

77 Stephen Blank, "Russia's New Caspian Base," http://www.caspianpolicy.org/news/russias-new-caspian-naval-base/, October 12, 2017.

78 *Ibid.*

79 Quoted in "Russian Media Comments Following Tripartite Sochi Summit: A New Yalta That Excludes The Americans," *MEMRI*, November 27, 2017, https://www.memri.org/reports/russian-media-comments-following-tripartite-sochi-summit-new-yalta-excludes-americans.

80 "Russia Plans Navy Bases in Libya, Syria, Yemen: Report," https://www.reuters.com/article/us-russia-navy-mideast/russia-plans-navy-bases-in-libya-syriayemen-report-idUSTRE50F3H120090116, January 16, 2009.

81 Moscow, *Interfax-AVN Online* in Russian, October 31, 2008, *Open Source Committee Foreign Broadcast Information Service, Central Eurasia* CEP 20081031950354, (Henceforth *FBIS SOV*), October 31, 2008.

82 "Russia Seeks Influence in Libya," http://www.dw.com/en/russia-seeks-influence-in-libya/a-36663867, December 6, 2017.

83 Samuel Ramani, "Moscow's Shifting Strategy in Yemen," https://www.al-monitor.com/pulse/originals/2017/07/russia-ambassador-yemen-houthis-hadi-military-influence.html, July 26, 2017.

84 Maher Farrukh and Tyler Nocita, "Yemen Situation Report," https://www.criticalthreats.org/briefs/yemen-situation-report/2017-yemen-crisis-situation-report-april-28, April 28, 2017.

[85] "Russia Seeks Naval Base In Egypt," *Middle East Monitor*, January 30, 2014, https://www.middleeastmonitor.com/20140130-russia-seeks-naval-base-in-egypt/.

[86] "Russia May Build Military Base In Somaliland-Media," https://southfront.org/russia-may-build-military-base-in-somaliland-media/, April 4, 2018.

[87] Stephen Blank, "From Sochi To the Sahel: Russia's Expanding Footprint," *Eurasia Daily Monitor*, November 29, 2017, https://jamestown.org/program/sochi-sahel-russias-expanding-footprint/ also in Real Clear Defense, November 30, 2017, https://www.realcleardefense.com/articles/2017/11/30/russias_expanding_footprint_from_sochi_to_the_sahel_112703.html; David D. Kirkpatrick, "In Snub to U.S. Rusia and Egypt Move toward Deal on Air Bases," *New York Times*, November 30, 2017, www.nytimes.com.

[88] Isabella Ginor, and Gideon Remez. *Foxbats over Dimona: The Soviets' Nuclear Gamble in the Six-Day War.* New Haven and London: Yale University Press, 2007; Isabella Ginor and Gideon Remez, *The Soviet-Israeli War 1967-1973: The USSR's Military Intervention in the Egyptian-Israeli Conflict, London: Hurst Publishers, 2017.*

[89] *Ibidem.*

[90] Theodore Karasik, "Russia's Financial Tactics in the Middle East," The Jamestown Foundation, December 20, 2017, https://jamestown.org/program/russias-financial-tactics-middle-east/.

[91] Henk Houweling and Mehdi Parvizi Amineh, "Introduction," Mehdi Parvizi Amineh and Henk Houweling, Eds., *Central Eurasia in Global Politics: Conflict, Security, and Development*, International Studies in Sociology and Social Anthropology, Leiden, the Netherlands: Brill, 2004, p. 15.

[92] Ilan Berman, "Demography's Pull on Russian Mideast Policy," The Jamestown Foundation, March 8, 2018,

https://jamestown.org/program/demographys-pull-russian-mideast-policy/; Valdai Discussion Club Analytical Report, 2013, www.valdaiclub.com, pp. 100–105.

[93] Leonid Gankin and Vladimir Serebryakov, "Islam Receives Vladimir Putin," Moscow, Kommersant, in Russian, October 16, 2003, *FBIS SOV*, February 7, 2005.

[94] "Islam In Politics: Ideology Or Pragmatism?" pp. 100–105.

[95] Morena Skalamera and Andreas Goldthau, *Russia: Playing Hardball Or Bidding Farewell To Europe? Debunking the Myths of Eurasia's New Geopolitics of Gas*, Geopolitics of Energy Project, Belfer Center, Harvard Kennedy School, Discussion Paper, 2016-03, June 2016.

[96] Corey Johnson and B. Matthew Derrick, "A Splintered Heartland: Russia, Europe and the Geopolitics of Networked Energy Infrastructure," *Geopolitics*, XVII, NO. 3, 2012, p. 495.

[97] Cited in Keir Giles, *Russian Interests in Sub-Saharan Africa*, Carlisle Barracks, Strategic Studies Institute, US Army War College, 2013, p. 26.

[98] "The Energy Fix With Nick Trickett," Bear Market Brief (BMB) Russia, www.fpri.com, August 7, 2018.

[99] Stephen Blank, "Energy and Russia's High-Stakes Game in Iraq," EGS Working Paper 2015-2-1, Center for Energy Governance and Security, Hanyang University, 2015.

[100] Charis Chang, "Is the fight over a gas pipeline fuelling the world's bloodiest conflict?" https://www.news.com.au/world/middle-east/is-the-fight-over-a-gas-pipeline-fuelling-the-worlds-bloodiest-conflict/news-story/74efcba9554c10bd35e280b63a9afb74, December 2, 2015.

[101] Aurangzheb Qureshi, "The Qatar-Russia Energy Deal That Might Lead the Way To Peace In Syria, https://www.middleeasteye.net/columns/can-qatar-russia-energy-ties-translate-peace-syria-1234735369, December 21, 2016; "Russia and Qatar Discuss S-400 Missile Systems Deal TASS,"

https://www.reuters.com/article/us-russia-qatar-arms/russia-and-qatar-discuss-s-400-missile-systems-deal-tass-idUSKBN1KB0F0, July 21, 2018.

[102] Jensen, "Russia in the Middle East," 2017.

[103] Stephen, Blank, "The Spirit of Eternal Negation: Russia's Hour in the Middle East," Stephen J. Blank, Ed., Mediterranean Security Into the Coming Millennium, Carlisle Barracks, Pa.: Strategic Studies Institute, U.S. Army War College, 1999, pp. 443–513.

[104] Matthews, "Russia Replaces America," 2018.

[105] Fyodor Lukyanov, "Why Iraq Refused Russian Arms," *Russia Beyond the Headlines*, November 15, 2012, www.rbth.ru; Blank, "The Spirit of Eternal Negation: Russia's Hour in the Middle East," pp. 443–513.

16. Implications and Policy Recommendations

Theodore Karasik

Introduction

The findings from the Russia in the Middle East Project demonstrate that the United States is being outplayed in this region. As Stephen Blank notes early on in the body of this research, Russia's foreign policy in the Middle East—as initially articulated by former Russian prime minister Yevgeny Primakov—has featured both continuity and innovation.[1] Primakov formulated the basic intellectual framework and threat assessment used by Russia to assess the Near East today. Primakov and his successors, namely Vladimir Putin, restored the anti-American and neo-Soviet outlook in Russia's overall national security policy by penetrating the Middle East by using an assortment of optics and tactics with such success that the model is being expanded outside of the Middle East region.[2] Tactics involving arms sales, finance, minorities and energy are all opening doors to Moscow that were previously closed. Russia's policy evolution in the Middle East clearly shows the enduring Soviet-like if not Tsarist worldview that drives Russian foreign policy.[3] Vladimir Putin's double visit to the Gulf in 2007 guaranteed Moscow's position in the Middle East today and was a masterstroke as described by Theodore Karasik.[4] And with Moscow's current control over the Syrian future, Russia's policy allows Moscow deeper access to the Middle East and ultimately Africa.[5] The challenges to America are many.

Timeless Pursuit of Imperial Goals

As Blank points out, Moscow's ingrained resort to cooptation tactics in all of its guises is not new. Rather, the Kremlin's call to arms at home and abroad is part of the larger push by Moscow to expand Russian influence. Indeed, it is a summons to a permanent state of war, even if it may take a non-kinetic informational aspect rather than a purely military character. But in either case, this summons to perpetual war by Moscow against Western interests in the Middle East is a landmine under the current international order. Furthermore, it is a landmine under the continuity of the very Russian state Putin seeks to preserve and extend.[6] As such, the key issue of sustainability of Moscow's push into the Middle East becomes paramount.

Europe's Division Is Moscow's Gain in the Middle East

The overarching security dimension of Russia's push into the Middle East has had a dramatic effect on Europe. Pavel Baev argues that disarray and discord are nothing new in European foreign policy, so the spectrum of different views on Russia's policy in the Middle East is presently perhaps only marginally wider than at the start of this decade, when, as he suggests, the arrival of a new cold war first appeared.[7] The erosion or even complete disappearance of US global leadership is a major factor shaping European views and policies in the greater Middle East. European political and business elites, as well as fractured public opinions, are at a loss about the trajectory of interactions between Washington and Moscow in this volatile corner of the world, and so "Europe" is missing a key reference point for assessing the consequences and risks of Russian policies in the region. Middle Eastern leaders, meanwhile, may see moves by some European countries like Austria to become friends and partners of Russia in a positive light. Yet, there is still widespread mistrust of Putin's intentions—although the unique feature of the political landscape in Europe is that Trump is trusted even less.

Russia's push into the Middle East and the Syrian civil war has put pressure on the EU to advance the Kremlin's cause there by creating divisions inside Europe. The application of this instrument is set to intensify, and Moscow will try its best to advance the proposals in favor of cooperation on rebuilding Syria while at the same "protecting" Iran from crippling US sanctions by including the Islamic Republic in a new, emerging economic space.

Importantly, Europe sees Russian-Turkish relations as highly unstable. The EU, as an institution, is in an awkward and dubious position, having to sustain the process of Turkey's accession while at the same time making it clear to the member states that there is no prospect of actually admitting Ankara into Europe. While European opinion is focusing on Turkish human rights violations since the failed coup attempt in July 2016, Putin, to the contrary, has expressed full support to President Recep Tayyip Erdoğan and has proceeded with rehabilitating the partnership interrupted by the November 2015 air skirmish crisis. Concerns rightly abound that Erdoğan is pushing Turkey further into an alliance of sorts with Russia that has several geopolitical implications. Primarily, those geopolitical issues of concern include Russian military equipment being used in a NATO country, Russia's creation of a Sea of Azov protection zone that also impacts Turkey, as well as Moscow's ability to use Ankara's deeply established ties in Africa, developed by Erdoğan over the past decade.

Nevertheless, as Baev argues, many Europeans find Putin's ability and readiness to maintain dialogue with all important parties to regional conflicts, from Israel and Saudi Arabia to Hamas and Iran, highly commendable and in sync with their preferences for carefully negotiated political solutions. And many Arab states hold a similar view.[8] This convergence of opinion is regularly missed by US policymakers and emboldens Russia to push further in the Middle East. A main point is that Russia can claim a role to play only as long as violent conflicts continue to rage in the region, and the Syrian civil war is notably now moving into a new phase requiring political work for post-conflict reconstruction. Baev states, "This propensity for conflict manipulation, combined with the appraisal of military force as the most useful instrument of policy, and compounded with the need to ensure an increase in oil prices, makes Russia a very particular kind of stakeholder in the overlapping Middle Eastern areas of turbulence."[9] Or, in other words, there must be unresolved conflicts for Russia to play any kind of serious regional role. Therefore, Moscow will exploit any opportunity to exacerbate those conflicts so that it becomes a necessary actor in the Middle East. For Europe, Russia's foray into the Middle East and the Gulf in particular is an immense security challenge. But so far, no good response to Moscow's push has been registered due to internal European disagreement.

Turkey Is Moving Away From the West and Embracing the East

From a Turkish point of view, Syria is the top security priority for Ankara. Mitat Çelikpala asserts that Turkey faces a long list of Syria-related priorities, including the re-emergence of the Kurds (politically embodied by the PYD/YPG/PKK) as an international actor, the existence of al-Qaeda derivatives on Turkey's borders, the future of Sunni regions after the defeat of the Islamic State, the increasing legitimacy of Bashar al-Assad's regime in Syria, the situation of the refugees, and the future of the pro-Turkish opposition in Syria.[10] Among these priorities, the immediate concern for Turkey is the military, diplomatic, and political support that the United States and Russia had been providing to the PYD/YPG/PKK since the beginning of the Syrian crisis.[11] This struggle continues to bedevil the West on what exactly to do with Turkey and Russia.

Russia is playing a decisive balancer role in the realization of Turkey's interests in Syria—despite Moscow's deceptive role as a political partner. In fact, Turkish decision-makers feel that they need Russian support to force the US to change its attitude toward the YPG in Syria.

The triangulation between Ankara, Moscow and Tehran is also part of the equation. The flow of events and Ankara's diplomatic initiatives indicate that Turkish officials are trying to keep Iran and Russia on Turkey's side in Syria. This paradoxical attitude is the result of the three parties' longtime geopolitical competition in the region, which drives their periodic conflicts as well as their cooperation. These current developments apparently have made Turkey an actor again on the Syrian battlefield; but in return, Russia is playing the Kurdish card with a much louder voice, thereby making Moscow a factor in Ankara's relations with the West and enhancing Russia's leverage in Iraq, Syria and Turkey. This complex web of relations results in an unbalanced, obscure and, at times, self-contradictory Turkish foreign policy.

From the Arab point of view, as noted by Shehab al-Makahleh, Russia is boosting its involvement in the region in order to protect its own national security interests.[12] Increased Russian engagement is noticeable through its calibrated military intervention in Syria and the formation of alliances with a number of Middle Eastern states, even at the expense of the United States due to Washington's withdrawal from the region under Obama's presidency and the multiple twists and turns of the Trump administration.

Iran Is Subservient to Moscow in the New Middle East

From the Iranian point of view, as articulated by Alex Vatanka, Iran's ideological commitment to compete with the United States in the Middle East and beyond has certainly been a major geopolitical boon for Moscow since 1979.[13] It is a reality that in effect weakens Iran's hand—as Tehran's stance on the US is a non-starter for a majority of the states in the region that enjoy close ties with Washington—and compels the Iranians to turn to Russia for a host of military, economic and diplomatic requirements. And yet, some quarter of a century after the fall of the Soviet Union, Iranian opinions on Russia vary greatly.

Vatanka argues that Russia and Iran primarily have a limited tactical military-security relationship out of necessity; but Moscow now holds the upper hand. [14] When it comes to the generals from the Islamic Revolution Guards Corps (IRGC)—the political-military guardians of the Islamic Republic and Moscow's principal Iranian collaborators in the Syrian war—one will mostly hear praise vis-à-vis Russia. These are the stakeholders in the Iranian state that speak of a "strategic overlap" of interests with Moscow in everything from combating Sunni terrorism to rolling back American power in the Middle East. Still, even among such pro-Russia voices in Tehran, the relationship is not always easy to justify, as was conveyed by Defense Minister Hossein Dehghan's statement about Russian "betrayal."[15] Nevertheless, for the IRGC, it is the flow of Russian arms, intelligence cooperation and other practical benefits Moscow offers that make it a special partner. Russia has already been able to take advantage of this relationship, as demonstrated by the Caspian Sea Agreement of 2018 but also by the on-again-off-again use of Iranian territory for Russian aircraft landing and taking off from Shahrokhi Airbase. Meanwhile, Tehran undoubtedly quietly agrees that Russia has historically taken far more from Iran than it has ever contributed to its national interests.

Arabs Appreciate and Value Moscow More Than Washington

When the Arab Spring turned into civil wars in Syria and Libya, Russia returned to the Middle East on a self-defense policy platform, seeking to counter Western ambitions in the region. This grand strategy required an application of diverse tactics in order to achieve its goals, all while benefiting from the weakness of the European

Union and the distancing of the US from the Middle East in favor of the Pacific region.

Moscow's return to the region on the counterterrorism platform was justified by the Middle East's close proximity to Russia's southern borders. This geographic closeness and the gravity of the terrorist threat gave Russia the justification to intervene to safeguard its own national security. Simultaneously, the fast-moving events compelled Russia to cooperate with key regional powers such as Iran, Turkey, Egypt and Algeria, in an attempt to reestablish the equilibrium of power in the conflict-ridden region.

Shehab al-Makahleh pointed out that despite official narratives echoed by the media in parts of the Middle East and the West in particular, many Middle Easterners do not view Russian intervention in the region as something negative, nor do they see Russian presence as colonialist or intruding.[16] On the contrary, they view the Russian role in the region as a *fait accompli*, a situation that cannot be easily challenged or transformed. At the same time, Arabs understand that each of the major world powers pursues its own objectives in this strategically located region, which controls most of the global energy resources.

Russia's Gaining Superiority in the Information Sphere Is to the US's Detriment

Donald Jensen argues that the projection of Russian power into the Middle East in recent years has been accompanied by an impressive Kremlin information warfare effort intended to advance Moscow's foreign policy objectives.[17] The media tactic is an important tool in Russia's arsenal. This campaign was been somewhat successful across the region, especially in Syria. But the effectiveness of that effort is undermined by several factors.

First, government censorship in the Middle East is much more prevalent than in more open media areas such as Eastern Europe, where we have seen Kremlin disinformation campaigns be effective. This fact enables host governments to block Russian messaging they oppose. Second, Russia in general receives a mixed basket of popular praise and disapproval. Research by Pew finds that 35 percent of those polled in the Middle East see Russia as a threat; but 35 percent have a favorable view of Russia.[18] These findings, moreover, have been consistent over the last few years. Third, there are few cultural, linguistic, historical or other ties between Russia and the peoples of the Arab world. In no country are there ethnic-Russian communities large enough to be mobilized by Kremlin information activities. Finally, Russia is geographically distant from MENA, making its messaging harder to sustain.

Conversely, Moscow can be expected to place more efforts on enhancing Russia's media presence and strengthen its influence through culture, art and education, in order to familiarize Middle Easterners with Russian civilization and values. Traditionally more conservative than the liberal and secular West, Russia has many more things in common with the Middle Eastern ways of life. And both Russia and the Middle East could reap great benefits from enhancing their cultural ties in the coming years, even while challenging US interests. This process is now ongoing and could push American cultural icons out of the region over time.

For the United States, Russia uses its information warfare capability as a tactic, especially its *RT Arabic* and *Sputnik* news services, to advance its foreign policy goals in the Middle East. Those foreign policy goals include becoming a great power in the region, reducing the role of the United States, propping up allies such as Bashir al-Assad in Syria, and fighting terrorism. Evidence suggests that while Russian media narratives are disseminated broadly in the region by traditional means and online, outside of Syria their impact has been limited. The ability of regional authoritarian governments to control the information their societies receive, cross cutting political pressures, the lack of longstanding ethnic and cultural ties with Russia, and widespread doubts about Russian intentions will make it difficult for Moscow to use information operations as an effective tool should it decide to maintain an enhanced permanent presence in the region.

Financial Tactics Are Growing

Theodore Karasik pointed out that for Russia, the Kremlin sees its historical mission coming to fruition in the MENA region, where it is using financial tools that are helping to guide these states firmly within Moscow's orbit and influence. The Kremlin's move is smart and timely. The status and prospects for Arab-Russian bilateral relationships are growing, and both the Arab states and the Kremlin are expanding their financial connectivity. The United States needs to pay closer attention to Russia's financial tactics in the Middle East in order to gauge Moscow's successes and failures over the coming years.

The growing financial cooperation and interconnectivity between Russia and Arab Middle East states raises a number of troubling questions that Karasik[19] points to as critical for understanding these monetary relationships: To what extent are Gulf states enabling Russian foreign objectives? What is the impact of Russia's financial tactics on the interests of US allies in the Middle East? How do these activities affect their relations with Washington? How do East Asian countries, and specifically their sovereign wealth funds (SWF), interact with Arab SWFs that conduct business with Moscow? Is there a triangulation effect ongoing that shifts the geo-economic center of global economics eastward?

Russia's ability to use finance as a tactic is new to the Kremlin's arsenal, with most of the financial activity seen in the Gulf states. The goal is to build greater ties between the two regions. Arab states that are open to and engaging with Russia's financial tactics are enabling Moscow to further cement itself in Middle Eastern affairs. Washington's Gulf allies are conducting business with Russia, a country that sees itself on a historical mission.

Overall, Russia's financial tactics in the Middle East undermine US foreign policy. Additionally, they contribute to an unhealthy financial environment for the United States by manipulating local economies in order to win the hearts and minds of civilians but also of the civil servants, soldiers and employees of the states supported by Moscow in the region. Russia's use of finance to build a presence in the MENA region and specifically the Gulf is a critical part of Putin's foreign policy. The US would be wise to track these developments and assess their implications for Washington's foreign security strategy.

Energy Tactics Are the Future for Russia in the Middle East and Africa

Shehab al-Makahleh argues that Russia can be expected to continue to interfere in many countries' politics, especially those that were part of the former Soviet Union, in a bid to annex them.[20] It will also start exploration in the North Pole for oil and gas in order to maintain its ability to use energy as a weapon against other countries. After the Syrian civil war ends, Russia, along with Iran, Qatar and Syria, will together export more than 70 percent of the world's gas. This factor is a serious threat to many countries, including the United States because gas will be used to twist the arms of multiple US allies and partners. The next decade will prove to be confrontational, with Russia and Arab states agreeing on many issues that will challenge the US.

Rauf Mammadov asserts that disagreements between traditional allies in the region have helped Russia become a player there.[21] By building economic ties with its energy rivals in the area, and working with international organizations such as OPEC to pursue its goal, the Kremlin is doing what it has always excelled at: divide and conquer. Russia has tried to use its energy diplomacy in MENA both to bring the region under its influence and to drive a wedge between the United States and its traditional allies, especially in the Gulf.

In its more muscular role in the MENA, Russia has been putting pragmatic energy policies above political differences. A key question is whether it can continue cooperating with regional energy players while disregarding its geopolitical differences with them. In other words, how sustainable will Russia's energy diplomacy in the region be? And how will international oil prices affect Russia's relations with energy-exporting countries in the area over the long term?

The United States has become far less dependent on oil imports and even less dependent on Middle Eastern oil than just a decade ago. But the global nature of energy markets exposes the US economy to oil and gas price fluctuations. Both a recent explosion at a natural gas terminal in Baumgarten, Austria, and China's decision to slash coal production roiled global energy markets, underscoring how interdependent they are. Washington must ensure that Moscow does not outmaneuver it to increase its influence over global energy policy, and thus prices. This means the United States must keep a close eye on relations between its most important allies in the Gulf as well as its rival Russia. Gulf countries, especially Saudi Arabia and Qatar, will remain among the world's biggest energy exporters for many decades to come. And US oil companies are still major oil and gas producers in the region. The United States needs to keep open lines of communication with Middle Eastern oil producers given this region's indispensability to the global energy industry. Russia, meanwhile, is itself keen to further expand its energy cooperation in MENA to prevent volatility in energy commodity markets in order to maximize revenues gained from the exports of its own hydrocarbons.

Russia's Arms Sales Complicate the US's Relationships With Arab Armies

As Anna Borshchevskaya points out, there is also no denying that Putin is making great strides since May 2000 to use weapons sales as a tactic to garner closer relations with Arab states at the expense of the US and Europe.[22] Moscow's military reform efforts since 2008 have clearly paid off, and arms sales have been an effective tool in Moscow's foreign policy arsenal, especially in the Middle East.

The advantages Russian arms offer to this region continue to outweigh the disadvantages, both practically and politically. While most US defense experts believe Russia will be unable to produce much next-generation weaponry, Moscow is making significant strides with its existing technology. Russian arms are sufficient for most of Moscow's clients—particularly those who cannot afford top-of-the-line Western technology. Borshchevskaya says that Russian weapons—generally speaking—are well made, sometimes on par with the US, well-suited for the region's operational and prestige needs,[23] and usually more affordable than Western offerings. Politically, Russian military products come with few strings attached and thus are a great choice when a country wants to diversify away from the West, or at least signal such an intent.

When it comes to arms deals, Moscow has made inroads with traditional clients such as Iran, Syria, and Egypt, but also diversified toward countries with closer links to the West, such as states in the Arab Gulf as well as India, Morocco and Turkey. Borshchevskaya notes that the Russian defense sector has problems, but it has also demonstrated improvements, learning and flexibility.[24] And in the context of US retreat from the region, Moscow has stepped into a vacuum where the Kremlin's efforts generate a multiplier effect of real power. As long as US leadership in the region is absent, Russia's arms sales to the Middle East and North Africa will remain a serious problem for American interests over the coming years.

Potentially hampering Russia are not only the above-mention problems with its domestic arms industry but also the fact that China wields a level of commercial influence Russia simply cannot compete with. Indeed, some countries, such as Algeria, are increasingly looking toward China, even as Algiers signed its blockbuster deal with Moscow. China is also starting to dominate in high-growth areas such as unmanned aerial vehicles (UAV), where Russia is no match. Another element is Western sanctions on Russian dual-use high-technology imports, especially effective toward Russia's defense industry. Commercially available technologies such as microelectronics and quantum computing have increasingly important modern military applications, but Russia cannot produce them independently. It has tried to resort to import substitution, but so far with poor results. Finally, Russian weapons on the whole met no real opposition in Syria. Therefore, despite Moscow's tests and displays, questions about the full extent of these weapons' capabilities remain.

Russian PMCs as the Deadliest Tactic

In the final analysis, by cultivating a growing number of private military companies (PMC) like the Wagner Group, Russia has created both a powerful and convenient weapon of non-linear warfare as well as a tool for the Russian elites to achieve their own geo-economic goals. Sergey Sukhankin argues that, from a military point of view, Wagner's operations in Donbas and Syria appear to have, in part, been designed to test its ability to "control the territory," a concept strongly emphasized by Valery Gerasimov and the Russian General Staff.[25] Importantly, PMCs offer Moscow deniability and conceal its responsibility for deaths of Russian soldiers in operations abroad. Additionally, Russian PMCs and especially Wagner allow for the potential integration of foreigners (from impoverished parts of the post-Soviet space), which provides the Kremlin with another powerful tool of influence to use overseas. Undoubtedly, the Wagner model is here to stay.

The Nexus of Demography and Ideology

Ilan Berman notes Russia's changing demography fundamentally alters its engagement with the Middle East and the Muslim World more broadly. As the country's demographic transition progresses, Russia's involvement in the politics of the region can be expected to increase, even as its potential to serve as a reliable partner for the United States there will continue to diminish. Fundamentally, Russian policy in the Middle East (and toward the Muslim World more broadly) is already competitive, seeking to assert Russia as a counterpoint to local US alliances and interests. The demographic pressures exerted by Russia's swelling Muslim minority are likely to reinforce these tendencies over the next several years. In the process, they will almost certainly exacerbate Moscow's already unconstructive, zero-sum approach to the Middle East.

2024: Putin and the Middle East

Gazing into the future, to 2024, is an important part of the Russia and Middle East project.[26] Specifically, Yuri Barmin argues that as Syria gradually falls from the top of Russia's political agenda in the Middle East over the coming years, Moscow will be looking for new ways to stay relevant in the region.[27] Russia's permanent military bases in Syria have the potential to change the power balance in the Mediterranean. Moscow has already created a heavily guarded perimeter in the Eastern Mediterranean by deploying air-defense capabilities to Syria, which complement its permanent naval force in these waters. Together, these deployments and growing capabilities will become a challenge for NATO as Moscow spreads its presence into the Alliance's naval underbelly in the Mediterranean Sea. Down the line,

Russia is also managing to expand military cooperation with Egypt and the future government in Libya, and is expanding its naval presence in the Red Sea.

Politically, however, hard power will over time produce fewer benefits for Moscow, and at higher costs, which is why the Russian government will need to discover new ways to remain relevant in the regional arena. Having used Syria to rebuild its image as a regional power, Russia is faced with the challenge of how to balance its relations with Saudi Arabia and Iran, neither of which is a true ally for Moscow. In order to forge stronger regional alliances, Vladimir Putin might revisit the idea of a global anti-terrorist coalition, which feeds into the concept of a regional system of collective security widely discussed by Russian policymakers.

Trying to insert itself in regional politics in the post-Syria era, Russia is likely to rebrand its image in the Middle East and position itself as a regional referee in an attempt to offset the negative impact of the Syrian conflict on its profile. Being a regional referee, however, does not necessarily translate into being a supporter of democracy. The legacy of the Arab Spring and Russia's own experience with democratic movements led Putin to believe that authoritarian stability may help the Middle East overcome its security problems. And Russia's military campaign in Syria has further crystallized this notion for the Kremlin that Russia has *carte blanche* in the region.

In addition, Russia's relentless drive in the Middle East is obviously tied to the future of energy markets through 2024. As both Barmin[28] and Mammadov[29] point out in their respective works:

- Russia's regional energy goals can be summarized as finding new markets for its oil and gas; attracting investment to replace Western capital blocked by sanctions; working with other energy exporters to stabilize international oil prices;

undermining Europe's efforts to diversify its natural gas supplies; and helping Russia deliver more oil and gas to Asia.

- A favorable geopolitical environment coupled with higher oil prices has eased the Kremlin's efforts to build bilateral energy relations with the regional powers.
- Energy contracts give Russia presence, but actual control over regional infrastructure projects remains undetermined. This again raises questions about the sustainability of Moscow's energy push into the Middle East during Putin's fourth term.
- Resilience of the American fracking industry to the low oil price environment and the future of the Iran nuclear deal will be among the most significant elements influencing Russia's future in the region, and particularly the strength of its continued cooperation with Saudi Arabia.

And as Ilan Berman notes, Russia's policy on the Islamic world will form a unique nexus with Arab states through 2024 and beyond:

- Demography is among the most underappreciated drivers of contemporary Russian policy in the Middle East. Ongoing population decline—and the expansion of Russia's own Muslim minority—has exerted a significant influence over Moscow's attitudes and activities in the region over the past several years.
- The growth and radicalization of "Muslim Russia" has helped propel the Kremlin into assuming a leading role in the Syrian civil war, and will play an important role in shaping Russia's regional objectives for years to come.
- The nexus between Muslim Russia and the Islamic Middle East is an extraordinary driver in Moscow's current and future relationship with MENA. Muslim Russia and the Islamic Middle East build on historical, governmental and business ties, and are now focusing on counter-terrorism and messages of peaceful co-existence and tolerance.

- Russia and the Gulf states are leading the moderation of Islam. Saudi Arabia and the UAE, are articulating the same message now. The relative success of this trend will strongly reflect on Russia's perceived policy accomplishments in the region.[30]

Implications for the United States

Considering the circumscribed and frenzied role the United States currently plays in the Middle East, Russia is wide open to do as it sees fit there—and without too much push back from Arab powers.
Role of Optics

Much of Russia's ability to project power and influence into the Middle East under Putin has to do with the role of optics in media reporting. Russia's regional presence is subject to sustainability issues. A departure point is the sustainment level of a Syria-type action including force projection throughout the Middle East. Some analysts believe that Moscow's posturing is merely for show and that, in reality, Moscow is likely "a one trick pony" and staging a "Kabuki Theater."[31] Protracted conflict in Syria keeps Russia financially strapped to the Levantine campaign. Thus, while Moscow is set to expand its presence, Russia's footprint and optics must be taken into consideration by policymakers. Furthermore, Russian actions in the Middle East must be measured in terms of influence, credibility and authenticity. It is possible that Russia does not need to do much to generate the optics necessary for strategic and tactical success in the future because of media amplification.

Role of Sustainability

Undoubtedly, questions remain regarding the sustainability of Russia's push into the Middle East through 2024. The key issues, as noted by both Barmin[32] and Mammedov[33] are:

- Russia is operating with limited resources everywhere in the world. It is doubtful that it can sustain a large continued military presence in the MENA region.
- While Moscow tries to expand its presence, footprint and optics must be taken into consideration by policymakers. Russia's actions in the Middle East must be measured in terms of influence, credibility and authenticity. It is possible that Russia does not need to do much to create the optics necessary for strategic and tactical success, because of media amplification.
- The US government needs a different set of metrics to measure Russia's future influence in the Middle East, including discerning key differences in actual projection versus optics of influence.

Energy contracts give presence; but questions regarding actual control over infrastructure remain undetermined because of the multiple layers of opacity. How much of the energy push into the Middle East is sustainable during Putin's fourth term is a key question that only market forces and geopolitics will answer. The strategy and cooperation between Russia and major OPEC producers exists now and will be coordinated more closely in the future. As Moscow expands its energy presence in the Middle East, it is important to watch for how Arab energy producers receive or reject Russian joint ventures, mediation, and controlling interests/ownership.

Moscow's ability to project its legacy navy relies on a hub-based strategy utilizing ports, airbases and berths. The question of cost impedes the arrival of new Russian naval craft until the late 2020s. It is possible that Russian maritime operations off the coast of Syria may not be easily duplicated off of other Mediterranean or Gulf of Aden/Gulf of Oman shores.

How Russia measures success will also be important in the timeframe out to 2025.[34] Public opinion is affected by body bags, and thus Moscow will continue to use proxies to influence conflict and terrorist zones. A favorable geopolitical environment coupled with plummeting oil prices has eased the Kremlin's efforts to build bilateral energy relations with the regional powers. Russia's presence in the region is nascent but growing quickly. Yet, will Russia be able to maintain its presence in the region? Will Russia or Saudi Arabia be interested in cooperation to extend the volume-cut deal now and in the future? This will depend on a number of factors. Resilience of the US fracking industry to the low oil price environment and the future of Iran nuclear deal will be among the most significant elements that influence Russia's future in the region.[35]

Demography's Pull on Russian Mideast Policy Not Understood

Demography is among the most underappreciated drivers of contemporary Russian policy in the Middle East. Yet Russia's ongoing population decline—and the expansion of Russia's own Muslim minority—has exerted significant influence over Moscow's attitudes and activities in the region over the past several years. Thus, the growth and radicalization of "Muslim Russia" has helped propel the Kremlin into assuming a leading role in the Syrian civil war. This same constituency will play an important role in shaping Russia's objectives in the region in the years to come.[36]

But there is a larger trend line that policymakers and stakeholders are missing: the nexus between Muslim Russia and the Islamic Middle East, which is an extraordinary driver in Moscow's current and future relationship with MENA.

Muslim Russia and the Islamic Middle East build on historical, governmental and business ties and are now focusing on counter-terrorism and messages of peaceful co-existence and tolerance. Russia and the Gulf States are leading the moderation of Islam. Saudi Arabia and the UAE, are articulating the same message now. How that message continues as Saudi Arabia undergoes its transformation in the future is driven by metrics of success and failure in the MENA region for Russia's policy in the region. Coordination among Riyadh, Grozny and Moscow on the issue of the future of Islam is critical to track and understand. Thus, we confront a multi-pronged and multi-dimensional Russian strategy with initiatives in energy, diplomacy, projection of military power, and use of Muslim populations on the basis of a cultural and political affinity.

Miscalculating the North-South Corridor

As Karasik notes, the North-South corridor of energy and economic linkages between Russia and MENA remains poorly understood.[37] Nonetheless, it clear that Moscow is achieving the ability to be the number one energy influencer in the Middle East.

Russia's moves to influence the energy market share and 91 percent of the entire future LNG industry in MENA—as calculated in 2016 by the Abu Dhabi Executive Council[38]—are well underway, from Iran to Algeria. And the Qatar-Russia relationship will be key in this regard. Moreover, Moscow is using the Peninsula as a lily pad to Africa, following in Beijing's footsteps, to enter key African states in the Sahel, East Africa, and Africa's core—notably, Mozambique—to gain presence for exploration rights, weapons sales, and access and export of strategic minerals.

Such North-South energy strategies are going to dominate the international market, especially between Saudi Arabia and Russia. From the Arctic to the Gulf, there is a flurry of activity that includes strategic minerals. Indeed, Saudi money will soon be financing Russian energy projects in the Arctic.[39] Arab states are helping Russia build the necessary bridges by sea and air to the Middle East. These strategies are moving Russia and MENA eastward in terms of operating outside of SWIFT or currency swaps with the West, while gearing their deals toward the Yuan/Renminbi. The activity of SWFs between the Gulf and Russia is thus an area of finance that is falling outside of US surveillance and understanding. Moreover, Russia uses the GOZNAK Joint Stock Company to print currency for MENA warzones.[40] Taken together, this gray area economic investment in the North-South corridor is poorly understood, as are the flows of illicit monies that deserve anti-money laundering (AML) attention: including connections among Gulf–Russian Federation, Belarus-Gulf, Balkans-Gulf, and Central Asia–Gulf.[41]

US Policy Recommendations

Russian ambitions in the wider Middle East are inimical to US interests and support forces like Iran, which are also hostile to our interests and values. This will be the case for quite some time. Expanding the cadre of those with long-term experience in both Russia and the Middle East will thus be necessary to ensure that key policymakers and stakeholders fully grasp the key projections and metrics of the evolving Russian-Arab relationships.

Establishing the contours of a well thought out approach to pre-empt Russian moves will require further examining and addressing the long-term issues surrounding the emerging nexus of Muslim Russia and the Islamic Middle East—including as this nexus relates to the future of ties that bind North and South.

More importantly, the US government needs a different set of metrics to measure Russia's future influence in the Middle East. This includes a more effective means to discern the key differences in Moscow's actual power projection versus optics of influence. A key point is understanding how Russia and the Arab states see their interests merging in new and complex ways, including what challenges this may pose for the United States.

A New Scholarly Approach to Understanding the New Geopolitics of Russia's Activities in the Middle East

The woefully inadequate understanding of Russian objectives and tactics in the Middle East has been observed by the authors throughout the duration of the project. The rising foreign policy cadres currently serving in government or studying at educational institutions are receiving the wrong instruction when comes to understanding the complex issues of Russia's vision toward the Middle East. What is missing is extensive field work in both Russian and Middle Eastern area studies via educational and or academic exchange programs. What we are seeing, in other words, is the failure of the US educational system to keep up with the demands of the geopolitical environment. Area Studies is increasingly neglected by universities, while cut-backs in Russian programs are hurting the country's capabilities to understand and anticipate Russian activities. A serious initiative like or akin to a Blue Ribbon Panel may be necessary to combine not only the disciplines of Russia and Middle East Affairs, but also Russia and Africa, and Russia and Latin America. The necessity to mix area studies disciplines to create a new breed of analyst that is cross-cultural is of paramount importance in order to not only see what Russia is doing and going to do but also to simultaneously be able to understand and fully appreciate the Arab point of view.

US Government Needs an Immediate Joint Fusion Cell on Russia in the Middle East

The US needs rigorous, in-depth understanding of the actors in the drama; thus, the establishment of a fusion cell that mixes Russia and Middle East analysts is beyond critical at this juncture. However, this task is currently prevented by the stove-piping prevalent within most Washington, DC, government institutions. Confusion reigns supreme because of a lack of understanding of the intricacies of Russian strategy and actions, compounded by the broad lack of awareness of the Middle East's many nuances. Throughout this project, the level of questioning from US government analysts illustrated that the Russian analysts do not understand the Middle East and Middle East analysts do not understand Russia. Desk officers who are responsible for Middle East countries are unaware or too narrowly focused on their country; and consequently, they are missing the extra-regional activity conducted by the Kremlin.

Accountability of Arab Partners

The US needs to find a mechanism by which Arab allies are held accountable for their interactions with Russia. The optics are particularly poor when, for instance, Gulf military officers come to Moscow and Washington simultaneously for training. What Gulf military officers are learning from Moscow and what they are sharing with Moscow about the United States are key unknown questions. These relationships deserve closer examination to determine whether sanctions need to be applied to key Arab leaders or companies doing business with Russia.

Sanctions on Arab Partners Necessary to Halt Russian Enabling

The United States' ability to use sanctions as a weapon against Russia is highly likely to be eroded or nullified as Moscow seeks to bypass them by relying on outlets in the Gulf. That said, it is still an open question how sanctions on Rosoboroneksport will affect Russia's weapons sales to the MENA region. The North-South Corridor is essentially a "gray zone" when it comes to observing illicit financial activity; it appears to be either off-limits or not even on the US policymakers' radar. The US Treasury, FinCEN, etc. must more closely examine the financial relationships between Russia and Middle Eastern states for irregularities. The toxic Russian state, where illicit behavior is a norm, cannot be allowed to negatively influence the reforms and transformations occurring across the Arab countries' energy and financial sectors.

The US needs to better understand the links between Russia and MENA. In contrast, Russians have a much clearer comprehension of MENA and its attributes than the US does. For Washington to address the threat posed by Russian activities in the region, this imbalance will need to be rectified immediately, for instance by introducing specialized training programs that bring cultural awareness to the analytical forefront. Presently, the US is missing the extremely important cultural drivers that are pushing Russia and MENA closer together. Understanding these attributes are key to generating an effective policy response.

Conclusion

Having returned to the Middle East, Russia is here to stay; forcing Moscow out of the region is highly unlikely. Although domestic problems in the Russian Federation may to some degree distract the Kremlin from its extra-regional goals, Russia's relentless drive south is now ever-present and amplified by the geopolitical and geo-economics transition occurring throughout the Middle East. As such, the US will only be able to contend with Russia's advances in this strategic region and beyond by understanding the key factors and drivers eluding Western scholars at the moment.

ENDNOTES

[1] Stephen Blank, "The Foundations of Russian Policy in the Middle East," Russia in the Middle East, The Jamestown Foundation, October 5, 2017.

[2] Ibid.

[3] Ibid.

[4] Theodore Karasik, "Russia's Financial Tactics In the Middle East," The Jamestown Foundation, December 21, 2017.

[5] Stephen Blank, "Russia Returns To Africa," GIS Reports, August 17, 2018, https://www.gisreportsonline.com/opinion-russia-returns-to-africa,politics,2631.html.

[6] Stephen Blank, op cit.

[7] Pavel Baev, "European Assessments and Concerns About Russia's Policies in the Middle East," The Jamestown Foundation, October 5, 2017.

[8] Ibid.

[9] Ibid.

[10] Mitat Çelikpala,"Russia's Policies in the Middle East and the Pendulum of Turkish-Russian Relations," The Jamestown Foundation, October 5, 2017.

[11] Ibid.

[12] Shehab Al-Makahleh, "The Arab View Of Russia's Role In the MENA: Changing Arab Perceptions Of Russia, and the Implications For US Policy, The Jamestown Foundation, October 5, 2017.

[13] Alex Vatanka, "Iran's Russian Conundrum," The Jamestown Foundation, October 5, 2017.

[14] Ibid.

[15] Bozorgmehr Sharafedin, "Russia says future use of Iran air base depends on Syria circumstances," August 22, 2016 accessed via https://www.reuters.com/article/us-mideast-crisis-russia-iran-idUSKCN10X0QP.

[16] Shehab Al-Makahleh, op cit.

[17] Donald Jensen, "Russia in the Middle East: A New Front in the Information War?" The Jamestown Foundation, December 21, 2017.

[18] Ibid.

[19] Theodore Karasik, op cit.

[20] Shehab Al-Makahleh, op cit.

[21] Rauf Mammadov, "Russia In the Middle East: Energy Forever?" The Jamestown Foundation, December 21, 2017.

[22] Anna Borshchevskaya, "The Tactical Side of Russia's Arms Sales to the Middle East," The Jamestown Foundation, December 21, 2017.

[23] Ibid.

[24] Ibid.

[25] Sergey Sukhankin, "'Continuing War by Other Means': The Case of Wagner, Russia's Premier Private Military Company in the Middle East," The Jamestown Foundation, July 13, 2018.

[26] Stephen Blank, "Russia's Middle Eastern Position In 2025," The Jamestown Foundation, November 20, 2018.

[27] Yuri Barmin, "Russia in the Middle East Until 2024: From Hard Power to Sustainable Influence," The Jamestown Foundation, March 8, 2018.

[28] Ibid.

[29] Rauf Mammadov, op cit.

[30] Ilan Berman, "Demography's Pull on Russian Mideast Policy," The Jamestown Foundation, March 8, 2018.

[31] Russia in the Middle East Workshop 1, September 25, 2017, Washington D.C.

[32] Yuri Barmin, op cit.

[33] Rauf Mammadov, op cit.

[34] Stephen Blank, "Russia's Middle Eastern Position In 2025," op cit.

[35] Ibid.

[36] Ilan Berman, op cit.

[37] Theodore Karasik, op cit.

[38] The Abu Dhabi Executive Council's 2016 assessment was never published in an open-source format.

[39] Nadia Rodova, et al., "Russia, Saudi Arabia To Ink LNG Deal Wed, Finalize 3 Joint Energy Projects Soon: Russian Official," S&P Global Platts, February 14, 2018 accessed via https://www.spglobal.com/platts/en/market-insights/latest-news/natural-gas/021418-russia-saudi-arabia-to-ink-lng-deal-wed-finalize-3-joint-energy-projects-soon-russian-official, February 14, 2018.

[40] Theodore Karasik, op cit.

[41] Ibid.

Author Biographies

Pavel K. Baev

Pavel Baev is a nonresident senior fellow in the Center on the United States and Europe at Brookings and a research professor at the Peace Research Institute Oslo (PRIO). Pavel Baev is a Research Director and Professor at the Peace Research Institute Oslo (PRIO). He is also a nonresident senior fellow in the Center on the United States and Europe at Brookings, and a senior research associate at the Institut Francaise des Relations Internationales (IFRI, Paris). Dr. Baev specializes in Russian military reform, Russia's conflict management in the Caucasus and Central Asia, and energy interests in Russia's foreign and security policies, as well as Russia's relations with Europe and NATO. His articles on the Russian military posture, Russian-European relations, and peacekeeping and conflict management in Europe have appeared in numerous publications. He has a weekly column in *Eurasia Daily Monitor* and is the author of the blog, *Arctic Politics and Russia's Ambitions*.

Yuri Barmin

Yuri Barmin is an expert at the Russian International Affairs Council, covering the Middle East and North Africa, Moscow's policy toward the region, as well as the conflicts in Syria and Libya. He regularly contributes his analysis to *Al Monitor*, the Middle East Institute, Al Sharq Forum and FARAS Center. Mr. Barmin holds an MPhil in International Relations from the University of Cambridge.

Ilan Berman

Ilan Berman is Vice President of the American Foreign Policy Council, in Washington, DC. An expert on regional security in the Middle East, Central Asia, and the Russian Federation, he has consulted for both the US Central Intelligence Agency and the US Department of Defense, and provided assistance on foreign policy and national security issues to a range of governmental agencies and congressional offices. Mr. Berman is a member of the Associated Faculty at Missouri State University's Department of Defense and Strategic Studies, and serves as the Editor of *The Journal of International Security Affairs*. A frequent writer and commentator, he has written for the *Wall Street Journal, Foreign Affairs*, the *New York Times, Foreign Policy*, the *Washington Post* and *USA Today*, among many other publications. He is also the editor of three books.

Stephen Blank
Russia in the Middle East Project Co-Investigator

Dr. Stephen Blank is an internationally recognized expert on Russian foreign and defense policies and international relations across the former Soviet Union. He is also a leading expert on European and Asian security, including energy issues. Since 2013, he has been a Senior Fellow at the American Foreign Policy Council, in Washington. From 1989 until 2013, he was a Professor of Russian National Security Studies at the Strategic Studies Institute of the US Army War College in Pennsylvania. Dr. Blank has been Professor of National Security Affairs at the Strategic Studies Institute since 1989. In 1998–2001, he was Douglas MacArthur Professor of Research at the War College. Dr. Blank's MA and PhD are in Russian History from the University of Chicago. His BA is in History from the University of Pennsylvania.

Anna Borshchevskaya

Anna Borshchevskaya is the Ira Weiner Fellow at The Washington Institute, focusing on Russia's policy toward the Middle East. In addition, she is a fellow at the European Foundation for Democracy and was previously with the Peterson Institute for International Economics and the Atlantic Council. A former analyst for a US military contractor in Afghanistan, she has also served as communications director at the American Islamic Congress. Her analysis is published widely in journals such as *The New Criterion*, *Turkish Policy Quarterly*, and the *Middle East Quarterly*, and she also conducts translation and analysis for the US Army's Foreign Military Studies Office and its flagship publication, *Operational Environment Watch*, and writes a foreign affairs column for *Forbes*.

Originally from Moscow, Ms. Borshchevskaya came to the United States as a refugee in 1993 and has since received an MA in international relations from The Johns Hopkins University School of Advanced International Studies (SAIS) and a BA in political science and international relations from the State University of New York at Geneseo.

Mitat Çelikpala

Dr. Mitat Çelikpala is Professor of International Relations and the Dean of Faculty of Economics, Administrative and Social Sciences at Kadir Has University, Istanbul. He teaches graduate and undergraduate courses on Eurasian security, energy and critical infrastructure security/protection, Turkish foreign and domestic policy, and the Caucasus. His areas of expertise are the Caucasus, North Caucasian diaspora groups, people and security in the Caucasus and Black Sea regions, Turkish-Russian relations, energy security, and critical infrastructure protection. He has published multiple academic articles and analyses on the above-mentioned areas, and he regularly appears in the media to discuss these topics.

Prof. Çelikpala is a board member of the International Relations Council of Turkey since 2004 and the Managing Editor of the *Journal of International Relations: Academic Journal*. He previously served as an academic advisor to NATO's Center of Excellence for Defense Against Terrorism, in Ankara (2009–2012), particularly on regional security and critical infrastructure protection. Moreover, he was a board member at the Strategic Research and Study Center (SAREM), Turkish General Staff (2005–2011), as well as an Academic Advisor to the Center for Strategic Research (SAM), at the Turkish Ministry of Foreign Affairs (2002–2010) and to the Caspian Strategy Institute, Istanbul, Turkey (2012–2013). He was a Senior Associate Member at St. Antony's College, Oxford University, UK (2005–2006).

Donald N. Jensen

Donald Jensen is a Senior Fellow at the Center for Transatlantic Relations, Johns Hopkins School of Advanced International Studies (SAIS), and Senior Fellow with the Center for European Policy Analysis (CEPA), where he is editor-in-chief of the CEPA Stratcom Program. A former US diplomat, Jensen provided technical support for the START, INF, and SDI negotiations and was a member of the first ten-man US inspection team to inspect Soviet missiles under the INF Treaty in1988. From 1996 to 2008, he was Associate Director of Broadcasting and head of the Research Division at *RFE/RL* where he helped lead that organization's expansion into new broadcast regions after the end of the Cold War and the adaptation of multimedia technology to deal with the broadcasting challenges of the 21st Century. Jensen was a foreign policy advisor to the presidential campaign of Governor John Kasich in 2016. His work has appeared in the *The American Interest*, *US News*, *Newsweek*, the *Voice of America* and the Institute of Modern Russia. He is a regular commentator on

CNBC, Fox News, RFE/RL and the *Voice of America*. He has lectured at a variety of universities, including Johns Hopkins, Harvard, Oxford and The George Washington University. In 2016, he was a Visiting Scholar at the NATO Defense College in Rome. Jensen is currently an adjunct professor at the Krieger School of Arts and Sciences, The Johns Hopkins University. He received his PhD and MA from Harvard and BA from Columbia.

Theodore Karasik
Russia in the Middle East Project Co-Investigator

Dr. Theodore Karasik is currently a Senior Advisor to Gulf State Analytics and an Adjunct Senior Fellow at the Lexington Institute, both located in Washington, DC. Dr. Karasik spent 2004 through 2016 in the GCC, the Middle East and Russia. For the past 30 years, Karasik worked for a number of US agencies involved in researching and analyzing defense acquisition, the use of military power, and religious-political issues across MENA and Eurasia, including the evolution of violent extremism and its financing.

Dr. Karasik was an Adjunct Lecturer at the Dubai School of Government, where he taught graduate-level international relations, and also an Adjunct Lecturer at University Wollongong Dubai, where he taught labor and migration. Karasik was a Senior Political Scientist in the International Policy and Security Group at RAND Corporation. From 2002 to 2003, he served as Director of Research for the RAND Center for Middle East Public Policy. He is a specialist in geopolitics and geo-economics for the MENA and Eurasia regions and frequently conducts studies and assessments of future security trajectories and military requirements.

Dr. Karasik received his PhD in History from the University of California, Los Angeles (UCLA) in four fields: Russia, Middle East,

Caucasus and an outside field in cultural anthropology, focusing on tribes and clans from Central Asia to East Africa. He also holds a CPhil and MA in History and International Relations from UCLA and Monterey Institute of International Studies, respectively. He wrote his PhD dissertation on military and humanitarian operations in the northern port city of Arkhangel'sk and their impact on political institutions during the Russian civil war.

Shehab al-Makahleh

Shehab Al-Makahleh is a senior media and policy adviser in Jordan and the United Arab Emirates. He has been working for a number of media outlets as media consultant. He is president of the Jordan-based Political Studies of the Middle East Center and the executive director of Geostrategic and Media Center. Al-Makahleh has been working for several Middle Eastern countries as a political, military and security expert. He has been working as a media advisor for notable personalities in the Middle East. As an anchor journalist and columnist at various media outlets and think tanks, al-Makahleh has published many academic and political books. He has taken part in many international conferences in the United States, United Kingdom, France, Germany, Norway, Russia, Jordan, Turkey, Lebanon, the UAE, Bahrain, Iraq, Switzerland, Austria and Sweden. He has chronicled the modern history of his country in *Jordan's Spiritual Leader: King Hussein's Charismatic Qualities* and *His Majesty King Abdullah II's Traits: Leader and Teacher*. Al-Makahleh has obtained unprecedented access to extremists who traveled to Syria and Iraq to fight and are now serving time in prison, which helped him finish his book: *Into the Terrorist Minds: Through Their Own Eyes*. Al-Makahleh holds a PhD in politics, first Master's Degree in Media, second Master's degree in international politics, a BA in Media and a BA in Economics and Statistics from the University of Jordan.

Rauf Mammadov

Rauf Mammadov is resident scholar on energy policy at The Middle East Institute. He focuses on issues of energy security, global energy industry trends, as well as energy relations between the Middle East, Central Asia and South Caucasus. He has a particular emphasis on the post-Soviet countries of Eurasia. Prior to joining MEI, Mammadov held top administrative positions for the State Oil Company of Azerbaijan Republic (SOCAR) from 2006 and 2016. In 2012, he founded and managed the United States Representative Office of SOCAR in Washington, DC.

Sergey Sukhankin

Dr. Sergey Sukhankin is a Fellow at The Jamestown Foundation and an Associate Expert at the International Center for Policy Studies (Kyiv). He received his PhD in Contemporary Political and Social History from the Autonomous University of Barcelona (UAB), with his thesis discussing the transformation of Kaliningrad Oblast after the collapse of the USSR. His areas of research interest primarily concern Kaliningrad and the Baltic Sea region, Russian information and cyber security, A2/AD and its interpretation in Russia, as well as the development of Russia Private Military Companies (PMC) after the outbreak of the Syrian civil war. Dr. Sukhankin's academic articles, expert opinions and commentaries, as well as policy-oriented analyses have appeared in leading international think tanks, research institutions and publications, including The Jamestown Foundation, ECFR, CIDOB, *Diplomaatia*, RIAC, *New Eastern Europe*, *Kyiv Post*, *The New Republic*, *Business Insider*, *Rzeczpospolita*, *El Mundo*, *El Periodico* and *El Confidencial*. He was a Visiting Fellow (2016–2017) and subsequently taught a course entitled "Foreign and Security Policy of the Russian Federation" at The Institut Barcelona d'Estudis Internacionals (IBEI). He is based in Edmonton, Alberta, Canada.

Alex Vatanka

Alex Vatanka specializes in Middle Eastern regional security affairs with a particular focus on Iran. From 2006 to 2010, he was the Managing Editor of *Jane's Islamic Affairs* Analyst. From 2001 to 2006, he was a senior political analyst at Jane's in London (UK), where he mainly covered the Middle East. Alex is also a Senior Fellow in Middle East Studies at the US Air Force Special Operations School (USAFSOS), at Hurlburt Field, and teaches as an Adjunct Professor at DISAM, at Wright-Patterson Air Force Base. He has lectured widely for both governmental and commercial audiences, including the US Departments of State and Defense, US intelligence agencies, US Congressional staff, and Middle Eastern energy firms. Beyond Jane's, the Middle East Institute and The Jamestown Foundation, he has written for such outlets as *The Christian Science Monitor, Foreign Affairs, Americas Quarterly,* CNN.com, *Al Monitor,* the *Journal of International Security Affairs, BBC Persian Online, The National Interest, The World Today, PBS, Daily Beast,* the *Jerusalem Post, Journal of Democracy,* and the Council on Foreign Relations. Born in Tehran, he holds a BA in political science (Sheffield University, UK), and an MA in international relations (Essex University, UK), and is fluent in Farsi and Danish. He is the author of *Iran-Pakistan: Security, Diplomacy, and American Influence* (2015) and is presently working on his second book, *The Making of Iranian Foreign Policy: Contested Ideology, Personal Rivalries and the Domestic Struggle to Define Iran's Place in the World.*